THE LIE OF THE LAND

by the same author

Paul Carter

THE LIE OF THE LAND

LONDON · BOSTON

First published in 1996 by
Faber and Faber Limited
3 Queen Square London WC1N 3AU

Photoset by Parker Typesetting Service Ltd, Leicester
Printed in England by Clays Ltd, St Ives plc

A CIP record for this book
is available from the British Library

ISBN 0–571–14101–3

10 9 8 7 6 5 4 3 2 1

For Winston
who would have had it simpler

Contents

List of Illustrations

Acknowledgements

The origins of this book go back to 1978, when a British Council scholarship enabled me to spend a year in Venice. More recently, fellowships from the Australia Council and the Australian Research Council have provided me with time to write. As for space, hospitality and day-to-day help, that the Australian Centre, The University of Melbourne, provided. My thanks to them all for their unquestioning support – and patience.

In preparing my account of Strehlow, I benefited from conversations with Philip Jones and Catherine Ellis, both of whom also made available to me unpublished research, research materials and *pensées* of their own. In 1989 a travel grant from the Victorian Ministry for the Arts made possible a research trip to Adelaide. At that time Dr John Tregenza graciously oversaw my first forays into the Light archives held at the Mortlock Library, Adelaide, while the Art Gallery of South Australia kindly made available to me Light's sketchbooks.

With great generosity of spirit, Geoffrey Bardon shared with me his unrivalled knowledge of the early Papunya Tula painting movement. More, Dorn and Geoffrey Bardon invited me into their home; the conversations that took place there on 13–14 May 1994 revealed to me the emotional core of what had at times seemed a solitary, and nebulous, enquiry.

Paul Carter
Buninyong
December 1994

Introduction

Friday's Other Foot

I escaped the Thunder, and fell into the Lightning
George Herbert, *Jacula Prudentum*[1]

Observing the machines at work removing hillsides, bulldozing topsoil, blasting away reefs of rock, scattering swathes of gravel, concrete, tarmac in the still raw wounds of the levelled site, one might conclude that our culture was indifferent to the beauties of natural localities. Yet within a few weeks or months, the ochre-grooved and battle-scarred Martian surface has miraculously sprouted pavements, driveways, gardens and houses; emerald lawns and conifers grow up supernaturally young and bright. And house-buyers live inside these alighted architectural satellites and, as they say, begin putting down roots: fences, washing-lines, gnomes and little fountains. And inside, photographs in rows, views through curtains, views of views (framed on the wall), wall-to-wall carpets are the modest argot out of which a new vocabulary of place is being improvised. And before long, what the property developers promised in their brochures begins to feel true: the lucky new residents are proud to have a place they can call their own.

At first it may seem bare, raw, unlived-in, but before long it acquires personal associations; it becomes a refuge from a world of contingencies that the television simultaneously brings to our living-rooms and miniaturizes as distant; it becomes, at least if the rhetoric is believed, another womb, whose homeliness this time round is palpable; and even if the other houses spoil the view, the fragment of horizon, the allotment of stars keep us in some sort of contact with Nature. All of this occurs without any enquiry, without any curiosity, as to what was sacrificed in order to create this place we inhabit, where we gather together our books, our dreams, our children. No one appears to worry about what was cleared away when the streets were laid out according to a two-dimensional plan, when the natural topography was neutralized and in its place artificial vistas were carefully mortgaged. At no point in the process of arrival, survey, settlement and residence does the ground make any claim upon our attention.

We may say, 'But we walk on the ground', yet we should beware of an ambiguity. For we walk on the ground as we drive on the road; that is, we move over and above the ground. Many layers come between us and the granular earth – an earth which in any case has already been displaced. Our relationship to the ground is, culturally speaking, paradoxical: for we appreciate it only in so far as it bows down to our will. Let the ground rise up to resist us, let it prove porous, spongy, rough, irregular – let it assert its native title, its right to maintain its traditional surfaces – and instantly our engineering instinct is to wipe it out; to lay our foundations on rationally-apprehensible level ground.

We do not walk with the surface; we do not align our lives with its inclines, folds and pockets. We glide over it; and to do this, to render what is rough smooth, passive, passable, we linearize it, conceptualizing the ground, indeed the civilized world, as an ideally flat space, whose billiard-table surface can be skated over in any direction without hindrance. The house we are so inclined to fetishize, locating within its purlieus that sense of place that lends us our identity and dignity – that intimation of the cosmic in the intimate that enables us to remain childlike even into old age – never touches down. We live in our places off the ground; and, it is our thesis, we idolize the picturesqueness of places because we sense our ungroundedness, the fragility of our claim on the soil. Our carefully enclosed and ornamented places, with their artillery of hedges, views, roads, boundaries and horizons, grow out of the sacrifice of the ground and are, in this sense, non-places.

Our homes are tumuli erected over the slaughtered body of the giant ground; only our nervous decoration, our attention to monumental detail, our preoccupation with property, give us away. The monumentality of the places we create – our cities, harbours, highways, even our provincial cottages – is an attempt to arrest the ground, to prevent it slipping away from under our feet. We build in order to stabilize the ground, to provide ourselves with a secure place where we can stand and watch. But this suggestion that the ground is treacherous, unstable, inclined to give way, is the consequence of our own cultural disposition to fly over the earth rather than to walk with it. Is it not odd that ours, the most nomadic and migratory of cultures, should found its polity, its psychology, its ethics and even its poetics on the antithesis of movement: on the rhetoric of foundations, continuity, genealogy, stasis? Is it not decidedly odd that a culture intent on global colonization should persistently associate movement with the unstable, the unreliable, the wanton and the primitive?

But perhaps it is inevitable; for a culture that is ungrounded, movement, however integral to its survival, must always constitute a threat. For fetishists of the clearing and the ziggurat the in-between space of the unroaded surface must always appear hostile, bent on thwarting its purposeful journeys. If we were grounded, the cultural opposition between movement and stasis would disappear. But this optimistic formulation begs the question of what it means to be grounded. What is the 'ground' in question which we inexplicably fail to touch? Philosophers may urge other philosophers to ground their thought more thoroughly, but this is merely a metaphor and assumes (once again) that the ground itself can be taken for granted. What is that fundamental surface that seems to inform every dimension of our oneiric, physiological and architectural fantasy but which remains, hitherto, metaphorical, metaphysical – ungrounded?

But to formulate the question in this way may be to perpetuate the problem. It implies that our better groundedness in the world depends on continuing to do what Western philosophers have always delighted in doing: stripping away appearances to uncover a firmer, bedrock reality. Western philosophy has in this respect operated little differently from the tunnellers, the earth-movers and the bulldozers: its first priority has always been to clear the ground of accidental impediments, to peg out its definitions and lemmata. Indeed, it is hard to imagine a philosophy, any more than a polis, founded on uneven ground, on ground that shifts or which already, by virtue of its natural obliquity, furnishes an infinity of positions, poses, points of rest to anyone prepared to traverse the ground in different directions. To write that in-between ground, where stability is a function of measured motion, might be the province of the poet rather than the philosopher.

In other words, if we are to avoid the *reductio ad absurdum* of the philosopher's search for unimpeachably firm foundations, we may need to respect the environment of knowledge, the tacit dimension of the ground that our flights of fancy seem so often designed to ignore. But again, this is not to advocate a different subject-matter so much as a different process of knowledge-garnering. Rilke expresses a familiar urban, post-Enclosure Act nostalgia for the solidity of the land when he writes, 'If one only had nothing but work memories from the beginning: how firm the ground would be underneath one's feet; one would stand.' And he compares the labourer's grounding of memory with the memories of the idler, for whom 'there isn't a moment when one isn't sinking in somewhere . . .'[2] But this alteration of perspective is perhaps superficial; at any rate, the self-possession so admired remains Athenian, cognate with the cleared and levelled agora where the orator stands up and holds forth.

There is absent from Rilke's picturesque reverie any identification with the process of field-work, the slow motion of folding and unfolding the earth associated with ploughing, harrowing and their sublimations, sowing and scything. There is no sense of the labourer's lean, of a figure set at an angle to the ground's grave resistance but on the move; no sense of the liaison between the variable softnesses and hardnesses of the earth and air and the evolving moods of the man who measures himself against them. A. G. Sturt is a more reliable witness here: 'Drizzling again after dark: and underfoot, slushy mud. Would that such conditions could find their way into biographies, for they tell. Tonight, for instance . . . if I could have walked out in dry hard clear frost, I feel that my mind would have been more sane and cheerful.'[3] To make the lie of the land an object of the mind, it has to be printed with steps; and the steps, their depth, their space apart, will bear witness to the gravity of the passage and its motive.

In wondering, and wandering, about the lost surfaces of the world, our aim is not to restore them, to 'landscape' them, to bring the irregular ground back into the poetic and historical picture. To restore the lost ground, as they have in the new housing estate, raising a small hill here, remarking a lost brook there, by fetishizing the environment as a concatenation of sacred groves, only contributes further to the ungrounding of the ground. Just as the bulldozer desecrated the ground, so the landscape architect resacralizes it; and neither moment, with its implicit divisions between inside and outside, sacred and non-sacred, ever recognizes the openness of the ground, the ground as process, adjunct to walking and supporter of shadows. There is, worst of all, nowhere where one might fall down or become inexplicably prone. The fantasy of standing up, a surveyor of horizons, so unquestioningly associated with sanity, vigour, command, may also bear witness to a paranoia, a fear of growing old (or young) associated with the lie of the land.

The old man has no use for open spaces; he takes advantage of the bank to rest. The child has no use for plains; he rolls in the useless sand. As for the earth's parabolic basins, even an upright young man like Ted Strehlow, the anthropologist, can sense their appeal. Returning in December 1932 to 'my old Finke, the Father of Centralian Rivers,' he wrote in his diary, 'it was delightful to be able to camp in the shade, to roll around, now at last in the sense of perfect security.'[4]

To avoid compacting the ground, rendering it another stable point of departure, we need to tread it lightly, circumspectly. The approach must be poetic rather than philosophical. For restoration of the ground does not mean treading it down more firmly or replacing it; it means releasing it for movement – in the same way that metre or speech pattern releases language for movement. We must recover the earth's metrical properties, seeing that its topographies are first and foremost systems of metricalizing movement. If the world were perfectly flat, there would be no motive for going anywhere; we would have no conception of absence, apparently. It is the irriguous uncertainties of the ground that introduce us to the adventure of taking calculating steps, of engaging with in-between spaces; and this adventure translates itself into stress and breath patterns. So that – to walk in the other direction, to turn this argument almost on its head – the achievement of a world society capable of living on and with the earth depends not simply on the evolution of democratic polities but on the achievement of an environmentally-grounded poetics.

In its simplest terms, the challenge that confronts us in the next century is to move differently, to learn to dissolve the emotionally-catatonic and historically-destructive opposition between mobility and stability – with its confrontationist vocabulary of special places and inviolable boundaries – and to find instead a different, more measured, more diplomatic means of moving about; if this were to happen, and we learned to ground ourselves differently, Shelley's old description of poets as the unacknowledged legislators of the world might yet prove to be accurate. But for this to happen, *poiesis* – all that is comprehended by the Western arts of representation – would need to undergo a renovation. It is not only the surveyors with their plans, the real-estate agents with their clipboards, but the painters at their easels, the writers mesmerized by walls of lines and symmetrical paragraphs, who need to imagine their 'field' of endeavour differently.

'The Natives were well pleas'd with our People until they began clearing the ground at which they were displeased and wanted them to be gone . . . ,' William Bradley of the *Sirius* observed in January 1788.[5] But clearing was the *sine qua non* of progress: it was the work that gave the infant colony at Sydney Cove its reason for being. The resistance of the trees to being chopped down defined the colonists' sense of a historical destiny. 'When I left Port Jackson in February, 1788,' John Hunter, another First Fleet annalist, reported, 'the ground about Sydney-Cove was covered with a thick forest, but on my arrival at this time [April 1790], I found it cleared to a considerable distance, and some good buildings were erected.'[6] And, as I intimated in *The Road to Botany Bay*, these processes of clearing and enclosure were as much rhetorical as architectural. The scatter of barracks, storehouses, convicts' quarters and little houses found their ideological counterpart in the accumulating clouds that hover over the scene in early engravings produced back in London; they serve to suggest that the bush (the uneven hills and valleys, and even the unpredictable weather of the region) come after the event, providing theatrically-conceived 'history' with a picturesque backdrop.[7]

The result of ground-clearing was to institute one system of memorialization at the expense of another. It was as if the colonists set out to erase the common ground where communication with the 'Natives' might have occurred. To found the colony, to inaugurate linear history and its puppet-theatre of marching soldiers and treadmills, was to embrace an environmental amnesia; it was actively to forget what wisdom the ground, and its people, might possess. Only a few years later the admittedly effusive traveller Joseph Arago could see in Sydney another Europe, in parts peculiarly British, and wonder how many ages the town had stood.[8] It was as if the colony had successfully blanked out its own origins. So successful was its mimicry, so dazzling the masquerade, that the casual visitor was blinded, and it did not occur to him to ask what ground it occupied. The replica was so convincing, it was as if nothing had been forgotten.

This was the visual and spatial rhetoric of colonization – the means by which it legitimated its presence – and it depended for its power on a poetics of representation, on a belief that manufactured objects (whether gates or costumes or proclamations) were physical images that figured forth a metaphysical reality. The tiny verandas at Sydney Cove, no less than the coquelicot-tiled *fazendas* of Rio de Janeiro or the whitewashed belfries of Cape Town, signified an idea of civilization: they pointed towards another world. In the absence of the ideal city, they 'stood in' for it; and to do this they had to subjugate the local lie of the land, and by taking possession of a neutralized ground rise up as monuments, as ruins, if you like, or preliminaries of a golden age. In any case, the poetics of representation depended upon a primary idealization of the object, its displacement from the environment – which henceforth must be seen as an ambiguous setting, picturesque when it backed off towards the horizon, recalcitrant when it opposed passage.

Poetry, no less than painting and town-planning, seemed to be implicated in this process of colonization by mimesis. 'The language of Poetry,' Keats wrote after William Hazlitt, 'naturally falls in with the language of Power.' We 'read with pleasure of the ravages of a beast of prey' and the 'same principle that makes us read with admiration . . . reconciles us in fact to the triumphant progress of the conquerors and mighty Hunters of mankind, who came to stop the shepherd's Pipe upon the Mountains and sweep away his listening flock.'[9] An apologia for epic over pastoral, this is also a vindication of the advent of the migratory Homeric muse: story-telling, history itself, might be the conceptual breakthrough needed to make imperialism possible; it was as if the arts of representation provided a transportable territory, an artillery of movable *genii loci* that could be set down wherever they were needed and, provided a plinth could be made for them, firm and level, begin to wink or flutter like flags.

As Keats implied, this one-sided appropriation of the ground incurred great loss. It not only meant silencing 'the shepherd's Pipe'; it meant deposing the shepherd's animistic communion with his non-human surroundings, 'his listening flock'. Where instructions for getting on had to be issued, where the conqueror's discourse was all of signs and signposts, there was no place for the 'baaing' of barbarians. Communication had to be regulated, and speech, like the ground, subjected to grammatical rules. And it was characteristic of this process that it could not tolerate ambiguous mimicry: look-alikes and sound-alikes had to be ruthlessly suppressed. This was the paranoia of the colonist: that his claim to belong to a higher destiny might prove to be empty, the mummery of foreign strollers, and it in part explains his over-sensitivity to supposed mockery or slight, his gratuitous aggression, his assertion of superiority.

The colonists' repetition of the word 'kangaroo' (derived from Captain Cook's North Queensland vocabulary) led the Sydney people to assume it was the foreigners' word for 'sheep'. But instead of convincing the whites of the falseness of their own representations, this intelligent mimicry provoked the opposite effect: 'Whatever animal is shewn them, a dog excepted, they call *kangaroo*: a strong presumption that the wild animals of the country are few.'[10] The Aboriginal willingness, their easy diplomatic preparedness, to enter into conversation was turned into evidence of a cultural backwardness, an environmental poverty. Tench could not comprehend that their politely encouraging mimicry originated in a mistranslation of his own, and that the paranoid lumping-together of everything was his. In any case, one thing was clear: despite the poet Southey's notorious surmise that in Australia 'for the music of the bleating flocks,/ Alone is heard the kangaroo's sad note,'[11] a discourse of univocal signs could not tolerate an environment of in-between sounds or rumours.

This was another aspect of ground-clearing: that it set aside sounds. It was true that the 'chaos' of landing, of 'clearing ground for the different encampments' and the like, meant that 'the spot which had so lately been the abode of silence and tranquillity was now changed to that of noise, clamour and confusion,' but this was only a temporary aberration: 'after a time order gradually prevailed every where. As the woods were opened and the ground cleared, the various encampments were extended, and all wore the appearance of regularity.'[12] To neutralize the lie of the land is to substitute a new silence for the old one. In fact, the 'silence' that is attributed to the ancient landscape is an important rhetorical weapon in the silencing process: by supposing that the land was formerly inarticulate, David Collins, another First Fleeter, justifies the colonists' articulation of it, their new eloquence of 'regularity'.

The lie of the land is associated with a noise that must be silenced. To inhabit the country is to lay to rest its echoes. And these strategies do not belong uniquely to remote episodes in the history of European imperialism – to the first report of arquebuses in the Bahamas, say, or to an ill-advised salute of cannon devised by the 'Feringis' [Portuguese] in Canton harbour in 1517;[13] they continue to be the traumatic weapons we use to quieten down the voices of the old ground. The odd silence of the housing estate, sans birds, sans chatter, sans water running, is a deafness produced by months of dynamiting, drilling, earth-moving, earth-stamping, and their hectic offspring, radios blaring to no other end than to mask with their little noise the larger noise of power or 'progress'. And both serve to suppress that other 'noise' arising from the natural lie of the land, its weathers, hydrology, vegetation and population, which never lay on an axis between hearing and silence but was an analogue of environmental time, another kind of history.

Ours has been a culture that, in George Herbert's words, has 'escaped the Thunder'; or, better, turned a deaf ear to its portentous voices. The question might be: how long can it also avoid falling into the lightning? Private Marine Easty was not a good speller, so perhaps it does not signify when he reports the weather off the east coast of Australia for 1 January 1788 as 'East Dark Clowdy att Night with Scaquals & Lighting'.[14] On the other hand, a habit of passing off lightning as theatrical lighting – a tendency to treat the evolving environment as foreign to our human drama – has been symptomatic. Our intellectual (certainly our Edisonian) Enlightenment might be characterized as lightning's silent arrest: short-circuiting its discharge to earth, we have made of it a permanent illumination. In any case, the knowledges we have privileged, the technologies we have designed to represent them, have always assumed the linearization of time and space, the elimination of its curvilinear and non-linear dimensions.

The opening of the woods, the clearing of the ground – these historical activities are cognate with the process of intellectual enlightenment, the ideology of progress. To remove the bushes, to render the ground as smooth as a billiard table, is to enclose the land within a permanent ring of light. The open field is a rebuke to clouds or other evidences of primitive chiaroscuro: the colonists' eagerness to remove every vestige of vegetation cannot be explained simply as a mistaken theory of agriculture; it expresses an overwhelming need to clear away doubt – not to make the land speak in accents all its own, but to silence the whispers, the inexplicable earth and sky tremors which always seemed to accompany colonization.[15] Progress, it seems, is built on the ruins of process; in order to stand erect, man must, it seems, stamp the earth flat, turning it into a passive planisphere.

From the beginning, as it were, this ideology ran into difficulties. If movement were suspect, if stasis were king, how was the colonist, let alone the trader and the traveller, to justify his shifting for himself? He must account for it psychologically, or else ascribe it to the will of God. In any case, as Robinson Crusoe repeatedly finds, it takes him into the heart of the tempest. 'All these Miscarriages,' he reflects, 'were procured by my apparent obstinate adhering to my foolish inclination of wandring abroad.'[16] And he adds, 'I was born to be my own Destroyer' – a philosophy that at least has the advantage of making the storms and shipwrecks that litter his life allegorical, evidence of God's hidden, but providentially guiding, hand. Had he remained at home, as his father bade him, nothing of this would have happened.

As an introduction to the psychology of the colonizer, Defoe's great book remains unequalled. What Phillip and his men set about at Sydney Cove, Defoe had already imagined a century earlier: 'My Thoughts were now wholly employ'd about securing my self against . . . Savages' – in which cause 'I resolv'd to find a more healthy and more convenient Spot of Ground.' And Crusoe's manipulation of that ground is instructive. A little plain with a rocky backdrop disclosing itself, 'On the Flat of the Green, just before this hollow place,' he pitches his tent; and his first act is to turn a disclosure into an enclosure: 'I drew a half Circle before the hollow Place [and] pitchd two Rows of strong Stakes, driving them into the Ground . . . '[17] This gives him a sense of security, but such is the paranoia at the heart of binary logic, it also creates a little theatre in which to contemplate his insecurity. The dramatic agent of this sudden new self-awareness is the storm, but 'I was not so much surpris'd with the Lightning as I was with a Thought which darted into my Mind as swift as the Lightning itself. O my Powder! My very Heart sunk within me, when I thought, that at one Blast all my Powder might be destroy'd . . . '[18]

Defoe's insight is to understand that the colonizer produces the country he will inhabit out of his own imagining. The colonizer is also a novelist, making the lie of the land an index of his own fears and hopes. Crusoe heeds the lightning only because it mimics the operations of his own mind. Likewise, the environment only signifies in so far as it supplies him with a *tabula rasa* whereon he can inscribe a hemisphere with himself at its centre. Crusoe holds no dialogue with his surroundings, only with himself. His island is of his own making and is conceived concentrically as the distribution of his own interests. Its very topography answers to the hierarchic command he claims over it. Nothing here can answer back, unless it is the parrot imitating his own voice; and certainly there can be no question of entering into negotiations with the island's other inhabitants.

The single footprint that marks the breaching of his Eden stimulates an extraordinary sequence of mental events which, taken together, are a brilliant anatomy of the colonial mentality and its images. Coming across the mark in the sand, Crusoe at first stood 'like one Thunder-struck', and then 'came Home to my Fortification, not feeling, as we say, the Ground . . .'[19] Unable to say what the impression signifies, he is filled with fear; in which condition his fancy projects on to it every fear of his own, including the image of Satan. This train of thought in turn produces its opposite: a revival of his Christian faith. That he should now 'tremble at the very Apprehensions of seeing a Man, and was ready to sink into the Ground at but the Shadow or silent Appearance of a Man's having set foot in the Island,'[20] suggests the odd workings of Providence. But there is no end to the ricochets of this mirror-logic; thoughts of the invisible are reflected back on to the footprint: 'it came into my Thought one Day, that all this might be a meer Chimera of my own; and that this Foot might be the Print of my own Foot . . .'[21]

On the single 'Print' or signature of presence is built an entire system of Heaven and Hell. This is the self-absorbed madness of colonial logic, repeatedly to project on to the environment its own chimeras. This much Defoe makes brilliantly clear; but in order to achieve this clarity, he has to make a remarkable assumption. The value of the footprint as a stimulus to the fancy depends in large part on its singularity. Nowhere in the narrative does Crusoe express any interest in locating the other footprints that might be logically associated with it. His own train of thought – his own wildly associative logic – depends on abstracting the print from the environment and, instead of regarding it as the trace of passage, interpreting it as a supernatural sign.

That footprint, we might say, is already enclosed within the clearing of the colonial gaze. As a signature, as a sign of absence, as something standing in for something else, it is not understood in relation to the lie of the land, as a dialogue of left and right marking the ground, as a historical passage. It is denied its other foot, its sense of direction, and it is this prior bracketing of the environment, symbolized by the absence of the other footprint, that precipitates the extraordinary fantasies that afflict Crusoe. There is, in other words, a direct connection between the clearing of the land and the erasure of its natural histories, and the identification of knowledge with semiosis, the science of signs. The interpretation of signs, as Christopher Columbus's diary of his first voyage eloquently testifies,[22] presupposes a world beyond, and its corollary, a deceptive present. It makes the breaching of the horizon natural. As for the lie of the land, unless it lies down it signifies nothing, or worse, the mendacity of the savage mind.

What would have happened if Robinson Crusoe had found another footprint? Then he would have found another and another, and a pattern would have emerged, a track. A system of memorialization would have come into focus, a different way of regarding the ground. He would not have needed to invent an explanation: traces, not signs, the footprints would have ceased to be enigmatic. He might have grasped that the ground he stood on vibrated to the passage of other feet, and constituted an open network of social communication. His hysteria might have died down; he might have relaxed, and instead of seeking to efface every trace of his own history on the island, he might have contemplated the arts of diplomacy. Certainly, when at last the man he had been waiting for ran towards him, their meeting would have been different: 'he . . . kiss'd the Ground, and laid his Head upon the Ground, and taking me by the Foot, set my Foot upon his Head . . . in token of swearing to be my Slave for ever.'[23]

This attention to the ground should not be mistaken for reverence. It is because he has nowhere to stand that the fugitive kneels down. He acknowledges Crusoe as his master by making away the ground. Ceding it with a kiss, he enters into the European way of seeing things, where signs operate more powerfully than substances. He submits to allowing Crusoe to be the ground and author of his own life; what he does not see – at least not yet – is that by setting his foot on Man Friday's head, Crusoe makes him the ground of his own mastery. How different these stiff, not to say ludicrous, transactions are, compared with the flexible exchange between equals which Montaigne, for example, describes: 'The word is half his who speaks, and half his who hearkens to it. The hearer ought to prepare himself to the motion or bound it takes. As between those that play at tennis, he who keeps the hazard, prepares, stands, stirs and marches, according as he perceives him who stands in the house to look, stand, remove and strike the ball, and according to the stroke.'[24]

A short history of British imperialism might be derived from an inventory of the billiard tables manufactured and supplied to the colonies during the nineteenth century. For the modelling of movement as a sequence of ricochets calculated on a level, two-dimensional ground might be said to characterize the colonial experience more generally. How were the executive officers of the Crown to communicate the need for order, for a symmetry of causes and effects, for a destiny played out on a 'level playing-field'? In these frustrating circumstances a game of billiards not only provided relief; it was cathartic, providing experimental proof of the validity of the social relations the colonists wanted to put in place. But, as Goethe understood, the corollary of flattening out space and time was that no convergence of interests could ever be discovered: no dimples, folds or slopes remained in the social field where different folk might 'roll' together or significantly depart: 'We see men of a certain importance, but with no trace of a similar tendency and a common interest; each one as an isolated being goes his own way, without sympathizing in the exertion of others. They seem to me like billiard balls; which run blindly by one another on the green cover without mutual knowledge, and which, if they come in contact, only recede so much the further from one another.'[25]

This mimicry of communication, where perfectly circular projectiles only 'kiss' in order to separate, depends on excluding the third dimension, the heights and depths that define the scope of the game in which Montaigne's two players take part. The introduction of the third dimension changes the dialogue profoundly, rendering it non-linear, non-reversible. It is true that, while they may lack a third dimension, the motions of the billiard balls imply temporality, a fourth dimension. But as, in principle at least, every future movement – every angle of rebound, every collision, every consequent linear displacement – is predictable, so, to adapt La Place's dictum, every past move can be retrodicted and restored.[26] Time is spherical, like the balls, and continually folds itself up into an eternity of instances. Introduce the third dimension, and this predeterminism evaporates: curvilinear trajectories are introduced, and because their outcomes cannot be reliably calculated, some environmental element of chance always persisting, time and space are materialized, are felt as the medium of corporeal actions that are genuinely historical, because contingent on a dialogue with other forces.

These ballistic considerations are not eccentric to our purpose; they have poetic and political implications. In the poetic sphere they imply a break with theatrical representations and the cultivation instead of what in this book is called a 'reverent miming'. The Russian poet Mandelstam grasped the necessity of this shift of emphasis when he reflected, apropos of the peripatetic Dante: 'We describe just what cannot be described, that is, nature's text brought to a standstill; and we have forgotten how to describe the only thing which by its structure yields to poetic representation, namely the impulses, intentions and amplitudes of oscillation.'[27] But it goes without saying that, where the ground is imagined as flat, as a potential field of dimensionless lines, there can be no curvature, and none of the contracting, the folding and unfolding, that are associated with amplitude. And without amplitude, a science of vibrations, there can of course be no sounds, no traces of movement. There can indeed only be the little silences of signs.

As for the politics of an environmentally-attuned poetics, these are glossed negatively by Chekhov who, writing to Suvorin, remarked, 'We depict life as it is, but we refuse to go a step further. We have neither near nor remote aims and our souls are as bare and flat as a billiard table. We have no politics and we do not believe in revolution . . . But he who wants nothing, hopes for nothing and fears nothing cannot be an artist.'[28] To depict life as it might be, Chekhov implies, it is necessary to breach the two-dimensional depiction of reality. The question now is: does this mean climbing to a commanding point in order to see further? Or on the contrary, does it mean renouncing this nostalgia for horizons, and focusing instead on the ground at our feet, beginning to pay attention to its folds and inclines? For where it rises up to meet us, there is no need for 'remote aims'; equally, where it turns away it is pointless to seek to see it, as it can only be known by a directed movement taking account of the lie of the land.

To bring the ground back into the historical picture, to suggest that the lie of the land can be a critical tool in reconceptualizing the history of colonization, is perhaps to open a path into that vexed and nebulous realm of the post-colonial. Currently, it seems to me, this is a territory occupied by strategists whose tactics remarkably recapitulate those employed by the very colonizers whose habits they mean to eradicate. It is not only the eighteenth century which, 'forced to walk along the ocean bottom as on a parquet floor, turned out to be pre-eminently a century of moralising';[29] our own demonizers of the politically-incorrect strut the same submarine line. After the deterritorialization of the Modern and the post-Modern, there is a call to 'reterritorialize';[30] but this can produce nothing except the renewed noise of destruction and reconstruction unless it occurs within and upon a different, more ample ground, one that is folded, vibrant. This zone will be 'open', but not in Hunter's sense. It will not be a penetrative breach, a widening scar, like the white pages of an opening book. It would more resemble the field disclosed by Montaigne's players.

The first step may be to understand that the historical ground we pride ourselves on clearing and possessing, conceptually as well as by force of arms, is a telescopic contraction of the environment. It is a ground evacuated of depth and height, of its capacity to partake in the flight of objects and their underground report. The smooth surfaces we pour over it may facilitate our faster flight, our greater leaps, but they also attest to a frustration, to a sense that the ground has lost its aura, its power to harbour local echoes, memories. As I write this, an article appears in a daily newspaper lamenting the loss of a creek – 'it was consigned years ago to a barrel drain and tied up in a ribbon of freeway asphalt' – which, the writer recalls, held a 'strong, almost mystical' attraction for him as a child. And he singles out one particularly memorable event which he associates with 'our patch of wilderness' – the day that he found himself alone with 'Ronny' and his bow and arrow.[31]

Perhaps what followed when, 'Without pausing, he aimed the arrowhead straight into the air, pulled back and released', had an obscurely symbolic, Freudian meaning. Perhaps it stays with him because of the more mundane calculation that an arrow fired straight up must come straight down, perhaps killing him (the 'deadly splinter' in fact lands a few metres away). But in retrospect, the real meaning of the event lies not in its beginning or its end, but in the space and time in-between, measured by the arrow's soaring arc: 'For me Ronny's arrow will never land. It will always be spinning and shimmering in the sunlight, a kind of airborne talisman connecting me to the time before expediency robbed us all of something beyond value.' In that moment, I would suggest, the boy felt disclosed to him a community between the lie of the land and the curvilinear laws of the arrow's flight. The 'ground', dangerous, uneven, unpredictable, was grasped not as a surface but as manifold surfaces, their different amplitudes composing an environment that was uniquely local, which could not be transposed. This enlarged ground not only belongs to the sacred precincts of autobiography; it makes possible an exploratory apprehension of the world; it gives meaning to the idea of historical contingency. Its plea for 'a less paved time' embodies both a politics and a poetics.

The amplification of the themes introduced here is the object of what follows, and hardly needs further preamble now. The three figures whose lives and works form our point of departure belong in their different ways to the history of European imperialism and its colonial outfall. This is obviously, perhaps too obviously, true of William Light, first Surveyor-General of the colony of South Australia and author of Adelaide's town-plan. T. G. H. Strehlow belongs to a later phase of that local history: the son of German immigrant missionaries to that state, he found himself caught within a multilayered colonial discourse, in which his father's work with the Aranda of Central Australia, although typically racist in its metaphysical assumptions, remained, in comparison with the racism of the wider Anglo-Saxon culture, relatively anti-colonialist. Less obvious, although equally telling, is Giorgione's place in this patriarchal pageant: to bring out the social and political implications of his praxis, he has had to be located in the light of the Spanish conquest of Mexico; in whose vulgarly golden glow, it is suggested, the new Venetian investment in the art of colouring assumes not only a poetic, but an anti-imperial, import.

Iron filings in a magnetic field, these figures operated within, were aligned to, the forces of patriarchy so instrumental in shaping the conceptual tools necessary for the assumption of empire. But although aligned, they managed in some way to trace out a counter-trajectory of their own, to preserve an awareness of another way of being, one taking account of the lie of the land. The use Giorgione makes of 'reversed perspective' is not only a method for preserving appearances – a reaction, say, to Florentine linearism; it is a way of folding together the elements of a world in danger of nuclear splitting and disintegration. Its function is analogous to that of Strehlow's elastically expansive 'musical phrase' which, enfolding linear elements and making them simultaneously present, provides the key to the genius of Aranda poetry. The counter-trajectory in Light's life is less easily identified, in part because his biographers have been intent on fitting him into the statuesque mould of hero and founder, but it is there in the interstices of his *Last Diary*, where a correlation between his tubercular breath patterns and the moods of the wind reveal a different subjectivity, one predicated on a rhythmic up and down that belonged equally to sea and chest.

What may need a word of explanation is the organization of the material. In his book *Science and Music,* Jeans remarks that 'When the wind or a blast of air encounters a small obstacle, little whirlwinds are formed which are the exact counterparts of the whirlpools which are formed when a stream of water strikes a rock,' and 'These whirlwinds are formed on the two sides of the obstacle alternately; as soon as one comes into existence, it begins to drift away in the general current of air, thus making place for others . . .'[32] This is somewhat how I imagine the life and work of my subjects taking shape: if the linear blast of air corresponds roughly to the patriarchal imperative, and to the linearist mode of world-shaping associated with it, the 'obstacle' is the ground, and the backward-spirals peeling off from the encounter are the traces of an impact that will not quieten down. Their dissonant forms correspond to the counter-trajectories I am interested in exploring.

But to suggest their nature it would perhaps be a mistake to 'unravel' them, to lay them out flat, as it were, for easier survey. It would be as if we were to remove the streaming flag from its pole and to stretch it on a table when, as Jeans reminds us, it is the little whirlwinds, 'chasing one another along it, first one side and then on the other', that produce the fluttering of the flag.[33] As this description suggests, the progression of whirlwinds is not without order. Their alternation suggests what might be called a soft dialectic, an endless modification of outlines produced by mutual interference and subtle modification or feedback – something remote, I hope, from the rigid oscillations of Crusoe's mental hopping on the spot, a mode of ratiocination which Canetti likens to the chattering of false teeth.[34] Besides, 'it is precisely these little whirlwinds of air that are responsible for the production of sounds in wind instruments,'[35] and it is that noise, rather than the clatter of artificial gums, that harmonizes best with the oceanic folds and edges that characterize the ground as it flutters, becoming the lie of the land.

To write in this way is, I realize, to make demands of one's readers, who may reasonably be impatient to get to the point, and who may find the sinuous byways and incidental curvatures along the way dangerously close to a baroque self-indulgence. But perhaps the impatience for a linear exposition is part of the problem; if our opening to the future depends in part on renovating our modes of historical narrative, then an attention to the processes of getting from one location to the next may not be self-indulgent but critical in establishing the value of the knowledge garnered. Cryptographers who are anxious to put some backbone into a book that advances from whirlpool to whirlpool, that seems bent on staying in the eye of the storm, may want to make out some secret connections. What, for example, is the cryptic link between Giorgione's art of chiaroscuro and the meditation on light said to illuminate William Light's life? Is the resemblance between the Strehlow-like figure on the banks of the Finke and the enigmatic soldier beside the unnamed river of Giorgione's *Tempesta* merely coincidental?

These questions are dealt with later; in a curvilinear environment there are no 'mere' coincidences – these are the logical artefacts of planar thinking. Similarly, the preoccupation with subterranean causes and hidden signs may arise in part from an indifference to the patterns that unfold before our eyes, those whirlpools that our ideological lines of latitude and longitude prevent us from assessing rationally in their motion. But more helpful in navigating the tides of the argument than a search for hidden reefs is to keep in mind two ideas or movement-images which continually shadow the argument. The first is the curvilinear flight of the spear; the second that of the storm. Neither of these topics, if such they are, belongs to what is usually understood as the concern of history, but from my point of view they signify the third and fourth dimensions that needed to be introduced if the historical significance of the subject-matter was to be localized and brought into relief.

Exponents of curvilinear space, they are also changed when viewed curvilineally, and in this way they become unifying threads for us. From a linear perspective, the efficiency of the spear's flight-path is proportional to its directness and rectitude: any rise or sag saps its energy; deviations towards the parabolic, and even the weapon's mere swagger and quiver, signify weaknesses. But as flight-paths whose motion is the historical trace, the unique instantiation, of a complex of gravitational, meteorological, physical and physiological forces, their value is quite different. It no longer resides in a power to pierce, but in their opening-up of a passage, their revelation of an environment that is 'dimpled', that continuously vibrates and shimmers like a dew-laced cobweb. As the trace of lively passage, the spear acquires its unifying meaning; the same fundamental impulse to enter into skilful play with the environment governs Giorgione's art of *macchiare*, Light's breath patterns, and the foot-marked Aranda chants reproduced by Strehlow.

Relocated environmentally, the storm also shifts its meaning. No longer a theatrical accompaniment of colonial invasion, a knot in the linear thread of progress, it is understood as a gathering-together, as a local event, a convergence of elements latent throughout the region. A highly-charged pressure-point within the meteorological regime, it slopes away infinitely subtly towards the plain blue sky. Its energy is never dissipated, only discharged and condensed preparatory to subsequent evaporation and reformation. This commonplace knowledge turns out not only to adumbrate a different model of territorial occupation, but a different conception of subjectivity, where the self is not a nuclear entity, a billiard ball 'in a game played by unskillful players, continually being nearly sent into a pocket, but hardly ever getting right into one,' as Samuel Butler put it,[36] but the player who, in dialogue with his multiplanar surroundings, continuously produces himself. In any case, it is where the spear-points turn into raindrops, in between lightning and thunder, that a poetics and a polity no longer colonial may converge and find common ground. It is in that place where the three figures of this book appear to die that they may be reborn.

Part One

A Reverent Miming

> It is my belief that when the strong web of future Australian verse comes to be woven, probably some of its strands will be found to be poetic threads spun on the Stone Age hair-spindles of Central Australia.
>
> T. G. H. Strehlow, *Songs of Central Australia*[1]

At Hermannsburg, the former Lutheran Mission west of Alice Springs (Plate 1), Strehlow is unremembered. When I visited the anthropologist's birthplace recently, I was, they told me, only the second person in two years to inquire after him. On the face of it, this is odd. Strehlow spent his childhood and early youth there, only departing from the place when his father, Pastor Carl, died in 1922. Ten years later, fresh out of Adelaide University, he was back, making Hermannsburg his headquarters while he undertook a series of field trips under the auspices of the Australian National Research Council to collect Aranda songs, myths and artefacts. During this time he involved himself spasmodically but familiarly in the life of the Lutheran community, now repairing the church organ, now helping to organize the Christmas festivities. More importantly, he undertook the revision of his father's Aranda translation of the New Testament.[2]

Nor did his attachment to his first home diminish after he began to attain a respectable place in the white academic community. His *Aranda Phonetics and Grammar* (prepared in the mid-1930s but only published in 1947), his monumental *Songs of Central Australia* (largely written in the mid-1950s but not published until 1971), and even his autobiographical account of his father's death, *Journey to Horseshoe Bend* (1969), bear witness to his loyalty to the land of his birth. Despite anti-German feeling during the Second World War, he maintained his links with the Centre; a patrol officer employed by the Native Affairs department of the Northern

Territory, he saw himself as a bulwark between his people (the Aranda) and the white authorities. In a lecture he delivered in 1967, Strehlow distinguished John McDouall Stuart from other nineteenth-century Central Australian white explorers; unlike one-time travellers (Colonel Warburton, say), unlike those for whom the Centre was incidental to their journeys (Ernest Giles, for example), Stuart had kept coming back, traversing Aranda country no less than six times.[3] In a way, this was Strehlow's ideal: to find a way of living that would enable him to keep coming back.

His scholarly researches, not to mention his numerous anti-assimilationist speeches made in the 1960s, suggest that Strehlow amply fulfilled the obligations which, as he reports in *Journey to Horseshoe Bend*, were placed on him by the mother of an Aranda playmate when he departed from Hermannsburg in 1922: 'You are not just a white boy . . . you are one of us. You belong to our people. You belong to the totem of the Twins of Ntarea, and you are a true Aranda. Go south and learn in the white men's schools, but then come back to us. No other white child born here has ever returned to us, but you must come back to us, to your own people.'[4] But here is the rub. This apparently verbatim speech is obviously a rhetorical invention. When questioned about the accuracy of his recollections of conversations heard forty years before, Strehlow replied that as a boy he had kept a journal;[5] but even if the Aranda mother's excellent Standard English speech glosses a historical fact, its value is clearly autobiographical. Retrospectively, Strehlow is giving his life's story a shape.

The speech Strehlow attributes to the nameless Aranda woman is a rhetorical way of asserting his right to call Hermannsburg home; but its theatricality produces the opposite effect. If Strehlow must wait upon an invitation to go back – one which, furthermore, he must write for himself – he evidently does not belong there. He may be 'a true Aranda' by affiliation – by virtue, say, of a lifetime of good works – but he can never stand in a filial relationship to Aranda elders, men and women. And indeed when, towards the end of his life, his high-handed management of the sacred objects he had collected in the 1930s caused a serious rift between him and the Aranda community, this was precisely the confusion of identity with which he was charged. Strehlow's error, another Aboriginal woman remarked, was to believe that he, the son of German immigrants, could be Aranda.[6]

This confusion, this profound sense of homelessness masquerading as an over-confident claim to membership of a group, cut the other way too: if his claim to be an insider risked making him an outsider in Aranda society, it also threatened to make him an outcast within the Lutheran community. In comparison with the Aranda system of social organization, which possessed sophisticated mechanisms for the provisional 'incorporation' of outsiders,[7] the Lutherans were notable internally for a propensity to schism, and externally for their dogmatic isolationism.[8] Religious exiles in their own land, the Lutherans were experts in exile's politics. So when in *Journey to Horseshoe Bend* Strehlow went out of his way to accuse the Immanuel Synod of South Australia of an unchristian combination of indifference and avarice that directly contributed to his father's premature death,[9] it would not be surprising if he were to find himself ostracized in the official local memory.

And it is true. At Hermannsburg, the presence of Ted Strehlow is conspicuously missing. There, proudly dominating the space at the centre of the Mission kraal, is the whitewashed church his father Carl built in 1897 (Plate 2); a plaque over the entrance testifies to Carl's pious industry as a translator. There is the residence Pastor Strehlow erected in the same year – nearly as tall as the church, lending the democratic scatter of the oldest Mission buildings an architectural hierarchy, it suggests patriarchal authority. There is the water tank, built in 1935 at the initiative of Carl Strehlow's successor F. W. Albrecht, storing the waters piped from Kaporilja and giving the Mission its first permanent water supply. There is the 'gallery' where the paintings of the Hermannsburg School of watercolourists – Namatjira and his sons, Pareroultja, Rubuntja and the rest (about whom Strehlow wrote so enthusiastically, so discerningly) – are on exhibition. Although the Mission's lands have long been returned to their traditional owners, Lutheran zeal keeps alive the memory of its founders and leaders. Ask about Strehlow, though, and you find yourself talking about someone else, or having to explain who you mean.

Now, according to many who knew him, Strehlow was a 'difficult' personality. He seemed to have a talent for alienating those whom he wished to attract. He was a passionate advocate, but a merciless critic of those who criticized his advocacy – a character awkwardly lacking the skills, the desire perhaps, to negotiate a middle ground. He accepted no authority, although he claimed it for himself; he demanded loyalty and obedience from his academic co-workers, but did not possess these qualities himself. He was touchy, tyrannical, sentimental. A gift for self-dramatization was combined with an insensitivity to the drama of other people's lives. His was a somewhat operatic temperament – and it might be easy, then, to make him the author of his own disappearance; as if only a regrettable quirk of personality prevented him from being added to the roll-call of Hermannsburg founding fathers.

But to seek to explain Strehlow's posthumous neglect as the legacy of his own psychology is to miss the point. It is equally half-sighted to represent him as a tragic hero labouring in the wilderness – the approach adopted in the permanent display at the Strehlow Research Centre in Alice Springs. Biographical and psychological enclosure acts of this kind are, as we shall see in our discussion of another tragic hero, William Light, among the basic strategies of colonialism: to make Strehlow responsible for his own 'mistakes' is simultaneously to write him out of history and to allow him a place in history only in so far as he departs from himself and learns to conform. But it was precisely this choice that Strehlow refused. To lay claim to a place of his own at Hermannsburg was to contest the Lutheran story, its patriarchal teleology that justified Carl's labour in the desert in terms of the acts of Moses and St. Paul – its assumption that Ted would inherit his father's ministry. It was to contest the very idea that notions of genealogy, lineage and descent had anything to do with living in a new country.

There was a sense in which to be memorialized as Carl's son, or even as a remarkable anthropologist, was to be denied a place of his own in history; and this might be literally as well as metaphorically true. As the name 'Hermannsburg' implied, the Lutherans regarded their mission on the Finke River as a spiritual clone of the Hermannsburg Mission Institute where they had trained. No allowance was made in this naming for the local lie of the land or the Aranda nomenclature. This was all very well for those pastors who had committed themselves to a wandering mission, and who intended to plant little Hermannsburgs wherever they went. But the child Strehlow was in a different position: like a second-generation migrant, his history, his identity, was tied up with the local difference of the environment where he had grown up. To name it, to invoke its indigenous name, say, was not simply to allude to an experience of place that Lutheran history ignored: it was to give himself a place in history.

Further, it was to assert the existence of a different kind of history, of affiliation rather than filiation. To downplay the significance in his life of mother and father, and capriciously to repatriate himself to Ntarea, a pool sacred to the local natives, could be regarded as the merest autobiographical kitsch; it was a convention of Victorian and Edwardian self-writing to claim descent not from one's parents but from some local sacred site, whether the orchard, the sand-hill, the folly, or father's library. But it was precisely this assumption of place that, as a migrant, Strehlow could not afford: to derive himself mythically from a place would have been to deny what was peculiar about his subjectivity, that it was not predicated on property, a prior historical enclosure act. The autobiography of a migrant could not consist of an inventory of special places, a genealogy as natural history; but its task might be to bring such places into being.

This process of bringing places 'into being' dissolved the distinction between autobiography and history; to affiliate successfully to the new environment was to be initiated into a new history, but also to envisage different ways of telling history. How was the 'ground' of one's existence – which for a figure like Strehlow had to be understood doubly, as the physical ground of the Finke River region and the metaphysical ground of one's self-knowledge – to be rendered? This was a poetic question, but it was also a political one: for evidently in renaming himself, Strehlow was also adumbrating a different system of cultural transmission, a future where patriarchal loyalties were replaced by an attunement to a historical environment. And if, as Strehlow thought, these new forms of writing must arise out of a synthesis of indigenous and foreign poetic modes, then to tell one's own life differently might be to help inaugurate a post-colonial polity – and literature – where the past was not a foreign country but the ground beneath one's feet.

So *Songs of Central Australia* is a detailed account of Aranda ceremonial songs, and also a demonstration of the poetic lineage linking them to the oral literatures of Homeric Greece and the Dark Age Germanic tribes of Northern Europe. But this cross-cultural perspective is developed not simply in the interests of rendering Aranda song traditions more easily comprehensible to Western readers: it is integral to the book's form. Strehlow's lengthy quotations from Anglo-Saxon charms, Greek tragedy, the Norse sagas and the *Prose Edda* go far beyond what is required to prove a thematic or a stylistic parallel. They are meant to be read in their own right, to enjoy an importance equivalent to the Aranda song texts they are supposed to contextualize. They are woven into Strehlow's narrative so that it ceases to be a linear exposition and becomes a poetic composition. Strehlow composes his book as the ancient Greek *rhapsode* is said to have made his poems, by drawing on a vast stock of poetic motifs and weaving them into a new pattern.[10] His is not simply a posthumous grammar, an elegy for a dead tradition; finding an equivalent form, it announces the possibility of a new, authentically Australian literature, of which it itself is the first example.

This, then, is the significance of Strehlow's work for our essay, that it sought to devise what we might call an environmental poetics, a theory of representation that took account of the local lie of the land. Triangulating between a colonialist heritage, a migrant present and the desirability of a bicultural future, Strehlow attempted to create a mode of memorialization more adequate to the representation of his, and his adopted society's, colonial condition. Affiliating himself to Aranda traditions, he did not forget his own learned Western traditions, but made the meeting-place of the two his life's work (his autobiography). The progress of his scholarship came to be the enactment of his own meditation on the problem of belonging. The aim was not the Odyssean one of going home loaded with an exotic treasure: it was, if anything, to inaugurate a history of disappearances, of lightnesses and temporalities, and by assimilating himself to an Aranda understanding of the environment to overcome the (Western) nostalgia usually associated with such transformational moments.

If a way of travelling could be found, a way of writing, that while it circled the Centre never settled down, one might disentangle oneself from an imperialist tradition, not by moving on but by continuing to come back. In this way Strehlow might affiliate to his adopted people, but he could also reaffiliate to Carl; by detaching his father from his patriarchal frame, by reauthoring him as it were, he could define his relationship to his father differently. By retelling his father's death, say, drawing it into the circle of his own coming into being, he could transcend the Oedipal curse of patriarchy and have Carl speak again, in accents at once similar to, and different from, his son's. But again, this meant writing history, not memoirs or confessions; and if that history were not to imprison the author solipsistically as the sole authority for his own experience, it had to be grounded locally – must indeed be a history of the ground.

So *Journey to Horseshoe Bend* is, as its title implies, a narrative of moving over uneven land; but it is also a skilfully-orchestrated meditation on the Western assumption that a narrative is a journey, a means of getting from one place to another. As Carl Strehlow is painfully transported down the dry Finke River, he meditates on another penitential journey, that of Christ to Calvary; as Theo follows his father's van over the sand-hills and through the mulga brush, he is aware of making the passage from childhood to manhood. And into this fourfold narrative at least two further threads are woven: a totemic landscape whose creative forces are everywhere visible and whose eternal influences bear down on the little party; and the landscape of colonization, its scored lineages of violence, expropriation and systemic racism. The effect is not fluvial in a Western sense: individual narrative tributaries building to a climactic flood, father's transfiguration. Quite the opposite: like the braided channels of the Finke itself, the parallelisms and convergences serve to slow progress down. A narrative corresponding to the anastomosing lie of the land emerges, and one effect is to put off the ending and its predictable nostalgia.

But before enlarging on Strehlow's poetic project and its historical corollary, a post-colonial culture both bicultural in some sense and authentically Australian, it is worth lingering on the ground already traversed, and seeking to deepen a little the grooves already traced there. To begin again with Strehlow's claim on Ntarea; if the totem of 'The Twins' had a personal meaning for Strehlow, it was in part at least because it symbolized a double identity that was perhaps second nature to those who found themselves caught in negotiations between colonizers and colonized.

The community at Hermannsburg could be characterized as a mirror-state, as a group that had reduplicated itself mimetically. Although within the broader Australian cultural landscape the Lutherans were an in-between group, occupying a border-land between the colonizing Anglo-Saxons and the equally repugnant savagery of the indigenous people, they did not see themselves this way. They certainly did not conceive of their experimental society as promoting any form of cultural (let alone racial) hybridism. If anything, their marginality, their need to unite against the twin barbarisms of white 'materialism' and black 'irreligion', reinforced their sense of internal unity and singleness of missionary purpose. At the same time, however, their group unity was self-defeating if it provided no means of annexing the people to whom they ministered. Less benignly, the Lutherans were parasitic on the Arabana, the Dieri, the Aranda; their own survival depended on persuading the latter that parasitism was symbiosis.

But the rigidity of the Lutheran outlook, its Mosaic (not to say typically imperializing) paranoia about preserving the purity of the spirit – represented territorially in an obsession with not-to-be-transgressed boundaries – meant that symbiosis could only be conceived as a form of traumatic engulfment: the Aranda was 'converted', like Saul instantly being reborn a Paul. It was as if the kraal gates opened, sucked him in, and closed with a cloud of dust behind him. The Lutherans duplicated themselves without compromising the rigid boundaries setting them apart from the physical and metaphysical wilderness where they had set down their tents. The new converts belonged to the chosen tribe by virtue of their ability to mimic the new forms, to say back to the missionaries their own words and doctrines. Within this world bound together by mimicry it was possible, as Carl Strehlow did, to take up ethnography. But there must be no question of being taken in by native beliefs: Carl Strehlow compiled his monumental inventory of Aranda and Loritja myths, but refused to attend the ceremonies and sites at which they were sung.[11]

These features of Hermannsburg's social dynamics, and the role that conversion as mimicry played in sustaining it, form an essential context for the emergence of Strehlow's poetic theory – whose object, we can say summarily, was to find a way out of the mirror-state and the mimetic poetics that maintained it. And first of all, we can see how they were embodied in the ambiguous meaning 'Ntarea' played in Strehlow's self-definition. Strehlow accepted the Lutherans' retrospective rationalization of their presence on the Finke, their humanitarian claim to have provided the hapless Aranda with a bulwark against the worst excesses of rapacious colonialism. Indeed, he went further, claiming a convergence of interests between the metaphysically-inclined founding fathers of the Mission and the no less spiritually-adept Aranda elders: 'It should be noted,' he wrote, 'that the most respected and upright of the converts on the early mission stations generally seem to have been persons who had been brought up in the old traditions – men who tried to preserve their old social organisation as far as possible, and who consciously sought to retain their pride in their native heritage wherever it could be harmonised with their new Christian beliefs.'[12]

But this last was a fatal concession, as the 'native heritage' mostly could not be harmonized with the 'new Christian beliefs' – a fact that the fate of Ntarea illustrated. The official 'desacralization' of the Manangananga Cave, the main *tjurunga* storehouse of the *ratapa* (twins) dreaming, occurred in April 1928 under Pastor Albrecht, but with the help of 'native evangelists' like Blind Moses, and six years later, when Strehlow visited the site, all trace of native awe had gone. 'A generation later, in 1955,' Jones adds, 'the taboo on Manangananga Cave had apparently been reinstated.'[13] On the occasion of Strehlow's second visit to the site, he discovered that he was 'the sole ratapa man able to chant the verses for this place.'[14] Nor can these metamorphoses in the cult of the Twins be attributed solely to the zeal of Carl Strehlow's successor Albrecht. By 1910 or so, the traditional ownership and maintenance of the sacred cave was already in doubt: 'with Ntarea,' as Pastor Strehlow had written at the time, 'after Loatjira the next in succession was the son Ubmelteraka and Kwalanke, who is already dead, and so Ngurtakangurla, the son of Arintja – our goat shepherd for many years – will be our next chief. Should he however die first, the now quite nominal title of chief will fall to Intjalka I. (=Johannes), the son of Karitjira.' And Strehlow added, 'Ntarea also is now a "given-up" camp. In recent times our station has become the assembling place for the rest of the western Aranda people.'[15]

Evidently, Strehlow's invocation of Ntarea as his own conception-site was not another instance of naïvely Modernist primitivism, or a latter-day flirtation with the Dionysiac Nietzsche. Strehlow was affiliating himself to a place from which the spirit had fled, and his object in re-authoring himself in this way was to reinvest the site with an aura it had lost. He was not a colonist (or a missionary, or an anthropologist) stealing away and destroying a local treasure, but a migrant, obliged to locate himself within a history of disappearances. Nor was it a question of posing as a pseudo-Aranda in order to mimic their tradition. In seeking to affiliate himself to Ntarea, Strehlow transferred his loyalties from a people to a place. As Carl understood, association with Ntarea had been a way of defining kinship ties, a place within the social group; for Strehlow it was different. Morton has noted that 'Since Hermannsburg Mission opened in 1877 hundreds of people, including T. G. H. Strehlow and other whites, have claimed twins as their conception totem.'[16] But Strehlow ignores this, construing affiliation purely, it seems, in terms of an attachment to place – not as admission to membership of a group.

Or rather, he seems to want to claim admission to a higher group than the one represented by the 'hundreds of people' casually associated with Hermannsburg – a group whose membership will be defined geographically, even topographically, rather than by common lines of descent. In keeping alive the verses not only of Ntarea but of a hundred other totemic sites throughout the MacDonnells and further east, Strehlow did not expect to preserve indigenous oral traditions – which he insisted were dying out – but he did want to find a way of transmitting the philosophy informing them: the conviction that identity was local, relational, environmental. In this sense, Strehlow laid claim to Ntarea for the future rather than the past, making its reconsecration foreshadow the way a future state might be constituted. But an identification with the lie of the land, with the poetics of the ground, could hardly be sustained inside the mirror-state of Hermannsburg, where spiritual insight depended on 'seeing through' the physical landscape, as if its appearances were deceptive or at best purely symbolic.

Because Hermannsburg's self-reinforcing mimicry did not appear this way to the inmates of that system; to them, it seemed that in their preaching they remained faithful to a tradition of sacred interpretation that understood the Bible as a system of representations, whereby invisible truths were rendered visible, and where, in the other direction, physical appearances were revealed as signs, as ephemeral guises in which the eternal manifested itself. In Christian hermeneutics the events of the Old Testament were to be understood figuratively, as the allegorical prefigurings of the Word made flesh. On the other hand, the full meaning of the physical deeds and sayings of Christ was metaphysical, only to be grasped by an act of historical transcendence. The difficulty was that, in the colonial situation, these rhetorical pretensions broke down: how were the uninitiated to tell a look-alike from the real thing? And if the look-alike was not real, how was the real ever to be grasped? The conventional nature of the Christian typology, the spiritual value it gave to certain signs, became obvious, and it proved impossible to distinguish mimesis from mimicry.

Nor were these idle questions of poetics; they critically defined the politics of race relations at Hermannsburg, and by extension defined the ideological context in which Strehlow set about finding an opening towards a mode of representing his place in the world that did not collapse either into the solipsism of mimicry or into the no less imprisoning system of sign-worship underpinning the authority of mimesis. In any case, the ambiguous slippage between mimicry and mimesis was a primary mechanism in advancing the ideological interests of the Lutherans, and it also (although more cynically) enabled the Aranda to find a way of incorporating themselves provisionally into a culture which, paradoxically, had no use for them except as potential souls. Consider, for example, the figure of 'Old Moses': what exactly was the status of his utterances? What was the significance of his appearance? Did he represent Christian doctrine? Or did he merely mimic its outward appearances? (And these were questions not only for the suspicious whites but for the Aranda, among whom 'mimicry' might have a different cultural valency.) And could not the same questions be asked of Carl Strehlow himself?

When the sacred *tjurunga* were removed from Manangananga Cave in April 1928, 'Albrecht delivered a sermon about the Biblical Moses and Aaron and the Golden Calf, likening *tjurunga* to the Golden Calf.' And prior to this, Aranda preachers were 'publicly ridiculing "*tjurunga* worship" '. Blind Moses, the former ceremonial leader and now evangelist, delivered a standard sermon entitled 'Churunga or Christ'.[17] At issue here was not simply the assimilation of Aranda tradition to a teleological reading of the Old Testament, but the passage from an outer light to an inner one. To remove the *tjurunga* from their site was to remove their power to signify; in effect, it was to deny their claim to signify regionally. In their place, a new order of universal signs was instituted: the cross, say, illuminating the world placelessly. And who was Old Moses in this? He represented the Old Testament prophet, but he was also an apostolic mimic. 'Old Moses with his silvery white beard,' Strehlow wrote in 1932, 'looks just like one of the early pictures of one of the Disciples; tall and erect, despite his blindness a sturdy walker – a voice in the wilderness, whose resolute tones invite outsiders to submit to the New Way, which experience has taught him is better than the old.'[18] Old Moses's sole surviving child was a daughter called Priscilla, a name that suggests perhaps Old Moses's other, Pauline mask.

Similar difficulties of interpretation surrounded Strehlow's own field-work. How was he to make the Aranda see their cultural traditions as he saw them unless he could persuade them to theatricalize or represent them? And what if such mimic performances meant nothing to them? These questions had another aspect: if Moses and his historical kin could glide over the ground carrying their spiritual horde with them, if Odysseus could return home confident that things would be much as he left them, because both stories belonged to cultural traditions in which the lie of the land had long been neutralized, then Strehlow was in the opposite situation. If he was to find any remnant of Aranda culture, he must be prepared to entertain an anti-Odyssean mode of travelling, one where no homecoming could be assured, where, carrying nothing with him, he must be prepared to stay empty-handed.

Strehlow's account of a visit he made in 1932 to Lukara, a sacred water-hole located about twenty miles south-east of Barrow Creek, is illustrative. Instead of marking a triumphant homecoming for Strehlow and the two Unmatjera men, the older Ilbaljurkna and the younger Remalarinja, the visit was experienced as a passage from absence to absence. Although Remalarinja 'knew the lay of the country even better than I; for I had been away a score of years at least [ ], he had never seen the *al'ipita* [sacred cave].' The old man finds himself in an even more embarrassing position: charged with the responsibility of locating the sacred site, he finds he is at a loss. 'At last Ilbaljurkna returned, almost in tears: "*Inkatai*," he said, "don't be angry with me; I was only a young man when I saw Lukara last; I have been away many years; I am grown an old man now; I have been away too long; I could not remember aright where the old place was, and the sand has covered the pit . . . ; but come and see what is left of the *tjurunga* of this greatest of places".' Not only has his memory failed him; the place itself has changed beyond recognition. As for the sacred *tjurungas* themselves, 'The old man trembled and removed the top stones. Broken pieces of old smooth *tjurungas* appeared, and he spread them out, and chanted the old songs over them – "*Iowa, namane jutjurna, iowa Lbaljukne jutjurne*" and he was not satisfied till I joined it too. We rubbed the sand off the shattered pieces – poor remains of an old treasure grove, and with shaking voices Ilbaljurkna and Remalarinja told me the story of the destruction of these *tjurunga*. This happened after the murder [of two white men in reprisal for their abduction of Aboriginal women] at Barrow Creek in 1874 . . .'[19]

The irony – at least for the anthropologist bent on collecting cultural treasure – is that he can only be assured of an authentic insight into the history of the people who are his subject where all physical evidence of their cultural traditions has disappeared. For at this point a theatrical mode of communication and exchange, based on ascribing symbolic value to certain objects, breaks down and there is nothing left to do but to enter into their distress empathetically. Again at issue here were two markedly different modes of poetic expression, and I think the changes that Strehlow made to his 1932 diary when he came to transcribe this episode for publication in *Songs of Central Australia* show he was conscious of this.

In the diary Strehlow reflects on what he has seen: 'I packed up the broken splinters to-night. *Sic transit gloria mundi.* I am living in the world of "Time was – Time has been – Time shall be no more".'[20] In *Songs of Central Australia*, however, he concludes: Ilbaljurkna's 'last plea to me' was to 'Tell the white *ingkata* down south what was done to us a long time ago in our own country.'[21] In the diary, Strehlow locates himself in the nowhere land of European elegy, within a historical tradition where the Aranda have no place; in the later version, however, he throws off this Homeric pose. A radiating space is acknowledged that holds the men together and implicates them in the same actions, the same history. This is not to argue for a progressive enlightenment, merely to identify a telling oscillation. And equally suggestive here is the replacement of the happy 1932 coinage, 'old treasure grove', with the more clichéd and literary 'ancient native treasure cave'; if the first suggests a numinous environment, the latter conjures up the Ithacan cave where Odysseus stored his treasure – a cave that could only be used in this way because it had been desacralized and assimilated to a poetry in which the lie of the land served merely to provide a theatrical stage set.

But things could not continue like this; Strehlow could hardly make a name for himself by travelling from absence to absence. If local presences were not easily located, they would have to be provoked; the Aranda must be made to represent what was absent, to mimic it as if it were there. Otherwise, his desire to deepen his knowledge of the Aranda would collapse into self-mimicry. As he noted in the diary of his 1932 Western MacDonnells expedition, 'I shall have to start tomorrow on a big job – mustering together as many natives . . . as possible. Else the University Party, as Tom remarked this morning, will only have us to work upon.'[22] This is the temptation of the Homeric pose: that it gives Strehlow the authority to pronounce upon what shall be kept (what shall be taken away). This is why Ilbaljurkna trembles, addressing the youthful Strehlow as '*ingkata*'. At the end of that visit the old man hands Strehlow 'a small *tjurunga* which he had picked up as a boy and carried about with him ever since.' Why should he do this, if not because Strehlow had impressed upon him that he possessed a more powerful story, one that could preserve the past over greater distances? As Strehlow put it, 'now that the *Ingkata* himself had come, he could gladly have all the pieces that were still left.'[23]

So the *tjurunga* pass out of the environment where they focused a culture of periodic performance into the realm of representations where, mere greasy stones, they risk becoming laughable. To protect his own dignity, the anthropologist must reinvest them with historic aura, but this can only be done by having his native informants re-enact the ceremonies and songs associated with them. But what if they have forgotten these? And even if they have remembered them, how is he to tell? The mimicry is essential, but it exposes the anthropologist to ridicule; because he is perhaps witnessing the representation of nothing.

'I had wished to take a movie of the dancers doing the *inkemarenama* around the *tnatantja* pole,' Strehlow writes on one occasion, 'but though I requested them this morning specially, nothing had been done to provide the *Inti iliara*. I felt intensely disappointed: the *tnatantja* was a work of art, and Tjeria a splendidly decorated imposing figure and fine actor; and now no *iliara* [newly initiated men], hence no real lifelike movie could be taken of the scene. I expressed my disappointment, and left without adding anything else. Everyone was very much upset, and since I was mean enough to delay giving out the flour and tea and sugar to-night, the poor old men were quite frightened, as Jim told me, as to what I would do. I said nothing more; only they offered to stage another Intia ceremony early to-morrow morning, and provide some iliara.'[24]

This sort of travelling left Strehlow feeling constantly 'edgy', poised between opposite destinies that looked frighteningly alike. The men dressed up, and it looked to all appearances as if Strehlow was about to be taken inside an ancient tradition; then, like the clouds of the region that gathered deceptively only to disperse rainlessly, everything seemed to reverse itself and melt away.[25] An imminent representation turned into its look-alike antithesis, empty mimicry; the curiously lifelike became the stupidly likelike. Strehlow's annoyance was exacerbated by his dependence on a particularly fragile technology of representation, but it also reflected a frustration stemming from the ambiguous nature of communication itself. The tendency of mimicry to colonize mimesis, as it were, not only made his ethnographic responsibilities harder to discharge; it characterized the entire Hermannsburg scene. Perhaps this was why Strehlow increasingly came to understand his task as the evolution of a poetics immune to mimicry's Gorgon look.

In August 1932, and presumably on other occasions, the Aranda congregation at evening service was treated to a slide show 'at which pictures were shown on the screen depicting the life of Christ'. Granted the far-famed mimetic powers of the Aboriginal people, events like this which were 'greatly appreciated by the visitors',[26] shed a very different light on the activities of the Aranda goatherds and shepherds at Hermannsburg. That in some ways most iconoclastic of Lutheran sects was creating about itself a film set which, in terms of its physical verisimilitude to the coasts of Samaria, far exceeded anything a Bible illustrator could manage. The men, the women and children with the walk-on parts may not have been waiting for the Second Coming; re-enacting what they had seen, they may have regarded their performance as an end in itself. At any rate, when anthropologists like Strehlow filmed them on or off the Christian set, it may well have confirmed the reality of their conversion – for was not their reproduction in this way proof that they walked in the footsteps of the saints?

In the semiotic maze such mirror ironies created, the irritation bordering on panic that Strehlow felt when an Aranda woman at Hermannsburg started telling him about her dreams becomes explicable. Before he could disengage himself from her, there was 'some mention of snakes . . . she also informed me that she often saw the Angel Gabriel in dreams.'[27] Strehlow was committing himself to preserving whatever remained of Aranda religious tradition. He had to assume an inner core of beliefs that had not yet been polluted, that survived intact beneath the Christian *persona*. The testimony of this woman seemed to disprove his hypothesis – consequently she rose up before him like his own nightmare. Historically, 'the brief Unmatjera Arenana [Carpet Snake] myth,' which Strehlow collected around this time may have had benevolent associations; but symbolically, who could say? In the Christianized imagery its status was at the very least ambiguous. Gabriel was unequivocally an advocate and herald of the new order. Besides appearing to Mary, he had come in response to Daniel's prayer for direction ('O Lord our God, that hast brought thy people forth out of the land of Egypt with a mighty hand . . . ')[28] But in a culture where, as Strehlow later wrote, those who have had visions and hallucinations 'have been firmly convinced of the absolute truth and reality of their experiences',[29] her dream also foretokened a fundamental shift of ground; for in accordance with Aranda conception beliefs, what the woman may have dreamed was the name of the spirit child with whom she was pregnant – a child whose conception site would lie, presumably, in the sky.

It may be that the men he worked with experienced a comparable edginess or sense of double-take. What were they being asked to represent? They became aware of the category of representation itself, the possibility that mimicry might be detached from the spatio-temporal matrix that gave it its magical or cultural efficacy and might be repeated for merely technological convenience, without regard for what it meant. The freedom the Aranda men feel to travel with him, to depart from the regular seasonal routes, reflects their sense of dispossession, their feeling that they travel desecrated ground where their passage does not perform a living place but merely recollects that experience, where the routes they take, the songs they sing, merely go through the motions. Doing it for the *ingkata*, they behave as if in a dream; it is as if they see and hear themselves for the first time as ghosts and echoes.

At least in Strehlow's diary, they spend much of their time in country that is distinctly European, picturesque, its indigenous names detached from their oral matrix and re-attached fragmentarily, as on a map. Strehlow evokes a landscape that suggests the watercolours of Albert Namatjira: 'I see to-night peaks around me everywhere; once their names were familiar to every child in the Aranda tribe, and there were sacred caves wherever you looked – at Ulaterka, at Ulamba, at Rubuntja. There still are a few Rubuntja *tjurunga*; but these have long ago been hidden in the sandhills E. of the mountain, to escape being stolen.'[30] A landscape, we might add, where speaking presences have been metamorphosed into, and disguised as, landscape features: Rubuntja, for example, was also a 'Northern Aranda informant belonging to the fire totem Urubuntja, born about 1880.'[31] The landscape becomes visible, that is to say picturesque, where the voices of these men are silenced.

It is as if the landscape is metaphysically as well as physically stripped, here and there silenced, bleached of sense and therefore standing up photographically proud, here and there still intoned and breathing, infolded and invisible to the European eye. And in their own way, the colonizers feel this metaphysical disintegration: the landscape that had been the Land of Promise has subtly turned into its look-alike antithesis, the parched plains of Egypt. Visiting Ulamba, a Western Aranda kangaroo and *arintja* [mythical man-eating beings] centre, a few weeks after Lukara, Strehlow commented:

> This is the last original cave with *tjurunga* in the Western Macdonnells . . . when Ulamba passes, another chapter in the history of the Aranda tribe will have closed. Another step nearer the grave. For the black man is one with the soil he inhabits, and now all this vast and populous territory is silent as the grave. Men have died and some have drifted to the centres of white man's civilisation and there degenerated [ ] for he does not bear transplanting into a different soil. Once there were firelight processions and chants and dance and song in these parts; now even the white squatter forsakes them. That last cave – it is as though Time had halted for a second and turned back and cast a pitying glance upon the dust of its sons; for these men were once a Great Race. And now – long live the White Man's civilisation! Welcome chaos in the world of to-day; for that is the modern youth's heritage from his own civilisation.[32]

Sentimental, this is also ironic. Strehlow's elegiac abandon depends on anticipating the absence of the folk whose disappearance it laments; it has the effect of hastening the very fate it appears to regret. This is its irony; and Strehlow's Homeric unawareness of this double bind constitutes a further irony. Indeed, an absence of irony, at least among Lutheran accounts of mission life, is an essential ingredient of the ideological enclosure act practised at Hermannsburg. The reality was, as we have seen, very different. It might be true (although Strehlow's elegy seems to give the lie to this) that the 'native heritage' occasionally found a place within Christian ritual; but this did not provide evidence of a convergent world view. The Aranda capacity to incorporate new cultural influences, evident both in their language and in their Christian chants, did not necessarily prove the 'transference of an age-old native practice to the new sacred forms introduced by Christianity';[33] rather, it demonstrated a gift for irony, for a politically-motivated art of mimicry.

Strehlow's advocacy of Hermannsburg as a community providing the detribalized Aranda with a distinct group identity – in Strehlow's view, painter Albert Namatjira became a 'nomad in no man's land' not when he failed to gain full initiation into his native traditions but when, leaving Hermannsburg, he tried to mimic the destructive individualism of white society[34] – this organic thesis should be set beside the description that poet Roland Robinson gave of his visits to the Lutheran mission and its outstations in the early 1950s. True, irony was written into his visit: to suppose, as many white artists and writers did in those days, that the Aranda would naïvely hand over their stories, was to invite deceit – and Robinson is duly duped. Nevertheless, Robinson's sense was that irony was systemic; that the Aranda adoption of white ways was purely strategic, a masking behaviour designed to preserve their own interests and traditions. Visiting Hermannsburg in 1954, he commented, 'They would pay lip service to the religion of the white man, but they would try to keep their own. They would avail themselves of the "cargo-cult" of the white man . . .'[35]

Particularly telling is the manner of his leaving Haast's Bluff. When Robinson announces his imminent departure for Hermannsburg, Namatjira offers to drive him; on the morning they are to go, though, the artist pretends to be surprised to find that he has no petrol: 'I knew at once that I had been "caught".' Provided with petrol by the Pastor, they set out, only to break down. Eventually the truck is brought in, and the mechanic comments, 'It's an old stunt of theirs. They'll always take a white man with them if they can. They know then that they'll always get help if they break down.'[36] So the helpless empowered themselves, and the powerful were framed. More fundamentally, and less sentimentally, Robinson's mistake was to suppose that the 'journey' had to do with a linear progress from one place to another. This was the idea that Namatjira satirized, ironically alluding to another tradition where movement might be a matter of deepening grooves and deepening obligations. Until that was understood, the poet was likely to travel superficially up and down a narrow line.

Ntarea begins to unfold a multiple significance. Or perhaps more accurately, it begins to resist being regarded merely as a site of 'significance'. The Western preoccupation with representations and their significance was cognate with the ideology of progress; it was the insignia of a migratory, if not nomadic, culture. To advance from one place to another, whether historically or geographically, to assert a connection across distances where there was none, meant translating the environment into a system of symbolic representations that could be set down anywhere, because they were nowhere localized. Symbolic representations had the convenient property of turning physical and cultural discontinuities into continuous lines leading from one place to the next. And the question becomes whether another form of movement is possible, a poetics of translation that is not bent on hurrying forward.

Perhaps Strehlow alluded to these matters when, at the close of *Journey to Horseshoe Bend* he addresses the Finke River in the guise of his thirteen-year-old persona Theo: 'The Lira Beinta was his own river: no matter what the future might bring, he would never cease to regard himself as one of the children of the Finke River.'[37] But the Finke River, of course, rarely flowed; and the deep pool of Ntarea, although it nestled in the bed of the Finke, rarely overflowed. Rather, pool and river occupied the same folded ground, the lie of the land enabling them to communicate with one another without either losing their identity. Further, when the Finke flowed, it flowed locally: local rainstorms fathered it, and it distributed its contents widely, disseminating a necklace of pools that soon dried up.

It was true, as Strehlow elegiacally reflected in his 1932 diary, that 'the waters of the mighty Finke lose themselves at last in the barren sands of the dead heart of this Continent.'[38] But this lapse into the rhetoric of the white pioneer intent on opening up the interior missed the point. The occasionally distributory system of the Finke was a foil to a culture intent on getting on; as the sign of a river it was deceptive. Symbolically, too, it was subversive: although it contained the dramas of birth and death, it drew no continuous line between them. It refused, in fact, to regard the ground as a surface on which to inscribe its own autonomous drama. The Finke *qua* river was nothing apart from its periodic performances of water movement. But these occasionally swelling tides of water did not signify release: they merely reinforced, reinvigorated the existing state of things, filling pools, deepening grooves. Embodying a different system of circulation, the Finke not only contributed to hydrological understanding; it modelled a non-patriarchal system of kinship, not to mention an environmental poetics.

There may have been another implication of Strehlow's attachment to 'The Twins'. We have spoken of an external, ironically self-conscious mimicry. But the situation at Hermannsburg, where Strehlow found himself somewhere between the colonizer and the migrant, was also, it seems, characterized by an *inner* mimicry – by what appeared to be a fortuitous resemblance between certain Aranda traditions and the psychological mechanisms that needed to be improvised if Strehlow was to ground his claim to belong locally historically and not merely rhetorically (or autobiographically). In Aranda society, 'All human persons were regarded without exception as the living reincarnations of immortal supernatural beings.' As humans evidently died, the doctrine of resurrection 'had as its natural corollary a belief in the twin personality of every human being.' This belief could manifest itself in an uncannily physical form: 'sometimes when a hunter returned from his quest and was still approaching in the distance, he appeared like two persons to his friends who were watching from the camp.'[39]

Here was an anthropological fact that glossed uncannily a commonplace migrant experience. To become the person who might legitimately live in the shadow of Ntarea, Strehlow had to rename where he came from. He had to embrace a different descent and invent a spirit double. To become worthy of his ancestry, he had to proliferate masks as well as strip away misconceptions. But this double life, while it might in another context cause psychological turmoil, focusing the migrant's dilemma, here seemed to be an essential condition of self-legitimation. For initiation into Aranda ways did not entail a European-style linear advance from obscurity to enlightenment, but quite the reverse, a gradual deepening of grooves, a reworking of masks. The figure most at home in the land was the master of masks. Strehlow explained admiringly, 'Obscurity in poetry was regarded . . . as a virtue rather than as a vice by the aboriginal clansmen; for it guarded the magical contents of their sacred songs against easy comprehension and memorization by the uninitiated.'[40]

Arduously circling his own country, crisscrossing it, peripatetically growing inward with a culture, step by step initiating himself into its historical pathways, Strehlow was evidently determined to return in his own way. He was not looking for a lost childhood, did not want to return to a simpler world, where things were laid out plainly. The appeal of Aranda culture lay in its complexity, in its seductive refusal to yield its secrets to the uninitiated. It was true that as a child Strehlow had learned to speak Aranda fluently, but:

> So great is the difference between the children's language, limited in vocabulary and poor in grammatical forms, and that of the adult initiated men, that upon my return to Central Australia in 1932 I

> avoided speaking Aranda as much as possible, not only because I had forgotten much of my earlier store of Aranda words, but also because I had no intention of betraying to the old men of the Aranda groups from whom I was endeavouring to collect my myths and songs how childish my Aranda speech had always been.[41]

To go back was to put behind him the toys of childish speech and, by acquiring the mantle of poetic knowledge, to achieve his initiation into manhood. To manage this entrance into adult society, Strehlow understood that he needed to mask his former self. He had to die to certain memories if he were to prove himself fit for resurrection as a new person, an initiated man. This second coming into being, culturally recapitulating the biological process, ensuring the initiate's passage into adult life, is a classic topic of anthropology; in Strehlow, it evidently coincided with an autobiographical motive. The anthropologist was a writer with literary pretensions; besides recording the sacred knowledge of an ancient culture which he feared to be on the edge of extinction, he wanted to take hold of his own life, to create out of it a significant narrative. To affiliate himself to a native culture was to furnish himself with a genealogy that mere filiation could not provide. Hermannsburg removed its mask and whispered its true name: Ntarea, 'his own home – the birthplace that bestowed upon him his Aranda citizenship rights which no man could ever take away from him.'[42]

In this context, the ambiguities implicit in Strehlow's view of Namatjira's life and art become clearer. In many ways Namatjira was Strehlow's spiritual elder brother, if not 'twin'. He had achieved in painting what Strehlow wanted to manage in literature: a synthesis of traditions producing a mode of expression accessible to that larger 'group' which, while Australian, was not locally attached to one part of its soil. According to Strehlow, Albert Namatjira's European-style watercolours were 'capable of setting the trees, rocks, animals, and persons of their own environment before the eyes of admiring spectators as their own rich verse had once conjured them up on the songs whose cadences had delighted the ears of Aranda audiences.'[43] Strehlow related this synthetic achievement to the conscious policy of the Lutheran pastors: 'During the critical first forty or fifty years of missionary endeavour at Hermannsburg, for instance, not a single youth ever refused to submit himself to initiation rites, which the authorities wisely refused to ban although they were personally not in favour of them.'[44] As a result, according to Strehlow, a bicultural, possibly multicultural, but still homogeneous community had evolved, one that gave the lie to the policy of assimilation. 'No man can stand successfully on his very own, as an individual divorced from the group to which he belongs by race, culture, and inclination'; and 'it is impossible to build up strong and lasting social structures on the shifting sands of illusive materialistic progress without the cementing influences of common ideals and concepts.'[45]

Strehlow's thesis is interesting, not least because it makes an explicit link between poetics – a mode of representation – and politics. The difficulty is that, as we saw, it sentimentalizes the political situation at Hermannsburg, and presumably therefore oversimplifies the poetics informing Namatjira's art. And while Strehlow could gloss over these difficulties for the purpose of a polemic, he could hardly avoid them when he came to set out his own poetic grammar in *Songs of Central Australia*. By dwelling briefly, then, on Namatjira's art, and on the circumstances in which the Hermannsburg 'school' came into being, we do not so much contradict Strehlow's account as deepen it. Just as Namatjira's superficially attractive paintings masked a complex response to the conditions of representation within the mirror-state of Hermannsburg, so the magisterial simplicities of *Songs of Central Australia* barely disguised a maze of ethical, religious and poetic enclosure acts against which Strehlow felt bound to rebel.

The point here is not to rehearse the by now commonplace observation that Namatjira was not perhaps brilliantly inweaving two cultures: that his paintings 'might conceal as much as they revealed . . . rather than represent a shared visual reality, they might mimic a European point of view and, by visualising the country in picturesque ways, perpetuate the white viewer's blindness to its spatial history.'[46] It is to go a step further and suggest that, even in supposing Namatjira mimicked the 'white' way of seeing the land, we remain the dupes of our own cultural frame of reference. As we have already said, the prospect of mimesis collapsing into mimicry may only have been frightening from a Western perspective; from a Central Australian viewpoint, the whole business of imitation may have appeared very differently. From within a performative tradition, the native evangelists (of whom Namatjira was one) may have imagined themselves incorporating mimesis into their own tradition. When they adopted Biblical names, they did not give up their other names; allowing themselves to stand in for representative figures in the Christian tradition, they metamorphosed these into living presences. And they achieved this by mimicking Christian forms, by copying what was said and shown. (This is not to question the sincerity of their Christian conviction; it simply alters the definition of conversion.)

This double mimicry whereby the Aranda copied the other in order to reassert their own identities may be exemplified in the work of the Aranda watercolourists. Strehlow's casual remark that Blind Moses looked 'just like one of the early pictures of the Disciples' not only lends support to my suggestion that he mimicked a pivotal figure within the tradition of Western mimesis; it throws light on the Biblical reference of Albert Namatjira's landscapes. It has become conventional to say that these express a bicultural understanding of the land, that they mimic a European way of seeing whilst more subtly asserting the painter's continuing attachment to his totemic landscape. But now another possibility emerges: that in mimicking the European way of seeing, he was copying the characteristic colours and forms used in Bible illustrations of the Holy Land.

According to Battarbee, the nearest parallel to the traditional *tjurunga* designs were 'the early Egyptian hieroglyphics.'[47] According to Strehlow (but not Battarbee), the Aranda first glimpsed the Canaan of representation in the coloured illustrations of the Bible.[48] With Battarbee and Gardner's help, the Red Sea of the ground swimming before their eyes parted, and a dry path (no doubt obeying laws of linear perspective) stretched away to where on the horizon lay the Promised Land of innovatory return. But suppose we were to keep both countries in mind, and to dwell on their ambiguous resemblances to each other – what after all, to go on with our metaphor, was there in the Bible pictures to distinguish the Holy Land from Egypt? From an Aranda perspective at least, the Red Sea might remarkably resemble its antithesis, the red centre; as for its sudden dryness, this would not have struck them as miraculous; on the contrary, to a people who welcomed turbulent floods as a way of staying at home, it would have suggested drought, not the prospect of plenty.

To write in this way is to some extent to suggest the kind of 'infolding' of narrative levels that a history of coincidences might essay; the simultaneous overlaying and metaphorical interpenetration of different visual and verbal data in the social, historical and religious life of the Hermannsburg community was commonplace. It is commonplace wherever colonizer and colonized attempt to improvise a *modus vivendi*, and it is causal, a primary mechanism for the generation of meaning. Yet, as I say, by linearizing the fluid dynamics of these situations we are liable to miss entirely their creative ambiguity, the irony that is critical to the commonalities improvised. Strehlow, for instance, ties the Aranda's artistic progress to the sight of 'coloured' pictures. Compare this with Battarbee's remark: 'I felt that colour was my strongest point and in my method I was able to take Albert right back to Nature. I was very nervous about the word "colour". Albert's knowledge of English was limited. His main language was Arunta and strangely enough the most freely used word in that language is the word "colour", which occurs in almost every sentence. It has several meanings according to the way it is used, but usually means "finish", and in some cases "ready to start".'[49]

Battarbee apparently alludes here to the Aranda word *kalla*, which on its own can mean 'completed', 'the tale is completed' and even 'he (she) has finished and now goes on a new quest, begins a new experience.' In the latter sense, Strehlow writes, it is used 'time and again in such legends as the A[litera] D[ialect] story of Kolbarinja's pursuit of his faithless son; here "Kalla" introduces paragraph after paragraph, and has the force of "away again".'[50] Leaving aside the fact that no reader unacquainted with the Aranda language could fathom the meaning of Battarbee's words, and that what he writes reproduces unconsciously the very ambiguity it purports to describe, it is evident that Battarbee alludes here to a troubling possibility: that it was not his skill as an art teacher that precipitated the new movement, but a mere phonic coincidence that, by temporarily masking an actual misunderstanding (or mutual incomprehension), seemed to create a common artistic ground.

Is it conceivable that this common ground consisted in the fact that a term which in English named one of the fundamental compositional units of naturalistic art signified in Aranda one of the key narrative markers of Central Australian song? Is it possible that Battarbee's colour instructions were heard as a narrative, that in painting certain landscapes in the style of Battarbee Namatjira was (despite the monumental appearance of the composition) narrating a story mobilely, tracing its gradual appearance, colour by colour, the routes taken, the places visited, the metamorphoses wrought? Colour/ *kalla* was a hinge word, opening a passage across the

Red Sea dividing cultures, but it depended for its efficacy on the fact that the common ground it appeared to define remained folded, enigmatic, its value provisional upon its power to preserve fertile differences.

If so, we might reflect on the word's meaning in Carl Strehlow's Aranda summary of the Bible, *Galtjindinjamea-Pepa*: there, *kalla* (which Carl spells *kala*, thus curiously recalling the classical Greek adjective meaning 'beautiful, lovely') occurs frequently.[51] By contrast, the many illustrations – whether of paintings by Leonardo, woodcuts by Dürer or engravings of works by Tintoretto – which punctuate the text are in a faded black and white. In that book at least, the phrase 'coloured pictures' would still have made sense; not as a visual description of the illustrations, but as an indication of their narrative function. The representations of the Fall, the Flood, the Burning Bush may have made little sense iconographically; they may have been understood as the Lutheran equivalent of their own *kalla*, a way of lending the story structural clarity and direction.

If this is true, Namatjira was not supinely assimilating his surroundings to a Western visualization of them. On the contrary, by representing it as the Land of Promise, he was painting it in the only way that the Lutherans and the white community could conceptualize it and make sense of it, allegorically, as a prefiguring of somewhere else. He not only mimicked Battarbee's style but the European way of seeing the ground in terms of representative images; that we do not see this, and assume that he was painting, say, the MacDonnell Ranges, may illustrate how blind we are to the cultural blinkers that determine our seeing. Our assumption that Namatjira represents the Central Australian landscape may demonstrate our incorrigible tendency to see through designs – to regard them merely as representations or signifiers. Perhaps Namatjira's art remained Aranda: it mimicked the iconography of Bible illustrations, not in order to assimilate the Aranda landscape to Christian conventions, but perhaps to mock our self-absorption.

Less negatively, by *participating* in its allegorical language, he was able to assimilate a European system of mimesis to his own traditions of seeing and drawing. By interpreting the Western tradition of representation performatively, regarding it as a way of re-enacting the iconography of Biblical illustration, he could preserve an indigenous conviction that the landscape was the creative original and abiding presence that lent these representations their meaning. Discovering the original of the oddly depressive images of Canaan, with its Plain of Sharon, its mountainous Hebron, its Transjordanian sandhills, he could revive their colour, bring them back to life. No genealogy was implied, merely a punning convergence or mimicry; but out of this mimicry a common ground might be created, where nothing was represented but certain performances kept alive the possibility of a differently grounded future.

In this context, Namatjira's infamous omission of the railway line from his painting of Heavitree Gap not only suggests how the place 'might have looked before it carried the colonists' iron signature';[52] it also ensures its resemblance to a Biblical landscape. In short, the nostalgia of the painting may be European, not Aboriginal; it may be our sentimental love of ideal representations that is represented, our voyeuristic preoccupation with the lie of the land in Eden that is projected there. If we attribute the missing signature of modernity to Namatjira's conservatism, thereby identifying him with the primitive other, incapable of change, of seeing the way things are going, we merely remain blind to the fundamentalism of our own gaze. If, as we see now, the original, violent intrusion of the railway signified our white indifference to the lie of the land, Namatjira's omission is not so much pre-Modernist as post-Modernist. Painting the Paradisal ground that blinded Europeans to the folded ground of history, he represented our dilemma: how our going forward has always been construed as a going back, how, as Francis Bacon pointed out, 'the vital direction of the sciences is toward the recovery of Paradise.'[53]

The circumstances in which the Hermannsburg School came into being, then, were anything but simple. If the European tendency was to isolate Namatjira, to see him as an original genius, his own object was to assist in the circulation of copies;[54] this latter had nothing to do with a post-Modern interest in simulacra, but expressed a performative conception of art production, one in which the value of representations lay in their power to induce imitations, thereby binding different groups together. Namatjira, the deep, still pool of wisdom, to whose genius two great cultural traditions had contributed; or Namatjira the distributor, the circulator, the *répétiteur* of a landscape that, having been largely secularized, could only be performed in this solitary way; this might be another way of representing his 'tragedy'. But the metaphors used here are not merely poetic, the allusion to the pool of Ntarea casual.

For at issue here were two conceptions of the ground, two ways of understanding its economy. If the Europeans saw the water-colours as a form of transportation, as a way of irrigating the coastal art-markets with images of the interior, Namatjira may have seen them as a way of him and his family staying put; a tendency to repeat himself, which the gallery owners found frustrating, was for him a way of not being drawn away from the places he loved. And where there was no urge to progress from one style or artistic phase to another, there was no danger of a periodic drought setting in, for the periodicity of his production ensured its elusive constancy.

In this context, there is a mythic fatefulness about the fact that the origins of the Hermannsburg School coincide with the tapping of Kaporilja spring and the provision of a permanent water supply at Hermannsburg. Kaporilja Tank, that 'marvel of the Water Supply', as Strehlow described it shortly after its completion in November 1935, meant that 'Hermannsburg will be proof against all droughts, it is to be hoped.'[55] But the piping of water from Kaporilja Spring, eight kilometres west-south-west at the base of the Krichauff Range, was not the only miracle Albrecht promoted in those years; in 1934 he had invited the watercolourists John Gardner and Rex Battarbee to exhibit the artistic fruits of their latest painting trip at Hermannsburg: 'For two days the exhibition continued and attendances never waned; a large number of the three hundred aborigines sat entranced by the pictures for hours at a time. Little did I realise that in this group of people was a man who viewed the pictures very differently from the average person.'[56]

Meanwhile, the trench-digging got under way.[57] It must have seemed extraordinary, from an Aranda perspective, to remove water from the folded declivities in the earth's surface where it periodically flowed or was naturally present. True, waters lost themselves in the sands, but there was another side to this: anastomosis of surface water, its tendency to spread out and seep underground rather than to run briskly in narrow grooves over the land and down to the sea, need not mean dissipation and death; it might simply signify a different form of circulation. The heart of Australia was not 'dead': in fact, the periodicity of Central Australian hydrology offered a genuine analogue of the heart's beat, its repeated distribution of life-giving fluid to the furthest reaches of the body. Where outstretched palms were stencilled on cave walls stained with water seepage, it was as if the common capillary action of flesh and rock were being traced.

If the behaviour of Central Australian water embodied a different conception of the economy of life, perhaps it also symbolized a different view of the after-life. In Christian eschatology the soul was resurrected from a grave that was conceptualized as a reservoir where the spirit lay imprisoned and motionless until spiritual vaporization, the condensation of immortality, occurred. But no such enclosure governed the Aranda soul: if, upon death, it disappeared like the rain underground, this was in order to return to the surface in a different form. It knew no immortality because it never died; its journey was a continuous coming-back, but never to the old country left behind. Thirty years later, writing *Journey to Horseshoe Bend*, Strehlow grasped this: reflecting on his father's death, his youthful persona Theo decides, 'this storied land would provide a far finer last resting place for his father than he could ever have found in some conventional cemetery in that distant country where he had come from. At Horseshoe Bend he was not sleeping alone: here he had joined forever the great company and congregation of the countless thousands of Aranda men, women, and children, who had lived and died in this Eternal Land.'[58]

But in addition to this, 'Men, animals and plants might indeed die and turn into dust; but the earth which absorbed their dust yielded new grasses and flowers, new trees and shrubs, fresh food for men and all other living creatures; and, according to Aranda belief, the second souls of all unborn children, too, emanated from the sacred soil of Central Australia.'[59] If the catalyst of new growth was rain, it was reasonable to associate rainfall with resurrection as well: 'Rain had hence come to be regarded as the visible symbol of life in Central Australia.'[60] But rain was not 'visible', it was blind; the totemic rain ancestor – 'No longer can he see any standing bushes'[61] – loses his way. What is visible is the trace of rain on the land, the water-courses; it is the anastomosing sand plumes, the cupped and sculpted river boulders, the transverse sand ridges of the river beds that are the resurrection of rain, its visualization or trace. In this sense, the lie of the land is not even the embodiment of 'life' but the form of the life essence itself. To borrow a Platonic term we shall explain later, its multiplicity of water shapes participate methektically in the One.

When the Hermannsburg Mission siphoned off water from Kaporilja spring, it contributed to the breakdown of this circulatory economy. Albrecht believed that by drawing off and storing a permanent store of fresh water he would contribute to the health of his community. But at a deeper level he weakened it. He was like the early nineteenth-century physician who recommended the application of leeches as a method of holding back the advance of tuberculosis. The supposition was that symptoms such as the flushed cheek and the burning forehead were signs of locally-high blood pressure caused by circulatory irregularities. If this pressure were not therapeutically relieved, it was argued, haemorrhaging was inevitable; if the infamous first symptom of TB, coughed-up pulmonary blood, was the result of capillaries bursting under an intolerable internal pressure, then the pre-emptive application of leeches was well-advised. But this mode of reasoning was, though reasonable, false, and the result of artificially drawing off the blood in an effort to restore equilibrium to the bloodstream merely had the effect of weakening the patient's resistance to disease.[62]

Similarly, Albrecht, by piping water from Kaporilja, imagined he was relieving a drought, but in reality he was weakening the capacity of the historical landscape to withstand invasion. By draining the spring he altered not only the physical but the metaphysical landscape; a spot that had formerly been a focus of animal and vegetable life gradually turned to dust and was deserted; perhaps more seriously, the efficacy of the totemic ancestor lodged there drained away. Kaporilja spring was sacred to Kantjia, the local rain totemic ancestor; to tap its water was to empty it of its potency to produce rainfall all over the land. By his artificial concentration of water, Albrecht weakened Kantjia's periodic capacity to distribute 'life' throughout Aranda country. With the drying-up of his water, his reputation also dried up.

An Aranda elder told Strehlow of an occasion in 1897 when a hail-bearing bank of clouds approaching the Mission from Kaporilja was miraculously arrested by 'the figure of a man emerging from one of these clouds.' The few Christian converts 'triumphantly insisted [that he] had been the figure of Christ who had protected them against these "evil foreign hailclouds".'[63] This was the effect of Christianization, which by converting the water as well, stopped the environmental circulation of things and turned the land into a pageant of empty representations. The vortical flow of water, which actively sculpted the trace of its passage into the sand, the sandstone, was channelled into pipes. Pipes could not force water to flow in straight lines that negated the physical laws governing hydrodynamics; but they could suppress these energy forms, modelling the transfer of energy as if the eddies in the slipstream counted for nothing. They could create the illusion that the sky-reflecting orbit of water collected in the tank at Hermannsburg was a faithful representation of the dark-light pool at Kaporilja.

Exactly the same transition from methektic trace to representational image occurred when the Aranda men took up Battarbee's mode of landscape painting. Strehlow likens 'the old style of pictorial art' among the Aranda (which he asserts had achieved perfection well before the advent of the whites) to that of the Celts as evoked by R. G. Collingwood in his book *The Principles of Art*:

> Suppose an artist wanted to reproduce the emotional effect of a ritual dance in which the dancers trace a pattern on the ground. The modern traveller [*sic*] would photograph the dancers as they stand at a given moment. A conventional modern artist, with a mind debauched by naturalism, would draw them in the same kind of way. This would be a silly thing to do, because the emotional effect of the dance depends not on any instantaneous posture but on the traced pattern. The sensible thing would be to leave out the dancers altogether, and draw the pattern by itself. This certainly is the explanation of much "primitive" art which at first sight appears altogether non-representative: spirals, mazes, plaits and so forth.[64]

But according to Strehlow, 'the weight of accumulated tradition' – and the metaphors are telling – had stifled creativity. In effect, traditional Aranda artists needed the influence of 'foreign artistic ideas' in order 'to explore new avenues.'[65] This stimulus Battarbee, and the Western mode of representation generally, supplied: 'the traditional habit of looking at everything from above limited the vision of the artist and frustrated his endeavours to express himself with freedom and clarity. The day of liberation came when white men first showed coloured pictures to the natives [who] now gazed with delight upon a world depicted as seen by eyes that have stopped staring at the ground in search of tracks and are looking instead at the landscape itself.'[66] In consequence, there was found 'an opportunity for releasing their pent-up creative energies.' In *The Australian Quarterly* in 1951, Leslie Rees described this change in metaphorical terms that make explicit the analogy with Albrecht's bringing water to Hermannsburg: 'the example of the "white art" has allowed the present generation of native artists to escape from a traditional bird's-eye symbolic illustration that needed myth to explain it, that had become "frozen" and sterile, that did not allow of extra creative enterprise.'[67]

In this account, the old way of looking at the ground imprisons the eye just as the ground imprisons the fallen water; it focuses attention on local patterns, surface features, traces of passage. Fieldmarks, and the traces associated with their creation, have ceased to be what Collingwood prescribed, patterns of living circulation. As a preliminary to colonizing the landscape with a European way of seeing, they must be turned into their antithesis: 'frozen' forms incapable of generating a creative current. The spirals, wavy lines and circles cease to be movement images and become instead outliers of a decadent baroque, ornamental offcuts of a once vigorous tradition. Evidently it is the photographic gaze of the 'whites' that freeze-frames them. But once characterized in this way, the role of the colonists becomes obvious: like Columbus protecting the Taino from an enemy of his own invention, the white painters pose as saviours. They would like the Aranda to share the experience of their patron saint, the Apostle Paul, who on the road to Damascus felt the scales fall from his eyes and who, seeing, saw that formerly he had seen nothing at all.

The new way of seeing jerks the head upwards through ninety degrees, the horizon comes into view, and seeing is divorced from the dance; as if, miraculously, the water at one's feet had been transformed into a pair of shining railway lines or a white waterpipe receding into the standing mirage.[68] But the ambiguity of these metaphors is unavoidable. For Strehlow at least, the old style of painting represents a damming-up of creative energies; Battarbee's example breaches the old walls of seeing – but to what end? Strehlow, like Battarbee, desires, paradoxically, to release the Aranda back into their own country. Therefore it is not enough to mimic brilliantly the European way of seeing, to represent the Central Australian environment as an endless sequence of photographic representations; this would merely be to release a 'deluge' of pictures that would both 'flood' the market and dissipate the Centre's unique appeal.

The Aranda artists must use this new mode of composition in order to go back to the 'aboriginality' which the decadence of their own tradition has stifled. They must see it as a way of raising the imaginative water-table, so that 'new avenues' of creative flow can occur. But these must be measured, or they will inundate and destroy what they attempt to reflect.

The universally applicable grammars of linear and aerial perspective must be relocalized; a new cult of the picturesque must be induced, a new community of *genii loci* commemorated. Only in this way can the new style successfully recapture the originally numinous nature of the land, and in addition render it authentically 'Australian'.

From this perspective, Namatjira is the most modern of Aboriginal artists and the most primitive. The most modern because he has mastered the style and technique of water-colour; the most primitive because he has advanced least far along the road towards recovering his lost aboriginality and integrating its style into the new artistic order. In this oddly paternalist context, the schoolmasterly judgements Battarbee passes on the Hermannsburg painters begin to make sense. Like Strehlow, he identifies the 'primitive' not with the backward but with the elementary and (in this, if in no other respect, a Modernist) the modern. So the surest way to sabotage Namatjira's development as an artist would be 'to improve his knowledge of art'.[69] Hans Heysen is said to have remarked, 'Why, Albert knows too much already.'[70] And Battarbee agrees; in demonstrating his ability to paint as well as a white man, 'the main thing he lost . . . was his aboriginal sense of decoration.'[71]

In this sense, Namatjira's followers and imitators are more (ab)original. Otto Pareroultja's work expresses, according to Strehlow, 'the same kind of distinctive Aranda feeling for balance, love of repetition and design, and sure sense of rhythm, that give such glorious vitality to their best verse.'[72] Battarbee is similarly positive: 'The Arunta people are permitted by tradition to draw only concentric circles and wavy lines, such as they have on their sacred *churungas*. Otto has developed this symbolism in his work and made it a style of his own. Here the rocks, mountains and trees are faithfully and well drawn, but the symbolism of circles and wavy lines is carried right through them without detracting from the picture, to which they give a primitive or aboriginal quality.'[73] And, following Strehlow, Battarbee compares the rhythm of his paintings to the rhythms of Aranda song.[74]

In these comments, viewing has given way to voyeurism. The art is appreciated for what it gives away of the artist's indigenous spirit; it is his artistic recidivism that appeals to the foreign viewer, the traveller with his repertoire of picturesque sites. Significantly, Battarbee compares Otto Pareroultja's brother Edwin with Gauguin;[75] as if he shares our nostalgia for the primitive, and unconsciously expresses (and legitimates) our desire to throw off perspectival restraint and re-enter the dithyrambic realm of the dance. But even this is not enough; to effect a complete union, more than a fortuitous interweaving of styles is needed. Ideally, a subtly new or hybrid subject-matter must emerge; for only this thematic synthesis can assure the status of the new art as authentically 'Australian' and not merely Aboriginal.

It is this synthetic subject-matter that Rex Battarbee appears to find adumbrated in the art of Albert and Rubena Namatjira's third son, Ewald, (Plate 3) and – intriguingly in the context of our reflections on the hydrologic cycle – it emerges in his distinctive interest in the weather. It is a combination of 'a sense of decoration, and atmospheric feeling' that persuades Battarbee that Ewald 'may be a genius with tremendous possibilities as an artist.'[76] Ewald 'has a leaning for clouds with rain falling out of them.' Of one painting, Battarbee writes, 'Apart from the beautifully drawn ironwood-tree, the mountain and cloud shadows cast on it, with rain falling, give a feeling that the country is really wet. This picture grows on one because it is so full of lively feeling.'[77] In Ewald Namatjira's painting, then, two cultures find common ground; like the idea of *kairos*, the sense of the eternal revealed in the temporal, which Strehlow describes as the distinctive feature of Aranda religion, the rainstorm's timeliness sustains what is timeless.[78]

Rain is an in-between phenomenon. In its combination of a regional identity with unencumbered, directed movement, it is the meteorological analogue of the creative spirit said to inform the Hermannsburg school of painters. It circulates the Central Australian landscape, periodically replenishing it, but it is not tied to one locality or another. It participates in the magic ceremonies whereby the yield of the country is assured; at the same time, it is sufficiently secularized to choose its own times and places. It belongs to the dance, but it also has a taste for making a theatrical entrance. Rain, and the weather generally, dwell between Heaven and Earth. The Aranda, Strehlow insisted, were exclusively Earth-worshippers; the post-Homeric Greeks and the migratory culture of the West have been exclusively Sky-worshippers.[79] About the weather – which neither culture deified, although both depended upon it – a synthetic subject-matter might condense, a repertoire of themes capable of representing historical contingency non-linearly, able to see the connection between a culture, its poetics and the lie of the land.

*

The coincidence of Battarbee and Gardner's exhibition with the construction of Hermannsburg's permanent water-supply turns out to be historically, and poetically, fateful. Two apparently unrelated activities prove to construct the world, grounding it ontologically, in identical ways. They mobilize the same metaphors; in particular, they imagine movement itself in much the same way, as a theatrical event occurring against a fixed and neutral background or landscape. It is from this initial schism between history and ground that the project of cultural, and poetic, reintegration begins. But the ideological nature of the schism itself is not open to question; Strehlow's linear reconstruction of the history of Aranda art depends upon an opposition between the static and the mobile, between the primitively local and tradition-bound and the progressively migratory and innovatory. But that opposition is a Western one, incarnated in Aristotelian metaphysics and physics. The linear conception of history it generates is similarly artificial. It is not only water that is parcelled into canals: our Western engineers of the intellect have similarly locked and weired the fluid of time.

Some instructive ironies emerge from the failure to perceive the ironies inherent in the colonial project of combining a return to the spiritually elemental with an advance towards the technological new. To enter the realm of representation (mimesis), as the Hermannsburg painters are said to have done, is to enter the house of Western history, with its books, its windows and doorways. It is no longer to see all around (with ears as much as eyes) a radiating environment of tracks and breezes; it is to be conscious of inhabiting a protective enclosure here and there breached by apparitional openings – doorways and windows – where spirits presumably enter and exit at will. Consciousness of a division between inside and outside, between what is present and what is absent, the quick and the dead, is instantiated in the architectural enclosure. The spiritual function of building becomes plain – to provide a site, a *tabula rasa* of foldless surfaces where this new division can be commemorated, a memorial of the outside which, now glimpsed fragmentarily as a receding landscape, seems to be in a state of ruin.

Again, this metaphorical way of speaking is not only poetic: it accurately glosses the historical ironies of Strehlow's situation. Writing of the Hermannsburg painting movement, Battarbee regretted 'One unfortunate gap in this art development': 'that because of the poor living conditions of the artists they and their people have not been able to gain the full appreciation of their paintings which comes of living with them in their own homes.'[80] Currently the kinfolk of the painters, and no doubt many potential artists, drift away to the cities, where they are 'sidetracked and lost in the slums . . . which become their graveyards.'[81] The implication of this is clear: in order to stay where they belong, the Aranda need to live in houses. And to what end? So that they can contemplate images of the landscape they no longer inhabit. The corollary of this logic is that the Aranda painters currently dwell amid ruins – ruins, what is more, of their own making. For they have abandoned one living-space, allowing it to fall into desuetude, and have failed to build up the other space so that its renovated walls can hang their memories.

No one, to be clear, is denying the right to adequate housing. The issue is a metaphysical one, to do with the enforced assimilation of one system of knowing and being to another, under the guise of preserving and promoting it. In Battarbee's logic, the Aranda must repair a ruin of their own making. Their paintings are wallpaper, whose decorative patterns disguise the cracks. But each piece fitted into the architectural grid blocks out another square of air and light. Thus an adequate representation of their totemic surroundings, its folded features and barely visible tracks, depends upon their fragmentation and ruin. Only by growing blind to what is can they bring into focus its representation. But to repeat, these paradoxes stem directly from the prior enclosure act of representation itself; once the 'instantaneous posture' is substituted for the 'traced pattern', as Collingwood puts it, the artist is radically redefined. No longer the dancer, disclosing the invisible, he comes to resemble a two-dimensional architect, enclosing the visible, placing it on permanent display. His task – his struggle, if we think of Lessing's Laocoön – is 'to save appearances', to breathe life back into what Western mimesis has rendered inanimate. But beginning with a ruin, he can only represent a ruin; and a large part of what we admire in his work lies in his ingenuity in disguising this fact behind the mask of beauty.

Strehlow himself was fully alive to these matters, and his poetic project in *Songs of Central Australia* could be glossed as an anti-architectural one, in which the ruins of time are repaired differently. Strehlow's propensity to elegy has already been noted, and even though he acknowledged the absence of elegy from the Aranda poetic repertoire,[82] he was prepared to maintain that the Aranda inhabited a country in a state of decadence. Like the poet of the Old English poem *The Ruin*, 'the native regards the natural objects at the sacred site and the surrounding landscape itself as the handiwork of his supernatural ancestors; and he is forced to admit that the present-day trees, rocks, and springs are at best only poor substitutes – ruins, as it were – of the original glorious features of the *pmara kutata* [totemic ceremonial centre].'[83]

An investment in the rhetoric of ruin is, as we shall see again in the Egyptian and Pompeian images Light brought to Adelaide, a fundamental rhetorical strategy of colonization; it is precisely the hypothesis of a prior breach that creates an opening for the colonizer. This, and the irony of the ruin that follows this prevision of ruin, is not in doubt; of more interest to us is the way Strehlow seeks to shift the ground of the argument, from the realm of the historical (and anthropological) to that of the poetic, to ameliorate the worst consequences of colonization, turning its penetrative destructiveness and assimilating it to a larger cycle of growth and decay which is ultimately restorative.

For the Hellenist Jane Harrison, the Aranda admission that 'present-day trees . . . are at best only poor substitutes' would have corresponded to what she describes as a 'gulf that is just opening . . . a possible division' between man and his totem. 'As a phase or stage of collective thinking through which the human mind is bound to pass,' she comments, it represents 'not so much a special social structure as a stage in epistemology.'[84] That self-styled psychoanalyst of the primitive, Geza Roheim, went further: it was, according to him, the phenomenon of *tjurunga* worship itself that evidenced man's primary division from his surroundings. Managing to assemble the anthropological literature in such a way that he could characterize Central Australian religion as stone worship, Roheim could understand the sacred caves and their associated rock emplacements as 'repressions' of the memory of migration.[85] The common ground has been rendered taboo, fetishized for the purposes of transport (and representation) as mobile stones, and in this sense the symbolic displacement of ancestor worship on to a stone suggested that the Aranda were both a migratory culture (like ourselves) and, also like ourselves, given to the pleasures of lithic enclosure.

Against the linearism of Harrison and the Cambridge Hellenists, against Roheim's atomization of the social and religious landscape, Strehlow's conception of the primary 'ruin' or consciousness of psychic division, is positive, opening up the possibility of a new group occupation of the ground. This is the political promise contained in the poetics of the

Hermannsburg school. Here, Strehlow said, was the artistic expression of a people who had been 'disturbed' by colonization but not destroyed, and whose 'artistic inspiration' had been stimulated by the experience of invasion because it had been freed 'from the restrictions imposed by "the totemic landscape".'[86] As a result, Namatjira had redefined the meaning of the group in Australian society. Transcending his local affiliations, he had created an Australia-wide audience for his work. This audience could, in theory, affiliate itself to Namatjira's way of seeing, thereby discovering a new spiritual unity.

This development – in which the artist reclaimed his ancient role of political leader and poetic seer – could not occur without a corresponding change in Australian cultural values. One focus of this change would be a critical reappraisal of the art gallery:

> In practice, definable art has no measurable existence apart from its public . . . Not only the primitive artists, but also the great European painters until a few centuries ago, had a twofold aim: to give pleasure to their patrons or public and to express their own personalities. A picture was normally created to embellish a particular building or a particular room, to adorn a particular wall or ceiling . . . The environmental context could never be ignored.[87]

The corollary is obvious. 'It is futile for [the artist] to think merely in terms of producing a painting for an Art Gallery or an Art Exhibition; for that means the creation of another museum piece.' The true and proper Art Gallery of the Australian people must be the domestic home: 'To be appreciated fully, art must be "lived with".'[88]

The 'domestic home' was not the Odyssean storehouse of the Westerner, where foreign objects were collected and displayed. It was not a repository or museum, but a 'treasure grove', a place dedicated to the restoration of group consciousness – a cultural place, that is, without walls where the interior assumed a different meaning. It was a place where abstractions like the outback, the dead heart, fell way – where ruins ceased to be signs of decadence, providing instead the open framework of a new mode of settlement. Essentially, abstract art was displaced art, a result of exhibiting art in the wrong environment, to the wrong audience. To cultivate it, as the Modernists did, was perverse, destroying the very conditions that made art possible. The sacred dot and circle designs of traditional Aranda art, executed by an artist who 'had always been an integral utilitarian member of a highly integrated society,'[89] were not abstract; they only became so when removed from the social and historical matrix that gave them meaning.

Strehlow's domestic art, then, is not localized, but retains its sense of being produced for a group; as the group of all Australians is not localized tribally but geographically, it seems logical that such an art must project an image of a homeland where all Australians feel that they can belong, a network of Ntareas if you like. And this homeland is conceived anti-architecturally, as a radiance of land.

> In the homely, kindly atmosphere of an Australian home the mannered cleverness of contemporary Europe and the dying magnificence of the older Europe both seem somewhat out of place. The art that would fit itself to such a home should reflect something of the airy, spacious freedom, the brilliant light, and the strong colours of our environment. Nowhere are these to be found in a richer measure than in the great central heartland of Australia.[90]

From which, it seems to follow logically, that homecoming entails the dissolution of the 'house'; as if by living with one's art, one could escape from the rhetoric of ruin. For ruins, it seems, are only displaced homes, the tortured ghosts of living spaces, memorials to murdered ground.

This sets the scene for *Songs of Central Australia*, a book intended to provide Australians with the outlines of a poetic homeland that they could call their own. That the poetry of the new Australian home must reflect the environment where it was produced was a nationalist commonplace with which Strehlow concurred:

> Neither the Greek satyrs and fauns, nor yet the English elves and fairies will survive transportation to Australia. Ours is a land of sunshine, colour, warmth, and airy freedom. If we are to develop a literature that will appeal strongly to an Australian audience, then our future writers and poets will have to garb their verse and prose with new trappings which will harmonise with the Australian background against which we are living our daily lives.[91]

The difference was that while he mimicked the suburban sentiments favoured by the Heidelberg painters and the *Bulletin* writers, and revived more recently by Ingamells in poems like 'Unknown Land', Strehlow viewed them from the outside, as a cultural in-betweener; and his object was to change the aspect of the future's inside – to make his outsideness part of it. In any case, he would never have made Rex Ingamells's mistake of protesting:

> Without a race, Australia is the plains,
> The mountains and the gorges, dusts and rains . . .[92]

Races existed, the mountains had names and affiliations, the gorges were breathing presences, the rains had their charms. The question was whether and how, with the inward drift of another race, Australia could be:

> Again what it has been before,
> A human Glory . . .

In short, 'a place'.[93]

In coming to *Songs of Central Australia*, we have not, after all, done more than continue to circulate the purlieus of Ntarea. It has often been pointed out that in that book Strehlow was at pains to defend his father's reputation as an ethnographer against the criticisms of Baldwin Spencer.[94] But this outward motive, the mask of filial piety, concealed a less obedient ambition; which was, as he had in *Journey to Horseshoe Bend*, to rewrite his father in his own name and so, by becoming father to the man, to affiliate Carl to his own history. Of his father's monumental collection of Aranda and Loritja songs included in *Die Aranda-und Loritja-Stämme in Zentral-Australien*, Ted had one criticism: although excellently recorded and accurately translated, they appeared 'only in their prose forms, not in their true metrical versions.'[95] This, then, defined the project: to revisit the ground of his father's work and by remetricalizing it, to translate it back into its true form.

Just as he had corrected his father's translation of the New Testament into Aranda in the late 1930s, so now the younger Strehlow set out to correct his ethnographic work. The correction was intended reverently, but it barely repressed a more violent ambition: by making audible what father Carl repressed and, notating it, to discover an authoritatively different voice of his own. In the non-verbal or musical interstices of Carl's account, in the silences produced by Carl's refusal to visit the sacred sites and attend the ceremonies, Strehlow would not only disclose the true sophistication of an indigenous chant tradition but identify the repression of the auditory. Strehlow's initiation into language had been violent: the constant threat of the rod hung over his stammering acquisition of ancient Greek, of English and German.[96] Language as semiosis was the voice of the father, and enjoined the pupil to enter the silent regime of writing and endless interpretation, translation. But language as *poiesis*, as auditory traces, as rhythmically and tonally significant shapes, as environmentally-localized occurrences: this held out the possibility of grounding knowing (and memory) differently.

To listen to the sound of what was being said, to its contours (which folded around one as the air), might be a means of learning to hear oneself speak. Less benignly, it could satisfy the Oedipal urge to shut up the father. In any case, it meant that *Songs of Central Australia* signified more than another pious act of filiation; by localizing his father's work, by bringing to the surface the historical and physical environment it had repressed, Strehlow created a place for himself. By remetricalizing his father's prose paraphrases, Strehlow reinserted them into a living-space where they resonated because they belonged. They ceased to be abstractions or ruins. Furthermore, they changed the way history was grounded: the father's work no longer belonged to the axis of linear progress towards enlightenment but approximated to a diary, an occasional grammar of cloudy peripateia. Posthumously at least, Pastor Strehlow made the pilgrimage to Manangananga Cave where, hearing the echo of his voice, he heard the unspeakable speak and was quiet.

Again, these spatial metaphors are not simply rhetorical; at the very least they mimic the meanings they evoke. To leave the high road was to enter a country where movement was influenced by the lie of the land. So 'to return to Ntarea' was not simply to strike out on one's own; it was to ground one's knowledge differently, to realise that irregularities of the surface, the sense the ground gave of being folded, embodied a different conception of one's place in the world. If prose was planar, the territory of translation, poetry, polysemous, untranslatable, was the discourse of folded ground. According to Strehlow, these insights were evident in the very constitution of the Aranda language, which was poetically and grammatically 'additive';[97] like undulating or cave-pocked country which bunches up planes, thus incorporating more ground, so Aranda verbal structures were able to expand flexibly, incorporating more or less material. And again, this elastic capacity to group syllables not only had its analogue in the lie of the land but also in the social organization of the Central Australians.

The revelatory insight of *Songs of Central Australia*, that 'the measuring unit of Central Australian verse is not the classical metric foot, but the smallest musical phrase into which the rhythmic measure of the line can be subdivided,'[98] is essentially a recognition of the flexibly incorporative, or folded, nature of Aranda song. Isorhythmic units, as they are called, with their 'capacity for expansion and contraction of formal units within established boundaries,' also characterize the musical system of the Pitjantjatjara people to the south-west, where Ellis contrasts them with the rigid bar divisions of Western music and comments: 'This difference between the rigid divisive thinking shown in the structures of Western music and the flexible additive thinking shown in the structures of Pitjantjatjara music . . . suggests a greater capacity for exclusion on the part of Western thinkers and for incorporation on the part of Aboriginal thinkers.'[99]

It also suggests, we might add, a non-architectural mode of structuring human relations. In his essay on Namatjira, Strehlow explained that the stability of a group depended on being able to 'build up social structures' that were strong enough to withstand the 'shiftless sands' of Western materialism.[100] Strehlow's architectural image may be the merest cliché; or it may deliberately conceal in order to reveal. What form, say, would the building of these structures take in a non-architectural culture like that of Central Australia? If the ground is not to be cleared for building, then the ground itself will have to be built up or grouped. If the kraal at Hermannsburg is remarkable for its flatness, the ground of the Aranda will perhaps be distinguished by unevenness, by subtle undulations, the notation of waterholes, passes and bluffs. The social group will define itself, then, by its manner of going over the ground, a ground ever-presently grouped by the totemic ancestors. Its social structures will in some way re-enact the grouping process.

This is exactly the claim that Strehlow makes in his monograph on Aranda grammar, when he maintains that the local lie of the land, and the manner of moving over it, provide an analogue of the Aranda language's grammatical structures: 'The Aranda language harmonises strikingly with the country which was once occupied by the people who spoke this tongue.' Strehlow sees a direct connection between the structure of the land forms and the structure of the language. If the landscape consists 'of wide featureless plains and barren sandhills . . . [where] every now and then you come upon rugged hills . . . Sudden gum creeks with lovely waterholes and clear springs in hidden valleys,' so too the Aranda language is 'plain, levelled down by analogy, and often lacking in the lighter graces. But it has a vigour and a ruggedness all its own. It is not incapable of grandeur or beauty.'[101]

This analogy between rhetorical and geological forms might seem to echo the prejudice discussed in *The Road to Botany Bay*, where explorers associate the 'primitive' state of the Aborigines with the primitive state of the landscape; in a country where isolated waterholes (and mountains) replace continuously flowing rivers and directionally significant ranges, it was little wonder if the languages specialized in localized names but lacked terms capable of making abstract connections.[102] But Strehlow proceeds from the inside, not denying the character of the landscape, but maintaining the complete efficacy of the tongue located there. If Aranda is at home in this country, it is because an evolutionary parallelism has been at work, with the result that no other language could be better adapted, more eloquent, more poetic. In achieving this harmonization, Aranda demonstrates its sophistication, however 'plain' or ancient the land.

When Strehlow says that the Aranda language is 'levelled down by analogy', he is not merely making a picturesque comparison with the region's geological history. It is not that the Aranda way of ordering language represents the landscape; rather, Aranda grammar may be said to re-enact the physical structure of the environment where it is spoken. The relationship is methektic (to invoke a term that will shortly be explained more fully) rather than mimetic. The simplicity, indeed the absolute regularity, of noun, adjective and verb inflections in Aranda arises by a process analogous to the erosion of the landscape: 'whatever irregularities there may have been in the Aranda conjugations originally have all long since been smoothed out by the action of the principle of analogy.' Aranda is simple because it is advanced, not primitive, in this sense resembling an indigenous plain English: 'Beside the conjugation of the Aranda verb even the simplest European inflexional system of verbs is hopelessly archaic and irrational.'[103]

Analogy, then, is a levelling process resembling the wearing-away of exposed outcrops. But it does not result in a wholly featureless, 'flat' landscape; rather, it means that the eroding forces settle into certain grooves or spread themselves more and more equably. Mountains yield to dunes; deep rivers silt up and in their place there multiply soaks, billabongs, ponds and springs. At the same time, those original features of the landscape, which correspond to the originary stories the Aranda tell about their totemic ancestors, retain their grandeur; indeed, if anything they grow taller, more impressive, more spectacular as their particular archaic poetic language stands out more and more sharply against the changed idiom of the plains that spread away from them on all sides.

Within these grooved plains, Aranda has developed a complementary grammar that transfers emphasis from the actor, the act and the acted-upon to the action itself. If a landscape is deficient in variegated points of reference, in progressive patterns of light and dark – if it lacks a European visual syntax – then one of two possibilities arises: either the human being must feel wholly at sea; or else he must derive his sense of place, his equilibrium, his sense of progress, from the measure of his own feet. He must articulate his relationship with his surroundings dynamically, employing the linguistic equivalent of an infinitesimal calculus to capture each successive moment of his movement over the ground. This logic finds its most sophisticated expression in the actions of the 'native hunter' and its equivalent, a language which, while it may be limited in vocabulary, has, for example, a verb which 'by means of agglutinating verbal suffixes and infixes, can express no less than ninety-five tense forms, four voices and three numbers.'[104] As the empathetic Strehlow explains:

> The native hunter is keenly observant of every minute change in the action described by him; and consequently each verb gives rise to a long set of derivative verbs which bear witness to the sharp eye for detail possessed by the nomad.
>
> Let us in mind follow the native hunter in his daily task of tracking an animal, say a mountain kangaroo [*euro*]. Let us assume that he contents himself by using various forms derived from the one verb '*ilkuma*' (to eat) in order to explain to us the various movements of the animal which he is tracking up. The mountain kangaroo comes down in the waning afternoon in order to feed on the more luxuriant grass on the plain below. Our guide will point to a trail leading down from the mountain slope, with nibbled-off grass on both sides of it; and he will remark: '*nala* (here) *era* (it) *ilkutjakalaka* (descended-eating).' If much grass has been nibbled off, this would show a long and slow descent,

> and the verb in the preceding sentence would be altered to '*ilkulb-ilkutajakalanaka*' ('descended-slowly-eating-all-the-while'); here the reduplication and the longer derived form indicate both the slow progress of the animal and its long-continued bout of munching grass.
>
> The trail has now reached the plain. '*Nala* (here) *era* (it) *ilkuetnalalbuka*,' will be the next remark – '*ilkuetnalalbuka*' meaning 'wandered-on-away-from-us-eating-on-its-way.' After a few more steps a cross track cuts the trail: the kangaroo, after going on a few yards further, had circled around and come back to where its pursuers are now –'*nala era ilkup-ilkuentjalbuka*' ('here it came-back-towards-us-eating-ravenously-the-whole-time'). After a while a particularly good patch of grass is reached: the tracks show that the animal feasted here for a long while, browsing about leisurely in big circles – '*nala era ilkup-ilkulanaka*' ('here it kept on browsing and browsing'). Our guide goes right around the outer edge of this patch in order to strike the trail of this kangaroo somewhere where it continued its journey. On finding it he will exclaim: '*Nala era ilkunaka*' or '*nala era ilkup-ilkuentjalbunaka*'; both verbs mean 'continued along, browsing'; the first form is used if the animal merely enjoyed a mouthful here and there; the second, expanded form is used to connote ravenous, greedy browsing.
>
> Having satisfied its main hunger during the afternoon and the night, the mountain kangaroo wends its way back towards the mountain fastnesses towards morning. Its tracks lead upwards into the rocks, and the guide will exclaim '*Nala era ilkutjintjika*' ('here it browsed on its way up').[105]

According to this account, there is a direct analogy between the impressions left by the feeding animal on the ground and the verbal expressions that describe them: light, fleeting passages elicit similarly succinct verbal forms, more leisurely progress produces a corresponding amplification and deepening of the verbal phrase. A sustained movement produces a polysyllabic elaboration which may be likened, not too fancifully, to the line of prints the animal leaves behind it. Equally important, the syllabic mimicry of the marks made by the animal's feet and browsing mouth serves to group them together into significant units. In contrast with a language like English, which segments one action from the next, which represents movement as a sequence of cinematic stills,

Aranda, it seems, is able by a process of agglutination to incorporate ever larger units of movement, and so represent the continuity of the animal's passage.

This process of verbal grouping presupposes a view of the ground quite different from the one customary in our descriptions of movement. Aranda forms are elastic, but this works in two directions; a verb stem that can be expanded to incorporate ever-larger patterns of motion also has the effect of making every part of that movement trace simultaneously present. The Aranda verb form is like a strip of elastic threaded through a hem; it can be stretched out to reveal more material, but in return, when it is contracted it compacts the material into folds. This property corresponds to the hunter's habitual way of seeing his surroundings: directing his searching gaze this way and that, always accompanied by a spirit double one step ahead of himself, he perceives the space as filled with elastic filaments (not unlike the flight path of the spear) by means of which distant moving objects can be brought suddenly close.

There is yet another dimension to this grammatical capacity for puckering the ground, grouping it into irregular but rhythmic units of motion. The marks the animal leaves do not resemble the ideal points of the geometer who, with his dividers, pricks out a track on the chart. It is true that they are signs: they signify a former presence that is now absent. It is true that by linking them together one can reconstruct the route of the beast. But they are also a trace of something more: the animal's size, its rate of progress, its business, its agitated or tranquil state of mind. These aspects of its progress cannot be plotted simply by joining up the marks; they depend on attending to the different depths of the individual marks, their variable directional accent, their indications of stress or rest. Only by recognizing the marks as the residue of impulses, as splash-points yielding widening circles of meaning, can they be fully interpreted.

Again, on Strehlow's account, Aranda grammar is able to bear witness to this accentual dimension of the ground. When infixes and suffixes are added to the verb stem, they not only expand it linearly, they also deepen the resonance of the verb stem itself, surrounding it with a widening range of resonance like concentric circles. Unlike a segmented language, highly differentiated lexically, which steps from one propositional state to the next and as it does so leaves the previous one behind, Aranda amplifies the semantic unit's power as it traverses a growing region. Like the 'dot' of traditional Central Australian 'dot-and-circle' painting, the verb stem always implies other dots, a pattern or grouping of marks. This implication does not arise solely from any pleasure we may find in turning isolated marks into visually significant patterns; it grows from the fact that the dots are the physical trace of the jabbing hand, as palpably imprinting the surface as the *euro*'s foot marks the ground. They are not the representations of ideas. They do not correspond to loci on a map. They are not the names of things, like nouns, but are better thought of as the units of a metrical pattern. They are not syllables or groups of syllables (words) but the stresses which, drawn into patterns, lend these words their rhythm, their poetic resonance. As such, their essential impulse is towards the grouping of marks; unlike Man Friday's solitary footprint, the elements of the agglutinative system cannot exist on their own.

The depth of the trace corresponds to the stress pattern of Aranda speech. The patterning of marks on the ground has its corollary in the gathering of syllables into poetically significant groups. And again, the essence of this process is that it presumes a logical as well as a physical environment that is folded rather than planar. A planar environment, one amenable to Euclidean modelling, has as its poetic corollary the clockwork metre of the heroic couplet. Rhyme, as Saintsbury has explained, 'when accepted by any language, gradually but necessarily breaks up prosody by versicles or sections merely, and substitutes prosody by feet.' Rhyme would be fatal to a poetry which, like the Aranda, has not 'given way to regular short metrical feet' but is composed of 'musical phrases' whose endings are implicit in their internal rhythmic and tonal structure.[106] Rhyme, it seems, presumes a metricated clearing, while Aranda song is about the constitution of that clearing in the first place. If one clears away folds likely to trip, the other reverently follows and reduplicates them.

So much for a poetic grammar that enjoyed a performative or methektic relationship with its surroundings, and which seemed to supply a mode of affiliation, a way out of the patriarchal enclosure. Its oddity is that it replaces the father less by erasing his trace than by deepening it. Strehlow's comprehensive reworking of his father's translation of the New Testament into Aranda is an exemplary case in point. Undertaken in the late 1930s, ostensibly in order to correct the many mistakes present in the old translation, Strehlow's new version is much more than a revision; employing his own idiosyncratic orthography, intended to capture minutely the nuances of spoken Aranda, and retranslating the Greek original with a minute and obsessive literalism, Strehlow so deepens the groove of analogy between Aranda and Greek that he reveals his father's work as a superficial approximation or representation. In Aranda terms, he reveals Carl's book as a mask narrative; when Hermannsburg elders complained that his new translation was too subtle and complicated, Strehlow reminded them that, as initiated men, it was their task to unfold successively more difficult truths.[107] Perhaps the analogy was more complete than he intended; 'obscurity', which Strehlow so admired in Aranda word-weaving, also afflicted his own work – the curiousness of its spelling might retain an accurate trace of Strehlow's own voice, but limited its practical usefulness to the local Christian community.[108]

Issues of translation were obviously critical to the enterprise represented by *Songs of Central Australia.* If some of the 'strands' of 'the strong web of future Australian verse' were to come from 'poetic threads spun on the Stone Age hair-spindles of Central Australia', then it was essential that a groove of analogy between Western and indigenous poetic traditions be found. It was not going to be enough to acknowledge the Aboriginal presence thematically, as the Jindyworobaks had, under the broader rubric of espousing environmental values.[109] Nor was a mechanically imitative rendering of indigenous verse-forms of the kind Harney and Elkin essayed in *Songs of the Songmen* likely to prove fertile. Posing as the empathetic bard, heir to all poetic traditions, Roland Robinson came closer in using English prose rhythms to emulate native story-telling idioms, but remaining linguistically uninitiated, he too was prone to a Panglossian sentimentalism that obscured the local history of the tradition he pretended to copy.

If Strehlow were to transcend the colonizing spirit inherent in the literary efforts of his contemporaries, he had to find a mode of translation that did not dilute and distantly echo but signified, in Husserl's words, the 'activity of concurrent actual production.'[110] Robinson had understood this intuitively, but not technically. The rhymed renderings of various Arnhem Land song traditions undertaken by Harney and Elkin were, Robinson commented, 'examples of outmoded, inadequate, prescribed traditions which modern poets have broken across their knees and used to stoke their fires. Their diction is cluttered with poeticisms, archaisms and inversions to serve the rhyme. Rhyme is, in any case, foreign to many traditions, certainly to Aboriginal oral poetry. Professor Elkin is an anthropologist, but not a poet. In the role of poet, he is an elementary verse carpenter.'[111]

Songs of the Songmen stood in the same relation to the originals that inspired them as the choreography that Beth Dean and Victor Carell devised for John Anthill's ballet *Corroboree*, whose challenge they explained as follows: 'We had to try to instil the depth and potent emotional beauty of aboriginal dance into people who had never seen an aborigine; to try to enthuse their will to picture in the mirror of their minds the excitement of an aboriginal ceremony which they had never known existed.'[112] And which, of course, never had existed, as the steps of *Corroboree* were a collage of different dance movements observed among the Tiwi, the Wongga, the Warlpiri. The translation envisaged is purely external, an animated going through the motions. It had to disguise the truth that it was a representational fiction: 'They had, we believed, to learn to feel the dance quality as we had felt it, and by so doing, to infect each audience with the beauty and thrill of this pristine ideal of the aboriginal mind – to carry the continuous line direct from the aborigines of Central Australia to Sydney. This was the difficulty, because steps devoid of mood, devoid of the aboriginal belief and atmosphere lose their potency and of themselves only seem unusual and weird.'[113]

The 'difficulty' lay in supposing that the in-folded song-dances of indigenous Australia could preserve their 'atmosphere' when unfolded and treated as a linear sequence, whether of syllables or footsteps. As Ellis has explained, dance-steps were associated with particular musical rhythms and oral texts. 'Rhythmic patterns are permanently combined with given song texts. As a result, the rhythm alone can convey the same meaning as the text to which it is tied. A rhythmic pattern consists of the shortest segment of rhythm which is repeated over and over again to produce a complete small song. (This is technically known as *isorhythm.*) Often the rhythmic unit is the same length as the text (which also must be repeated a number of times to complete a small song) but sometimes it is much shorter, requiring two or even four presentations to accommodate the complete text. The pattern, whether long or short, is built of rhythmic cells which also appear as units in other rhythmic patterns set to different texts.'[114]

Ellis comments, 'This makes it possible for many ideas to be communicated simultaneously. For instance, at any given point in the ceremony the painted design on the body of a dancer may have one specific meaning (e.g. "home") and the song text with its associated rhythmic pattern may have another (e.g. a description of a journey). If the rhythmic pattern is one which has a link to another small song, then the text meaning of the latter is also implied.'[115] And so the meanings radiate: 'Many pieces of information are presented simultaneously. The rhythmic pattern and song text can refer directly to one event in the story, and to others by implication. The body design on the dancers can signify a different aspect of the story. The dance step, which is tied to musical structure through the beating accompaniment, may depict yet another piece of information, while the dancers themselves represent the personality attributes and characteristics of those whom they portray. Melody, as well as indicating the nature of events taking place in the ceremony (painting, dancing, etc.) acts as a constant reminder of the essence, the "taste" of the ancestor.'[116]

In this context of a hierarchy of expressive languages endlessly folding one into the other, continuously reconstituting the ground of their own coming into being, and by this means ensuring that the physical ground is the metaphysical ground of their performance, Dean and Carell's progressivist figure of the 'continuous line' captures the essence of their mistranslation. As Western choreographers, whose art depends on the provision of a planar stage, uninscribed, free of impediment, empty of history, they lift dance figures observed on their travels and, assimilating them to a presumably universal dance grammar (another continuous line), form them into a picturesque sequence, a representation of reality that can be produced anywhere. Only by negating the lie of the land, by isolating the dance steps from the spirit double of the ground, could this aesthetic effect be achieved. Theirs was an irrigatory process: it brought certain currents to formerly sterile realms, but in the process sacrificed those analogues of the land's lie, the surface patterning, the weir-edge shimmer, the counter-whorls around boulders, which gave them their significance as a source of knowledge.

External mimicry of Aboriginal song and dance revealed too much because it implied too little; it flattened out what should have remained folded. It made what was deep appear shallow. And this had an ethical as well as a metrical aspect. Roland Robinson recalls how the earlier visit of Dean and Carell to Areyonga near Hermannsburg had stymied his own efforts to gain access to local songs and legends; these 'well-known Americans' had without permission published photographs of secret ceremonies, and these had inevitably got back to the settlement. 'Normally,' he remarks self-righteously, 'it would mean death if any woman or uninitiated man were to see any sacred ritual object.'[117] Evidently, Robinson regarded his own story-collecting as a different, more trustworthy, more inward kind of process. Of a story told him at Hermannsburg, he wrote 'when I re-tell it, it restores my sanity, my "*en-thos*" – "the god within". I love fairy stories, even though I know they are only the vestiges of myths . . . Look at that Aboriginal myth I have recounted. Look at its directness, its natural poetry. Look at its psychology . . . Is it not the repressed desire of most men to be capable, and to have the opportunity of, such sensuality? Look how it puts romanticism in its place.'[118]

But what exactly did this sensation of the god within mean? Robinson seems to have understood it orgiastically, as a Dionysian identification with the other; briefly, and rhythmically, he entered into the world of the native, thereby coming in touch once more with his own primitive being and enjoying a oneness at once multiple, nomadic and free of taboos – including the irrigatory taboo of rhyme. But these sensations, although ardently argued, remained subjective; they might justify Robinson's claim to belong to a poetic genealogy extending back to Homer and the first Aranda bard – 'kindly old men, heroes, fighters, song-men, sages, and custodians of their traditions'[119] – but they had little historical value. They could not initiate the poet into the life of the group; he remained an outsider, a Westerner nostalgically looking out and listening. It is symptomatic that Robinson's recollection of his journey north from Alice Springs is a self-conscious, and tasteless, pastiche of the sexually-punctuated wanderings of 'the man [and ancestral hero] Yoola who was always wanting women':[120] 'What uninhibited children of the earth we were. As we drove north through the mornings, Kristin would be rousing, stimulating my sexual urge until I saw the speedometer registering seventy . . .'[121] Like Chatwin, Robinson's true subject is the monadic consciousness condemned to inhabit a planar world; the lines which appear to converge, to point to a common origin, turn out on closer examination to have as much substance as lines of latitude and longitude.

Still, Robinson points us in the right direction. His term '*en-thos* – the god within' invokes a theory of poetic inspiration congenial to Jane Harrison and the Cambridge Hellenists. As F. M. Cornford wrote, 'The worshippers of Dionysus believed that, when they held their orgiastic rites, the one God entered into each and all of them; each and all became *entheoi*; they "partook" of the one divine nature, which was "communicated" to them all, and "present" in each.'[122] And in his study of the later Plato and of Parmenides, Cornford was exercised by the 'much-vexed problem of "participation"', or *methexis*, according to which the Platonic 'Forms' or 'Ideas' are able 'to be present in a plurality of things, and yet to remain one.'[123] For her part, Harrison lent these ruminations a decidedly local inflection when, in *Themis*, she illustrated her argument that totemistic thinking is based on group unity by reference to the Intichiuma ceremonies performed by the 'Central Australian tribes'.

Quoting Spencer and Gillen's description of the magical acts performed by men of the Emu totem 'to induce the multiplication of the totem' – 'the shedding of blood of the human Emu, and his counterfeit presentment of the bird-Emu' – she commented that they 'have for their object to bridge the gulf that is just opening, to restore by communion that complete unity which is just becoming conscious of possible division. The ceremonies are however still intensely sympathetic and co-operative; they are, as the Greeks would say, rather methektic than mimetic, the expression, the utterance of a common nature participated in, rather than the imitation of alien characteristics. The Emu man still feels he is an Emu; the feathers he puts on, the gait he emulates, are his own, not another's.'[124] And Harrison speculated that, as the primitive group unity broke down, magical practices yielding to religious ones and 'individual observation tending to take the place of collective suggestion', *methexis* would give way to mimesis, or 'participation to imitation.'[125]

Now in *Songs of Central Australia* Strehlow was at pains to demonstrate Spencer and Gillen's limited insight into Central Australian society – and by extension to dethrone the authority of J. G. Frazer and the Cambridge Hellenists, who had drawn so heavily on these writers for their own speculative reconstruction of the beginnings of Greek culture and Western art. It might seem far-fetched to insist on Strehlow's debt to Harrison and her kin, and to suggest that his conception of an environmentally-attuned post-colonial poetics is usefully glossed by their notion of participation or *methexis.* But Strehlow's relationship to these older scholars is not filial or prodigal; just as he side-stepped linear descent from his biological father, so Strehlow avoided confronting his intellectual mentors directly. Instead of engaging dialectically with them, he prefers to redraw the grooves they have made in the landscape of ideas, and by deepening them to disclose their indifference to the local lie of the land.

Strehlow's authorities were authorities *for him* – which perhaps explains why *Songs of Central Australia*, written mainly in the 1950s and published in 1970, seems to have been produced in a time-warp; in between Spencer and Gillen and the fashionable Aryanism characteristic of late Victorian and early Edwardian ethnographic theory had come Modernist anthropology, Modernist literary criticism and two generations of cultural theorizing. Yet hardly any trace of these more recent trends exists in Strehlow's book. A passing assertion that the concept of *mana* was unknown amongst the Aranda contradicts a major assumption of Durkheim's *Elementary Forms of Religious Life*, but otherwise the French school of anthropology forms no part of Strehlow's conceptual vocabulary. The Structuralist insights of a Lévi-Strauss (which would seem to gloss so usefully the symmetries between musical form and social life in Aranda culture), Mauss's account of the social and economic significance of the gift (obviously relevant to the Aranda sharing of ceremonies and songs) are totally absent; likewise any allusion to Jakobson's structural linguistics. Nor can Strehlow be said to be a functionalist in Malinowski's sense; if anything, his inclination is to invert the functionalist paradigm, to subordinate the economic, religious and social operations of the group to the poetic; to be sure, the Aranda's songs are 'functional' in the broadest sense, but their real interest lies elsewhere, in their poetic value.

Oddest of all, there is no reference in Strehlow's book to the discovery – surely inspirational in the context of Strehlow's project – of a living Homeric literature. Milman Parry's field-recording trips to Serbia and Bosnia-Hercegovina in 1933 and 1934 were contemporary with Strehlow's earliest studies of the songs of the Aranda. Parry's South Slavic studies enabled him to do what a study of the *Iliad* and the *Odyssey* did not permit: 'We can learn not only how the singer puts together his words, and then his phrases, and then his verses, but also his passage and themes, and we can see how the whole poem lives from one man to another, from one age to another, and passes over plains and mountains and barriers of speech – more, we can see how a whole oral poetry lives and dies.'[126] Surely this was Strehlow's ambition. If we add that Parry found that 'the singing tradition of both the Moslem Southslavs and their

Christian brothers is the same',[127] we have here, surely, a formula of cross-cultural mingling and synthesis extremely pertinent to Strehlow's project.

Relying on writers like Saintsbury for his knowledge of English verse-forms, or Chadwick for his model of the growth of Western literature, Strehlow was affirming the earliest influences on his own education at Adelaide University. Saintsbury and Chadwick were authorities, but so (by the 1950s) were T. S. Eliot and I. A. Richards; what counted was that the former were authorities for him, part of his personal destiny. Temperamentally, he would have shared Heidegger's preference, expressed in a very different context, for 'a turning away from all empty material exchange . . . finding the simple and noble need to act in a responsible way for the self.'[128] In this way, refusing to debate his own ideas, Strehlow sought to make himself an *ingkata*. In the Central Australian system of education, 'constant repetition is essential to thorough knowledge . . . the authority of the knowledgeable elders – "the people knowing many songs" – must in no way be challenged [ ] the student must be motivated to accept the elders unquestioningly as the models of master musicians and wise people, while at the same time learning the strictest self-discipline.'[129]

From this perspective, the cultural theses of the Cambridge Hellenists did not have to be refuted; they were 'mask' narratives which might mimic the truth outwardly, but whose superficiality a deeper initiation into 'primitive' culture would soon reveal. And quite properly, Strehlow associated the falling away of masks with the acquisition of the primitive's language. Gilbert Murray, Harrison and F. M. Cornford drew heavily on the ethnographic literature made familiar to them through J. G. Frazer's ever-growing compendium *The Golden Bough* for their argument that the emergence of the Attic drama represented the creative collision of two cultural streams: one indigenous and characterized by a group-based totemism identical with that still current in certain 'primitive' societies, the other, the so-called 'Homeric' tradition, foreign and invasive, characterised by its humanization of the gods and the universalization of their attributes. And there is no doubt that Strehlow found this thesis applicable to his own situation and ambitions.

According to Harrison, the poetry of Homer was the poetry of a migrant people. Thus the many 'single combats in *The Iliad* really reflect not the fights of individual heroes at Troy, but the conflicts of tribes on the mainland of Greece. When the tribes who waged this warfare on the mainland pass in the long series of Migrations to Asia Minor and the islands, the local sanctities from which they are cut loose are forgotten, and local *daimones*, eponymous heroes and the like become individualized saga-heroes. Achilles and Alexandros are tribal heroes, that is collective conceptions, of conflicting tribes in Thessaly. Hector before, not after, he went to Troy was a hero-*daimon* in Boeotian Thebes; his comrade Melanippos had a cult in Thebes, Patroklos whom he slew was his near neighbour, like him a local *daimon*. It is the life-stories of heroes such as these, cut loose by the Migrations from their local cults, freed from their monotonous periodicity, that are the material of Attic drama, that form its free and plastic plots.'[130]

Returning from Ionia during the fifth century BC, by some unidentified process of reverse migration, the sagas of humanized gods and godlike men became then the material of the Attic drama. But the rapidity of their literary transformation was only made possible by the existence of a mould into which the new material could be poured; an indigenous form of ritual having its origins in the ancient initiatory ceremony known as the *dromenon* or 'enaction of the New Birth into the tribe': 'In Greece, the chief seasonal *dromenon* seems to have been in the spring; its object, the magical inducement of fresh life, for man, for other animals and for plants. A particular form of this spring rite was the Dithyramb [from which the drama arose].'[131] The hero whose deeds Homer and the tragedians commemorate 'wears the mask and absorbs the ritual of an *Eniautos-Daimon* (roughly: Year Spirit) . . . The *daimon* functionary represents the permanent life of the group. The individual dies, but the group and its incarnation the king survive. *Le roi est mort, le roi vive*.'[132]

In other words, the plots of Greek tragedy may be largely derived from Homeric saga, but 'the ritual forms in which that content is cast derive straight from the *dromena* of the *Eniautos-Daimon*. Such forms are the Prologue, the Agon, the Pathos, the Messenger's Speech, the Threnos, the Anagnorisis and the final Theophany.'[133] 'The cult of the collective *daimon*, the king and the fertility-spirit is primary, Homer's conception of the hero as the gallant individual, the soldier of fortune or the gentleman of property, is secondary and late.'[134] But for its fruitful collision with indigenous traditions to produce the Attic drama, Harrison's view of 'Homer', the poetic body of knowledge representing 'Olympianism', is largely negative. It represents the patriarchal overthrow of a 'primitive form of society [ ] matrilineal not matriarchal,' an arrogant imperialism. The Olympian refuses to be an Earth-*daimon*, a *daimon* of air and sky: 'He will not die to rise again, but chooses instead a barren immortality. He withdraws himself from man and lives remote, a "jealous god".'[135]

The absorption of these ideas into Strehlow's work is evident. Why, he asks, did a Homeric tradition not arise here? 'In Central Australian verse we find literary matter probably not unsimilar to the raw material from which poets like Homer's predecessors hammered out poetry as an independent medium of artistic expression.' Yet poetry remained the prisoner of dance and music: 'with all its excellences and in spite of its mass-appeal, "primitive verse" needed to be freed from its bondage to music and dancing in point of form, and to religion and ceremonial occasions in point of themes and content, so that great poets could arise who could impress upon their creations their full individual genius without let or hindrance. This,' Strehlow concludes, 'is what, in fact, happened in ancient Europe.' He explains it in the same way as Harrison: 'the secularising process [through which independent poets like Homer emerged] was probably assisted and accelerated by constant wars and upheavals, which sometimes led to migrations on a national scale.'[136]

These passages might imply that Strehlow regretted the failure of a native Homer to emerge; but his position was subtler. He wanted to maintain the poetic significance of Aranda song, but also to hold open the possibility of further historical, and poetic, development. This was the other side of Strehlow's notorious contention that the decadence of Aranda song and dance had predated the European invasion; the 'thoroughness of their forefathers' in commemorating in story and verse the features of the Central Australian landscape had meant, Strehlow argued, that the modern Aranda had 'not a single unoccupied scene which they could fill with the creatures of their own imagination'; 'tradition and the tyranny of the old men in the religious and cultural sphere have effectively stifled all creative impulse.'[137] If this were true, then by analogy with Harrison's argument, contact with a migratory 'Homeric' tradition might stimulate, rather than stifle, the native tradition.

Strehlow writes in *Songs of Central Australia*:

> Had the Aranda and their immediate western neighbours, like the European peoples in the Heroic Age, been disturbed from their

> traditional homes by the coming of the whites, but been able to preserve their social institutions and most of their sacred traditions, they would have found that the new areas into which they moved were full of sites which were devoid of any myths known to them. Their own wanderings would have cast up new leaders, who would have brought order into the general confusion of religious ideas, and mitigated the disruption of the old social structure inseparable from such a vast upheaval. These new native leaders would in time have become legendary heroes, and many of the old mythological trappings would then have been transferred to their shoulders, as has indeed happened elsewhere on the globe.'[138]

And if this could still happen, a new Australian, not simply pan-Aboriginal, literature might emerge.

This transference, a desire to incorporate the past into the future, distinguished Strehlow's attitude to his intellectual forefathers. Much as he was influenced by their theory of Western poetry's beginnings, he rejected its primitivism, and its equally imperializing corollary, a progressivism that condemned, say, his own people to belong to the Stone Age. There was nothing 'primitive' about Aranda culture. To think there was simply testified to the linguistic ignorance of the white onlooker – a fact illustrated by Spencer and Gillen. 'Inaccuracies' in their accounts of the Engwura festival held at Alice Springs in 1896, which occur whenever they 'go beyond merely photographic descriptions of what they saw and attempt to give explanations of these spectacles,'[139] arise from a confusion of mimicry with mimesis. Their own anthropological biases, reinforced by the primitivist preoccupations of their distinguished correspondent J. G. Frazer, were part of the problem, but the fundamental difficulty was their ignorance of Aranda.

When they questioned their native informants in pidgin English, they found their own presuppositions parroted back to them – a mirror state possibly reinforced by the fact that 'where English uses "no" in response to a negative question, Aranda always uses "yes"; in the native language such a "yes" affirms the whole negative sentence which it answers.' And Strehlow comments, 'This is a feature that has led to many misunderstandings between the natives and their white questioners.'[140] Not knowing the language, they could not know that they were not meant to know: 'Spencer never seems to have realised that the sacred myths, ceremonies, and song verses used to be regarded as the private property of individuals or small totemic groups.'[141] One consequence was that Spencer had no inkling of Central Australian social organization; instead of recognizing a distributive system, where small groups networked across a large region, occasionally congregating at (totemically significant) nodal points, Spencer lumped the Aranda together, creating a nation where none existed.[142]

Not understanding the double movement that constituted Aranda social and ceremonial life, Spencer completely misunderstood the nature of the Alice Springs gathering. There was a major difference between the 'main "Western Desert" type of ceremonial gathering and the Aranda *ingkura* ceremonial festival.' If the latter events implied congregation, 'concerned with the staging of the great Aranda ceremonial cycles by the totemic clansmen before the members of their own local group and visitors from other local groups allied by myths with their own,' the former entailed rigid segregation, being 'arranged for circumcision purposes – circumcision being visualised as the main act of initiating the male novices into the spiritual world of eternity.' Spencer and Gillen missed this important distinction; what they described 'were actually commemorative ceremonies in honour of various totemic ancestors, and not initiation ceremonies in the generally accepted significance of the term.'[143]

Besides obscuring the social structures and religious life of the Aranda, their linguistic incompetence had two other consequences. It focused attention on the physical, visual and musical dimensions of the ceremonies at the expense of their intellectual and political content; and as a corollary, it confirmed the impression that Aranda society was 'primitive'. As Strehlow later emphasized, 'All incising of designs on the *tjurunga*, all work on cult objects, totem-poles, *waninga*, and ground paintings, all decorating of the ceremonial actors, and all sacred performances and ritual, took place to the singing of the appropriate song verses, believed to have been composed by the supernatural personages themselves.'[144] And these song verses, over which Spencer and Gillen passed in silence, were not 'a collection of sounds [which] cannot be translated',[145] but a mnemonically-infolded vehicle of religious and historical knowledge: 'to "possess" these songs by memorising them was once regarded as one of the highest goals in life by all ambitious young men.'[146]

Not understanding the activity of memory, the place of memorialization as periodic performance in Aranda life, Spencer and Gillen pushed these people back into a past which testified not to Aranda 'primitiveness' but to the anthropologists' own technologically-induced amnesia. Ashamed they had no songs of their own, but only their cameras and their wax-cylinder recording machines, they pretended to find the antics of the others theatrical, infantile. Against all this framing, this grouping of the imperial gaze, Strehlow satisfactorily rebelled. His group, for example, has nothing to do with 'collective suggestion'; it is a social and political unit that guarantees the freedom of its individual members. There is no hint in his writings of a group consciousness; as his essay 'Monototemism in a Polytotemistic society' makes plain, totemic worship amply accommodates the expression of an individual life experience.[147] Spencer and Gillen misrepresented what they saw: the term *inditjuwuma* (which they misspelt 'intichiuma') applied only locally; they 'mistakenly adopted it as the general Aranda term for all increase ceremonies.'[148] Elsewhere, different terms were used. The obsession with a Parmenidean unity gradually splintering is a European one; it makes no sense in a Central Australian context, where the people are locally grouped and where, therefore, any act of self-affirmation is of necessity relational, a matter of reaffirming ties with neighbourhood and neighbours.

Similarly, the anthropological preoccupation with the passage from magical rites to truly religious rituals is senseless where, from the beginning, totemic rituals comprehend both presence and absence: 'Normally the Central Australian increase ceremonies are acts of worship as well as magical rites.' They are, Strehlow writes, 'commemorative' ceremonies, and 'celebrate the lives and deeds of the totemic ancestors.'[149] Questioned about their belief that the landscape is the living trace of the totemic ancestors' passage and enduring presence, Aranda elders are quite able to appreciate the difference between then and now, to acknowledge that the landscape now is but a dim reflection of what it must once have been: 'The native was a realist: he knew that his totemic ancestors would never again wander over the landscape as they had done at the beginning of time.'[150] Theirs is a wholly spatio-historical awareness – one reason why they can have but little use for our concept of history as chronology, our impatient urge to put things behind us. They have no need to flesh out the bare facts, to make up a story to represent what once occurred; for them, time is already 'fat', multiply in-folded in the present.

Again, Harrison, drawing on Australian material, might have concluded that Olympian sky-worship was an inevitable, if partly regrettable, advance on the old totemic worship of the Earth. However, Strehlow could have informed her differently:

> It has been assumed far too often that aboriginal Australian religion emanated from the puerile phantasies of Stone Age men with immature children's minds – of men who could not perceive the physical differences between themselves and animals, of men who were ignorant of physiological paternity, and so on . . . It is far more reasonable to suppose that it was his full awareness of the harshness and insecurity of his existence which forced him to seek spiritual communion with the immutable things of his own experience, and to identify his mortal Time-bound self with what he believed to be unlimited and eternal in the unchanging landscape of his country.[151]

The genius of Aranda religion lay in its capacity to bring into dialogue the eternal and the temporal: 'During the performance of totemic ritual, transient Time and timeless Eternity become completely fused into a single Reality in the minds of all participants,' the experience that Strehlow likened to the Greek notion of *kairos*, 'the moment of time which is invaded by eternity.'[152]

It is this internal dialectic between the eternal, embodied in the immutable features of the landscape, and the temporal, embodied in the patterns of human life, that explains why an external dialectic between Sky and Earth is not required to motivate the seasons, the growth and decay of things; theatrical representations of Jovian lightning-bolts impregnating a resplendent but prone mother Gaia are an unnecessary hypothesis where there is no gap to be closed up, no Odyssean exile to be negated – where the ground itself is mother and father and vibrates to their companionable intercourse. Strehlow's remark that 'the aboriginal Central Australians had not been forced by recent migrations to transfer their earthborn supernatural beings into the sky, in order to continue to enjoy the protection of these sky dwellers after moving to new areas,'[153] was no more or less plausible than the culture-theorizing indulged in by the Social Darwinists.

The difference was that Strehlow could demonstrate the further point, that the Aranda had no need of a sky myth because the earth supplied them with both principles of creation. On the last day of the increase ceremonies associated with Krantji, a Northern Aranda kangaroo centre, 'the *tnatantja-pura* [approximately "totem-pole"], held by all the men belonging to the Krantji kangaroo clan, was twisted about over the central hole in the ground-painting; and the down-tufts stripped from both the *tnatantja-pura* and the ground-painting mingled with one another as they were thrust down into this opening . . . the totemites were engaged in a reverent miming of the act of intercourse.' This, says Strehlow, explains why 'the sky and its dwellers had no influence upon the earth nor any interest in it . . . maleness as well as femaleness were believed to have co-existed side by side in the Central Australian landscape.'[154]

Here, '*daimon* worship', far from signifying a Dionysiac suspension of mundane time and space, a theatrical transcendence of historical fate, reveals itself as a performative reaffirmation of an historical tradition. A vortical concentration of space-time occurs, analogous to that presumably involved in the upthrust of mountain ridges, in the furrowing of creek beds and the dimpling of water-soaks. But the emphasis is on their becoming, not their timeless being; the measures cannot be separated from what is measured, the trace from what is traced – so in a simple way the spaces in between Strehlow's woven word-tufts are as eloquent as the grouped phrases. They assert the fundamentally dual nature of existence – a conception remote from our preoccupation with binary oppositions. The elaboration of that relationship informs the design, the proliferation of the ground-painting's concentric circles, the rehearsed approaches of the spear-like, penis-like *tnatantja-pura*. Nothing is represented here – 'these two separate "principles" were not personalised in any way'[155] – as no separation has occurred. Any Olympian attempt to represent this fact misrepresents it, precisely because it assumes the theatrical space of mimesis itself, with its dramatic repertoire of *dei ex machina* bringing about miraculous events.

Strehlow's authorities for him provided the groundwork of his own cultural project; but characteristically, he departs from them not by transgressing their conceptual boundaries, but by deepening the grooves within their already-surveyed territory. By this means he gradually discloses the ideological nature of their descriptions, the temporal territorialization that has occurred, the racist enclosure acts that imprison both them and their subjects. The Cambridge Hellenists are not surpassed, any more than Carl Strehlow is surpassed. Nevertheless, by his own 'reverent miming' of their intellectual deeds, Strehlow distinguishes his own work from theirs. And it is in much the same spirit that we can gloss the meaning of that reverent mime, and begin to understand how it differs from Robinson's Dionysiac pose, that rhapsodic mask said to represent the coming of the god within.

After all, Harrison might characterize *methexis* as a primitive form of mimicry – both mimicry and *methexis* being superseded in her progressivist fable by mimesis – but her colleague Cornford took a different view, according to which the meaning of the term changed and deepened over time. In any case, for Cornford the term was one of philosophical rather than ethnographic import: 'This relation called "participation" (*methexis*)' is, from the first, 'a mystical, non-rational relation.' As he explains, 'The Idea is a group-soul, related to its group as a mystery-*daimon*, like Dionysus, is related to the group of his worshippers, his *thiasos*.'[156] But this is only a simile, as Plato's mysticism is not a naïve return to *daimon*-worship but rather belongs to the Pythagorean reformation of Orphism. 'Orphism was still a cult, in which the initiate, as Aristotle says, "was not expected to learn or understand anything, but to feel a certain emotion and get into a certain state of mind, after first becoming fit to experience it".' In terms of ritual, Orphism stood midway between the totemic rites and the Attic drama, and, Cornford says, it specialized in 'those dramatic representations of the passion and resurrection of the life *daimon*, which point back to the old mimetic dances of magic, and forward to the tragic drama.'[157]

'Pythagoreanism,' Cornford writes, 'presents itself as an attempt to intellectualise the content of Orphism, while preserving its social form . . . Like Orphism itself, it is both a reformation and a revival. Like all reformations, it means that much of the ceremonial overgrowth is shaken off: Orphism ceases to be a cult, and becomes a way of life. As a revival, Pythagoreanism means a return to an earlier simplicity, a disinterring of the essential form, whose outline is simple enough to adapt itself to a new movement of the spirit.'[158] Against this background, one is tempted to say that, in relation to the Orphic Robinson, Strehlow is a disciple of Pythagoras. This is not an idle comparison for, as the Italian poet Giuseppe Ungaretti reminds us in his Orphic poem '*Risvegli*', what is at issue here is the method of memory:

Every moment of mine
I have lived

some other time
in a faraway epoch
outside myself

I am far away with my memory
following those lost lives.[159]

Similarly, Robinson is haunted by 'Ancestral voices. A primitive ancestor in me', whom his poetry reincarnates.[160] However, reject this comforting legend and embrace, as Strehlow does, the Pythagorean doctrine of 'harmony', and the question of self-memorialization presents itself differently. It becomes passionately a matter of numbers, of plotting the 'processional movement out of unity into plurality';[161] energy is transferred to the mechanics of the eternal return, from orgiastic identification to poetic technique, and a proper knowledge of the just ratios or groupings of parts.

A Pythagorean poetics pervades *Songs of Central Australia*. For example, with regard to the *tjurunga* essence, a mindless group unity is neither achieved nor sought. Aranda sacred art, song and dance is not the primitive expression of 'participation'. Equally, it has nothing to do with Western mimesis, the personalized, naturalistic representation of heroes. 'Just as in Central Australian dramatic performances the actors tended to avoid completely realistic gestures, and used stylised and highly rhythmic movements in their miming techniques,' Strehlow writes, 'so the native artist avoided fully representational figures in his patterns.'[162] The state of mind evoked here is that of an Orphic adept on his way to becoming a disciple of Pythagoras, a 'passionate sympathetic contemplation (*theoria*), in which the spectator is identified with the suffering God, dies in his death, and rises again in his new birth. By these and other ritual means – the eating of flesh or the drinking of wine – the old sense of mystical oneness and participation can be renewed, and the *daimon*-soul of the group re-created in collective emotion. The only doctrine is the myth, the verbal counterpart of the action of the rite, the life-history of the God, which is also the life-history of the soul.'[163]

Strehlow's 'reverent miming' corresponds to the *theoria* of the Pythagorean adept. There is no question of the artist, the dancer or singer confusing himself with the power invoked (his totemic ancestor); his is not an instance of primitive *methexis*. Yet he does not occupy an empty stage; the ground-painting determines his steps, he is not free to represent the spirit using 'realistic gestures'. His is not the art of mimesis. Yet nor is his 'miming' to be confused with the Orphic pretensions of a Roland Robinson, or the frankly outward mimicry of the alien outsider. His philosophical *methexis* corresponds precisely to my term 'performance':[164] to perform – to echo Husserl's definition of intentionality – is always to perform something. There is never an actor on one side, something to be acted upon on the other; the two come into being through each other. Thus, in contrast with a theatrical drama, with its neutralized space, its exits and entrances that have to be motivated, what Strehlow calls a commemorative act always demands a physical ground – which, by his reverent mime, the actor brings back into historical circulation.

In this context, Strehlow's apparently casual admission at the close of *Journey to Horseshoe Bend* that his father's last illness 'had shaken and shattered his faith to its very foundations'[165] assumes a greater significance. In Strehlow's reconstruction, his dying father contrasts the 'indifference' of his clerical colleagues with the 'humanity, the sympathy, and above all, the practical helpfulness of the churchless bush people'. He recalls St. Paul's *First Letter to the Corinthians*: 'It was the failure of the Lutheran clergy to give due weight to the God-established supremacy of love that had constituted such a grave weakness in the doctrinal soundness of much of their preaching.'[166] This hypocritical coldness is cognate with Western society's prudish view of human sexuality, and the contrast with the 'Central Australian love-making pattern' could not be greater: 'It cannot be too strongly emphasised that such sires as Antijroba, Malbangka, and Kulurba did not rape the women whom they desired. They first roused them to a fever pitch of passion. Gratification came to the alkngarintja women only after their excitement had become an almost unendurable sensation of pain. Marital intimacy brought to them both physical pleasure and physical relief.'[167]

The 'marital intimacy' Strehlow admires is Pythagorean; it transforms the Dionysian orgy into something lawful, making it a way of life. And as, in the act of sexual intercourse, the partners are *mutatis mutandis* engaged in a reverent miming of 'the meeting of the two vital forces, symbolising maleness and femaleness respectively – the conjunction of the boundless virility of the ancestral sire and the charm-induced passionate self-surrender of the alkngarintja woman,'[168] the sexual act itself may truly be said to be methektic. Participation in it defines oneness as a temporary unity in difference, a concept remote from the self-transcendence of the Bacchic frenzy. Perhaps these meditations would have taken shape in an autobiographical sequel to *Journey to Horseshoe Bend* which, had it been written, must have described Strehlow's initiation into manhood.[169]

The appeal that a concept of 'participation' held for Strehlow may have been multiple. In the 'mirror state' of Hermannsburg, Western mimesis merged into mere mimicry. The coercion inherent in the poetics of representation became evident, and was unmasked as a device of patriarchy; as if, unable to bond with the earth, the itinerant male principle could only replicate itself one-sidedly – as if journeys consisted solely of right or left footsteps, and never both alternating. Here *methexis* offered a way out. In particular, departing from the high road of Western science, with its nostalgia for Paradise, it licensed a movement characterized by an attention to the lie of the land. *Methexis* was the 'non-representative' principle behind Celtic, and Aranda, art, whose spirals and mazes reproduced by an act of concurrent actual production a pattern danced on the ground.

As a psychological attitude, *methexis* did not signify a naïve and regressive identification with the other. Nor did it signify progress towards an integration of self and world – it did not approximate to the depressive state described by Melanie Klein in which 'whole-object' relations had been achieved.[170] In a sense, it refused the linearization of growing-up represented by these models. Instead of regarding birth as the first displacement, the first expulsion and ruin, it understood it as the primary emplacement, as the first choreography of the ground. A methektic identification began in a recognition of the duality of being; it assumed that communication began as an oscillation, a contract across difference. The twin double that Strehlow invoked when he claimed affiliation with Ntarea was not a clone of himself; it might be the *genius loci* itself. In any case, its irremediable and untranslatable difference was not an obstacle. On the contrary, it provided the reason for imitation. And again, the imitation engaged in was an act of love; it did not penetrate, so much as dimple or in-bend, the other's folded surfaces.

The spectators of the gladiatorial contests who, in Bulwer-Lytton's *Last Days of Pompeii*, were 'intent upon no fictitious representation – tragedy of the stage – but the actual victory or defeat, the exultant life or the bloody death, of each and all who entered the arena,'[171] witnessed, it is true, an end of representations; but they did not thereby embrace *methexis*. Rather they tasted, albeit briefly, the power the colonist and the missionary felt when they observed their representations crush the life out of the savage. In contrast with this identification with the father-figure of power – an abstraction made architecturally present in the form of the arena and dependent for its effect on banishing sympathy from the scene – *methexis* insisted on an empathy with that which was palpably present, not necessarily to the sovereign eye but certainly to the eye and ear in their physical association with the body's endless plotting of the ground.

Hostile to the stage, to the planar construction of the world as 'over there', *methexis* was equally hostile to the simple stratification of motifs: as if autobiography and ethnography could be kept apart; or as if, since both were performances in which before and after dissolved into the concurrent actual production, either could be divorced from internal questions of composition (poetics) and external questions of speaking position, implied audience and points of reference (politics). The fact that Strehlow could not disentangle these motifs of his life may make him susceptible to criticism on every specialist front; but it also ensures the enduring interest of his writing. Participating in the production of the history to which he wanted to belong, Strehlow could not afford the luxury of a colonized viewpoint. Near and far could not be so easily distinguished. While the Olympians manufactured heroic journeys, he spent his life, Penelope-like, weaving and unweaving a single pattern. Like Namatjira, he wanted to stay at home. The difference was that, as a migrant, this entailed devising a new way of travelling, and singing, the place.

Strehlow's definition of art as 'a reverent miming' had immediate implications for the practice of poetry. If *Songs of Central Australia* was to have any lasting value as the poetic primer of a future literature, it needed to devise a satisfactory method of translating Aranda songs into English; as the Aranda genius was not the Homeric genius, this inevitably meant subjecting the European muse to critical analysis. Strehlow's examination of Aranda song led him, for example, to conclude that the orthodox view of classical Greek metre as purely quantitative could not be sustained; it was, he thought, equally improbable that English or German verse had ever been purely accentual.[172] In finding a way of preserving the composite nature of Aranda song, whose elastic musical phrase is at once accentual and quantitative, Strehlow was also revising and reviving his own native traditions.

He was also implicitly mounting an attack on the efforts of his white contemporaries to incorporate Aboriginal elements into their art and science. Elkin might excuse the exterior mimicry of *Songs of the Songmen* – it uses 'forms, length of line, accent and rhythm that seem to convey best the feeling and atmosphere and, in the case of chants, the ritual "beat" ' – by explaining that many Aboriginal songs 'are almost codes, mnemonic in function, and for some purposes, secret,'[173] but this was because he was ignorant of the languages in which the songs were sung. The same ignorance that forced him and Harney to produce 'translations' that reproduced the most reductive features of their own poetic tradition, also obliged him to treat the music of indigenous songs as a thing apart. It is significant that in his musical transcriptions of the Arnhem Land songs (some of which formed the basis of Harney's verses), Trevor Jones indicates the vocal line solely by crotchets. Without the poetic information that might have allowed him to represent the union of poetic and musical measure, Jones had no choice but to divide the music into bars, but whether the bar divisions corresponded to isorhythmic units, or simply linearized and segmented the performance, was a moot point.[174]

The same linearization and flattening-out afflicted the attempts of white poets to render indigenous poetic forms. Thinking of Strehlow's image of the hunter whose grammar allows him elastically to incorporate more and more of the *euro*'s movement history into a story whose analogue is his own passage, his own reverent mime of the land's lie, the poet who wanted to imitate Aranda songs forms clearly had to essay a poetry of incremental movement. There was no room here for the fixed positions which made similes possible, for a dialectic between outsides and insides; a kind of word-weaving analogous to the patterns of turbulence which those surfaceless elements, water and air, create in their motion was needed. And this accounts in part for the provisional, and indeed incremental, nature of Strehlow's own translations.

Towards the end of *Songs of Central Australia*, Strehlow translates part of the Northern Aranda 'Honey-Ant Song of Ljaba', and comments on his own efforts. Sometimes the preservation of the formal structure has meant departing from the meaning: 'In verse 30 I have been unable to keep the refrain "dwell, ever dwell", and have replaced it with "tell, ever tell". This at least rhymes with the former, and so preserves some of the chime-ringing association for the English reader.'[175] A subtler flattening-out of poetic implication occurs in verse 25: 'In nectar immersed, with wave-rings adorned they dwell, ever dwell,' which, Strehlow says, means literally, 'The nectar keeps on marking their bodies with wave rings.' 'The reference,' he explains, 'is to the wave-rings and foam-rings which a flooded river leaves behind on the objects it engulfs and on the sides of the river banks.'[176] To preserve the rhythm the mobile has been rendered immobile, the present continuous of 'keeps on marking' turned into the past participle 'adorned'. But perhaps more serious than the linearization and segmentation of time is the sacrifice of physical depth associated with the process of marking. Here, it seems, is a natural progenitor of the dot and circle design; the pecked surface of water radiates rings that lap over and over against the river-bank, embodying a double movement, projective and sedimentary. But in translation the idea of dwelling ceases to belong to a dance figure re-enacting creative environmental forces; movement becomes a predicate defining a static staying at home.

It was Strehlow's distinction to recognize that these problems of rendering were not narrowly rhetorical, but stemmed from Western poetry's post-Homeric divorce from music. Commenting on the same 'Honey Ant Song of Ljaba' in an article published while *Songs of Central Australia* was in progress, Strehlow noted that the Aranda songs are poems 'intoned or sung because they are in metres which give musical, not spoken, length values to all the syllables in each line. Syllables containing long vowels may take up no more time in chanting than syllables containing short vowels: in the latter case consonant clusters may take up the remaining time value of notes on which the syllable falls.' And Strehlow concluded, 'For this reason native poems can never have their rhythms adequately represented by any English version which is intended only for recitation.'[177]

Nor could they be adequately 'represented' by treating them as abstractly musical compositions and setting them down under a musical stave, for the rhythmic grouping of syllables 'were intended to regulate the movements of ceremonial dancers.' Further, they were only one 'side' of the rhythmic context: 'When a song was being chanted, it was not unusual for the singers to bring out its strong musical stresses in their chanting while tapping out simultaneously a different rhythm with their boomerangs.' 'The musical notation of sung verse of this kind also presents very considerable difficulties; for there is no fixed melody in our sense of the word.' However, Strehlow suggested, the 'tune' of each verse could be represented by 'setting down the two constants that emerge during actual chanting. The first is the invariable rhythmic measure found in each verse of the song. The second is the "tonal pattern" traditionally associated with it. The "tune" of each verse then results from the combination of the rhythmic measure with this traditional tone pattern.'[178]

No wonder Strehlow was strongly drawn to the music theatre of Wagner, for here was a Western composer who, by writing both music and words, had created (to paraphrase another composer, William Byrd) a 'musical rhythm framed to the life of the words.'[179] But Wagner's example also points to the limitations of Strehlow's proposed model: the complete harmonization of language and music leads to a mutual reinforcement that, while aesthetically appealing, is ultimately enclosing, and that once again excludes rather than incorporates the lie of the land. This indeed is the significance of the 'numerous slurred notes' that 'play an important part' in the 'Honey-Ant Song of Ljaba'. The slur, which Strehlow defines as 'two or more notes sung on one long syllable',[180] embodies a notion of musical duration and continuously-changing pitch relations that the modern Western system of musical notation cannot transcribe. But, as Ellis shows, the slur is a critical element in maintaining the isomorphism of song text and rhythmic pattern.[181]

Figuratively, to return to our grammatically elastic hunter, the shallowly-arched and asymmetrical slur sign corresponds to the trajectory of the spear. Dispatched on its shallowly-curving arc, the spear is the foot of the hunter elongated. It is the ground puckered up and drawn tight as the throat of a purse. The thin projectile sings and quivers over the glinting space, its tone being its vectorial signature. In this composite 'action' the hunter's incremental motion is allied to the 'melody' or lie of the land. This is why the hunter, retracing traces and eventually striking down his prey, could plausibly describe the process as magical, an act of reverent miming not unlike that engaged in by the *rhapsode* when he invested his voice with ancestral tones. This was also why, at the end of *The Road to Botany Bay*, I invoked the image of the historian as hunter; for spatial history cannot be divorced from the manner of going over the ground. To be alive to the lie of the land is to understand writing and walking as cognate activities.[182]

A. D. Hope may have missed part of the point when he savaged Jindyworobaks Ingamells and Kennedy for investing in lines like

'Garrakeen, the parakeet, is slim and swift./ Like a spear of green and red he flashes through . . .' ('Kennedy and Ingamells may "write with their spears and throwing sticks beside them", but I should like to know for how many other Australians a spear is a natural simile for a parakeet, or taken from "the very world around".'[183]) As the description of a painting in the style of Arthur Boyd or Albert Tucker, Ingamells's poem has considerable merit. But that is the point, perhaps: it represents a representation, it reads movement back into what is static rather than catching it on the wing. It is not that this simile is unnatural, but that similes in general have no place in a poetics of *methexis*.

The Jindyworobaks turned the spear into a metonymy of Aboriginal culture, not to say a metaphor of the poetic process. 'Beside these ever-flowing falls were spears fashioned./ Beside the tall gum were songs sung,' wrote Ian Mudie.[184] In 'April 28th 1770', Hart-Smith's stereotypical Aborigine stands at the ocean's edge, 'my spear was raised to strike', observing the European landing. He retreats, and they 'came and took our spears', this one-sided exchange inaugurating a new universe of one-sided discourse. If before 'I made the waves' voices say what they would', 'Now they are asking the question,/ and turning over the question, breaking up the question.'[185] Robinson, as ever, is more animated: 'Would I might find my country as the blacks/ come in and lean their spears up in the scrub.' The stress here is not on a naïve identification with the 'other'. What Robinson perceives and admires – it may be another projection – is a poetry whose movement is physically embodied: 'I had no human word, beyond/ all words I knew the rush of ash-/ grey wings that gloomed, with one respond,/ storm-grey, to swerve with crimson flash.'[186]

In any case, while the Jindyworobaks tried to shift the ground thematically, lexically and rhythmically they stayed in the old country. With the partial exception of Roland Robinson, there was a depressing indifference to Pound's injunction to 'make it new'. Any 'word weaving', so characteristic of Aranda song, was absent from their monotonously linear lines. According to Strehlow, the only recent poet writing in English whose poetic practice remotely resembled that of traditional Aranda song was Gerard Manley Hopkins, whose 'sprung rhythm', with its capacity to incorporate into the poetic foot 'one, two, or three slack syllables . . . not counting in the nominal scanning', recalls the musical form of Aranda rhythmic measures.[187] Hopkins's metrical innovation was a way of 'folding' individual images into one another so that, instead of standing in a linear relationship, snapshot after snapshot, they were apprehended dynamically as a group whose constituent parts continually moved and remade themselves.

Strehlow may have denied that he was a poet,[188] but some of his translations of Aranda song are reverent mimes whose word weaving embodies an environmental conception of poiesis as kinesis – of the spear's flight – undreamt-of among the 'poets'. Rex Ingamells's 'Ulamba' may paraphrase a myth recounted in *Aranda Traditions*, but one sees at once why 'Mr. Ted Strehlow, from whose friendship I received much of my inspiration for all these poems, considers that the poem does not sufficiently capture the spirit of the legend.'[189] Ingamells's poem is a native picnic: the walk to the sacred cave is narrated as if through the lens of a movie camera hovering aloft, peering from a helicopter perhaps. The landscape it imagines is convex, has the sonata form of the poem itself, a linear ascent and descent. The quatrains of alternating ten-syllable lines segment the movement into self-contained scenes that, continually cutting off one moment from the next, render the whole poem elegiac, a sequence of epitaphs. Nothing is enacted as if it were here; all is narrated, or represented as over there.

In terms of physical viewpoint, 'Ulamba' should be compared with Strehlow's account, in *Songs of Central Australia*, of his visit to a cave containing some Loritja rain *tjurungas*. Strehlow, with a self-conscious sense of weaving his own autobiography into his argument, quotes lengthily from his '1933 diary account of my stay at Horseshoe Bend.' Ostensibly, the passage is cited to make the point that Aranda rain-increase rites depend as much on the act of blood-letting as on the singing of sacred songs; but the value of the diary entry lies at least as much in the sense it communicates of an intimate space, concave, textured, composed of irregularly-formed surfaces, where the bloody acts designed 'to honour their rain ancestors in the traditional manner' take place in the localized present. It is the localization of the action that prevents it from assuming the gaudy colours of a theatrical event and slipping into the picturesque past of our nostalgia for the primitive.[190]

Formally and metrically, Ingamells' ballad should be compared with Strehlow's attempts to render the Arintja 'Song of Ulamba' into English. 'The particularly easy rhythmic measure employed in the Arintja Song of Ulamba lends itself,' Strehlow comments, 'to reproduction in an English version.'[191] Encouraged by this, Strehlow then offers a second translation, 'to indicate [also] the effect of Aranda reduplications to the English reader by using double phrases for reduplicated compound words.'[192] What that 'effect' is becomes obvious when the translations are compared. For example, in the first 'rhythmic' translation verses 20–22 appear as:

> The avengers' stripes are flashing in the light:
> A [white] pair, they are flashing in the light.
>
> 'My own home, my dear home,
> Ulamba is lying yonder!'
>
> 'My own home, my dear home,
> [O] Ulamba, chasm-cleft!'
>
> 'The birds are speaking with many voices
> At Ulamba, chasm-cleft Ulamba.'

Insert the reduplications, and the same verses metamorphose into:

> Stripes erect, stripes of death, far they gleam, far they flash:
> White and long, closely paired, far they gleam, far they flash.
>
> 'Home of mine, home so dear, Ulamba, rocky-faced!
> Hark! The birds! Voices call, voices fall!
> Ulamba! Rocky-faced, rocky-based!'[193]

This second version cannot reproduce the tonal pattern of the Aranda original, but it does reproduce, or at least copy, its rhythmic measures. By grouping verbal phrases in this way, their subordination to the subject-predicate structure of a conventional English sentence is avoided. The theatricality of English grammar is side-stepped; qualifying phrases like 'in the light' or 'yonder', with their implicitly three-dimensional resolution of space into near and far, small and large, disappear, to be replaced by agglutinative word compounds in which the 'environment' of the thing named is contained within its own naming. Phrases like 'far they flash', 'closely paired' retain a 'Western' conception of time and space, but it is one where the perspective is reversed. The named radiate attributes, rather than concentrate them.

Further, the reduplication of identical or similar phrases describes the manner of their radiation; the 'Stripes erect' are experienced as pulsations of light, as rhythmic, dancing lightning. The analogy with the trochaic beat of feet and the panted breath-pattern of chanted verse is obvious. Less obvious is the analogy with body painting; the reduplicated phrases, subtly metamorphosing until they form concentric rings of meaning, correspond to the jabbing of dots and the emergence of undulating circles. The spacing of the phrases on the page, while it recalls the experiments of the Black Mountain school of poets and their search for a metrics of the breath, also has a local import; these phrases might in their arrangement reproduce the totemically-notated landscape of a Central Australian locality. Their distribution is not just a typographical metaphor for the physical performance of the singer; they may be spread out across the page as water-soaks, chasms, black-and-white stained cliff-faces are spread out in Aranda history – in a way where all parts bear witness to a metamorphosis going on wherever the footing voice alights.

Elastically extending the verse structure, revealing the measure and value of spaces (and sounds) in between, has the effect of making Aranda song entirely modern. By magnifying it so that the warp and woof can be examined, Strehlow reveals its internal dialectic. Aranda song is not the mindless repetition of traditional myths – this is the myth that is perpetuated so long as we attempt to enclose it within the architectonic structures of our own poetic tradition. On the contrary, it is the repeated performance of the ground, which here is not a given (an already demarcated and enclosed agora, say, corresponding to the rhymed enclosure of the stanza), but remains the other of the beat, the footmark, the exhaled breath, the thrown spear, even the rain-bearing cloud. Aranda song, Strehlow suggests, embodies a method of environmental management. It springs from a wholly historical awareness of the contingency of natural events. Its poetics, not its politics, are a pledge of human renewal.

But the poetics subtended a politics. To return to Ntarea, to memorialize it as a homeland, and not simply as a personal projection, implied a view of society. The constitution of 'the musical phrase' might model the constitution of society, but only if both derived their authority from their reverent mime of the lie of the land. Aboriginal music, writes Catherine Ellis, allows for 'varying degrees of fold,' a concept which, she says, informs Aboriginal thinking more generally; the ability to 'add to, to "fold" information', 'is also present in the flexibility traditionally shown over land usage. Boundaries between food gathering groups in desert areas were retained rigorously until times of disaster (floods, fires, droughts) when it was possible to "fold" the area available for a particular group by temporarily extending the boundaries (but never abandoning them).'[194] But while he recognized the importance of the traditional symmetry between song, land and ownership, Strehlow was less inclined, whether temperamentally or by virtue of his training, to accept the foldedness; for this implied an open-ended process of evolution that lacked a grammar (however subtle) and a clear sense of purpose.

It was this fear of the anarchy, the illicit desires and hybrid formations he associated with in-folding, his sense that the arbitrary amalgamation of fragments in fact signified that the centre could no longer hold, that defined Strehlow's ambiguous engagement with literary Modernism – of whose party he was, though he did not know it. After all, Hopkins had defined a point of bifurcation in English poetry. His reverent miming of Welsh and Anglo-Saxon bards anticipated an anti-Modernist trend in early twentieth-century English poetry, characterized by a desire to revive an indigenous cultural identity centred on the pre-Roman, even pre-Teutonic, world of ancient Britain. But it also looked forward to, and inspired, the likes of Ezra Pound, who cut his poetic teeth by paraphrasing the Anglo-Saxon poem *The Seafarer*, miming its poetic feeling rather than trying to represent its literal meaning, and who fancied himself as a modern Homer, heir to the entire European literary tradition.

Strehlow revered the mantic Hopkins but would have no truck with the later, and more self-conscious, *rhapsode* of the *Cantos*. 'In Old English poems,' writes Strehlow (but he might be describing Hopkins), 'the lines are bound together by alliteration and by kennings or poetical synonyms . . . In the Central Australian songs the division of each couplet into two similar or complementary lines likewise calls for a large stock of synonyms or poetic substitutes.'[195] Hopkins, like the Aranda singers, employs synonyms rather than similes, and the motives may be similar; rhythmically and alliteratively implicated paraphrases never break the surface of the poetic line – as the three-dimensional viewpoint implied by the simile might. Instead, they bunch up the line or swing it out, like the windhover alternately hovering and careening about its parabolic circuit.

In exploring the history of metrics, no less than in his in-weaving of heterogeneous poetic materials, Pound's practice built on Hopkins. It cultivated a learned but sonorous 'obscurity' intended, like the more enigmatic expressions of the Aranda singers, to remint the language and restore its purity. It also, if Maurice Bowra was to be believed, emulated the practice of Homer. Accepting Bowra's assertion that 'Homer's language was never spoken,' Strehlow found a parallel between 'the nature of the poetic vocabulary of the Central Australian songs and the general character of the ancient poetic language of Greece.'[196] But the same could be said of Pound; his language was a macaronic in-folding of poetic traditions with a view to creating an epic where all times and places were simultaneously present. It was a metalanguage designed to conserve as well as reveal. The difficulty, at least from Strehlow's point of view, was that such experiments did not spring from any living community. The self-appointed bard did not impersonate any group voice: 'It seems a peculiar thing that in our modern age, which boasts about its democratic tendencies and its ideals of universal education, literature, and the Fine Arts, should seek to disengage themselves more and more from the *profanum vulgus*.' 'Modern verse,' Strehlow concluded, 'cannot afford obscurity to the same degree as "primitive" verse.'[197]

What kind of obscurity, then, could modern verse afford? In a postscript to his verse epic *The Dawn of Britain*, C. M. Doughty (better remembered for his prose epic *Arabia Deserta*) said, 'it is the prerogative of every lover of his Country, to use the instrument of his thought, which is the Mother-tongue, with propriety and distinction; to keep that reverently clean and bright, which lies at the root of his mental life, and so, by extension, of the life of his Community: putting away all impotent and disloyal vility of speech, which is no uncertain token of a people's decadence.'[198] This orotundly lumbering pastiche of a sixteenth-century sermon makes Doughty's purpose plain: if Pound wants to make it new, Doughty intends to make it old. If Hopkins's instinct is poetic, to avoid obscurities 'so far as is consistent with excellences higher than clearness at first reading,'[199] Doughty's is didactic, to license them in the interests of purging vility and promoting mental cleanliness.

Doughty's revived 'Community' depended on a revised poetics; this is his interest for us. The object of *The Dawn of Britain* is twofold: to renovate the mother-tongue, and to justify this historically. The great mistake the modern British have made is to forget their pre-Roman, Celtic roots. By modelling themselves on Imperial Rome, they not only draw towards the brink of war with Germany, but they forget their true interests – which lie not in the colonies but in the recovery and defence of Britain's indigenous traditions. Poetically, this self-forgetfulness manifests itself in an ignorance of the quantitative genius of British verse, deriving from the 'fruitful Homeric tradition', which Doughty sees as a distinctive expression of the greater Celtic confederacy of nations that dominated Europe before the rise of Rome, and which, but for Rome, would have realized their historical destiny under the banner of Jesus Christ.[200]

After the Second World War, the association of quantitative metres with the resurrection of Britain's indigenous identity and, by extension, native polity, was promoted by the Scottish nationalist and poet Hugh MacDiarmid, who wrote in an essay on Pound, 'Wagner was right when he spent years studying word-roots. He knew (as Charles Doughty knew) that we were coming to another quantitative – as against accentual – period in culture.' And the new period would mark a return to origins – to the *pibroch*, say, of the great period which 'knew no "bar". They were timeless music – hence their affiliation with plainsong, with the *neuma*.' 'Unbarred music – quantity music – expresses itself in pattern repetition; hence the idea that the Celt has no architectonic power, that his art is confined to niggling involutions and intricacies . . . yet the ultimate form here is not symphony; it is epic' – which MacDiarmid equates 'with the classless society'.[201]

A kind of synthesis of anti-Modernist and Modernist myths of origin occurs in the work of the Anglo-Welsh poet David Jones. Sharing Doughty's mythopoeic imagination, Jones makes Celts and Christians one in their opposition to Roman colonization, and he suggests that the subtlety of their songs leaves them vulnerable to the stamp of more virile, if barbaric, poetic measures. At the same time, Jones understands the genius of the mother-tongue very differently from Doughty; like Pound or Eliot, his notion of purifying the tongue is to immerse it in an ocean of competing spoken idioms and half-remembered quotations, to elicit from words not a vague music but a local resonance. In *Anathemata* and in the fragments posthumously published as *The Roman Quarry*, Jones works out a kind of conflict theory of poetic genesis. He is interested in the phonetic mechanisms – the warp and woof of sounds as they ravel and unravel themselves across words, across languages – that enable symbols to transform themselves as they pass from one culture to another; and he finds these most powerfully revealed where one culture comes into violent contact with another, for here, in the no-man's land between warring forces, the tongue's tapestry is rudely rent, an in-between language irrupts, by turns idiomatic, allusive, baroquely intricate and involved.[202]

Against this (admittedly sketchy) background, we can make better sense of Strehlow's insistence that Aranda song is both accentual and quantitative. The distinction made in European literatures between quantitative and accentual poetry fails in the context of Aranda songs, which use a 'new system of accentuation' that 'brings out the strong beats of the rhythmic measure.' 'Verse rhythm in these songs does not flow from speech rhythm. It is hostile to the spoken language. It forms its own strong rhythmic patterns and then forces them upon the normal rhythm of prose. It is a mould in which the untidy scrap material of everyday speech is melted and reshaped. It wilfully changes the accentuation of the spoken language', with the object of ensuring that 'verse accent supersede[s] speech accent.'[203] The effect of this 'intoned poetry' can, Strehlow says, be compared to Gregorian chant or plainsong before musical rhythm became subordinated to verbal rhythm.[204]

But it could just as well be compared with Pound's conception of 'absolute rhythm': 'The music of free period, of a constantly varying phrase-length and rhythm-length, is a freedom from fixed lengths, but the symmetry must underlie, and the sense of this symmetry must be kept fresh and vivid, if not in the consciousness, at least in the subconsciousness of the performer.'[205] Absolute rhythm is not measured by the metronome; it occurs where a convergence exists between poetic and musical phrase, where a fixed element and a variable one miraculously fold into one another. It is hostile to the 'clock-work of bar-lengths'; thus it is historically no accident that 'both in Greece and in Provence the poetry attained its highest rhythmic and metrical brilliance at times when the arts of verse and music were most closely knit together, when each thing done by the poet had some definite musical urge or necessity bound up within it.'[206] Aranda song, then, is Modernist and anti-Modernist; it preserves what the West has lost and can only recover wistfully, experimentally – the tempo of the masterwork that is also the breath-pattern of the community.

This was the splendid scope of Aranda poetics, but by his studied rejection of the Modernists, Strehlow narrowed it, modelling the polity it adumbrated in terms of a return to origins, as an Australian analogue of the European nostalgia for the other country (the mother culture) obscured by patriarchy's imperialism. As a result, the homeland, although constituted poetically, remained to some degree 'groundless'; although localized, it still idealized the lie of the land. To be fair, the Modernists were equally prone to the temptation to fetishize the ground as territory;

Doughty's nationalism easily merged into Pound's Fascism. But at least their acknowledgement of the impurity of tradition, their willingness (under the aegis of Freud and Joyce at least) to recognize amnesiac processes of pidginization and hybridization as integral to the reformation of the common tongue, kept open the possibility of a poetics responsive to the brute facts of colonialism.

To ground a tradition in the past might be to un-ground it in the local present; groundedness might be a form of groundlessness. As we spiral backwards towards Ntarea, the surfacing of these ambiguities here is appropriate. If, earlier, the case was made for regarding Strehlow's autobiographical writing as the necessary form in which a migrant version of history must be cast, then now the reverse proves to be true; the most generalized and speculative features of his cultural theory prove to fold back into the most intimate and hidden aspects of his personal history and psychology. What form was the new ground to take? It must be free of totemic superstitiousness; but it must also be free of Western planarism. It must be simultaneously localized and universal. The higher group that inhabited it must likewise be proudly provincial and worldly-wise. Unlike the mundane Anglo-Saxons, they must also have their thoughts fixed, as the Lutherans' were, on the next world. Only now this was to be construed as a historical and territorial coming into being, not simply as a spiritual or metaphorical one.

Strehlow may not have been familiar with Heidegger's philosophy of Being, but the resemblances between his conception of a poetically-grounded polity and the open 'clearing' of 'Being' which the Swabian philosopher outlined in his wartime lectures on Parmenides are striking. Perhaps they need no special pleading. True, the Catholic fundamentalism that informed Heidegger's thought no doubt had its earlier counterpart in the Swabian Lutheran seminary where Strehlow's father studied; but both were heirs to a Kantian tradition of political philosophy in which the identification of a distinctive historical and poetic destiny went hand in hand with the idealization of the homeland. In any case, Heidegger's metaphysics usefully glosses Strehlow's thought, and in the process reveals how the movement it essayed still contained in it a nostalgia for return and stasis. From our point of view, it also reveals how an incremental and curvilinear trajectory, designed to disclose the ground gradually, could disguise a pre-emptive and prior enclosure act.

Certainly, a distinction between a peripatetic philosophy of disclosure and an empiricist and materialist philosophy of enclosure pervades the lectures Heidegger gave in the winter of 1942–3 at Freiburg on the fragmentary poems of Parmenides, 'The Way of Truth' and 'The Way of Seeming'. And indeed, if we bear in mind that, as Cornford puts it, Parmenides was 'a dissident Pythagorean' whose debt to his master's thought 'came out in his preference for unity, rest, limit, as against plurality, motion, the unlimited,'[207] then we can begin to see a genuine mental convergence between Heidegger's emphasis on a truth that lies hidden under layers of historical accretion, and which can only be disclosed by the philosophical adept prepared to tread the 'wood ways' unconditionally, and Strehlow's conception of Aranda knowledge as a body of wisdom that can only be approached gradually, obliquely, by yielding oneself unquestioningly to the teachings of the masters, and following in their footsteps over many years towards the sacred caves. Their similar casts of mind may even be reflected in their invocation of similar symbolic topographies, both favouring deeply-folded landscapes where a dramatic chiaroscuro of dark and light surrounds the road to revelation. Whether a clearing in the Black Forest or the open mouth of a sacred cave in the West MacDonnells, both liken the clarification of intellectual form received there to a lightning bolt accompanied by thunder.[208]

This parallel certainly helps to explain Strehlow's inability to integrate historical change – processes of cultural hybridization and poetic pidginization – into his imagined poetic republic. According to Parmenides, Being is continuous, indivisible; it completely fills the whole of space, it can countenance no void.[209] This is a doctrine that remarkably anticipates Strehlow's surely unproven conviction that already, prior to white invasion, the Central Australian landscape was completely filled poetically. The corollary in both cases seems to be similar. Parmenides maintains that 'there can never be a state of not-being in which what is could ever be; and there can be no transition from not-being to being or from being to not-being. Nor can there be any change of that which is; for that would mean that it is not at one time what it is at another.'[210] In the same way, Aranda songs can only be 'thought or known' while they are repeated without change; any modification to them wholly disperses their form; the divine essence bodied forth in them is not progressively weakened, but instantly flees. If our history follows the false way of seeming, narrating states of becoming and perishing, there can be no place in it for Aranda traditions.

Be that as it may, this logic suggests that Strehlow's conception of the totemic landscape and Heidegger's notion of a ground to be disclosed, rather than enclosed, have a common intellectual lineage. While the Cambridge Hellenists blamed the Olympians for transforming and falsifying an indigenous philosophical tradition, Heidegger's collective *bête noire* was the Romans. The 'Romanizing' of Greek thought enclosed its fundamental insights, turning them into concepts to be deployed instrumentally in the interests of imperial domination. Originally, Greek thinking had not been territorial in this way; it had enjoyed a different relationship with the ground whence it sprang, one that was essentially poetic. This had meant *inter alia* that the original Greek polis referred not to a political state; it had to do with 'the essential abode of historical man', where 'the Being of man in its relation to beings as a whole has gathered itself.'[211] In this sense, 'the essence of the polis' was the 'topos' – which was not simply a physical site but a place secured for Being.[212]

Heidegger glosses this last point further; using a term already familiar to us, he describes the place thus reached as *daimonios.* To translate this term as 'demonic' is to commit a typical Romanization of its meaning; rather it is to be understood as the 'uncanny, or the extraordinary, because it surrounds, and insofar as it [is] everywhere surrounds the present ordinary state of things and presents itself as everything ordinary, though without being ordinary.'[213] This is precisely the situation in the sacred landscape of the Aranda, where the *tjurunga*, for example, is at once an inert slab of painted stone and the place whence the sacred essence emanates. The Aranda's sacred site corresponds to Heidegger's 'uncanny district' or *daimonios topos.* Strehlow and Heidegger understand the 'work of art' metaphysically rather than aesthetically, as a 'disclosure' of Being.

Finally, Heidegger connects the 'leap into Being', which he regards as the essential achievement of early Greek philosophy, to a reconceptualization of the ground. Associating Parmenides's Way of Truth with a notion of 'the clearing, the lighted, and the open', he proceeds to imagine the thinking of Being as an escape from 'the ground and its cracks' where 'beings' (the realm of the plural, the transitory, the 'soil' of the factual) dwell, into the 'groundlessness of the open (the free) of Being'.[214] Heidegger elaborates this transition in terms that, allowing for terminological differences, remarkably recall Strehlow's most optimistic scenario for the future of Aranda culture. 'Being', Heidegger stresses, is 'never autochthonous'; it is detached from a 'soil' and a 'ground' because it discovers the security of the 'open'. To be sure, the open 'does not secure in the sense of a sanctuary man might hunt out somewhere within beings'; it 'does not provide a place of refuge'. But in compensation, it inaugurates 'the beginning of history' and a new figure, 'historical man'.[215]

Heidegger's passage from the ground to the groundless is not a transition from, say, the primitive to the modern; it is this turn of events that his philosophy is at pains to avoid. Rather, it seeks to join up the locally sacred haunts or *topoi demonioi* so that they form what might be described as a historically fateful homeland; the sacred does not retreat, rather it becomes pervasive in the form of a metaphysical sense of nationhood. This process finds its analogy in Strehlow's thought that 'after the native owners had moved out of their old group territories and mingled with different tribesmen in a new area, many of the old sacred myths, together with their songs, would undoubtedly have coalesced and undergone a unifying process.'[216] In Heidegger's terms, a plurality of illusory 'beings' would have yielded to the openness of 'Being'. Further, Strehlow speculated, 'once artistic inspiration had become freed from the restrictions imposed by "the totemic landscape", it would have been possible again for men of poetic skill to invent new themes and therefore new songs.'[217] These new 'men' would presumably have been somewhat in the position of the poet Hölderlin who, in Heidegger's theology, is the prophet of his nation's sacred destiny. Significantly, in view of the Strehlows' life story, the wanderer of 'Andenken' must undergo a distant peripateia or exile in order to understand what 'home' truly is. Travelling to India, 'the original homeland of the elders', he 'experience[s] the parental source and thank[s] them for guarding these beginnings that are now fulfilled in the German homeland.'[218]

This is not to recapitulate the kind of racist argument that Strehlow, along with many Australians of German extraction, experienced during the Nazi period; no guilt by ethnic association is implied. It is in any case too shallow, even too dangerous, to collapse Heidegger's metaphysics into an apology for National Socialism – dangerous because it mystifies the roots of his thought in modes of thinking common to a variety of political philosophies. Heidegger's Westernization of Greece, for example, while it may be borrowed from Nietzsche, also has precursors in European

Romanticism, where it was tied to an apparently anti-colonial Liberalism. In reality, though, the nostalgic homogenization of an assembly of cultures under one national banner provided, as has recently been pointed out,[219] a metaphysical ground for the West's writing of itself over the rest of the world.

However, Heidegger's idea of the double return – at once spiritual and geographical – usefully glosses Strehlow's conception of a post-colonial Australian culture. To come home, to be freed of a dependence on physical as well as metaphysical shelters and road verges, to step out into the world as home, to have disclosed to one the polis or 'historical place', implies a prior exile or marginality; only the wanderer can return. Strehlow, say, can only find his Fatherland because his father has voluntarily exiled himself from his Fatherland. But the new old country will necessarily be different from the one left behind; Australia, say, or Hölderlin's India, will only be 'Germany' because it is not the Germany remembered. It will be Germany refounded as the place of all places. The figure who finds his historical place, Heidegger writes, 'simultaneously becomes an *Apolis*, without a city or state, a-lone, un-canny, with no way out of the middle of being-in-the-whole.'[220]

In this context, we can make sense of one of the most extraordinary aspects of *Songs of Central Australia*, the arrangement of its longest section, 'Subject Matter and Themes', according to a thematic inventory derived from a Norse poem commemorating the magic charms of the Teutonic 'Father of Magic', Odin – or, as Strehlow insists, Othin. If Odin's song that brings help 'in sorrow and pain and sickness' finds its correspondence in a section of the Emianga song, then his resurrection charms find their counterpart in the Aranda increase songs. To strengthen the value of the parallel, Strehlow goes to considerable lengths to show a relation between magic spells and songs celebrating totemic ancestors. 'Othin,' he writes, 'is in many ways a figure strongly reminiscent of an old Central Australian ceremonial chief. The native ceremonial chief, too, derived part of his prestige from his prowess with the spear . . . [although] to win undisputed authority in the local group discussions he had to become first and foremost a master of mythological and magical lore.'[221]

But Strehlow's Odin is something more; he is the Homer of the new order, the *rhapsode* of those 'wanderings' that Strehlow imagined would throw up new leaders who, in time and through the genius of the bard, would come to be regarded as 'legendary heroes'. And this state is to be attained, poetically at least, by a going home that transforms 'home' into something different. Historical circumstance may have exiled Strehlow from his poetic heritage, but this proves an advantage; obliged to return to the poetic home he never knew, he finds its measures adumbrate life here. Odin, formerly a local *ingkata* or ceremonial chief, is transformed into the bard of all places. From this perspective, his primitive charms sound differently; they grow and transform themselves; they become the sacred patterns of a new race. They throw off their paternity, their nostalgia for autochthonous purity.

Strehlow's conception of the national future as a gradual resurfacing and regrouping of elementary forces, as the disclosure of what was immanent in the place and its dual history, was grandly Wagnerian, but clearly involved some fateful enclosure acts. It committed Strehlow to a form of cultural racism; for while he could broker an ideal marriage of indigenous and European poetic forms, he could not countenance the historical mechanisms that all around him were bringing something else – a mimicry more powerful than his representation, perhaps – into being. His irritation with the Aranda woman's Christian dreaming was symptomatic; he could not accept what has more recently become plain at Papunya and Yuendumu (and if Philip Jones is right, already characterized Namatjira's situation[222]), that occupation of an in-between ground not only formed the condition but the subject-matter of a post-colonial art.

The Stuart case, in which Strehlow acted as an expert linguistic witness on behalf of Rupert Max Stuart, a part-Aranda man accused of violent murder, illustrated the inner tension his attitude must produce. There was a moment in the case where the prosecution read a carefully-nuanced statement prepared in consultation with the accused, and commented, 'it would be interesting to know how Mr Strehlow translated this into Aranda.' Rising to the bait, 'Strehlow wanted to state there and then that the Aranda language contained idiomatic equivalents for almost every expression contained in the English language.'[223] He was apparently restrained from doing so. Saving Stuart from hanging may have been a triumph for Strehlow, but the court proceedings also showed him at his most rigid and legalistic. This was particularly ironic in view of the in-between dialect – variously called 'Northern Territory English' and 'pidgin English' – Stuart spoke, and his presumably partial knowledge of Aranda.[224]

The defence that Stuart could not have written the affidavit said to have been prepared by him was further complicated by the fact that, during the nine-month course of the trial and Stuart's daily exposure to the English of his warders, the accused man's English appeared to have improved a lot.[225] Strehlow was in the invidious position of having to ascribe full linguistic dignity and stability to a 'half-caste dialect'.[226] He had to defend an idiolect that, even as it was identified and fixed, was becoming something different. If Strehlow made an impression on the court, it was because he shared the Law's abhorrence of ambiguities; because he made Stuart speak his language. But ambiguities, ironies and mere coincidences were the argot of resistance within a colonial culture, and the opening towards a post-colonial future depended on incorporating them, not suppressing them. More than this, they characterized discourse generally – which outside Eden has always been prone to misunderstanding. Even Strehlow's beloved Aranda was in this respect thoroughly modern.

While Strehlow brilliantly grasped the additive nature of Aranda thinking, which he found expressed in Aranda grammar's agglutinative system of verb formation, he seemed not to grasp fully the possibility that what distinguished the culture of the Aranda might be its capacity simultaneously to hold in place multiple views and meanings, to think, not in terms of paradoxes and contradictions, but in terms of a lesser or greater folding of the ground. The immediate consequence of this view was a tendency to disparage the song performer if and when he departed from the received song-text. For Strehlow, authority was vested exclusively in the song itself; the performer was judged by his capacity to repeat the sacred text flawlessly. The corollary was inevitable; the performer who did not reproduce the totemic verses with all the reliability of a tape recorder revealed a forgetfulness justifying Strehlow's prediction of the imminent disappearance of Aranda song traditions.[227]

Conceiving Aboriginal musical education passively, Strehlow could find no room within it for individual creativity. Add to this poetic proposition Strehlow's historical contention that 'the thoroughness of their forefathers' in commemorating in story and verse the features of the Central Australian landscape had left the present-day Aranda 'not a single unoccupied scene which they could fill with the creatures of their own imagination', and that 'tradition and the tyranny of the old men in the religious and cultural sphere have effectively stifled all creative impulse,' and the implication was clear. Like Rome, the Aranda nation was doomed to collapse from within; European colonization might have been managed more humanely, but it could not be held solely responsible for the disintegration of Aranda social and spiritual cohesion. But this is not only to invoke a Western notion of creativity, but to import it in a way that masks the creativity of the Aboriginal music education process where, as Ken Hale writes, with Strehlow's historical thesis explicitly in mind, 'the learning of a song is a creative act': 'the room for creativity is inherent in the complementary doctrine according which young adult learners must acquire even the most difficult or "tricky" (Warlpiri yajiki) poetic chants on the basis of the evidence of the most elementary sort. In effect, one does not really learn the songs by rote; rather, one re-creates them on the basis of the evidence made available in choral singing and associated (often piecemeal) mythological narrative.'[228]

Recent work by Ellis glosses the nature of this 're-creativity' in an interesting way. Strehlow understood the trickiness of the songs anthropologically, as an integral part of the process of socialization. But Ellis finds that the difficulty of the songs is inherent in their musical structure. Their complexity may not be transitional but constitutional, and consist in part in their capacity to infold paradoxical alternatives. In a teaching session, a song-text may be repeated until the students are familiar with its internal isorhythm and its relation to a melodic section; a new internal isorhythm using the same structural format may be introduced next; then a new internal isorhythm is presented; and so on. 'Gradually the structural units involved in this fitting are changed so that the original concept of division into four (or three) is dislodged, but no explanation is given. Paradoxical structures are simply left with the students, the expectation being that sooner or later the performers will make the perceptual transition to another hierarchical level of the interlocking structures, or recognise the "other side" of the structural ambiguity that will then make sense of the new material presented by the song leader, and imitated by the uninformed performers.'[229] It is through this 'structural play', 'within this subtle structural iridescence that the performer has great creative scope without affecting adversely the timeless communication of the ancestor.'[230]

These findings place Strehlow's view of Aranda song in a usefully critical perspective. Strehlow's logic left, strictly speaking, no room for creativity. Where, then, he found evidence of the Aranda artist's pleasure in creating beautiful patterns, he was bound to draw one of two conclusions: either the artist was distorting the received tradition, or his innovations were purely decorative or ornamental flourishes without a serious social or historical significance. Central Australian Aboriginal artists might have a very small repertoire of pictographic motifs at their disposal, but they were able to elaborate these at will:

> The plain circle found in the sand drawings was normally elaborated into a figure of ten, twenty, or even more concentric circles, or into a cleverly executed spiral containing the same number of convolutions. Similarly, single lines or U-figures were rarely found: they were generally doubled, trebled, or repeated still more often. The best artists showed a keen feeling for the beauty of line and contour; and some of their freehand circles were remarkable not merely for their elaboration, but for sheer beauty.[231]

Likewise, among the songs there were 'verses which exist for purely artistic reasons and for giving pleasure to the listeners'; for instance, 'the couplets and quatrains which try to echo in words noises made by humans or sounds heard in nature.'[232] These mimetic flourishes were not 'abstract', as they arose and were appreciated within a definite social and physical context. In relation to the sacred poetic or pictographic matter, they had much the same role as the 'architectural decorations for a room, ceiling or wall.' For example, in 'the veined and mottled surfaces of polychrome marble slabs in such buildings as the Château of Versailles and the Walhalla of Regensburg . . . and the decorative motifs expressed in lacquer, paint, and gold leaf in the Goldlack Zimmer . . .', 'the principles of abstract art are applied',[233] and are functionally, because decoratively, 'of high importance'. If we allow that Strehlow's praise of the Aranda singer's onomatopoeic flourishes aligns him with Rousseau who, identifying the essence of music with melody against the claims of harmony, advised the musician, 'Let him realise that he will have to render noise in song; that to produce the croaking of frogs, he will have to have them sing,'[234] then his view of Aranda creativity was that it was essentially baroque.

This might have been no bad thing, had the baroque carried positive connotations in Strehlow's poetic universe. Baroque elaboration is characteristic of cross-cultural exchange in colonial societies:

> The baroque substitutes a grammar of gesture for the syntax of sense. It proliferates a multiplicity of particulars at the expense of the design of the whole. Instead of communicating a clear meaning, representing and expressing an underlying form or structure, the baroque communicates only itself: its own ebullient presence and process. The baroque does not represent a meaning. Rather it mimics the process whereby meanings are communicated. Indeed, by rendering the surface unreadable it mocks Renaissance reason and its presumption of a unified (and middle-class) perspective. The baroque introduces noise into the system; it introduces redundancy . . . As a mode of behaviour, the baroque is the characteristic means by which peoples of different cultures first make contact in the absence of a common language.[235]

But for son as for father, baroque elaboration suggested irreverent mockery, not reverent miming. Commenting on the fact that initiated Aranda and Loritja men used a secret language in talking amongst themselves, Carl Strehlow thought that it could not be greatly useful as it swarmed with ambiguities and *double entendres* that must be disastrous for the communication of plain sense. One word is used to mean 'old man, father, wallaby, the burrowing mole, wild turkey, *Podargus*, cormorant, drake fan-palm, and a blazing fire.' Another term, *eroatitja*, can signify 'woman, mother, wife, black cockatoo, white cockatoo, mountain pigeon, duck and the sun.' The elder Strehlow comments, 'The *rukuta* [partially initiated youth] speaks in riddles when/if he tells his watcher he has seen *eroatitja*. Without doubt many things are wanting in these incomplete expressions, or misunderstandings. The stuff (*sic*) is productive of laughter eg. when not only the *rukuta*, but also the stars are *injitatjuta*, i.e. are referred to as dogs or when he calls the shelter where his fellow camp-mates dwell: *waramba* (= the shelter that a lying-in woman occupies) etc . . .'[236]

But in view of Ellis's remarks, the suspension of certainties may be intentional. To be born a second time, socially rather than biologically, is to enter again a world in which signifiers have yet to settle into fixed grooves of meaning; where word-sounds, the pre-semiotic vocal gestures out of whose nebulae constellations of sense will eventually condense, retain their magic power to conjure up the world. If Strehlow's material is even partially accurate, the secret language does not represent ideas, it evokes the spaces in-between them, inviting the initiate to discover the logic that links them. That logic is not linear or associational (although clearly the things denominated *eroatitja*, for example, are all associated with the feminine principle); it is not Borgesian, exemplifying an exotic taxonomy that holds up a mirror to our Western way of organizing the world. It appears to be open-ended, provisional, unfixed, so that it is of the essence that the initiate stumbles, and misnaming himself and the world, becomes again as an infant. To grow up, the initiate must don the fool's persona. To be born fully into language, the voice must issue forth from a fool's mouth.

Evidently there is a connection, even if it is merely coincidental, between the Aranda system of education and the migrant's sensation when, on seeking initiation into his adopted culture, he finds that 'language no longer functions non-contextually, but is become a gestural, almost physical device.'[237] Out of this latter experience can come, I have suggested, poetic forms that nose their way 'into the starless interstices which, because they are ambiguous and may lead punningly in many directions, do not remove us from the ground but rather create an atmosphere, the beginnings of an air we can breathe, in which sounds may begin to map a speaking-place simply by virtue of their internal orchestration, their pattern of echoes.'[238] The suggestion that Carl Strehlow's semantic constellations should be read poetically does not ignore the fact that these relationships were premeditated, arising from classificatory categories long-established in Aranda social and religious tradition; because no exploration of the trajectories linking terms ever occurred on level, historically-evacuated ground. The lie of the land is always implicit both in the poetic connections that are grasped, and in those that remain concealed. Just as the constellating metaphor creates a pattern where unlike things seem to share a common space, so the folds of the ground determine our perspective. The ground curves out of view into the valley, but in compensation the mountain opposite is suddenly close.

Strehlow was also of the baroque party without knowing it. He admired 'elaboration', the spontaneous unfolding of ever more densely woven figures, but he feared their abstraction. The challenge, at once poetic and political, was to preserve their unfolding forms without losing sight of the ground. It was to ensure that the patterns they made remained functional in the social life of the group. Somehow, they had to be mobilized in a way that brought the ground back to life; they had to be detached from their illustration of uncanny places and allowed to wander over a larger region. At the same time, the new 'groundlessness' their wanderings inaugurated must not mean the abandonment of the land, or an indifference to its physical form, its regional grouping. Reverently miming the land's coming into being, the Aranda had illustrated the principle of *kairos*, the ceremonially-induced intersection of the eternal and the temporal. But the country had been desacralized, the *tjurungas* sold or stolen; a different source of animation must be found.

This, I think, was the role which that most baroque (but regional) of everyday phenomena, the weather, came to play in Strehlow's life and writing. It may be pure coincidence that, according to Jane Harrison, the weather was one of the first victims of the Olympian ascendancy. But it is not by chance that *Journey to Horseshoe Bend* culminates not in Carl's death but in the advent of a life-giving storm; for it is the storm that, in alliance with the earth, subverts the empty, inhuman pledge of immortality vouchsafed by the sky. The changelessly changing middle air, with its time to time instress (as Hopkins might say) of accumulating clouds and life-giving rainfall, inspires some of the most rhapsodic (in the etymological sense of most elaborately stitched together) passages in *Songs of Central Australia*. Obliged to weave his own story out of different histories, he is like the Aranda rainmaker who only commands the storm by submitting his will to the open divagations of the air: 'Our clouds are still wandering about: they are going north, south, east, and west; and when they have wandered about sufficiently and become tired, they will pour down their rain.'[239]

So with Strehlow's mode of composition; it wanders about. After the rainmaker's words, Strehlow makes rain himself, quoting a 'description of the rainstorms that ended a long break of hot, dry weather at Jay Creek in January, 1937.' This powerful invocation – 'Men, beasts, birds, trees, and grasses – all would become reborn through the transforming power of the rain' – is in turn woven into a description of the blood-letting Loritja rites practised to ensure adequate rainfall. There follows an extended quotation from the 1933 Horseshoe Bend diary, while simultaneously, as it were, a further thread is being added to the rain-making history; a lengthy footnote draws our attention to the bloody rites once associated with the cult of Thor 'who ruled over thunder and lightning, wind and rains.'

And all of this is by way of a masking or initiatory narrative. Only now does Strehlow bring us to 'the Hale River area, which includes several notable Eastern Aranda rain totemic sites', and to 'by far the finest rain song I have been privileged to record in Central Australia,' one that extends to some eighty couplets, 'which reveal great metrical ingenuity on the part of their author or authors.' But again the homecoming, the lightning of the clearing, is withheld. Instead of transcribing and translating this master-work in full, Strehlow quotes but two or three fragments designed to illustrate its most common rhythmic measures; and these fragments, what is more, have already been quoted earlier in *Songs of Central Australia* in another context, so that our exploration of a totemic song turns out also to be an exercise in textual memorialization.

Finally, in another putting-off of the end, having rendered these fragments in two different metres in an attempt to suggest their metrical ingenuity, the web of Strehlow's rhapsodic composition is completed by a pious return to his father, as a Western Aranda rain song originally collected by Carl is extended and returned to its metrical form.[240]

The coming of rain, its spears of lightning and rolls of thunder, especially engaged Strehlow's imagination; it is, say, the rain chants associated with Kaporilja that inspire Strehlow to attempt a translation that preserves 'the rhythmic measures and the number of syllables found in the Aranda originals'.[241] The central myth connected with the same site, one in which the son of Kaporilja is successively killed by his father and resurrected by him, is fertile in literary analogues; Kaporilja recalls Odin in his guise of 'God of the Hanged' as described in the *Havamál*, not to mention *The Golden Bough*. And not only literary analogues: Kaporilja's mythic association of the thunderstorm with the struggle between father and son may have spoken personally to Strehlow, providing a secret reason, a totemic motivation or topographical metaphor for the journey from Hermannsburg to Horseshoe Bend, defining it as the reverent enactment of patriarchy's 'primal scene', the son's rebellion against his father and the father's tragic revenge.

It is not necessary to ascribe Oedipal motives to Strehlow or his *persona* Theo. Where the father's will is law, the drama arises from the situation itself. So, bound to follow his dying father, Theo must himself die to the old world of the Mission and, resurrected at Horseshoe Bend, face his initiation into manhood. The journey becomes, in this sense, a passage through the underworld; it occurs between the 'flash of lightning' that strikes the son down and the 'shower of rain' that brings him back to life. As for the narrative, it is the thunder that speaks. At any rate, the weather plays an important role in the dramatic structure of *Journey to Horseshoe Bend.* The chief totemic sites presiding over the Finke River landscape traversed by Strehlow's dying father are the sacred rain site of Mborawatna, the 'accursed ground' of Uralterinja, 'looked upon fearfully as the very home of Death', and Mbalka, 'the most potent of . . . primal fire sites.'[242] The narrative of Strehlow's last days and hours is woven out of various threads, metaphysical, historical, autobiographical, but it is clear that their coming together, the fateful pattern they weave, occurs under the direction of these powerful places.

This might suggest that they act in the role of *dei ex machina,* as zoomorphic equivalents of Olympian gods, but their role is not theatrical; they do not manipulate the human drama invisibly, from outside. Their peculiar power is that they seem to radiate their designs far beyond their physical sites; partly this reflects the mythical fact that they are links in song lines that network the whole region, but partly it suggests the way in which they seem drawn into the human paths that bend past them, appearing to colour those tracks, to determine the outcome of the direction they take. In this sense it is not exactly correct to suggest that Strehlow's final struggle is represented baroquely, allegorically, in a battle between fire and rain presided over by mocking Death. These contrary forces coexist as alternative narrative shapes, as interference patterns grooving the historical and physical ground, so that advancement (fictionally or factually) depends on picking one's way through their web of marks.

When Death comes to Father Carl, it is not immediately accompanied by a thunderous apotheosis of the kind that orchestrated Beethoven's passing, or that of Our Saviour; when the whirlwind sweeps down the Finke valley some while later, it comes because it was always coming; because ever since passing Mborawatna some days earlier, 'the rain ancestresses were awakening from their sleep, and these hot winds were bringing clouds into the sky – clouds that might pour down refreshing showers on this desiccated and parched country within the next few days.'[243] Similarly, death does not catch up with Father Carl at Horseshoe Bend; nor was it lying in wait. It was simply with him, a spirit-double, from the time he crossed Fifteen Mile Creek: 'What the totally exhausted sick man had been forced to suffer on his rough night ride through the

Land of Death was almost beyond imagination.'[244] If, on the Thursday morning they arrived, 'Horseshoe Bend was fully living up to its mythical reputation as a heat-creating totemic centre,' there was nothing personal about it.[245]

Coming there, Carl Strehlow was letting his life be a reading of the ground. This was his apotheosis: to throw off the shadow figure of biography (of the Christian pilgrim sans home, sans ground) and to find his spirit's journey laid out before him. Understood properly, the river, the sandhills and the mountain represented life's plot; they located its essential features of travail, death and rebirth spatially, as a relationship, at once physical and poetic, between places. To enter their powerful field was to begin to feel one's life grounded, to escape at last from the lifelong sensation that the earth had been slipping away from under one's feet. It was as if a spirit equivalent of the barred sandhills lay across one's path, as elastic breaths of air faintly retarding progress, making even the lightness of passage seem grave and slow. One thing was certain: there was no going back from this exploratory pacing; this was not a dance, it represented nothing.

Re-enacting the landscape in this way, the *ingkata* did not die. Rather, he became at last his ambiguous other, an Aranda ceremonial chief. 'At Horseshoe Bend he was not sleeping alone: here he had joined forever the great company and congregation of the countless thousands of Aranda men, women, and children, who had lived and died in this Eternal Land for hundreds, and perhaps for thousands, of years past.'[246] What prevents this ending from being merely sentimental is Strehlow's acute sense that this different immortality must be grounded historically; an environmental catalyst must determine this cross-cultural convergence, enabling hard and fast boundaries to dissolve and reform. This is the meaning of rain's coming, its timely intervention: both literally and symbolically, it overwhelms the desiccated surface, transforming it into a necklace of rivers; what is flat becomes grooved and folded. 'According to Aranda belief, the second souls of all unborn children . . . emanated from the sacred soil of Central Australia. The existence and the continual re-creation of all these forms of life depended on the fertilizing and quickening power of rain.'[247]

Le roi est mort, vive le roi . . . but Strehlow is not reverting to old Dionysus. His accents grow dithyrambic because he wants to enact another cross-fertilization, between the declaimed measures of the New

Testament and the musical word-weaving of Aranda song. 'To the boy the rain that was falling on his father's grave had come to represent the symbol of life, the promise of life, the assurance of life, and the certainty of life. Life could not be finally conquered by death; for the power of life was greater than the destructiveness of death. Life was from eternity to eternity.'[248] Was this the meaning of Horseshoe Bend, that it provided a way out of the autobiographical solipsism of returning to Ntarea? By burying his father here, Theo made a place for himself. Forgotten at Hermannsburg, he is by his own act of self-memorialization remembered downriver.

How, then, to return there? Not by arriving peremptorily and taking a photograph. To judge from photographs, Horseshoe Bend has always been a ruin. In fact, in comparison with a shot taken in July 1994, 'The broad sandy bed of the Finke River at Horseshoe Bend, with Mount Engoordina in the distance'[249] suggests that the site was more denuded of vegetation, more 'ruined' sixty years ago. However, the lines of casuarina-like shrub that striate the channels and adjacent banks are not what they seem. Mrs Libby Morphett, wife of the present station owner, recalls years of repeated floods that swept away the coolibahs and red river gums, and let the exotic *atholl* colonize the river bed; she laments the sweet waterhole that previously existed.[250] These recollections postdate the old photograph; they postdate the ruin and destruction of the Horseshoe Bend Hotel where Carl Strehlow died.

Memorialized as a sequence of fallings-off, it seems that Horseshoe Bend has always been in a state of ruin; even its best times have been repairs and renovations. But this may be the point: to accept the circulation, the alternating bands of black, red and grey corresponding to different phases of its life-cycle. Strehlow describes in *Journey to Horseshoe Bend* the fires produced by the crow ancestor Mbalka; in these, many ancestral parrots perished, and as a result, 'in the Aranda-speaking area the pink and red feathers of these parrots and cockatoos were taken to symbolize the colour of the leaping flames, the black feathers the dead bodies of charred birds, and the grey feathers the ashes of birds totally consumed by the blaze.'[251] Then the rain ancestors approached from distant Erea, with their stripes of quivering white, their lightning lances, and 'the crow ancestor himself was drowned by the overwhelming fury of this rainstorm.'[252]

But nothing is finished; the ill-advised performance of Mbalka's fire rites can still revive his scorching power.[253] And this repetition in difference does not simply explain the ruination of the country, but establishes ruin as a creative principle, as a process of keeping things the way they are, in a continuous state of becoming to no end. But to comprehend this, it would be necessary to inhabit the land differently, to remove one's gaze from a horizon that is as much historical as visual,[254] and once again turn to tracing patterns in the ground. This return to ground-tracing would involve a different conception of movement, one that deepened grooves, that to the noviciate at least might seem like running on the spot, but to the initiate would appear instead as a way of 'marking time', of metricalizing the ground and so keeping the place in play.

There is a moment when, approaching the termination of the journey in the wake of his father's van, Theo grasps this possibility: 'The last few miles were covered, chain by chain, yard by yard, step by step. Theo put down one bare foot before the other almost mechanically, sometimes wondering whether the long-expected station lights would ever come into view . . . Because of the darkness which blotted out all the more distant objects, such as the hills and the dunes, it often seemed that neither the van nor the team was moving forward at all. In spite of all movement the travellers seemed to be marking time; and even the closer trees passed by them seemed to reappear again and again.'[255] Strehlow compares this state to sleepwalking, but from another viewpoint it might have been a form of *sleepwaking*, where the ideological nature of 'journeys' becomes plain. It was wanting to reach Horseshoe Bend, the desire to measure progress, to assemble the road as a series of backward views, that brought about Carl Strehlow's death, an ending marked, significantly enough, by more than one 'asphyxiating bout of asthmatic breathlessness.'[256]

And again, how to return there? Over there, winking like windows or mirage pools in the red ochre shimmer, is a trinity of headstones. The middle one, Carl's (Plate 4), bears a quotation from St Paul's *Letter to the Hebrews*: 'By faith we perceive that the universe was fashioned by the word of God.' This might be an answer – by reading differently . . . by walking differently. The bed of the Finke River at Horseshoe Bend contains many surfaces, whose hardness corresponds to the antiquity of the last flood to pass over them. The lowest lying parts are softest, composed of a silk-fine sand that slides like slow water underfoot. Ribbons of sand higher up preserve the minute corrugations of the wind's passage, while over the banks a chrome-coloured crust scintillates with tiny lights of mica. These surfaces are not only historical traces, maps of the weather as far away as Hermannsburg; their variable resistances translate for the walker into variable rates of progress.

I have sometimes wondered whether the different strands of Strehlow's book might not correspond to these different metres of the ground, and whether a suitably devised peripateia of the locality whilst reciting his book might not be arranged. It might break the drought, the solitary figure on the edge of the river bank silently intoning, unaware of the lightning bolt behind him, but already seeing the ground turn to green.

Part Two

About Canoes

. . . the Venetians are grown the most eminent of all nations for the noble art of mimicking . . .

Joseph Spence[1]

Of course, photographs give you no inkling of the *Tempesta*'s austere colouring (Plate 5). Nor do they preserve the curious sensation that the place where all parts converge, the place in the near foreground where all parts converge, is the water in the shadow of the bridge. There is a centrifugal effect out of its whirlpool. A mass of shadow, accumulating near the soldier's right foot, finds its counterpoise in the foliage of the forked tree growing on the mound behind the gypsy mother. Only it has been transformed; just as, crossing the same patch of water, the group of spindly saplings to the left of the broken columns has been transformed into the sturdy, forked tree, like the mother before it, bearing and sheltering saplings of its own. Lastly, in the pairing of objects flung out oppositely, the gypsy's breast finds its counterpart in a Byzantine dome on the horizon.

There is a centripetal effect. All parts bend over, drawn into curvature by the pool's force of attraction. The trees and grasses which grow on its margins bend over it. Their outlines are tattered, as if the centre's suction strains to rip them out by the roots. The green masses circle like birds drawn to their own reflection. The bridge tilts and the towers beyond lean silently. The broken columns are steps, leading down into the depths or out of them. The gypsy's right leg is in contact with every plane of the curved hillside. Every part, near and far, from every side, climbs a curved field of force to the lip of the volcano, the convex shield's hollow boss. It is a dark well and, like a well, shares the structure of a tower. It is the north pole of a bar magnet, warping the stray world like a current-combed sea anemone into its maw, or spraying it out to recompose, to blossom like a flower. A magnet, an ideal tower which all parts make their point of reference, a column of space which connects them, and idling about their roots, carving them back, flows between and separates.

What I describe here is difficult to assess in the gloomy room of the Accademia where the painting is normally exhibited. The way the towers down the right-hand side of the river grow taller towards their further edge; the way in which, similarly, the marble base on which the broken columns stand seems compacted towards its nearer edge; the sensation that the balcony, above and just beyond the bridge, turns towards us; these visual facts, henceforth referred to collectively as Giorgione's 'reversed perspective', have been passed over in silence. But the difficulty of seeing these visual facts is, I want to say, more to do with method than with reflections off the glass.[2] Whether the myriad interpretations of its meaning have lessened or added to its 'enigma' may be a moot point, and my business here is not to offer another speculative exegesis. It is to suggest that these interpretations, whether iconographically, biographically or sociologically based, have one thing in common: an assumption that the meaning of the painting lies behind its surface. The painting is enigmatic because it hides what it intends. The enigma may be a product of our historical distance, it may be intentional, an expression of Giorgione's free spirit. Either way, our discourse about the painting has conventionally had the function of supplying a missing underground dimension.

This vertical third dimension (not to be confused with the horizontal third dimension or depth recuperated by linear perspective) is a relatively modern idea. Its history might be: between the mid-fifteenth and late-nineteenth centuries, a scenographic conception of space dominated Western thinking, but towards the end of this period its theatrical logic broke down. Mathematical, technological, anthropological and even poetic developments made the scenic model of reality unsustainable. Signifiers grew harder to pin down, or harboured contradictory meanings. Appearances became melodramatic, gesturing towards what could not be said. Decipherment became essential and, as the surface failed to cohere, meaning entailed excavating beneath the surface. As Rosalind Williams writes: 'Convictions that surface reality can be misleading and that the truth is found only by descending to uncharted depths . . . are central assumptions of modern intellectual inquiry. In history, economics, psychology and linguistics . . . the process of excavation has become the dominant metaphor for truth seeking.' And, she adds, pointing to a contradiction, 'The modern quest for knowledge is framed in the same spatial construct as the ancient quest for buried secrets.'[3]

Schliemann's excavation of Troy, Freud's theory of the unconscious, and the literary-symbolic interpretations of the *Tempesta* (beginning, significantly enough, in Vienna, where in 1895 Wickhoff claimed to find in the painting an illustration of an episode from the *Thebaid* of Statius[4]) express the new attitude. The seven or more levels of ancient Ilium, the three storeys of consciousness have their counterpart in the X-ray-assisted discovery of the *Tempesta*'s three surfaces or phases of composition. And they all depend on treating the ground, physically as well as metaphorically, as the most recent deposit of an historical process, and its present topography therefore as remotest from the original, primitive forces thought to underlie it.

Oddly, this new conceptual space, and the intellectual mining operations it facilitates, preserve the Euclidean conventions of the scenographic space whose ground it undermines. While early twentieth-century scientists and artists and philosophers came to grips with the fact that the old ground was crumbling, turning back into dust and air, the sign-miners continued to extend their tunnels as if the solidity of the matrix was not in doubt. Theirs was, in fact, an ambitious attempt to save the ground, to preserve the idea of an original, bed-rock meaning; so Schliemann cuts through thousands of years of history and risks his men being buried alive in order to get to the bottom of things – but no further.

It is predictable that scholarly exegesis of the *Tempesta* should be blind to its reversed perspective; but there is a more fundamental point. The conceptual space of the underground is a social and historical space, not simply a mental construct. Freud may advocate an unlocking of doors, the removal of prohibitions on ancient pathways, but his psychopathology of everyday life has the opposite effect: to produce a world of broken pavements, war-shattered buildings, walled, deserted gardens and reversed signs – where only further destruction can lead to the recovery of what has been lost or repressed, trodden underfoot. It is as if the ground, its irregular natural and historical topography, wears a double aspect. On the one hand it marks the site where something lies buried; on the other, its mere accumulation over time signifies a forgetfulness which must be corrected. Schliemann and Freud present themselves as historians; they want to unearth the earliest layers of human consciousness. But in fact what they have in mind is an open space inscribed with writing, a text, a poem. The lumpy topography of history offends them as a kind of interment or abandonment of the original inscription, the place's true name. Like Odysseus, they want to penetrate the Troy of the past in order to plunder Pallas Athene's palladium; as if everything since has been a patriarchal imposition.

The space they invoke may seem neutral so long as we regard it as a mythic or mental sphere of operations, a mere hypothesis; but once we extend it into the social and historical world of our experience, it loses its neutrality, serving among other things to reinforce the techno-pragmatic view of social space as a locus of unpredictable, panic-inducing and destructive events, whether undertaken in the name of town-planning or military invasion. The lost text is also the map and the archaeological dig's outlines of foundations; it is the surface reduced to its linear calligraphy, bare of shadow, voices, directions; an original without beginning or end. The science of the underground appears to disturb the foundations of Cartesian thought, to disrupt its logocentric linear perspective, but in fact reinforces it, reproducing its conceptual space symmetrically underground. And with the same destructive results: curvilinear environments are treated as deposits lacking any spatial integrity of their own. Eyes sharp as spear-points scan the surface for flecks of gold that can satisfy their nostalgia for a genealogy, another home, a larger enclosure. What Lefebvre says of semiotic theorists applies more generally to the science of the underground: it promotes 'the basic sophistry whereby the philosophico-epistemological notion of space is fetishized and the mental realm comes to envelop the social and physical ones.'[5]

To return to the *Tempesta*; its reversed perspective is ignored by our modern nominalists not simply because their eyes (and minds) are elsewhere, but because it belongs to a different conceptual space, enigmatic precisely because it conceals nothing. And this is true whether or not the *Tempesta* has a 'subject', and whether or not Giorgione fashionably concealed it to flatter a patron's taste for puzzles. The composition of the *Tempesta*, which modern writers characteristically describe as 'dreamlike', embodies a scientific view of the production of space. It does not represent an idea, a mental space. It expresses a way of looking. In this sense, projecting a social and historical space free of cryptography, it criticizes the critics.

'Reversed perspective' is synonymous for some writers with the 'inverted perspective' of Trecento painting, Byzantine mosaics and even Roman frescoes.[6] I use the term differently: to suggest the resistance of Venetian painting to the orthodoxy of Florentine centralized perspective. The buildings in a landscape of Titian's *Noli Me Tangere*, or Titian and Giorgione's *Venus Sleeping*, refuse to narrow towards their more distant edges. Relative to Florentine expectations of convergence on a common vanishing-point, they splay out, and even though viewed obliquely, turn to face us.

Evidence that reversed perspective was a well-remarked feature of the Giorgionesque style comes from the designs of Domenico Campagnola. Domenico copied his father's engravings, some of them derived directly from Giorgione, and himself worked with Titian. In Domenico's Pierpont Morgan Library drawing, 'Buildings in a Landscape', there is not a single architectural element, whether square window, roof or rough wall, but it widens towards the left hand and further edge.[7] Elsewhere, linear and reversed perspective coexist: in Giulio Campagnola's *The Astrologer*, dating from about 1509, the ground floor of the obliquely-viewed palace is drawn in linear perspective, the *piano nobile* in reversed perspective – with destabilizing results.[8] Similarly toppling buildings resulting from attempts to insert Florentine perspective into a northern setting occur in, say, Benedetto Montagna's *Woman and Satyr with Cupids* (c.1506–12) or Palumba's *Satyr group in Landscape* dating from 'soon after the turn of the sixteenth century'.[9]

Another key figure in the development of reversed perspective is, of course, Dürer. Around 1500 Jacopo de' Barbari visited Nuremberg, where he gave Dürer lessons in perspective. We know that this was not linear perspective; and Dürer's 'gothic' engravings (which were already known in Venice – witness Giulio Campagnola's reproduction of the three-storey, half-timbered house in Dürer's *Madonna with the Monkey* of c.1498 in his own *Ganymede* of c.1500–3) already display a robust, northern reversed perspective.[10] Presumably Jacopo imparted the wisdom evident in his own wonderful *Map of Venice* (1500), that wedge-shaped buildings corresponded to wedge-shaped spaces, and could therefore constitute a principle of composition.

Jacopo de' Barbari's famous engraving provides the naked anatomy of the perspectival construction used in the *Tempesta*. Jacopo wanted his 'map' to be an image; he wanted his two-dimensional layout of the city to preserve a third dimension, a sense of recession towards the mountains beyond the Lagoon, an illusion of buildings standing up and holding their ground. In linear or Euclidean terms, he confronted a paradox: a uniform map projection would ensure that every part was represented equally in two dimensions – but at the expense of preserving a recognizable image. Who, after all, could connect the plan view of a piazza or palace with a familiar place? On the other hand, suspended over the Lagoon somewhere south of the Giudecca, how could a bird's-eye view of recognizable sights avoid seeing nearer things relatively larger?

De' Barbari's solution is synthetic. He recognized that appearances could only be preserved if Venice were conceived as a concave bowl with the eye suspended at its focal centre. But while this might preserve equality in different directions, it did not overcome the problem of relating different views; a map with no viewpoint was now transformed into a view with as many visual pyramids as the arms of a starfish. The question was how to stitch these different recessions together; how to make radiating views curve round and converge on the eye wherever it looked.

This was the office of reversed perspective. Inspecting his map closely, we find that, just as in normal vision our gaze widens with increasing distance, so wherever we look in de' Barbari's map we find individual buildings splay out, everywhere turn their facades towards us. Generally the buildings grow smaller, but individually they refuse to narrow and recede: fat, wedge-shaped, they yield nothing to linear space. Reversed perspective is the means of harmonizing a multiplicity of viewpoints. It lends mere mobility a sense of perspective. It transforms comings and goings into a distinctively-shaped city. Turning geography into history, it re-enacts a spatial history.

What I am suggesting, then, is something more than a remarkable correspondence between Giorgione's art and the physical and spatial aspect of Venice where he painted. This resemblance has frequently been remarked upon; Adrian Stokes wrote lyrically about 'the curvilinear yet pyramidal character of several Giorgione compositions', finding there an amalgam of the circular and the rectangular, 'the two shapes in relation of which we are never so conscious as when we are surrounded by stone building searched by water.'[11] Stokes saw in Giorgione's paintings another amalgam, that of art and science: 'Beside his dreams there lay unanxious an inductive spirit.'[12] But if, as this implies, Giorgione put together the bits and pieces of his life – the Castelfranco countryside, the easeful style of the *frottola*, the water-reflected, warped and combined forms of Venetian building – to show how they cohered, adding up to a space others could inhabit, then the implication is still that Giorgione derived his space conception from somewhere else. Stokes may not ask us to look behind the painting; but he still implies that we can step to one side, and seeing Venice, see more clearly.

Lefebvre tries to lend this impression that Venice and its art produced in each other a dialectical edge:

> In Venice, the *representation of space* (the sea at once dominated and exalted) and *representational space* (exquisite lines, refined pleasures, the sumptuous and cruel dissipation of wealth accumulated by any and every means) are mutually reinforcing. Something similar may be said of the space of the canals and streets, where water and stone create a texture founded on reciprocal reflection. Here everyday life and its functions are coextensive with, and utterly transformed by, a theatricality as sophisticated as it is unsought, a sort of involuntary *mise-en-scène*.[13]

Venice is a test case for Lefebvre's thesis. If, as he says, space is 'produced', it ought to be possible to identify inductively the forces (social, historical, environmental) that produced it. But in Venice, on his own admission, the distinction between production and product, between audience and theatre, breaks down. Venice does not represent itself to itself; it is not a city of mirrors. It continues to reproduce itself, to generate its own history. This feedback phenomenon needs to be taken into account. True, in a weak historical sense Venice is 'produced' by a particular history and environment; but Venice also continues to produce itself, its environment, its history.

When Giorgione composes forms in a way that recalls the curvilinear environment of Venice, with its lightning-bolts of marble and its waters deeply-foliaged, he does not simply represent a historical product; he contributes to its production. His paintings do not add to the views of Venice available. They do not clog up passageways with picturesque associations. Quite the reverse: painting something else, a river, a hillside, he avoids bringing Venice to a standstill. Choreographing its space, as a network of formal and chromatic relations, he avoids confusing seeing with the accumulation of objects. True to Venice's pre-capitalist economy, he encourages circulation, trade between places.[14] But this will be missed if we regard Giorgione's art, like the space of Venice, as a product of historical forces. Giorgione is not a scenographer; his paintings are part of the performance. 'Venice,' Adrian Stokes maintained, with Giorgione's sparsely populated canvases in mind, 'inspires a sense of affinity, of equality of emphasis in the visual world, of an unchanging emblematic showing that embraces the movement of the waters. Venice, but not the population. They appear matchstick-like, out of place.'[15] This may be true of the figures in Longhi, Canaletto or Carlevaris, trapped in the equally match-like orthogonals of linear perspective, but it slanders Venetians.

The gondoliers, say, move through Venice's canals as if the amphibious environment were made for them. Their progress is curvilinear in a double sense, as their vessels rock backwards and forwards on parabolic paths. Again, these figures are not products of Venetian space; they mould it, make it. Rubbed angles, abraded tie-stones, their calls round blind corners; these are coeval with Lefebvre's 'oft-repeated gestures . . . of carpenters and masons, sailors and stevedores.'[16] And Venetian painters, to generalize, produced Venice similarly, by the spatial relationships they built on in their painterly navigations. 'As the gondolier at the stern steers with the oar,' Boschini remarked, 'so the Venetian painters use the paintbrush.'[17]

Like the gondoliers, Giorgione performed Venetian space; he inhabited it as they inhabited it. And the parallel may be neither picturesque nor sentimental. Giorgione's compositions were built up layer by layer, paint being applied directly according to the blot-technique. The way in which the brush blotched the surface, taking care to build up all parts of the canvas at once so as to maintain an equilibrium or tension between different compositional elements, was identical with the manner in which the gondolier's oar dabbled the surface of water, unfurling highlights here, deepening whorls of shadow there, as, keeping its leaning balance, it stayed abreast of the marbled glaze. In this performative environment, to represent Venetian objects rather than Venetian space would be to take an outsider's point of view. Adopting a different, perhaps Florentine, perspective and seeking to represent Venetian forms independently of the space they harboured, would be equivalent to colluding in her social and spiritual collapse, turning her into a picture-book. It would have been to see Venice scenographically, as foreigners did, as, later, Canaletto painting for foreigners did – and as, in Giorgione's own day, artists like Carpaccio and Gentile Bellini did.[18]

This, then, is to imply a dialectic of a different kind; if Giorgione avoided painting gondolas, processions, argosies and funnel-shaped chimneys, it may have been because he felt their mimicry of individual objects blinded the eye to seeing the subtler identities in difference which, for him, constituted the key to community. Carpaccio's and Gentile's public commissions were exercises in visual rhetoric; they persuaded the viewer to identify with the artist's artistry, to compare his representation with the real thing. But in the comparison lay the fault. Venetian space could not be represented in this way, and to divorce Venetian forms from their curvilinear setting was to begin to prepare them for transport to other places or, inversely, to prepare the way for translation and invasion.

I am suggesting that Giorgione's paintings did not effortlessly embody the Venetian point of view; they jostled for position among a number of competing space conceptions. If Giorgione's *Tempesta* appears to us to have elicited better than any other artist the character of Venetian space, it is because he understood it historically. According to Panofsky, 'Just as it was impossible for the Middle Ages to elaborate the modern system of perspective, which is based on the realisation of a fixed distance between the eye and the object and thus enables the artist to build up comprehensive and consistent images of visible things; so was it impossible for them to evolve the modern idea of history, based on the realisation of an intellectual distance between the present and the past which enables the scholar to build up comprehensive and consistent concepts of bygone periods . . .'[19] Inversely, if Giorgione understood perspective differently, it was because he understood history differently.

Panofsky's periodization of history (and philosophy) is, of course, overdrawn. Few fifteenth-century Florentine painters, and even fewer northern artists, adopted the principles of linear perspective undiluted. Besides, as Francastel has put it, Brunelleschi's geometrical rationalization of the third dimension is not a new method of representing space; it is a transformation of social space itself. 'Columbus discovered America because he had the astrolabe'[20] – and, we might add, because he belonged to the culture that, via Alberti's treatise on geography, provided 'the methods of surveying and mapping and the instruments . . . responsible for the new scientific accuracy of the depictions of towns that date from the late 15th and early 16th centuries.'[21] The new way of looking at objects, defining them in terms of the spaces between them, harmonizing them according to a supposedly ancient principle of 'just proportions', accommodated different, even contradictory, tendencies. It suggested the closed space of Alberti's viewing cube, with its sense of forms converging on a well-ruled centre; it made possible the organization of an open space – the world could suddenly be imagined as a continuous planar surface on which, at intervals, objects (islands, mountains, cities and populations) were located. It theatricalized what could be seen, and then insisted that beyond the horizon an infinity of other theatres could be found.

The principle that held these proliferating fields together was that of repetition, both historical and spatial. Brunelleschi's painting of the Baptistery and the Piazza del Duomo was not simply an experiment in perspective: it was a way of harmonizing seeing with ancient forms – the Baptistery was supposed to be Roman. Brunelleschi was seeking a perspective that would coincide with the view of the Ancients. He wanted to create a symmetry between his view and theirs which would ensure his own architectural innovations repeated their principles and so were in harmony. In effect, he wanted to synchronize past and present by visualizing them spatially.[22]

The principle of repetition could be applied universally as well as locally. If Brunelleschi and Alberti invited contemporaries to step inside a cube, geographers and surveyors imagined stepping outside, treating the earth itself as a solid equilateral box. The roundness of the globe may have been formally respected, but its various zones were talked about as if they occupied different 'sides'. These sides were symmetrical with regard to each other. Thus what occurred here could be predicted to occur there; the globe could be discovered in advance of its exploration by the simple rhetorical principles of repetition, inversion and antithesis – underlying all of which was the new assumption of the uniformity of space in every direction, and therefore the symmetry of its parts.

The new geometry was a critical as well as a descriptive technique. Columbus is said to have kept the 'true' distance covered each day to himself, giving out to his crew a consistently lower figure.[23] In this way the lie of the land could be neutralized and, wherever it eventually hove into view, could be said to have been found in the place predicted for it. In the meantime, whatever came unpredictably between the navigator and his projected goal, the central point on which his ships converged, must be regarded as an impediment to progress. Like the Florentines, Columbus regarded himself as a voyager into the past; he too was looking for the lost proportions of the Ancients, those balancing lands of Paradise and Atlantis that would restore history's harmony. Peoples who came in between, obstructing his journey home, disturbing the symmetry of his enquiry, could not be unmotivated. Blocking his free circulation, they resisted historical enlightenment; it was logical, symmetrical, to interpret them as the Devil's kin. Far from respecting their right to belong where they were, their mere standing on the beach was suspicious, even provocative, indicating their displacement.

The appearance of the 'blacke Moores which are in Africa', one George Best explained, was not due to 'the distemperature of the Climate', but to 'the curse and naturall infection of the blood'. The alleged cause of the curse is also instructive. It is the legacy of an original departure from the law: Cham, Noah's eldest son, laid claim to 'all the dominions of the earth,' and while yet in the Ark, 'used company with his wife . . . to disinherite the offspring of his other two brethren.' To punish his 'disobedience of parents', God made Noah's son 'blacke and lothsome, that it might remaine a spectacle of disobedience to all the world.' The racism of this passage may be crude, but the mutual reinforcement of history and geography it displays is subtler. Reproducing their blackness, the blacks repeat history; but their history is also their geography – they are punished by having to occupy 'a cursed, dry, sandy, and unfruitfull ground, fit for such a generation to inhabite in.'[24] Both their illicit mobility (their original imperial ambitions) and their actual stability are suspect. They lack the proper ambition to travel properly and so redeem their dark origins. Why, enslaving them to a higher purpose, transporting them to another country, might be a way of redeeming them.

To travel properly was to be able to fix one's position. In this way, the Aristotelian dialectic between stasis and motion reasserts itself. Further, now that motion can be more accurately mapped, rectilinear and circular motion can be reconciled; one sets out to the horizon with a view to coming back. The world is a planar surface with the odd property of extending its lines to infinity; or where, which is the same thing, every beginning marks another ending. Rectilinear motion minutely hooped about the earth comes to resemble cosmic motion; the notion of the still, fixed axle-tree of the universe is preserved. Later, and perhaps daily in

Venice, this characterization of movement seemed retrograde; stasis came to be understood as relative motion. The planets moved in the puzzling way they did because the earth moved. The consciousness of a Montaigne did not revolve about a stable self; the self, a comet rather than a ponderous world, wobbled under the influence of the knowledge of others, and was at all times largely in shadow. The motion of the blood was tidal – another Venetian intuition – and, Sarpi asserted, the very ground beneath one's feet shifted.[25]

Giorgione's art positions itself relative to these critical implications. When some sculptors claimed that their art was superior to painting because, in walking round a statue, one could see every aspect, Giorgione – according to Vasari – replied that painting was superior in just this respect, that it could make all positions apparent at a glance; and he painted a nude in a turning position, flanked by reflective surfaces (clear water, armour, and a mirror) to prove his point.[26] This may or may not be apocryphal; the *controposto* nude suggests the *Tempesta* or the surviving fragment of the Fondaco dei Tedeschi, while the apparatus of mirrors is more in the theatrical manner of Titian. But in any case it begs a question: what if it was precisely a sense of the peripateia that needed to be evoked?

Stokes finds in the notion of composing a painting 'for one glance' (*una sola occhiata*) a key to the art of both Giorgione and Piero della Francesca: 'Their inspired emphasis upon simultaneity entailed a lack of emphasis in any particular, but a much heightened accent upon brotherhood, upon a conception of form stemming from the ceaseless inter-communication of textures and surface colours.'[27] This, as ever, is revelatory, but what exactly is meant by 'brotherhood'? How exactly is this 'inter-communication' conceived? In Piero, this is exactly the expressive function of linear perspective, in conjunction with that *amicizia* of colours recommended by Alberti. In Giorgione's paintings, however, these terms of reference have to be established.

Readers of Stokes will know that these questions go to the heart of his life as well as his aesthetic; his advocacy of stability and depth as against baroque decoration, his desire for community, are not unrelated to certain fundamental emotional themes.[28] But as Stokes balanced the temptation of immersion and self-dissolution in the other with a keen awareness of identity in difference – which he associated not only with certain art but with other choreographies of space (including tennis) – so we may temper his account of Vasari's Plinian anecdote. Giorgione's reversed perspective, accommodating let us say a non-baroque *controposto*, is a technique for evoking relative motion. There is no question of the eye stalking the subject photographer-like, no intention to represent her cinematographically as a montage of successive positions collected together. It is the motion of the eye that touches rather than sees which Giorgione copies. The gondolier scatters images; polished armour dazzles; only mirrors see through space.

Giorgione's landscapes gather in a way foreign to Piero because Giorgione wants to visualize seeing; not to construct elaborate machines for the manipulation of (rectilinear) reflections, but to present the curvilinear environment. As the curvature of space only becomes visible when we attempt to project our visual experience on to a two-dimensional surface, the science of painting becomes definite: to reveal what is normally overlooked, the world's curvature but for whose parabolic field things would fly apart or collapse into the black (eye-) hole of centralized perspective's vanishing-point. This indeed is the aim of Leonardo's synthetic perspective, 'a spherical space which is homogeneous, but by no means simple, and which possesses some of the qualities of Einstein's finite infinity.'[29]

It has also been the aim, rather more recently, of the artist Albert Flocon, who commenced his serious study of linear perspective while in a French prison awaiting deportation by the Nazis: 'I sat in that hole with my dreams of escape and drew scenes on the scanty sheets of paper I could set aside, scenes breaking through the walls into the far-beyond, my first attempts at perspective drawing.'[30] Out of this escapism, from this double exile of the eye from its everyday curvilinear environment, there grew a desire not to see through or into, but to compose things as they are all about. Flocon's curvilinear or hyperbolic perspective became a way not only to represent appearances but to construct a new living-space for himself; to inhabit a spherical enclosure that, like the world, disclosed rather than imprisoned. 'If all goes well, is it not sufficient that as I gaze at a wide seascape and as it penetrates me, horizon, ocean, beach, dunes, and clouds join in forms that grow on all sides into a picture?'[31]

As this suggests, not only are two kinds of perspective involved; two modes of seeing are implied. If rectilinear space asks us to focus on forms, to scrutinize them as signs of space, then reversed perspective, with its subtle bending of shapes about each other, tends to dissipate the gaze, inviting us to look without distinction at an animated sea. Western seeing at least harbours this paradox: that to gaze fixedly at something is to lose sight of everything about us; conversely, the useless activity of 'staring into space', allowing the world back in, may be to see everything at once. We classify these two ways of seeing hierarchically: the hunter keeps his eyes skinned, staring about him, alive to every chance movement, because this is the way things come into view; the scientist daydreams or goes for a walk because this is the way he can later solve the problem. But it may be that these two phases of seeing constitute different forms of knowledge. Not to see one view at the expense of another keeps the whole of one's surroundings in play; it is, for example, to hear as well as to see. It may be a method for keeping on the move while staying where one is.

Rectilinear space is a machine for firing eyesight into space. It imagines seeing as a spear, capable of striking through the chaotic maze of appearances and finding the loop, the way to the vanishing-point, where all comes together and the enigma of the environment's multiplicity is commanded and reduced to order. And this power of focused projection is often regarded as a prerequisite of cognition as well as perception. Arnheim, for example, influenced by gestalt psychology, maintains that visual perception is selective, and he associates the ability to pierce the visual field and to distinguish sharply shapes from their ground in part to the physiology of the eye: 'Because retinal sensitivity is so restricted, the eye can and must single out some particular spot, which becomes isolated, dominant, central.'[32]

It is relevant to our later argument that Arnheim embraces the traditional Western identification of seeing with thinking:

> Audible information about the world is quite limited. Of a bird it gives us little more than its song. It is limited to the noises things make. Among them are the sounds of language, but they acquire their meaning only by reference to other sensory data. Thus music by itself is hardly thinking about the world. The great virtue of vision is that it is not only a highly articulate medium, but that its universe offers inexhaustibly rich information about the objects and events of the outer world. Therefore, vision is the primary medium of thought.[33]

Against this one might advocate cognitive chiaroscuro: 'Perhaps the opposite of light, i.e. darkness, as brought out in Heidegger's thinking can lead us towards the explanation of reality in terms other than those of light. For in darkness we cannot see, and thus we must begin to hear . . . our traditional conceptuality and metaphors fail us. It is then that the silent *cogito* begins . . .'[34]

Curvilinear space, as Flocon says, works in the reverse direction, letting the world penetrate the eye. This conception of seeing is shield-like: the arched sky, the earth bent like a bow, gather round the wandering eye protectively, shielding it from the piercing prospect of nothingness. Seeing in this way is to be seen, one's own gaze answering the look of the world. Again it is Arnheim who, with his usual perspicuity, appears to gloss this attitude, calling it 'passive reception': 'As I open my eyes, I find myself surrounded by a given world: the sky with its clouds, the moving waters of the lake, the wind-swept dunes, the window, my study, my desk, my body.' But, he continues, 'is this awareness of the world all there is to perception? Through that world roams the glance, directed by attention, focusing the narrow range of sharpest vision now on this, now on that, following the flight of a distant seagull, scanning a tree to explore its shape. This eminently active performance is what is truly meant by visual perception.'[35]

But is it? There are at least two other ways in which visual perception might perform actively without narrowing to a sharp, spear-like gaze. It is interesting that both Flocon and Arnheim use coastal prospects to illustrate their ideas; the wide, uncluttered horizon, the low, featureless dunes, the formless clouds provide the maximum resistance, as it were, to the eye intent on focusing. (It is the same world, spawning smudges of clouds and mud-banks, which forms Venice's physical environment as well as the mythic basis of the Venetian art of *macchiare*.) These horizontally-banded spaces, where zones continually melt into one another – as many horizons as wave edges, as many glazes as weathers – suggest a way of seeing which is pre-attentional, which is active but unfocused.

The narrowness of the roaming glance may be inescapable, but within its narrow field a host of part-shapes, the glitter of waves, the throb of the mirage, coexist; and these field events do not ever resolve themselves into shapes, but persist as it were on the edge of vision, defying attention to reduce their glare, to detach them from the ground. This undirected attention can be likened to the perceptual conditions obtaining where colonizers and indigenes meet for the first time – it is usually on the beach – where, however briefly, it would be dangerous to distinguish the significant from the insignificant, and where as yet, from all the things swimming into one's ken, nothing is picked out.

But a quite different mode of seeing comes into play when, instead of focusing on the mobility of the eyeballs within the eye-sockets of the stationary observer, we contemplate the runner, the dancer, the walker or the gondolier. Then the limitations of conceiving visual perception in terms of an observer and an observed become apparent. The person on the move keeps his eyes on the ground but does not focus on this or that feature. His eye drives ahead, keeping the path open. It attends, without seeing sharply, to a parabolic world that fattens on either side to accommodate the body's passage and swiftly slips away behind. But nothing is pierced here; the field ahead is merely paced. The space around, the lie of the land, are neither 'given' nor intermittently resolved into stable forms; they are seen in relative motion, as choreographic extensions of the mobile body.

If the eye does have a projective function, it is to continue to identify the spaces in-between, where the body fits. This is not a one-sided process but essentially involves measuring out the ground, 'scanning' what lies ahead in rhythmic as well as visual terms. Without this instinctive ability to gauge intervals, the gondoliers would collide, the dancer would miss his turn, the walker would trip up. Seeing of this footed, bipedal kind is genuinely musical; preoccupied with convergences and divergences, it is also curvilinear.

These different ways of seeing are not merely modal or developmental, but historical. Columbus's discoveries, say, were the offspring of a way of seeing. As far as possible he allowed nothing to come to him: the surface of the sea, the screen of the sky, were tirelessly scanned for signs (birds, spars of wood, shoals of fish) which, when spied, were construed purely in terms of what they might indicate about what lay ahead.[36] Fluctuating flights, irregular appearances and relative motion were turned into further rectilinear projections confirming Columbus's own way. Ultimately, everything must prove familiar. So, hearing as he saw, Columbus identified among the singing birds of the Bahamas only the Spanish nightingale.[37] Columbus forced on what he saw a rate of exchange; he insisted on its yielding a profit, whether semantic or material. But the trading was one-sided: he turned what approached back on itself, as if it were a false representation.

Besides the spear-like gaze of relentless semiosis, the other weapon Columbus carried with him was Minerva's gorgon-bossed shield of mimesis. This, commonly imagined in the Renaissance as made of crystal and reflective like a mirror,[38] was a device for stopping natives in their tracks and making them wonder who the actors were – themselves or the reflections. They might well feel surrounded by visions and speared to death. And if Columbus pointed to scars on their legs, they might well suppose he understood what was happening now. So, like the rounded surfaces of the sea, the physical appearance of the Taino warriors counted for nothing. These men 'were very well built with fine bodies and handsome faces,'[39] but their nakedness, their failure to conceal themselves, to clothe themselves with representations, made them dull. True denizens of the coast, they seemed to defend no interior. Not deceiving, they defied communication.

And then Columbus 'saw some who had wound scars on their bodies and I asked them by signs how they got these and they indicated to me that people came from other islands near by who tried to capture them and they defended themselves.'[40] Looking past the men, Columbus invited them to act a part; and the play they improvised under his direction was the prologue to conquest. The Taino, Columbus noted, 'have extreme fear of the men of Caniba or Canima', further observing 'they say that they have but one eye and the face of a dog.'[41] Far from finding this puzzling, the *Journal* remarks, 'the Admiral thought they were lying and felt that those who captured them must have been under the rule of the Grand Khan.'[42] What could be more natural where a dog-king reigned than to find a dog-faced folk? In any case, the Taino provide Columbus with a role to play; as their defender and liberator, Columbus was not inaugurating the end. On the contrary, freeing them from the threat of slavery to the Caribs, he turned the clock back to the Golden Age. Who knows, he might even strip them of certain geo-imperial delusions under which they currently seemed to labour. In any case, who could doubt that he would help them see the world more clearly, with both eyes?

Such are the ironies of a mimicry harnessed to the colonial fantasy of representation or mimesis. Nowhere in this dumb-show is attention paid to the curvilinear forms and gestures of animated beings; their faces and scarred limbs are studied like photographs, on which the slap of curveting prows and the parrot-like whistle of parabolic spears leaves no trace. And such ironies were not confined to the Caribbean basin. In the first half of the twentieth century the students of the underground were opposed by proponents of the aesthetic gaze – a way of looking at art as a purely formal arrangement of elements, whose meaning was only grasped when these elements were seen as a unity. In this view of things, which lent itself admirably to the appreciation of 'primitive' art, the meaning of a statue, a painting or a view resided entirely in the harmony created by the internal structure of its parts – which structure was only to be apprehended aesthetically. According to Roger Fry, a poem consisting of nonsense syllables could create the same effect as a poem by Milton, provided it sounded well.[43]

At first glance, the aesthetic gaze seems similar to the passive, shield-like seeing evoked here as a foil to the spear-thrusting imperial vision. It seems to involve suspending an irritable longing for resolution, an extractable story or point; it values the composition as a whole rather than in its particulars. Yet its passivity is apparent only; it still at bottom insists on grasping the object as a whole, in a single glance. And the aim of this is not to sustain the engagement but to conclude it, to carry the painting or view away in one's mind. There remains an unbridgeable gulf between the stillness of seeing and the peripateia of everyday life.

Leo Stein expresses this position lucidly when describing his experience of the view he had from his villa near Settignano above Florence. After twenty years he was about to sell his home, when:

> Suddenly, and for the first time, I grasped the structural character of that view, and at once it became in itself superfluous. Before that happened, I could remember what the view was like, though I could not in any proper sense remember it. Now I can see it any time in the mind's eye. Not only that, but I can see it anywhere. That view had offered in an almost obvious way a form which was still beyond my capacity fully to realise. I was rapt by it into a higher experience than I could digest. Now I can not only remember it and sketch from memory, but I can see its essence in any landscape whatever . . . in the world of aesthetics there are heights beyond heights for him who has an adequate method and persists.[44]

Stein's verticalism is not just metaphorical. His 'aesthetic vision' is born in an elevated place, and it has the effect of carrying him yet higher. To grasp a view aesthetically is to be elevated above it, to see it at a glance. To see in this way is to overcome the land's resistance to being seen. Reversed perspective, I am suggesting, grows from an antithetical ideology of the eye, where to see is not to penetrate and transfix but to dwell on the directional lie of the land. In this latter situation, it is the chiaroscuro of the view, the gradients of blindness, that count, giving the impression of a landscape gathering round.

Perhaps the emergence of Florentine perspective had something to do with the heights from which the Roman grid of planar Florence was habitually viewed. Most of the Florentine artists came down from the surrounding mountains. The landscape which Baldovinetti painted for his *Nativity* in the atrium of SS. Annunziata (1460–2) bears witness, in its meticulous placing of chessmen towers on a chequerboard plain, to his training as a mosaicist; it also perhaps captures the genuine astonishment of hill dwellers on first catching sight of the Arno plain.[45]

In any case, despite appearances, the aesthetic gaze is a method for seeing beneath appearances, grasping their underlying formal grammar. Its efficacy depends on the unchanging passivity of what is seen – the gaze is still totally one-sided – and the object is to render the view in itself 'superfluous.' The viewer's mystical sense of being carried to a higher realm is calculated; it means, in effect, experiencing the no-place of seeing all places in terms of a single formal key. Stein's experience is finally the colonizer's. Having learned the formal language of the country, he feels no obligation to descend into the human and historical particulars of what lies about him: 'I now had an adequate method both in speculation and in seeing and it was as though I had nothing to do but to enter into my kingdom. I started to paint . . .'[46]

The difficulties of moving beyond the aesthetic gaze are comically and sadly experienced by Italo Calvino's Mr Palomar who, named for a dome, takes an interest in domelike particulars. Observing a young woman on the beach, her bosom bared, he walks by, discreetly looking away. But, he thinks, it is reactionary to behave so conventionally. He walks back 'so that his gaze touches with impartial uniformity' the waves, the boats, the bath-towel, the nipple, the coast. But, he thinks, this means 'flattening the human to the level of things.' He walks back again, 'his glance . . . making a curve that accompanies the swell of the breast from a certain distance, elusively but also protectively.' But this also, he reflects, seems too dismissive. Walking firmly towards the woman, he plans to 'linger on the breast with special consideration, [then] quickly include it in an impulse of good-will and gratitude for the whole.' Too late: irritated by his attention, the woman scrambles up, grabs her towel, marches off. Palomar reflects bitterly on 'the dead weight of an intolerant tradition', but what creates his tragi-comic dilemma is the back and forth of his footsteps, not his thoughts.[47] In refining his ideologically correct gaze, Mr Palomar forgets to look where he is going. And, like Leo Stein, he overlooks the fact that the world is looking back.

Calvino whimsically dramatizes the fact that curvilinear, as well as linear, seeing has its history. To want to see environmentally, he has to pass beyond the frozen aversion of the Victorian gaze, focused sightlessly on infinity. He has to surpass the aesthetic gaze which sees everything flatly, stilly (as if looking at a painting). He has to transcend its antithesis, the merely roving, environmentally-mimetic gaze which, darting here and there, perpetuates a paranoia of its own. He would like to, but cannot, find a way of having his seeing converge on his touching, to re-enter a nurturing world where the breast, no longer fetish object, seems at home. Failing to take account of his own progress across the sand-dunes, persisting in thinking himself another Palomar, an observatory of distant stars equipped with a far-piercing telescope, he fails to measure the distance between himself and the woman. She has for him the same function as Arnheim's seagull, whose motion serves to stabilize the roving glance. Focusing his thoughts, if not his eyes, exclusively on her, Palomar loses sight of their relative motions, of the curvilinear field that embraces them both, within which a genuine convergence, obliquely by other paths, might be possible.

Different cognizances of the visual field provoke different histories; a refusal to see eye to eye not only blights gender relations but determines the fate of empires. Pursuing his thesis that pre-Homeric cultures were 'bi-cameral', social control occurring through the medium of auditory hallucinations channelled via 'the god-king', Jaynes ponders the apparent ease with which Pizarro effected the overthrow of Atahuallpa and the Inca empire: 'Not subjectively conscious, unable to deceive or to narratise out the deceptions of others, the Inca and his lords were captured like helpless automatons. And as its people mechanically watched, this shipload of subjective men stripped the gold sheathing from the holy city . . .'[48]

Despite its elegant guise, this is cultural and historical determinism at its most reductive. Far from relying on 'bicameral voices coming from the sun,'[49] the Inca aristocracy was perfectly capable of narrating and recording its own history. Referring to the *quipucamayocs* or official historians of the pre-contact period, the Andean noble Guamán Poma de Ayala commented that 'they kept count of the content of the Inca's storehouses; they helped to administer the Inca's provinces; they carried messages, and, in sum, they were repositories of wisdom and information.'[50] This hardly squares with the notion of a people so preoccupied with a buzz of voices that they could not count what was happening before their very eyes.

Nor does Poma de Ayala's account of the origins of the Inca suggest a people unable to narrate deception. Maria Antonia Garcés notes that he represents the advent of the Cuzco rulers as 'the usurpation of the Andes . . . from its true masters.' Further, we owe our knowledge of this original deception to the 'first chronicler': 'In this way, Waman Puma establishes a metonymic connection between the inventor of the "historical fables" of the Inka state and the idols and ceremonies introduced, into the Andean scenario, by Manqo Qhapac and Mama Waku.' Mamu Waku, who 'seems to have contrived a highly elaborate fiction involving a dowry from "her father, the sun",' is 'associated with artistic invention.' Garcés expresses the view that 'these fables spring from the earliest rituals of this culture.'[51]

Jaynes's interpretation does have the merit, though, of recognizing ways of seeing as historically critical. As Prescott long ago made clear, Atahuallpa's mistake was not that he yielded up his right to spear-like vision, passively allowing Pizarro's image to enter his retina; it was, like the first Mr Palomar, to pretend to see nothing at all. At the first meeting with Pizarro, the Peruvian monarch 'seemed to discharge all expression from his features . . . He remained silent, with his eyes fastened on the ground.' And when a Spanish charger was put through its paces and brought to a dramatic halt a few feet from him, he 'maintained the same marble composure as before.' That this not-seeing was feigned is clear from the sequel, in which Atahuallpa 'turned his head to look at Pizarro, smiling . . .'[52] Pizarro's conquest of Peru is more plausibly explained in terms of Cortés's comparable success in Mexico; as Prescott notes, Pizarro's plan to kidnap Atahuallpa was modelled on Cortés's capture and confinement of Montezuma.[53]

In any case, early communication between the Aztec leader and the Spaniard illustrates the point that different ways of seeing do not represent insuperable cultural differences but flexible, if diverse, historical visions; there is no single 'primitive' mode of seeing, but within the modalities of vision available to us as binocular creatures there are certainly emphases that are not typically Western. The value attached to mimicry is a case in point. A rectilinear conception of seeing is not only one-sided. In making the viewpoint of the spectator symmetrical with the vanishing-point of centralized perspective, it renders the viewer proof against being seen. A world conceived as a quiver of orthogonals converging on the vanishing-point cannot look back. Except as it flatters the viewer's authoritative point of view by rendering it transcendent, invisible, it cannot mirror him. The viewer looks through a window; he is by definition absent from the composition his viewpoint creates.

Here, to introduce mimetic elements into the field of vision is, as Arcimboldo revealed, to disclose the formidable foreclosure on seeing that linear vision entails. The world that seems to compose so well is, in reality, a pattern of wedge-shaped pieces whose imagery might come from anywhere. In Arcimboldo's designs, a collage of heterogeneous visual material successfully mimics a realistic image because the parts fit exactly inside the structuring lines that constitute 'realism's' language of representation. Similarly, architectural prospects – receding colonnades and narrowing rooflines – mimic seeing; only this we do not see. What we see instead is the triumph of rectilinear space which, by its very invisibility (its masquerade as a prospect), conceals from us our blindness, our imprisonment.

In other cultures mimicry, far from spelling disaster, might be proof of seeing clearly. And to see clearly might mean for the Aztecs, as it meant for the Spaniards, glimpsing a clearer outline of the future as well as the past. Diego Durán, relying on Mexican testimony, reports that when Montezuma received from one Tlillancalqui detailed descriptions of the Spanish, he had the best painter in the city brought before him, and ordered him under Tlillancalqui's instructions to paint their ships, their faces, their variously-coloured clothes, their caps and swords, leaving nothing out. Montezuma then ordered a succession of the most senior painters from neighbouring cities to inspect the images, asking them if they could identify the figures and objects displayed there, and whether 'their ancestors had left behind any information or pictures or statues relating to them.'[54] At length, Quilaztli from Xochimilko, a man famous for his collection of ancient paintings and for his skill in interpreting them, comes forward. Quilaztli prophesies the Spanish conquest, describing what will happen in cinematic detail, and concludes: 'So that you will give credence to what I have said, here is the picture which has been handed down to me from my ancestors,' from which it appears that Quilaztli's prophecy is nothing more than an *ekphrasis* of an ancient picture in his possession.[55]

Montezuma may not have welcomed Quilaztli's news, but it enabled him to place the Spaniards in an historical perspective. They have been in Mexico before; they are returning. In the context of the Aztecs' circular conception of historical time, their mimicry of past appearances makes ominous, frightening sense; typically, the indigenous philosophers interpreted the Spaniards' arrival, not as a political and military threat, but more fundamentally as a sign that the present epoch of the world was coming to an end – and, as all had been foreseen, had perhaps at a similar moment in the past already happened, what could be done to prevent it happening again?[56]

From a Spanish point of view, the uses of mimicry were very different. According to Bernal Díaz, who viewed the invasion from a wholly Spanish point of view, shortly after Cortés's landing Montezuma sent messengers with instructions 'to make realistic full-length portraits of Cortés and all his captains and soldiers, also to draw the ships, sails, and horses, Doña Marina and Aguilar, and even the two greyhounds.'[57] A week after the pictures had been sent to Montezuma, a second embassy arrived, 'led by a great Mexican chief, who in face, features, and body was very like our Captain. The great Montezuma had chosen him on purpose. For it is said when Tedile showed him the portrait of Cortés all the princes present exclaimed that one of their number, Quintalbor, looked exactly like him.'[58] This perception was shared by the Europeans: 'We in the camp', writes Bernal Díaz, 'called them "our Cortés" and "the other Cortés".'[59] Recognizing his likeness, Cortés should have acknowledged a deeper, familial kinship. Unlike Odysseus, a nobody in his own land after so many years away, Cortés was being accorded immediate recognition; he was being invited to regard his triumphal procession as a homecoming.

From the Spanish view, again, it looked very different. The other Cortés undermines the authority of the real Cortés by revealing the theatricality of the rectilinear gaze. In a world whose space is unified, forms can only exist in so far as they occupy a unique position; a form that slips and slides, occupying more than one place at once, is a contradiction in terms. If the maker of history (Cortés) can double up and be an actor in his own drama, then whose point of view is authoritative? It was with an intuition that likeness mocked, rather than reinforced, identity that Cortés had previously forwarded to Montezuma 'a crimson cap with a gold medal engraved with a figure of St George on horseback, lance in hand and slaying the dragon', together with instructions that, when they met, Montezuma should 'wear the cap on his head'.[60] Cortés invited Montezuma to mimic a European war-lord, to put on his badge of authority. Cortés's other did not signify a mimetic bridgehead to diplomatic exchanges; he illustrated the delusory nature of appearances. Montezuma dressed up as St George did not represent an alliance of powers; it was a humiliating mime, a pantomimic parody of the Aztec's imperial pretensions.

It was as if Hernán Cortés was already inviting Montezuma to take part in the conquistador's Triumph, and had in mind the kind of pageant put on for Henri II in 1550, where the conquest of Brazil, complete with forest landscapes, sham combats and erotic interludes, was staged, 'over fifty Tabbagerres and Toupinaboux Indians [being] freshly imported for the occasion'.[61] Of this, Mullaney writes: 'The ethnographic attention and knowledge displayed at Rouen was genuine, amazingly thorough, and richly detailed; the object, however, was not to understand Brazilian culture but to perform it, in a paradoxically self-consuming fashion. Knowledge of another culture in such an instance is directed toward ritual rather than ethnological ends, and the rite involved is ultimately organised around the elimination of its own pretext: the spectacle of the Other that is thus celebrated and observed, in passing.'

This excursion into the New World takes us less far from Giorgione than might be imagined. At issue in these cross-cultural exchanges was the status of mere coincidences. A philosophy of history based on the idea of rectilinear progress had no choice but to relegate them to the ghostly realm of superstition; a curvilinear conception of time might view them differently, though, as demonstrations of identity in difference. There is no question here of supposing Giorgione subscribed to a cyclic view of history, but his curvilinear perspective did imply an environment where convergences, ambiguities and metamorphoses might be the order of the day.

From a non-European point of view, it was the Spaniards who behaved like automata. Durán reports that before consulting Quilaztli, Montezuma spoke to the painters of Malinalco, who showed him a picture in which their ancestors had represented 'men with only one eye in the middle of the forehead, like the Cyclops,' saying they would one day invade and take possession of Mexico.[62] This powerfully evokes the appearance of a soldier in armour, his head encased in a cask of gleaming iron, sporting, where his face should be, a gaping hole and visor eyelid. Suits of armour did not simply sheathe the body; they represented an external anatomy of its movement. The cuirasses of overlapping plates and hinges which billowed around shoulders, elbows, knees, fingers and toes, were early automobiles.

These military developments had painterly implications. They encouraged, for example, the study of light. It is no accident that among the reflecting surfaces turned on Giorgione's *contraposto* nude is a suit of armour. Breastplates, greaves and helmets were not only proof against spears; out of light they generated their own phalanx of glittering spear-points. The swords these metal Arguses brandished were merely the most sharply-focused of a hundred eyes. Painters too had to learn to shield themselves from the onslaught of highlights, finding ways to reduce the gleam or otherwise dissipate its tendency to swallow up the world in its metallic mirrors.

An early painting by Giorgione, the Castelfranco *Madonna with Saints*, illustrates these points (Plate 6); it also suggests how the dissipation of highlights could be a weapon in the attack on linear perspective. Painted between 1504 and 1506, before Giorgione adopted the method of painting direct, the Castelfranco *Madonna* was a public commission, quite possibly obtained through Giovanni Bellini himself, and Giovanni's influence on the composition is clear, notably in the adoption of a frontal viewpoint, a pyramidally-arranged subject and a symmetrically-disposed pair of distant landscapes.[63] But as the perspective of the chequerboard floor reveals, these compositional conventions are invoked critically, even ironically.

It is not a question of demonstrating Giorgione's ignorance of Brunelleschi or Alberti; it is well known that Florentine linear perspective was little used in the Lagoon. At about the time the Castelfranco *Madonna* was painted, Giorgione's friend Albrecht Dürer, on a visit to Venice, wrote of his plan to go to Bologna 'to learn the secrets of the art of perspective, which a man is willing to teach me.'[64] Again, Jacopo Bellini's studio drawing books feature many linear perspective constructions, apparently the result of the master visiting Florence himself, but as Joost-Gaugier observes: 'His [Jacopo's] compositions lack the cohesive character of a single fully developed and carefully formulated method of representation.' Like other northern painting schools, though, the Venetians were familiar with chequerboard or two-point perspective, which might lack theoretical prestige, but had the practical advantage of imitating the natural behaviour of the eye – which did not gaze motionlessly at paintings but roved left and right, up and down.[65]

Besides, perspective in Venice was understood rhetorically or theatrically, as a compositional stratagem rather than a scientific theory. As the Venetian Pomponius Gauricus wrote in 1505: 'The intervals between people depend on perspective; the clarity of the *istoria* depends on these intervals; but this clarity is also a function of the number and disposition of the figures; these in their turn determine their intervals; therefore the number of people is a concern of perspective'[66] – propositions exemplified in Gentile Bellini's *Procession of the Cross*. But even within this provincial tradition, the Castelfranco *Madonna* seems heterodox. Take the Virgin's extraordinary altitude, isolation and physical inaccessibility: if Giorgione was imitating Bellini's similarly-enthroned Madonnas, surely his version reduces them to absurdity?

Again, suppose we say that her mountain-top remoteness is determined by the vanishing-point of the chequerboard floor; if the picture space converges on her head, what are we to make of the landscape beyond and behind her? The converging orthogonals of centralized linear perspective define the limits of what can be seen; a landscape behind their pyramid is a visual contradiction. It is as if Giorgione satirized the rhetorical inflation of Bellini's paintings; if centralized perspective 'worked', there would be no need to create a useless pyramid for the Madonna to sit on – her central position would be assured. Alternatively, if, as is evidently the case, the ziggurat's sole compositional function is to draw the viewer's eye towards her, then the chequerboard floor is an irrelevance. Further, this perspectival duplication makes explicit what is merely enigmatic in Bellini's own paintings: the purely rhetorical nature of the Madonna's connection with the landscape. Behind the red screen another picture begins; or perhaps there is no beyond, and the Virgin is flanked by painted walls. In any case, the two landscapes beyond are purely decorative, sharing no spatial community with the foreground or, for that matter, with each other.

At the same time, having dramatized the incoherences of Bellini's method, Giorgione seems intent on overcoming them by his own means. We notice, for example, the subtle concavity of the picture plane; while our viewpoint is sufficiently elevated to be able to see the Madonna's hand resting on the arm of her throne – and consequently down over the wall into the countryside – it is also low enough to make out the features of St George underneath his helmet. Linear perspective's narrowing ramp has been bent back towards us, as if the relationship of the painted space to the painting's plane were that of a bow to its string, and we looking in were archers. More obviously, having created geometrically incompatible spaces, Giorgione sets about weaving them together compositionally. And he does this not by theatrically manipulating the parts, but by emphasizing an identity in difference. The angle of St George's lance, subtly mirrored in St Francis's wedge-shadowed form, creates a widening 'V' that functions contrapuntally in relation to the pyramid of the Madonna.

The lance, the sole foreground feature that overlaps decisively with the background, does not, however, dissipate attention; it brings it to the tower, whose form, picked up by the left-hand edge of the Madonna's dais, brings us back to the foreground. The lance has another effect: it suggests a border, and consequently invites us to explore the territory inside it more fully; so by this and the inclination of St Francis, attention is drawn to the right-hand landscape, its parleying knights in the middle distance and behind them, in a minor key as it were, another tower, itself perched between a pyramidal crag and a 'V' of dark foliage. Is it an accident that the knights, whose armoured highlights recall us to St George, are located at the cusp of an equilateral triangle whose base is St George's lance; that the road sweeping by them might be a bow-string just released?

A series of formal resemblances between the gestures, appurtenances and disposition of the foreground saints and architectural and landscape events in the background has the effect of creating a radiating distance that converges on the foreground. A diagonal links St George and the knights; but another diagonal subtly links St Francis to the left-hand tower behind St George – the portico to the tower's left exactly mimicking the waist-high base of the throne extending left of St Francis. In this way, saints and landscapes seem implicated in a common choreography, as if, governed by the same formal force-field, they could easily change position.

Perhaps these formal resonances are over-determined, purely phonological echoes without semantic significance – 'audible information' in Arnheim's sense – but even if this is so, it is these mere coincidences that create compositional significance. It is as if by the exact placing of similar forms in ways that assured their independence, Giorgione wanted to find a visual language free of merely symbolic connections. In poetic terms, he wanted a language free of metaphors. Metaphors have to do with bringing distant things close; they are a means of making unlike things bend towards each other and intersect. But what if the world were from the beginning *curved*, and meetings bound to occur? Then the challenge was to mark those pathways, locating the like-minded forms they generated at intervals along them.

This account of the Castelfranco *Madonna* might be complemented by a similar analysis of Giorgione's Benson *Holy Family*, a small, intimate work which on the face of it has little formally in common with the public altarpiece (Plate 7). The figures in the Benson *Holy Family*, probably executed a little before 1504, owe a good deal to the Bellini studio where Giorgione had trained; his Joseph, for example, could have been derived from a Nativity sketch by Jacopo or from Giovanni's predella *Nativity* for the Pesaro altarpiece – one of the few asymmetrical compositions, incidentally (the Frick *St. Francis* is another), where Bellini attempts the measured progression between planes characteristic of Giorgione from the beginning. From a compositional point of view, though, the Benson *Holy Family* marks a considered departure from these masters, and in particular a rejection of Giovanni's best-known composition, the Madonna and Christ child in an architectural or landscape setting.[67]

One way to characterize Giorgione's painting is to describe it as a Bellini composition viewed from two or three paces to the right. This simple shift of viewpoint slides the holy family aside from the window-framed landscape. Instead of being symmetrically posed, the family is now located between two contrasting settings: a glimpsed crag and tower bathed in warm light, and an angle of half-lit, half-shadowy wall. As a result, both architectural and landscape elements are rearranged; no longer self-evidently symmetrical about an imaginary vanishing-point, they strike us as two unrelated backgrounds whose only point of convergence lies in the foreground.

The division and separation of the background does not result in compositional slackness or disorder; no longer organized as a theatrical stage-set, wall and window assume a human role in the picture. No longer stiffly representing an idea of holiness, they are free to mimic the human group, to converge sympathetically on their event and to be caught up in it. Mary's unconventional pose, holding out the child towards Joseph, creates a trinity of highlighted figures whose 'V' is also the place where both backgrounds converge.

The convergence is achieved in a variety of ways: an alternating rhythm of light and dark ensures that the left-hand wall is felt as a widening shadow emanating from Joseph; the muted colours of vestments are echoed in the distant landscape; most obviously, the inverted pyramid of the holy family is imitated by the distant crag sloping to the base of the tower. But in any case, the result is to create a setting that curves around the holy family, as if they exerted a gravitational attraction on their surroundings; notice, for instance, the wedge-shaped rock to the right of the Madonna. The effect is not claustrophobic, rather the reverse. The unforced, mimetic alignment of natural and human forms makes it possible to contemplate greater divergences, remoter contingencies. Held together by their mere coincidence in the holy event, the surroundings are valued for their separateness, their difference. This is not the indifference of Florentine painting, where citizens go about their business apparently unaware of what is happening behind them, but the sense a community might provide which composes its world, not according to the logic of the emotionally unaligned, all-seeing eye, but cognisant of compassionate curves, spaces neighbourly because partially concealed from one another.

This account might be extended: a curvilinear projection evidently informs the Madonna, as if she were painted on a convex surface bulging towards us, magnifying her form and especially her forward thigh at the expense of Joseph who, despite his planar proximity to Mary, seems warped away, depicted on a slope receding from us. But enough has been said perhaps to demonstrate the point that, from the beginning, Giorgione understood composition critically, as a process of eliminating the rhetorical licence of his masters and grounding his compositions environmentally through the use of a reversed or curvilinear perspective.

And again, the perspective was historical as well as poetic. For instance, the northern convention of locating the subject in the middle foreground and treating the landscape as two separate views flanking the subject provides an obvious precedent for the Castelfranco *Madonna*. The dissonance between the left and right-hand landscapes in such paintings also paves the way for Giorgione's conscious asymmetry. In this, as in so much else, Giorgione may have been anticipated by Leonardo. Gombrich has noted that in the *Mona Lisa* 'the horizon on the left hand side seems to lie much lower than the one on the right,' and suggests that the elusive expression and pose of the lady owe a great deal to this simple visual enigma.[68]

Gombrich would no doubt derive Leonardo's romantic landscape from northern sources.[69] This certainly applies to the landscapes of Leonardo's studio companion Lorenzo di Credi, with their curious assemblage of gothic towers and Alpine valleys. The lovely tondo, *Madonna and Child*, in the Quirini Stampalia Gallery in Venice (Plate 8) is typical in this respect. It also serves to highlight Giorgione's compositional originality. In the tondo, partly to give a superficial unity to two fanciful and unrelated backgrounds, partly in order to concentrate attention on the foreground figures, di Credi has placed mother and child directly in front of a monumental vertical: the wooden upright of what is presumably the cross. The compositional value of this or any similarly divisive vertical was well known to Giovanni Bellini (witness his *Crucifixion* in the Correr Museum, his *Madonna with Peter, Catherine, Lucy and Baptist* in the Metropolitan Museum of Art, New York). But neither Bellini nor di Credi seems to understand the vertical as an element of reversed perspective.

Giorgione did not pluck his forms *ex nihilo* – he inherited them from the visual lexicon of fifteenth-century painting, where they had conventional thematic associations. But he adopts these forms as if unaware of these associations, as if their significance will have to be discovered methektically, by exploring the peripatetic relationships between forms, the way they might bend space round themselves and so, as they migrate, appear to perform it, here drawing it out, there flinging behind them little vortices. This substitution of a processual mimicry for symbolic representation is not regressive; it presupposes the curvature of space. It assumes that within space's tense field of converging and diverging forces, forms do not occur at random, but crystallize at nodal points.

The meaning of Giorgione's paintings is determined metrically, by the exact placing of forms in relation to chromatically and spatially-associated neighbouring forms. To paraphrase a song is not simply, like any translation, to lose the richness of the original, but to lapse back into assuming that such works conceal their meaning, that a representable core of sense exists which can be extracted and taken away. But such works seek a coincidence between the naming and the thing named. They do not use ingenious metaphors to draw distant things near, to make them more visible; they work metonymically, to preserve the original proximity of things, their identity in difference.

To liken Giorgione's paintings to particular kinds of verbal composition is not to employ a merely poetic metaphor. At least it is no more metaphorical than their conventional comparison with music. In the early eighteenth century, Berkeley could maintain that 'visible figures represent tangible figures, much after the same manner that written words do sounds. Now in this respect words are not arbitrary, it being not indifferent, what written word stands for any sound.'[70] In this case, it was from an aesthetic point of view simply a matter of deciding which of the two media represented the world more vividly – a question Renaissance painters usually decided in favour of painting.

Think, says the Marchesa Vittoria Colonna in Francisco de Holanda's *Roman Dialogues*, of the effort a poet goes to in order to convey the impression of a storm. He usually uses too many words, and besides, each image replaces the previous one, so that by the end one has forgotten more than one has remembered. 'Now, how much more does the painter speak to you who depicts all at once the storm together with lightning-flashes [*lampi*], thunderbolts [*saette*], waves, shipwrecks, ships and reefs . . .'[71] If Giorgione's *Tempesta* is so unlike this storm, it is in part because Giorgione is talking a different language; one where, while nothing or little is represented, the environment of history is rendered tangible.

To make forms tangible, to put them back in touch with their surroundings, means abandoning any literary programme and rendering forms according to the curvilinear principles inherent in the physiology and psychology of visual perception. This is a point that Berkeley makes clear, and which is also implicit in Leonardo's researches into perspective: that the divorce of seeing from the other senses comes about from the attempt to model sight according to the rules of linear perspective. 'In vain,' protested Berkeley, 'shall all the mathematicians in the world tell me, that I perceive certain lines and angles which introduce into my mind the various ideas of distance; so long as I myself am conscious of no such thing.'[72]

Berkeley maintained that the judgement we make about the location of objects within the visual field is derived from experience. That is, it is in origin tangible. But, as is clear from a passage in his *Theory of Vision, or Visual Language, Vindicated and Explained*, our experience of the world is that it grows larger, not smaller, as it recedes. Imagine, Berkeley writes, a squared, diaphanous sheet held perpendicular to the plain: 'Those [parts and objects in the horizontal plain] that occupy most squares have a greater visible extension, which is proportional to the squares. But the tangible magnitude of objects is not judged proportional thereto. For those which are seen through the upper squares shall appear vastly bigger than those seen through the lower squares . . .'[73]

A similar intuition informs Giorgione's reversed perspective; to preserve our tangible experience of the environment, our sense of distant things growing in stature, it is necessary to resist the ideology of the vanishing-point and to insist on the curvature of space, which alone can account for our sense that distant things are magnified and draw close. Here, visual forms are not a kind of writing so much as the equivalent of poetic speech or song. The dialogue they maintain amongst themselves corresponds to the poet's assonance and alliteration. But more significant than this internal coherence is the implication that such paintings are performative; that they are mimetic histories of the environment, their composition representing a spatial mnemonic, a choreography.

If Giorgione was an historian of space, we can venture another Mexican parallel. The Mexican painters were historians because they were masters of the glyph. The hieroglyphic writing used by the Mexicans differed from the Europeans' alphabet in still retaining a physical link with the world it prolonged. Although its signs were like a slipstream stretching out behind objects and ideas, warping them towards a kind of thin immortality, the crouched chubbiness of the figures, temples, animals and dots they featured was not delusory. The style of the signs bore witness to the physico-mimetic origins of the gesture involved in drawing them, which was at once a stylized representation of a visual form and a visual cue to the oral memory. Charles Dibble explains that the pre-Columbian codices of the Aztecs functioned as memory images. The ideographs (glyphs) that conveyed the essential historical facts had to be complemented by an oral tradition capable of fleshing out the glyphic skeleton. 'The act of reading,' he writes, 'consists in reciting from memory under the stimulus of the glyphs.' The glyphs were as much heard as seen; the person entrusted with 'reading' the glyphs regarding it as his duty to recite aloud from memory while, perhaps, pointing with a finger to the 'text', thus ensuring that the glyphs would serve to revive the appropriate sounds when he was gone, and hence to keep history alive.[74]

The environmental reference of 'the old script of the Mexicans' was, in fact, brilliantly intuited nearly two centuries earlier by Herder. It was, he wrote, 'a living language. In it the great harmonising power of gestures provided, as it were, the order and sphere where things belonged . . . And where no picture came to mind, they agreed on strokes, and the coherence of it all must be supplied by the world in which it belonged and from which it is divined.' In line with the primitivism inherent in his evolutionary model of language, Herder imagined that the glyph was fundamentally imitative and grammarless, likening it to the 'detached signs' used by 'individual mute and deaf persons';[75] but as Sacks has reminded us, a deaf language can be 'at every level – lexical, grammatical, syntactic – a linguistic use of space: a use that is amazingly complex, for much of what occurs linearly, sequentially, temporally in speech, becomes simultaneous, concurrent, multilevelled in Sign. The "surface" of Sign may appear simple to the eye, like that of gesture or mime, but one soon finds that this is an illusion, and what looks so simple is extraordinarily complex and consists of innumerable spatial patterns nested, three-dimensionally, in each other.'[76]

But even Sacks's thesis may preserve a residual primitivism: to internalize the movement of the mind is not necessarily to advance. Sachs sees Sign as 'a unique evolutionary alternative',[77] but in view of the thesis about the origins of speech which Le Cron Foster has championed, it too may involve a foreclosure on the four-dimensional environment operating on speech, at least in its beginnings. According to Le Cron Foster, language may have originated in the mimetic translation of 'states and movements in space' into 'spatiosonant articulatory counterparts.'[78] Be this as it may, in the Mexican system writing – the silent symbolization of concepts – remains subordinate to recitation. The glyphs serve as a cue for speech. The ambition is to revive the voice. The visual images are notations for a vocal performance; and if these pedagogical displays occurred in public and employed ritualized physical gestures, then the glyphs may be considered as a kind of performance text. Rudolph Laban, the pioneer of dance notation, suggested that the Aztec signs involved 'a kind of choreutic symbol writing, now practically forgotten.'[79]

In any case, this connection with performance helps to define their character further. For the Nahuatl signs are not free-floating. They are not letters that can be combined to represent any sound; they remain tied to concepts. Furthermore, their order is not negotiable, but is fixed by the oral memory they themselves fix. Implicit in their appearance is an order in space as well as time. They allow certain steps or permutations of steps but not others, certain gestures but not others. European writing, by contrast, was a system for making things disappear. Letters might obey certain rules of combination, but these owed nothing to the nature of what they represented. There was nothing sculptural or remotely architectural about words, however much printers spliced them into lines and columns. The alphabet did away with the necessity of speech. Phonetic script presupposed that sounds could be represented independently of sounding them. Reducing voices to a kind of equivalence, making possible (in theory at least) their transportation and immediate reproduction elsewhere, letters were like coins; they facilitated trade, the exchange of unlike things, whilst remaining themselves unchanged, constant.

As Herder's contemporary – and a less romantic philosopher of language – Rousseau remarked: 'This [phonetic] way of writing, which is ours, must have been invented by commercial peoples who, in travelling to various countries, had to speak various languages, which would have impelled them to invent characters that could be common to all of them.'[80] Noting how script substitutes 'exactitude for expressiveness', he commented that 'This is not exactly to represent speech, but to analyse it.'[81]

The object here is not to seek to demonstrate a linear connection between Giorgione and the art of Mexico; it is to locate Giorgione's art historically, to suggest that the *Tempesta* is not an exercise in enigma but represents a view of the world achieved dialectically, through an engagement with the 'New World' of linear perspective. Nor was Giorgione alone in this. Settis does Giorgione a disservice, I think, when, in an attempt to place the *Tempesta* in an historical context, he identifies the artist's tastes and interests with those of his patron Gabriele Vendramin.[82] In my view, Vasari's association of Giorgione's art with Leonardo is far more persuasive, if only because it acknowledges Giorgione's scientific interest in the visual appearance of things.

Writing of the freer style Giorgione adopted at some time between painting the Castelfranco *Madonna* and the *Tempesta*, Vasari attributes his new mastery of chiaroscuro, his ability to create 'living forms and other things, soft, blended and shaded in the dark parts,' to the influence of Leonardo: 'Giorgione had seen some works by the hand of Leonardo, with a beautiful gradation of colours, and with extraordinary relief, effected, as has been related, by means of dark shadows; and this manner pleased him so much that he was for ever studying it as long as he lived, and in oil painting he imitated it greatly.'[83]

Presumably the two artists met in Milan, at the latest by 1507, during the time that Leonardo was writing notes for his proposed *Treatise on Painting*.[84] In any case, Leonardo's paintings, like Giorgione's, were heuristic: they were not humanistic explorations of symbolic images, but hypotheses about the nature of seeing. Chiaroscuro was part of a broader search for a perceptually accurate 'method', capable of imitating the true appearance and relation of things. Rejecting Alberti's imaginary lines, Leonardo studied a natural instance of rectilinear flight: the phenomenon of light. And what he found was that, invisible in itself, light was visible everywhere as colour. This was not only a physical discovery; it defined a philosophical bias. The truth was to be known by its effects, by its passages from one surface to another; and the effects, the differently-textured and positioned surfaces, were not accidents but the conditions of its becoming knowable. Knowledge in this sense was fundamentally environmental, a matter of understanding the historical migration and transformation of forms spatially.

Statements such as 'The surface of every opaque object partakes of the colour of the adjacent object. The painter must take care in placing things among other objects of different intensities of light and illuminated by different colours, keeping in mind that no subject is ever seen entirely in its true colour,'[85] or 'Since the end of one colour is the beginning of another, it must not be called a line, for nothing intervenes between one colour placed in front of another except its end, which is imperceptible even when viewed near at hand. Therefore, painter, do not accentuate it in distant objects . . . '[86] clearly gloss Giorgione's practice. One only needs to look at the steady alternation of foliage and tower, dark and light, differently affected by light and shadow, or to see how sky, tree and water partake of each other's colour, to feel the *Tempesta*'s debt to Leonardo. It is as if Leonardo had Giorgione's painting in mind when he remarked of lightning at night behind buildings, 'it suddenly seems, when it lightens, as though the height of the buildings were diminished.'[87] No wonder René Huyghe, who specifically linked Leonardo to Giorgione, could say '*Venise applique, en somme, la pensée que Leonardo da Vinci avait déjà exprimée et qui était si chargée d'avenir.*'[88]

But prophetic or not, Leonardo's observations were experimental, attempts to describe the psycho-kinetic appearance of light. They are directly related to his famous statement:

> The body of the atmosphere is full of infinite pyramids composed of radiating straight lines, which are caused by the boundaries of the surfaces of the bodies in light and shade, existing in the air; and the farther they are from the object which produces them the more acute they (the pyramids) become and although in their distribution they intersect and cross they never mingle together, but pass through all the surrounding air, independently converging, spreading, and diffused. And they are all of equal power (and value); all equal to each, and each equal to all.[89]

In this formulation, the nature of physical objects is entirely dependent on the positions from which they are seen, and as these positions are infinite, we can never have complete knowledge of them. To look at a landscape (or to paint it) is not to strive for a truthful representation of objects; it is to take as truthful a cross-section of 'the body of the atmosphere' as we can. For the forms we see do not exist over there, but as projections on to the eye; we know them as the curvilinear edge of air where they enter the eyeball. Wherever we stand it will be the same; this is what we will see, a cross-section of airborne, coloured forms.

The fact that no subject is ever seen entirely in its true colour underlines further the environmental nature of seeing. To see something in its true colour would be to see nothing at all. To see is always to see a field of mottled, textured colours; forms are merely their graded arrangement and to remove any one of the neighbouring tones would be to destroy their identity in difference. It would be as if the eye, instead of being a translucent shield on to which the world is projected and there further gathered, its roundness reinforced, were a spear which, believing all things met in the vanishing-point, pierced the air, looked into the eye of light, only to find nothing there.

And these are not fanciful images; they allude to a practical question of brushwork. If patches of colour are the primary constituents of curvilinear space, they cannot be applied, as they were in the Bellini studio, to fill in a space previously delineated in outline. They must mime the experience of seeing, our grasp of the environment in terms of mobile chiaroscuro. They must suggest forms as they converge on the eye, and not according to an ideal viewpoint; and they must limn the complementary and contrasting pathways between forms by advancing all parts of the canvas at once, maintaining an equilibrium throughout the field.

Only in this way, by *methexis* rather than mimesis, can the painting avoid coming between us and the environment; such painting will not represent nature but provide a performance of it, a choreography of marks that mimes the experience of looking. Vasari praised Giorgione's drawing: 'nature favoured him so highly, that he, having become enamoured of her beauties, would never represent anything in his works without copying it from life.'[90] But he is decidedly critical of Giorgione's '*invenzione*', contrasting Titian's scrupulous preparation with Giorgione's willingness to improvise, and observing that, for all his admirable sincerity, Giorgione 'failed to see that, if he wants to balance his compositions and to arrange his inventions well, the painter must first do various sketches on paper to see how everything goes together.'[91]

But is this interpretation sustainable? It provides an alibi for generations of critics who have passed over the composition of the *Tempesta* in silence, but it hardly explains why an artist dedicated to copying from life should abandon one method (that of Bellini and his school) for another (that of Leonardo) if the latter was likely to prove less reliable. True, Giorgione gave up preparatory sketches, producing the asymmetrical compositions deprecated by Vasari. He composed as he went along; where the soldier stands in the *Tempesta*, X-rays show that Giorgione originally painted a nymph (Plate 9). Later, it seems, he painted her out or replaced her with the gypsy mother who now occupies the picture's right hand. Later still, where the nymph had once been Giorgione painted the soldier.[92]

But these revisions, though they suggest an evolving idea, hardly betray formal uncertainty; the soldier and lance only enhance the emotional identity in difference that Giorgione sought when he doubled up the nymph. In effect, he replaced a mirror (the nymph) with a genuine admirer (the soldier), whose reflection on her would not collapse into mere repetition. And to enhance the subtle drama both of their meeting and of their parting, he reversed their chromatic relations; across the water from a mother whose earth-warm flesh tones glow against a white shawl thrown over her shoulders, a soldier stands, white-shirted, a crimson jacket thrown over his shoulders.

The effect of this is to define a second convergence within the painting: the gypsy is located at the focal point of a sideways-flowering 'V', although it might be more accurately likened to a tensed bow. The upper arm of this widening wedge is formed by the right-hand edge of the trees immediately behind the broken columns and continues by way of a stormlit cloud-edge across the river interval to the trees above the mother's head. The lower arm is a diagonal, defined by chiaroscuro, that originates about the soldier's turned face, follows the foliage edge across the plinth of the columns, and is picked up in the grassy border at the gypsy's feet.

Perhaps in earlier drafts of the painting the nymph at the lower left-hand corner harmonized with the light-dark arrangement of parts used to articulate this bow-like form; but little more. The addition of the soldier, his colourful jacket located exactly where the arrow might rest on the archer's thumb, turns that widening wedge on its head. We reverse our gaze, passing down the narrowing 'V' of buildings on the river's flank, and find ourselves on the light river bank, which by way of a purely rhythmic contrast of light and dark brings us to the soldier. It is not that the original focus of the painting is neutralized; rather that the elastic structure of the space is more tightly tuned. We have a sense of diagonals stretched across curved spaces, and that these diagonals, like projection lines on a globe, borrow the curvature of the bounding space, to this end wrapping themselves in the rope-like warp of storm clouds and leaves wind-strained like iron filings in a magnetic field.

It may be that, like Leonardo, Giorgione was not interested in the kind of poetry practised by Bembo and Poliziano; that he reacted against the humanistic cult of representation, with its repertoire of symbolic images and literary *istorie*, wanting to develop a visual language more akin to mimicry, a metrical interpretation of world. It was not a question of creating an illusion; Giorgione did not want to trick viewers into thinking they were looking through a window. Nor, like the Flemish, was he interested in baffling the eye with such richness of detail that a viewer's first reaction was not to take in the painting as a whole but to inspect the surface and to marvel at the technique. By mimicry he seems to have understood the environmental history of light; and this, it should be stressed again, was not simply a matter of esoteric taste. It represented a definite view, not only on aesthetic matters, but with regard to such apparently unrelated matters as the basis of the Venetian economy, the heliocentric theory of the universe, and the nature of human communication.

According to Acosta, the artists of New Spain were skilled in making 'images of feathers'. 'Some Indians,' he writes, 'which are good and expert workemen in this Art will represent perfectly in feathers, whatsoever they see drawne with the pencill, so as the Painters of Spaine have, in this point, no advantage over them.' And, he added, 'It is a goodly thing to see the lustre which a greene, an orange tawny like gold, and other fine colours do cast, and, beholding them another way, they seeme dead colours.' Acosta further relates that, when presented with a 'square . . . wherein was the figure of St Francis', Sixtus V 'desired to make triall thereof, touching the table with his fingers, to see if it were feathers, for that it seemed strange to see them so properly fitted, that the eye could not judge nor discern whether they were naturall colours of feathers, or artificiall, done with the pencil.'[93]

Acosta's report serves to characterize anecdotally the situation of artists like Giorgione, Titian and Tintoretto. On the face of it, the Venetians and the painters from the Mexican village of Pascaro shared similar interests. Both gemmed their designs, as Boschini would have said, with jewel-luscious colours. Both, it seems, sympathized with Leonardo's view that there were no lines in nature, that lines were simply the edges of overlapping colours. Both embraced his dictum that the colours of adjacent objects interacted with one another. Both understood Leonardo's observation that 'The lights which are produced from the polished surface of opaque bodies will be stationary on stationary objects even if the eye on which they strike moves. But reflected lights will, on those same objects, appear in as many different places on the surface as different positions are taken by the eye.'[94] Indeed, as the natural iridescence of parrot feathers exceeded anything achievable with pigment, the masters of Pascaro may be said to have out-Veniced the Venetians in exploring the behaviour of light. There was in their 'tables' a direct relationship between the mobility of the viewer and the appearance of nature. What looked lustrous here, there might look dead.

But there were also important differences. As no feather paintings have survived, we cannot comment on them. We can, though, interpret the European reactions. Whether or not the terms in which they praised them corresponded with the artists' intentions must remain a moot point, but they certainly throw light on an ambiguity at the heart of the Western doctrine of mimesis. As the feather paintings showed, mimesis, the representation of nature, was always in danger of collapsing into literal imitation or mimicry. The mathematical organization of external reality which centralized perspective intended was, in this context, an attempt to save mimesis from collapsing into mere mimicry. The Pope's desire to touch the painting, to ascertain whether the figure of St Francis was a visual or a tangible illusion, may reflect his unfamiliarity with Mexican aesthetics; but in any case, it indicates a Western tendency to confuse visual wealth with material wealth. If iridescent plumage is most highly-esteemed, it is because it creates the strongest visual illusion. In Venice, the equivalent of this would be the use of gold to represent gold, where gold (presumably like the Mexican plumes) symbolizes metaphysical light (the Sun, the Serpent) because of a literal resemblance.

The history of the aptly named Pala d'Oro in the apse of St Mark's is instructive in this regard. The Pala d'Oro was given its present appearance by Venetian craftsmen around 1345, but it incorporated a number of older, Byzantine enamels. The late Byzantine panels of the top register, representing the Six Holy Days of Our Lord, preserve a balance between the blue figures and their gold setting. Originally, no doubt, they were typical of the balance of blue and gold obtaining throughout the panel. But now, in their new setting, they have been reduced to little more than jewels, meant to flatter and highlight the face of gold. In the ninth and tenth centuries, cloisonné enamels filled the whole available space: 'The background extending around figures and objects, in particular, is entirely enamelled.'[95] By the middle of the tenth century, gold was acquiring a new prominence in the design: 'It became the practice to confine the enamelling to the subject represented, which was thus made to stand out against a gold background.'[96] This was technically simpler, and encouraged Venetian artists to schematize their designs. As a result, 'the fillets tended to grow thicker, the network of golden lines patterning the surface became increasingly conspicuous, to the detriment of the areas of colour which they were originally intended only to delimit and throw into relief.'[97]

Byzantine artists had conceived of all colour (and not simply gold) as 'light materialised'.[98] In Venice, however, gold and light became punningly confused. What had been a technique of symbolic representation became over time a substitute for it, a way of mimicking wealth in every sense. The vulgarization of light as gold was not confined to the Pala d'Oro; as far as one can judge, it extended to the physical aspect of Venice during the fourteenth and fifteenth centuries where, increasingly, colour yielded to gold or to gold's best equivalent in stone, marble. Ruskin imagined Venice in the thirteenth and early fourteenth centuries as 'a city of graceful arcades and gleaming walls, veined with azure and warm with gold, and fretted with white sculpture.' He surmised that it was the interior of St Mark's that inspired Venetians to decorate water-bordering palace exteriors in the same way. Statues, too, he said, were frequently gilded.[99]

Since we know so little about Gothic polychrome statuary,[100] this latter statement cannot be verified, but Ruskin's broader picture seems confirmed by Pietro di Natali who, in a poem written about 1382 describing the meeting (in 1177) between Barbarossa and the Pope, imagines the dignitaries sightseeing: they admired the gilded [*dorate*] churches, but most of all they were impressed by 'the resplendent houses and how many beautiful palaces there are built and buildings in every corner, with lead, gold and marble adorned, with columns, turrets and high towers, worthy of kings and cardinals.'[101]

By Giorgione's day, however, the chromatic character of Venice seems to have undergone a significant change. Philippe de Commynes, writing in 1495, comments: 'The houses are exceedingly large and high, and of good stone, and the ancient ones all painted. The others built within this last hundred years are all faced with white stone brought from Istria, a hundred miles away, and yet have many a large piece of porphyry and serpentine on the front.'[102] Some idea of the ancient aspect of Venice can still be gained by visiting the islands of Burano or Chioggia, where the single-storey fishermen's cottages, with whole walls intensely burnt sienna or egg-yolk chrome or forget-me-not blue, stand a permanent rainbow along the water's edge.

In view of these, it seems incontestable that 'at least in intensity and variety of colour the face of Venice has not grown, but diminished, with the centuries' passing.'[103] Ruskin, who shared this view, was even prepared to provide a cause: Roman pride and Florentine geometry. In the early Renaissance, he protested, 'the architects began to be too proud to receive assistance from the colourists.'[104] Besides investing in Istrian marble – which, as de Commynes implies, was a dullish stone without the crystalline lustre of true marble – the richest Venetians began to import the much flashier and richer-looking stone of Carrara. Carrara increasingly replaced coloured stone, notably the *broccatello* of Verona; and, as it shone from mantelpiece and balustrade, it seemed to contract something of gold's prestige.

Outside, Carrara's first significant appearance in Venice occurs in the crocketed coping of the west façade of St Mark's and in certain of the statues there, executed in the early part of the fifteenth century, where it was conceived as the stone counterpart of the gold mosaics in the doorways below, still visible in their glory in Gentile Bellini's *Procession of the True Cross*.[105] Inside, gold and its equivalent, marble, shone everywhere, if we can extrapolate from what Pietro Casola saw in 1494. 'The fireplace was all of Carrara marble, shining like gold,' he writes of a lying-in chamber belonging to the Delfini family, and adds, suitably impressed, 'The ceiling was . . . richly decorated with gold and ultramarine . . .'[106] De Commynes, visiting Venice a year later, makes the same report. There are usually, he observes, at least two bedrooms '*qui ont les planchez doréz, riches manteaulx de cheminées de marbre tailléz, les chalitz des liztz doréz, et les ostevens painctz et doréz, et fort bien meubles dedans*.'[107]

To judge from the sumptuary decrees passed in 1512 in the wake of the formation of the League of Cambrai, the love of gold had never been so indulged. 'The value of golden necklaces . . . was not to surpass 100 ducats and the use of golden or silver threads or of golden belts was prohibited.' Like dress, decoration was to be less opulent. A maximum of 150 ducats was to be spent on gold leaf or painting, and 'the householder was forbidden to buy vain gold objects – boxes, mirrors, vessels.'[108] Another indication of the changing times: it is recorded that Bartolomeo Buon's earliest recorded commission, a wellhead executed in red verona for the *cortile* of the Cà d'Oro (another palace to benefit from incandescent Carrara), was replaced by more precious porphyry when it became available.[109]

During the fifteenth century coloured stone was on the retreat. It survived, if at all, in the form of precious wall jewels of serpentine and porphyry; but these had no constructive value – they swam in an increasingly brilliant sea of gold and marble. 'There are those who use gold immoderately in their paintings,' wrote Alberti no later than 1435, 'who think that gold lends their paintings majesty. I do not praise them.'[110] And in the use of colours, Alberti advised the painter to take account of a certain '*amicizia*' between them, so that they lend each other dignity and grace.[111] Evidently, Venice's builders and sculptors were not heeding this advice.

In short, the impoverishment of colour in late fifteenth-century Venice was associated with an increasingly vulgar mimicry of light. The old equilibrium between parts suggested by an *amicizia* of differently-coloured façades had been replaced by a fashion for façades that were Venices in themselves – a Lagoon of Istrian stone in which were set precious islands of porphyry, serpentine or fragments of patterned marble. It is hard to believe that this new anxiety to have the city masquerade as golden was unconnected with the discovery of gold in the New World, and with the accelerated shift of power and influence away from Venice that this meant. As the income from Venice's former sea empire dwindled, it became harder to maintain appearances; gold became an obsession and, as the alchemist Mamugnano was to discover, in this matter the Venetians could easily be gulled.

The Venetian governor of Famagusta, Count Marco Antonio Bragadini, captured and killed by the Turks in 1571, was said to have left behind him a son called Mamugnano. This Mamugnano, having enjoyed great success in the East as an alchemist, came to Italy in 1578. In Brescia he won the favour of the Margrave Martinengo, who furnished him with introductions to the noblest in Venice. He demonstrated his powers of turning quicksilver into gold in the house of the Nobile Cantareno. His fame spread rapidly. At this time the Senate received (monthly, it seemed) reports from Spain of gold bullion arriving from the Americas. It lost no time in cultivating the newcomer. It protected him from the Pope. It patronized him.

In such congenial circumstances, the alchemist blossomed. In 1590 the renowned Bragadini 'holds banquets daily for five hundred people and lives in princely style in the Palazzo Dandolo on the Giudecca. He literally throws gold about in shovelfuls.' His cup ran over. '*Illustrissimo*' he was called by the greatest in the Lagoon.[112] The Doge addressed him in the second person. Then he made a promise he could not keep: he proposed to manufacture fifteen or sixteen million sequins. But they were not forthcoming. It was rumoured that he defrauded Venice. 'It was realised that his craft did not go beyond one pound of quicksilver, however much various persons begged him to produce more.'[113] People looked for themselves; what the alchemist claimed to transmute into gold was not quicksilver, but gold itself! Retribution came as swiftly as fame, the punishment sneeringly Venetian: Mamugnano was hanged from a gilt gallows, in a garment studded with gold spangles.[114]

Wanting to dramatize the wages of false representation, Marlowe need have looked no further than the history of Master Bragadini. The deeper meaning of his play, though, would have been its rehearsal of the tragic dumb-show of colonization, the career of men like Columbus and Cortés who, in the name of gold, insisted on interpreting every eye-catching ear-ring as a vanishing point viewed from the other side; but hop through its eye and a widening pyramid, a treasure-house would be found, its riches increasing the further they penetrated. No wonder they regarded the diplomatic mimicry of those they came across as an elaborate deception. The Spaniards persistently mistook the Indians for alchemists; the choice was theirs, to produce gold or to pay the price of counterfeiters.

To disguise poverty by trading profitably with the eye: this was a permanent Venetian preoccupation. In 1786, visiting Il Redentore, Goethe noted 'the side altars all covered in what looked like a magnificent arabesque embroidery. I was particularly impressed by the tendrils and leaves embroidered with gold thread, and when I looked closer I discovered an ingenious trick. Everything I had taken for gold was actually straw, pressed flat and painted on paper in beautiful designs. The ground was painted in vivid colours and everything was executed in excellent taste . . .'[115] But we may surmise that the question of what constituted false 'gold', and what true, assumed a particular political and economic urgency in the early 1500s.

Conquistadors frequently fancied that the gleaming white walls of the Mexicans' cities were wrought of silver or gold. Gomara comments: 'I doe believe that with the imagination and great desire which they had of golde and silver, all that shined they deemed to be of the same metall.'[116] This, in effect, was the object of the Venetians: to make foreigners see wealth where there was none, or less than might be thought. And Venice's reputation also worked in the opposite direction; Hojeda, Vespucci's first captain, coming upon 'the finest harbour in the world', named it the Gulf of Venice, at the same time congratulating himself that he had 'discovered gold, though not in any great quantity . . .'[117] Provided appearances did not lie, what was Venetian by name should prove Venetian by nature.

This form of sympathetic magic masquerading as inductive logic had painterly implications too. If, as Acosta claimed, the expert workmen of Mexico were able, using feathers, to match the painters of Spain (among whom Acosta would have counted Titian), there was an argument for giving up traditional painting techniques; even the jewel-like colour which Giovanni Bellini achieved using Antonello da Messina's new method of painting in oils could not rival the brightness of feathers. Their lustre could produce 'an orange tawny like gold' no Western painter's palette could equal. If the object of art was to mimic wealth's symbol, gold, as closely as possible, to trick the eye into seeing (even touching) what was not there, then the Venetians should have fashioned arrows out of their paintbrushes and taken to shooting birds.

These were not choices available to Giorgione or the youthful Titian; feather paintings did not become known in Europe until the 1530s. But the interest they aroused, and the reasons for which they were admired, point to the vulnerability of artists who, however original their *invenzioni*, might find themselves outmanoeuvred technologically. Before gold poured into Europe from the New World, the Venetian cult of gold had had a symbolic value: it represented unattainable as well as attainable wealth, even if the spiritual was increasingly collapsed into the material. But the gold bullion produced by melting down Cuzco and Tenochtitlán made it unnecessary to mimic gold; it defined those who used gold leaf sparingly and showily as the newly impoverished.

In short, the material wealth flowing from the New World changed the position of painters. What did it mean now to employ 'jewel-like colour'? What cultural anxiety was implied when Pietro Aretino praised the '*aureo colore di porpora ornato*' (golden colour suffused with purple) of his friend Titian?[118] Between the Florentine science of representation and the new world of mimetic effects, how was Venetian painting to define its interests? As is clear, this was not simply a question of technique or taste; it reached to the very heart of Venetian identity. In particular, it might reflect a measured judgement on a society which, after facing eastwards culturally and economically for the best part of a millennium, had in the preceding century begun to turn its attention (and its investment capital) towards the Italian mainland.

When the Veronese Bartolomeo Cipolla acknowledged that what was elsewhere an undoubted reason for social inferiority was permitted in Venice for the sake of a '*necessitas loci in quo nulli alii redditus vel fructus nisi ex mercimonio haberi possunt*,'[119] he caught both Venice's strength and her weakness: her wealth, her promotion of the circulation of goods, was born of necessity. Her overseas connection had made her wealthy because her physical location yielded nothing. She was rich because she was poor. But let the arteries of trade harden and clog up, as they did after the fall of Constantinople and under the growing maritime power of Portugal and Spain, and her lifeblood was denied her.

Aware of the way the trade winds were blowing, Venice had taken the thoroughly un-Venetian step of looking to relocate her empire on the Italian mainland. As early as 1405, for example, her troops had taken Verona. But this was not simply the pragmatic redirection of trade routes: it was a change of economy. Venice's colonies in the eastern Mediterranean had been little more than a chain of military outposts designed to protect Venice's trading routes. Little or nothing was drawn from the local economies. By contrast, the control of Verona had nothing to do with the encouragement of trade; it was a purely imperial arrangement – the Veronese territories were to provide what Venice could not provide for herself:

> The country around Verona is rich in corn, oil and wine, fruit and excellent stone, in rivers, waters and lakes: amongst which is Garda, the most beautiful and delightful lake in the whole of Italy: and it has many restorative springs which, one imagines, were used in antiquity as baths, as they are still hot and traces of wall can still be seen round them. But what shall we say of the city's most noble position? In truth, is there anything more beautiful, more delightful to behold? Never was there a painter, however skilful, who drew a more smiling, more agreeable countryside. Almost all the city is either a plain or faces towards the south, as towards the east and west, and the land rises pleasantly towards the north. The mountains here curve round neatly and agreeably so as to form almost a theatre, lightly embracing a valley which lies between them and contains vineyards and most attractive gardens; these are so pleasing to anyone who sees them at a distance that his heart is at once uplifted with joy.[120]

The terms in which Venice's official historian Sabellico describes Verona and its environs represents a profound change of orientation. Here, it is implied, is the Roman pedigree the Venetians longed to established; here the building-stone they lacked, the fresh water they wanted, the fruit for the picking they must trade for. Here, we notice, was even the curved space the Venetians had to construct for themselves; here, perhaps, was Giorgione's commission. Here, certainly, was the natural wealth which Venice could only imitate. Venice was a magnificent masquerade, but you only had to peer beneath the surface of its painted faces, or let a low tide drain the colour from its opaline waters, to detect the putrid shallowness of its foundations, and to fathom the desperation that shadowed its magnificent boast. As Grand Tourist Joseph Spence remarked, "'Tis the most melancholy and the most gay place in the world.'[121]

There were romantics who refused to acknowledge Venice's vulnerability. Pietro Aretino, overlooking the Rialto market, could write, 'I have here vines in barges, game and small birds in the shops,' and could declare, 'What do I care about seeing streams that water the fields, when every dawn I see the water covered with every kind of produce the season has to offer?'[122] But the tide of economic history was turning against him. Better the bird in the hand than the bird in the air, as Aretino's enemy Francesco Berni advised.[123] When the Venetians gained a foothold on the mainland, they grew less content to rely on sea-borne fruit and vegetables; they wanted to grow their own frugal jewels, and, Molmenti says, the number of gardens in Venice and its surrounding islands rapidly increased.[124]

Venice owed a chromatic debt to Verona, to her painters, her masons, her stone. But it is the same story. As with the blues of Byzantium, so with the greens and reds of Verona; in Venice, they drain away. To an extent it was unavoidable. Granted that the dampness of the Lagoon made fresco difficult to handle, and the expense of mosaic, the Venetians could not import Giambono's coloured walls. The Ducal Palace was a partial exception. In general, the Venetians confined ochres and *verdes* to transoms and ship's figureheads. If Gentile da Fabriano, in whose studio Jacopo Bellini trained, encouraged the Venetian love of gold, then Pisanello (who helped paint the Ducal Palace frescoes lost in the fire of 1577) represented Veronese taste. Giambono, Stefano and Pisanello replaced the blue and gold beloved of the International Gothic style with red and green. Not until Giorgione's *Tempesta* does green, the layered aquamarine green, turbulent, coiled and faceted, of Pisanello's *St George*, find Venetian acceptance.

With stone, with Verona's pink *broccatello*, the growing bias against decorative colour is clearer. Whatever has been lost inside the Ducal Palace, outside it stands as Verona's great triumph. And, understanding what gleaming white stone came to signify, its rosy foliage flowering on a marble espalier, symbolizes the convergence and synthesis of Byzantium and Verona, Orient and Occident. Yet the later Piazzetta façade shows a distinct decline in chromatic complexity. Along the older Lagoon facade, the centres of the brick diamonds may be black or white or red, but on the Piazzetta side the formula has become mechanical; the centres are almost invariably of red Verona.

It is as if jostling lozenges of water have been frozen; as if a hand-stitched shawl had been replaced by a machine-produced garment; as if the elastic chiaroscuro of light in flight had yielded to a chequerboard of stuck-on feathers. Vastly outnumbered by their white neighbours, the two red columns in the Piazzetta's upper arcade are the last survivors of a colourful temperament apparently doomed in the Lagoon. Whatever its provenance, colour in Venice seemed to be absorbed into a generalized, mesmeric golden light. We have mentioned the fate of Buon's well-head. By the middle of the following century the use of *broccatello* had so declined in Venice that Vasari was frankly perplexed: 'Notwithstanding the fact that the Adige makes it easy to transport mixed and other kinds of stone from Verona, you see few things executed in them here.'[125]

The picture I have tried to paint here, while no doubt overdrawn, is one in which the *Tempesta* cannot be regarded as the effortless expression of a spirit and a culture in equilibrium. That painting's curvilinear perspective, achieved as much chromatically as formally, needs in my view to be seen as the expression of a historical moment, as a point of convergence. In it, in the art of Giorgione, there met critical questions about the nature of seeing. These could not be resolved theoretically, by recourse to Florentine perspective. Nor could they be satisfied by persisting in the jewel-like colour of the Bellini brothers, even if we can endorse Rosand's view that Giovanni's tonal values opened a way to Titian: 'The rationality of Brunelleschian geometry, its clear linear articulation, is muted by the irrational glow of golden mosaics and by a tonal envelope that obscures the precision of contours.'[126]

Colour had lost its constructive value, becoming increasingly arbitrary, local and subservient to gold. Even light, which gold was said to imitate best, was under threat. It had become hard, as if manufactured by looking-glasses. To see differently, neither mimicking appearances nor construing them as deceptive appearances, meant finding a different mode of painting, one more akin to methexis, capable of re-enacting an environmentally mobile and implicated vision, one that settled nowhere because it circulated familiar country. This would entail giving back to colour its constructive function as a way of defining the relationships between forms. It would also mean developing a choreography of the brush corresponding to our own navigation of our surroundings and the continuous rearrangement of appearances this produces.

A chromatically-organized passage back and forth across the visual field would not collapse into arbitrariness. It would resemble the way in which non-Western peoples are said to find their way through country which to Western eyes is featureless: by composing contiguous, but unlike, features into a network of remembered pathways. These describe not an autobiography, a merely personal journey, but a repeatable topography, a mnemno-kinetic device for inhabiting the land and traversing it without reducing it to so many signs – those semaphores, flashing lights and scarlet pennants so characteristic of colonization.

To paint in this way would be implicitly to ally oneself with Venice's oldest cultural attachments: to the open circulation of precious goods, and to a system of visual design which refused the opposition between false and true representations, regarding all representations as merely strategic positions, as poses whose value was choreographic, a matter of timing and opportunity. A painting produced under these conditions might be able to embrace the paradox of a silent thunderbolt, a peaceful storm. For as nothing was represented, nothing was denied; the sudden tongue of light was not sudden after all. It had been foretold by the general discharge of forms that occurs endlessly across spaces, across seas, across glances. The mistake would be to arrest the process of exchange, to suppose it meant anything.

Such an art would be a parabolic return to origins. It would revive the Byzantine love of mobile light without divorcing it from historical contingencies. Lindsay remarks how 'Plotinus takes over Aristotle's idea of the relation of energy and potency,' but removes it 'from the actual world of change and becoming'. The concept of *energeia* comes to be used to describe the nature of the One: 'The trinity of *ousia, dynamis, energeia* (being, emitted potency, actualisation or fulfilment) . . . is taken over by the pseudo-Dionysios and was adopted by the Christians.' And Lindsay observes that by rendering matter inert and passive – 'a concept close to that held by Plato of Space (comparable to a mirror or a screen)' – Plotinus provided the metaphysical basis for a purely mechanical, or we might say rectilinear, theory of motion: 'The complex qualitative as well as quantitative unity of the object, organic or inorganic, is disintegrated.'[127]

Mathew speculates that 'The custom of gazing at a decorated surface is perhaps essentially Western,' and certainly the mosaics of St Mark's and Ravenna conform to the Byzantine sense that 'Only by moving the eyes could all the surface be touched by visual rays.'[128] They seem to assume a projective theory of sight akin to that propounded in Plato's *Timaeus*, where it is maintained that 'the organ of vision' consists of 'fire', and that colour is 'a flame given off from bodies': 'Assuming that there is this effluence and that [effluence and organ] must unite, he holds that the [visual stream] issues forth for some distance and coalesces with the effluence, and thus it is that we see.'[129] This accords with the impression that, in Byzantine art, 'depth was considered more important optically than width or height, but it was conceived as being in front of the mosaic or picture, not behind it . . . The "picture space" of Byzantine art was primarily that of the church or the palace room in which it was placed, since art was considered a functional part of architecture.'[130]

Venetian painters from Giorgione to Tintoretto and Tiepolo also seem intent on creating a visual space that converges on the spectator's own standing room. Rosand has written of Titian's 'reluctance to exploit orthogonal recession; rather, deliberately countering the spatial momentum of perspective construction, he favours a shallow foreground stage.'[131] Even Tintoretto, who specializes in steeply-raked perspectival coulisses and theatrical back-lighting, employs these depths 'in reverse', producing vertiginous convergences about the surface in the centre of the composition, where linear perspective would have left an empty space. But unlike the earlier mosaicists, these artists do not metaphysicalize the dynamics of energy transfer, nor do they subject its behaviour to rectilinear laws.

In this sense only the Venetians remain Aristotelian. They imagine light as the force continuously applied to objects, as the medium of their attraction, transaction and transformation. The dramas of light that they paint propose light as *dynamis*, as the energy that projects forms into history, into connection with one another. *Energeia* or kinetic force also derives partly from the omnipresence of pressing light, but what lends light its shape (and its non-Aristotelian, curvilinear harmony), are the forms themselves that it illuminates. Their different tones and shapes carve back light, cooling it or warming it, reflecting it or absorbing it, mingling it with neighbouring tones, lending it the substantial body of shadow. They are not dead *materia* nostalgic for an after-life; re-enacting essential environmental relations, they are absorbed in one another. Like the half-moon of green cloud, which is the gypsy's breast by another name – which is also the Byzantine cupola in a different axis – they turn towards one another, lovers, making of chance coincidences a different history.

The critical step in developing a methektic mode of representation was the evolution of the blot technique, the art of *macchiare* so lyrically described by Marco Boschini in *La Carta del Navegar Pitoresco*. The art of blotting comprised every aspect of the Venetian use of colour: from the application of oil paint in thick solid masses (*impasto*) and the manner of the brush's 'attack', to the harmonizing of colours, the rounding-out of figures with deepening tones, and the use of glazes. But, as Pallucchini argues, Boschini understood the *macchia* in two particular senses: as the physical gesture of making a blot, and as the process of building up the picture surface, almost like the mosaicist, 'with the brush's bruising blow.'[132]

The highly original point is that the *macchie* out of which the Venetian design develops are not natural blots: they are impressions left by physical gestures. They are brush-mediated handprints, brushprints whose features – depth, contour, physical size, drag and lean – can be read exactly as the native tracker might read the spoor of a beast of prey. Leonardo had famously referred to the *macchie* in nature which, like Rorschach blots, could stimulate the artist's *invenzione*, but Boschini's blots have a subtly different provenance. Not fortuitous discoveries mimicking forms, they are exploratory gestures on their way to becoming forms. They produce forms rather than reproduce them. Halfway between projections of the mind and images of nature, they foster a system of composition based on mere coincidences.

As Boschini writes: 'One sees how Nature with such great Art agrees in wanting to make herself immortal; and with blots of colour very often studies to imitate figures in marbles and planks. And granted she does not achieve perfection, she at least approaches somewhat the true light by imitating the Venetian way of painting, regarding that method of blotting [*macchiar*] as both beautiful and good.'[133] The Venetian art of *macchiare* understands these suggestive blots of colour not as proto-images in the Tuscan manner, but as steps or marks orienting the painter to the true path to composition. 'O a thousand times glorious road, which represents Nature superficially with blots of colour and wandering tints. The same art of the blot tenderly unites in a good design light and dark, detaches forms and shapes them truly, with plastic feeling, rounding them out in wonderful ways.'[134]

The Venetian artists respect the jewel-like colour of their Byzantine precursors but interpret it differently, physically rather than metaphysically. Colour, the relationships between colours, is for them a means of mobilizing the picture plane, a way of getting from one part of it to another, uniting all parts, bringing all parts forward equally, deepening here, lightening there: 'The Venetians block in the histories [*Istorie*] with those colours that come to hand, designing and composing at one and the same time.'[135] Figures are formed, grounds in between them fixed simultaneously. But even when figures are detached and brought forward, they remain grounded. They are like the crests of waves; the shadowy setting flowing round them, the troughs in-between. As spaces look forward to the human drama, so the figures are 'rounded', keeping physically present the curvature of space about them.[136]

Colour alone could not mobilize the picture plane. 'Those rosy flesh tints and bruises of colour, those streaks made with the finger, that rough outline [which] makes living figures move,' depend for their effect on the use of chiaroscuro. It is the passage between light and dark that the painter has to keep continuously in play; light and dark, like left and right footsteps, supply the mechanism and the points of reference.[137] The art of *macchiare* is a process consisting of the gradation of light and dark, the relative depths of tones. As Boschini explains, the Venetian artists first filled in the outlines with solid colour:[138] 'Their great object at this stage was to distinguish the advancing from the retreating portions, that the figures might be relieved by means of chiaroscuro – one of the most important departments of Colour, Design and, indeed, of Invention.'

Having corrected his forms from nature, but not before, the artist painted the colour of flesh. When this layer was dry, he began to reassert the chiaroscuro, 'scumbling over this or that figure with a low tint to make it stand out from its neighbour.' Then he began to add new highlights 'on a head, a hand or a foot, thus detaching them, so to speak, from the canvas, as you can see in Tintoretto's *San Rocco in Prison*.' This process of adding highlights and deepening shadows consists, Boschini warns, 'not in covering entire figures, but rather in gemming them [*gioielandole*].' At the end, the painter left 'the bodies of great masses in middle light, still with many dark areas and few lights.'[139]

This peripateia of the picture plane, this accretion of surfaces, defines the difference between those New World mosaicists, the feather-painters of Pascaro, and the Venetians. 'The imitation of nature in painting is therefore justly called colouring; but the painter arrives at his end by indirect means. He gives the variety of tones in masses [*macchie*]; he smartly impinges lights, he clothes his preparation with more delicate hues, he unites, he glazes; thus everything depends on the process. For if we look at colour abstractedly, the most positive may be called the most beautiful, but if we keep the end of imitation in view, this shallow conclusion falls to the ground.'[140] It also distances Giorgione and Titian from the local cult of golden light. Unlike the Flemings and other *copiisti*, Boschini writes, 'If by chance one of our great painters depicts a coat of armour, a golden vase, a reflecting mirror or other similar object, he makes it gleam [*straluser*] with colours.'[141]

One begins to see that Titian's 'golden colour suffused with purple' was not simply a representation of gold by indirect means. The dimpling of the picture plane was equivalent to the goldsmith beating out gold leaf until it became a basin of light whose hammer-bruises glowed so intensely they looked dark. In a similar vein, Boschini describes the armour of the Roman emperor Claudius in a lost painting attributed to Giorgione as 'well-tempered with his brush'.[142] The lancelike paint brush of the great artist could be likened to a sword or to an arrow flawlessly finding its mark, but either way, its object was not to pierce, to cut through, but to lay open what was concealed, to create a coloured passage for light.[143] In the same way, the gondola, averse to being swallowed up in water's underground, sliced open water to duplicate light out of darkness. In the same way, the Taino canoes sped obliquely towards the water's lip, where they did not shrink to nothing but turned into the vertically elongated brushstrokes of mangroves and palms.

These analogies may not be wholly fanciful. To bring forms forward, to suggest their continuity with the environment out of whose depths they sprang, Venetian painters increasingly adopted dark grounds. Even when they represented autumnal forests or brooding thunderous suburbs, they had in mind reflected light, water's curvilinear cuirass. A gesso ground might give the colours a luminous quality, but to paint highlights, white on white, or shadows, which merely deadened the luminosity, was hardly possible unless a second, darker ground was added. The glow of Bellini's paintings, based on a white ground, has little to do with the light Titian created. His understanding of aerial perspective enabled him subtly to diffuse and lighten distant mountains, but the foreground figures remained quite detached, defined by line and local colour.

To free themselves of this genial, timeless serenity, to capture light in movement, the thunder of history, Titian and Tintoretto covered the white ground with a layer of red or red-black gouache, which could then be highlighted with white.[144] By this means, they did away with the underground space or metaphysical depth signified by the white ground of the Florentines, replacing it with successive layers of paint, each of which served as a further surface to be painted over. But not simply to be covered; the art lay in allowing the under colours to shadow through. And to this end, the artist not only added glaze upon glaze but carved back the surface, revealing here and there forgotten depths, sculpting odd knots of highlight; and in general treating his canvas as a miniature topography of Alpine hills and valleys, or even more locally, a storm-whipped sea.

Titian at least carved wood as well as painting. Wood carving meant 'the "liberation" of the drawn line from the wood', taking account of the forces and stress lines inherent in the matrix itself, differentiating and articulating these – a process directly analogous to building up and paring back the picture surface. Rosand and Muraro remark of Titian's monumental woodcut *The Triumph of Christ*: 'At once preserving the energies of the basic drawing and recording the very carving process by which it is realized, its complex of black and white marks, broadly impressionistic in effect yet retaining the individual force of each stroke, is the graphic equivalent of the Venetian *pittura di macchia*.'[145]

It is as if these artists brought into accord the lance and the shield, understanding that the 'point', although a geometrical necessity, was never sharp in the phenomenal world. The point was a zone of relatively high pressure which might be represented as accurately by a shield-shaped cloud as by a flint-tipped dart. It is also as if they understood the world metrically, timing their brushstrokes to the changing moods of things, taking their opportunities flexibly, agilely, like hunters after their prey. It is because foreign painters do not understand the art of *macchiare*, Boschini says, that they start again if they make a mistake; but the Venetian painter goes on, circling, coming back.[146] In a similar spirit of humility, not pride, Montaigne could remark, 'I rarely repent.'[147]

It was as if, in contrast with the Mexican artists who had to shoot the birds in order to portray their iridescent flight, the Venetian artists found a way of catching light on the wing; which is to say, as it was reflected and, according to rules of crossplay determined by the environment, went about its business of *macchiare*, lending the outlined shells and ammonites in stone the appearance, not of marine animals come to life, but of embryo forms, whose constitutional chiaroscuro rendered them capable of evolving not only an infinity of forms, but of shadowing forth their common genealogy.

To be clear, this intuition of a structural resemblance or community between superficially unlike things was both physical and metaphysical because it was kinetic, at once invisible and visible, taking the curvilinear tracks of things as a natural condition of their being in the world, defining their composition as an environment. It was based on the kind of dynamic conception of the environment explicit in Sarpi, which enabled him to conceive of the circulation of the blood. Venetian space was conceived of as a medium; it was built up, as the painting was built up, not through the proliferation of little bridges from one part to another but in reverse as it were, through the continuous vibration of the medium itself, whose varying tones produced locally different forms, intensities of colour and rates of progress.

Rosand recognizes the role the rough cross-weave of the painter's canvas played in stimulating fantasy,[148] but what of the plastic properties of oil paint? Oil paint was a colloid suspension that had perhaps something in common with D'Arcy Thompson's dynamical conception of the cell, where

> We then deal not with material continuity, not with little bridges of connecting protoplasm, but with a continuity of forces, a comprehensive field of force, which runs through and through the entire organism and is by no means restricted in its passage to the

> protoplasmic continuum. And such a continuous field of force, somehow shaping the whole organism, independently of the number, magnitude and form of the individual cells, which enter like froth into its fabric, seems to me certainly and obviously to exist.[149]

True, we cannot prove the existence of this environmental surface tension, but its existence in microcosm must have been an everyday experience for the painter. The fixing of pigments in a colloid suspension preparatory to painting depended on the availability of a medium (gum or egg-white in tempera, or vegetable oils in the case of the secret method of oil painting brought to Italy from the Netherlands by Antonello da Messina[150]) which was invisible and internally cohesive. It was the internal force field of the chosen medium that ensured the equilibrium of pigment particles, for as D'Arcy Thompson noted, surface tension is a phenomenon by no means limited to outer surfaces: 'within the heterogeneous emulsion of the cell . . . we have a multitude of inner surfaces.'[151]

So in a painting by Titian, thirty or forty glazes[152] create a chromatic environment isomorphic with the viscous, curvilinear appearance of the Venetian world. Sized colours, translucent but tangible, somewhere between water and glass, actively assisted and guided the process of composition. Although leaving little trace beyond a deepening of shadow with successive glazes, their drag on the brush lent painting a tempo. The localization of colour, the steady alternation of light and dark, expressed the temporality of the medium. The thirty or forty glazes Titian applied to a painting, going over worked ground, advancing every part of the painting together, were like dance figures. The successful composition grew out from the hand's well-tempered choreography.

And this was a microcosm of circulation in Venice, where curvilinear perspective served to keep the uniquely flat surface of the Lagoon creative, capable of crystallizing islands and towers. It was as if the oil and tempera canvases of Titian and Giorgione were cross-sections of a curved force field; the art of *macchiare* consisted in identifying nodal points in the painting's flat surface where oblique lines of convergence poured up through the surface or entered it, plunging back into the third dimension. To keep all these forces in play, to prevent the stretched canvas warping and folding up, it was necessary to tap these force-lines and, lending them a crystalline structure along this plane, to induce an equilibrium. So with

Venice's leaning towers: their inclination was not a weakness, but a sign of their connection with the elastic environment, and the mutual balance and convergence of parts.

After a false Renaissance of Carrara and gold, patriotic Venetians found the renovation of colour attractive. Writing in 1557, Dolce says: 'Outside, many prefer their houses and palaces painted by hand, rather than covered with white marbles, porphyries and serpentines inlaid in gold.'[153] It seems reasonable to associate this return to origins with the prestige of artists like Titian and Giorgione, who in addition to their works on canvas were energetic painters in fresco, collaborating most notably in the now largely lost allegory for the Fondaco dei Tedeschi next to the Rialto Bridge – a work which Zanetti, writing in the middle of the eighteenth century, could still liken to '*un vivo raggio di cocente sole*' (a lively ray of burning sunlight).[154]

To judge from the single surviving fragment of the Fondaco frescoes in the Accademia – a female figure still remarkable for the luminous warmth of her flesh tones – it was the golden light of sunset Zanetti had in mind when he compared Giorgione's colour to the sun. In fact, writing of Titian, Zanetti recorded, 'Certain masters today hold it as certain that in many works Titian wanted to imitate the light which one sees towards the setting of the sun.'[155] This then was the revelation of their methektic practice: to turn gold into flesh by way of atmospherically-suffused sunlight, and so to reassert human, even erotic, interests. Eastlake remarked that, for the larger part of his life, Titian occupied a house looking out across the Lagoon towards Murano and the mountains.[156] The deepening flesh tones of the Venetians as, towards sunset, they passed to and fro in their gondolas, may well have been Titian's habitual study. But even this is too naturalistic, too external.

Boschini, alluding perhaps to the dark grounds that Lagoon painters favoured, compared Venetian painting to the dawning sun illuminating the night.[157] If Venetian painting was a way of dealing with darkness, this accords well with the city's reputation for sharply mingling joy and melancholy. One recalls that, at the time of his premature death, Giorgione was working on a painting called *La Notte*. And bearing in mind that Giorgione painted where, a year before, all had been flames (the fresco commission had been occasioned by the rebuilding of the Fondaco after its destruction by fire in 1504), his fiery colour suggests a typically

Venetian taste for ambiguity, for expressing opposite possibilities in a single form, and interpreting the mastery of their mere coincidence as a cause for self-confidence. And this reversed perspective, in which distant interests converged and were united, was not only chromatic: it may have been peripatetic.

As the frescoes have disappeared, it is difficult to assess the relationship between the figures and their architectural milieu. Valcanover's reconstruction of the scheme Titian and Giorgione devised for the Fondaco dei Tedeschi makes its clear that the figures were more than life-size, equal to the tall windows they flanked, and in the case of the figure of Justice, rather larger.[158] The effect would have been the opposite of match-like – these giant forms seeming to loom large in the distance and, closer at hand, leaning over and looking down – and therefore, I am speculating, creating an effect of reversed perspective. There was a vernacular precedent for this disproportion between figure and frame: it used to be a habit in Friuli to fresco the west façades of churches with an enormous figure of St Christopher. To the weary traveller, bent beneath his burden, it seemed to bring the end of his journey near as it glowed deeply in the sunset.[159]

Perhaps this was what drove Columbus to hallucinate; that he looked in vain, at sea, on land and in the sky, for the giant Christopher who might harbour and give succour to his fantasies. He was nowhere to be found, and in consequence, however near Cathay seemed to draw, it remained, like a mirage, just as remote. It was as if the power of transformation eluded him – but this was exactly the gift the Venetian artists laid claim to with their 'fieriness'. In the poetic sphere, fieriness signified the ability to 'forge' striking metaphors. The warm glow of Giorgione's figures suggested 'liveliness', their power to re-enact the painter's will, as extensions of his arm and brushstroke to preserve the body's curvilinear kindling of space. 'A fiery people reveals its boldness in its metaphors, whether it inhabits the Orient or North America,' remarked Herder,[160] while Magellan's secretary, Antonio Pigafetta, reported two kinds of parrot in the Moluccas, the white and the red. It seems that the red parrots were valued at one bahar of cloves on account of their speaking more perfectly than the white ones.[161]

In any case, it is a sober fact that the paintings of Giorgione and Titian represent the appearance of the world after sunset and before dawn. Their cloud tones, the chiaroscuro of their forests, the glow of flesh hues may be seen by us by daylight, but they give us access to what the sun itself never sees: the dawning of darkness. They represent a light, a time of day, where they grow too dark to be seen. They make an appeal to daylight to complete them, but they also make it clear to the daytime viewer that his light is not theirs. Mediating between the visible and the invisible, they invite the viewer to discover a fiery ray projected from the eye, answered by the canvas. They invite us to see through the rectilinear invisibility of daylight to the tangible aspect of darkness.

Painting the hour when, as Byron wrote, 'The moon is up, and yet it is not night;/ Sunset divides the sky with her; a sea/ Of glory streams along the Alpine height/ Of blue Friuli's mountains,'[162] Giorgione and Titian made Temanza's picturesque claim that the five streams feeding the Lagoon were associated with different colours, 'so as to be easily distinguishable for a considerable distance,' seem believable.[163] Where gondola-knives scumbled the bruised-cloud reflections of sunset, the Porto de Tre Porti known as the yellow, Sant' Erasmo the azure, San Nicolò the red, Malamocco the green and Chioggia the purple nightly mingled, hatching life. Painting like this, these artists worked methektically. Their 'activity of concurrent actual production' did not represent the Lagoon; they wove it as Penelope wove her winding cloth, tracking back and forth across it lest the surface coagulate and freeze.

The old distinctions between accident and substance, figure and ground, dissolved. The waterborne were detached from their bodies. Their voices alone remained. Ripples of laughter among lantern-lit waves. It grew impossible to say where voices came from, or where they were muffled up, or when. Near and far infinitesimally bent towards each other, met, crossed, became each other. Phrases, entire sentences, whole histories belonged to other people. Silences; shadows. An oar's unguarded plash, betraying passage. Unmoored, no longer anchored in fixed positions, myriad destinies met in the coved, imaginative ear.

It was the same with colours. They enjoyed a life of their own. They emerged from torch-lit doorways. Luminous wave-edges and pale masks jostled on the water steps. Silk stockings: Istrian bollards. Gondolas converged like black windows. The water was a waiting palette. Alighting from their *fondamente*, the masses took to it. (It was as if they smuggled the body of light away.) The parent palaces glowed ghostly in the evening. In their lee, like a school of gnats beneath a poplar, there grew towards sunset a *perpetuum mobile* of black knives, circling. Fans fluttered like moths. Balconies leaned over to envy the view. The gondolas were long-armed brushes, carrying highlights to the shadow, producing frilled cuffs.

When suddenly, somewhere else, the sky was on fire, and the gondola's wake dabbed the trailed silk with gobbets of gold. Shadows deepened and were scumbled with the sky: features were pink and brown blots advancing. The canal was petalled with faces. May became autumn's russet. The prow-spliced waves ignited. Mooring posts were painted torches. By the molten water, kindled by it, Phoenix-like, from their wooden rafts, the palaces rose, glowing like flesh. Their cinders settled on the flowing gold. The water was stained marble.

Glaze by glaze, the gondolas, which were purple now and gilded, plied and applied the paling colour before it dried, cooled down, until the canvas was crowded. Later, they would ferry home to bed skulls and empty capes. But now, just now, the bridges opened their wings, the palaces wore a bloom upon them. They were avenues of blossoming trees the lovers threaded. The *campi* were filled with children's games. The bottle-glass windows glowed like bunches of golden fruit, or thunder-clouds. The well-heads were crèches of roses. Venice did not need the spring; it came to her each sunset in an access of gold . . .

Such passages may seem literary if read as novelistic interludes. Alternatively, they may be episodes from a Venetian history of light. In any case, they bring us parabolically back towards the implications for spatial history of reversed perspective. If Titian, Tintoretto, Giorgione and the rest were not mere mimics of Nature, if (unlike the Florentines) they did not merely represent ideas – if, in short, their art was in our terms methektic, a physical re-enactment of the environment (taken in its broadest sense), the question remains: what did these painters understand by 'Nature', by external reality? What was their licence for supposing that the dance of the brush as it enunciated forms provisionally, ambiguously, spontaneously, corresponded to the look of nature?

What, for example, does it mean to say, of Titian's late canvases, 'in our necessarily immediate engagement of this textured surface, we learn to make distinctions, to separate flesh from fur, leaf from bark, to distinguish proximate object and distant horizon.'?[164] If it means anything, it is that these painters were responding to the new look of history, where the evidence of the eyes could no longer be interpreted unequivocally. Rosand not only evokes an art that takes us back to the child's first efforts to gain a visual purchase on the world; he uncannily characterizes the experience of a Columbus, or any European, trying to come to terms with a world that looks like the one he left behind, but which fails to answer his piercing glance.

The art of *macchiare* was an art of peripateia. It visualized a relationship with one's surroundings that was mobile and performative without being merely theatrical. It perceived the environment as an inexhaustible matrix of pathways and viewpoints. It thought not in terms of solitary vantage points, but of meeting places reached by way of curving routes. It imagined distant parts of the world bent towards one another in secret dialogue: the folds in the earth were the evidence of their inclination. Stability, whether hydrological or commercial or emotional, was explained in terms of fluid mechanics, as the graded but continuous flow of energy between parts; and the histories these processes related was that of the continuously self-transforming lie of the land.

More formally, this art of staying at home depended upon conceiving Venice as an open region within a closed region. An open region 'is usually characterised as a region for each point of which there is a surrounding that lies entirely within the region.' A closed region is one where boundary points have been fixed and where therefore 'each surrounding of a boundary point contains points which do not belong to the region.'[165] If the latter encourages binary thought patterns, leading to what Wilden characterizes as the paranoia of digital communication, the former encourages cultivation of the local, a respect for the territories contained within the surface at one's feet, the sand, the clay, the rock which, being carved, displays an infinity of surfaces.

To inhabit an open region within a closed one is to introduce into one's topological reveries the dialectic of history. It is to understand the *poesia* of one's style as an ethical inevitability, not simply an aesthetic choice. In particular, it is to reject the teleological rhetoric used to legitimate the European colonization of the rest of the world. Imperialism inverts the regional hierarchy, construing the world as an inexhaustible reservoir of closed regions (other cultures) within an open, and unlimited, region (the flat plane of Euclidean geometry). This may in the short term be good economics, but it is bad theology, worse geography, and in the end makes impossible the fulfilment of desire. 'Imaginary exchange values [ ] true to the myth of progress under capitalism, know no such [socio-ecological] limits. Imaginary structures are those we associate with symmetrized relations of either self or other in "zero-sum games". In the personal sense, the Imaginary *when dominant* is the domain of that loss of perspective and confusion of levels we know as paranoia and/or psychosis. In the socioeconomic sense, the Imaginary when dominant is the domain in which (apparently) unconstrained competition is dominant over cooperation, and exchange values dominant over use values.'[166]

In this sense, the Venetian artist, who could 'artfully turn fugues, marches, capriccios [*bizzarie*], toccatas, improvisations, fantasias, and could move back and forth between one form and another',[167] and whose reversed perspective preserved a curvilinear perception of the lie of the land, advocated an anti-imperializing mode of communication with his surroundings. His provisional masks, changes of direction, his intriguing 'enigmas', were not evidence of shiftiness, loose morals, or a disposition to political or personal treachery, but could be construed as aspects of poetic, as opposed to paranoid, communication. Glossing Jung's identification of Mercury with the unconscious, James Hillman writes: 'Elusive, mercurial, the unconscious is not a place, nor a state, but an obscurely ironic brother, a sister who echoes, so you do not forget . . .' Hermes, the thief, Mercury full of tricks, a malicious imp, is the psychopompos who leads to the hidden truth, saving us from literalism and paranoia. 'Deception and duplicity . . . save from delirium because false belief and true belief always occur together, together with revelation.'[168]

So Venetian artists understand the canvas, their Hermes the brush. But these remarks also map out an alternative approach to communicating across differences. The non-Europeans, with their obscurely ironic mimicry, implied a parabolic return to humanity; so that the conquistadors might not forget who they were. Hermes is not only the thief, he (more often she) is the go-between Malinche, the mediator who negotiates different levels of meaning, enabling all parties to avoid literalism and paranoia. Against the Dominican and Franciscan zealots, who cannot tolerate ambiguity (who castigate duplicity as Devil's work), he embraces mere coincidences as revelations. Victory (not least over colonial paranoia) must mean successful communication, yielding to rather than dominating the other. Linguistically, yielding up is not a retreat into language games (another form of paranoia); it is to relocate words in the world, to come upon the self in someone else's self-portrait – an effect that twilit paintings create when they look back at us from somewhere else with a remembered light.

*

'Revelation, then, is always an act of displaying phenomena . . . each thing in its image, each word in its *echos*.'[169] And, against Arnheim's deprecation of auditory phenomena, we can say that in these environmentally-attuned situations, the *echos* is not to be understood as a degradation of the original. For *echos* takes in what we call the primordial world, as it sounds and swells all about us and within us, as we are borne aloft on the crest of life,' writes F. Joseph Smith, 'We would not talk so much of *eidos* as of musical *tonos* or of a fundamental *echos*, that describes things not only as seen but as felt and heard.'[170] The psychological counterpart of this auditory intuition – something remote from Jaynes's bicameral hallucination – is wonderfully glossed by Montaigne, who understands that selfhood can only be achieved performatively, by a concurrent mode of self-production (in his case by writing): 'We are entirely made up of bits and pieces, woven together diversely and so shapelessly that each one of them pulls its own way every moment. And there is as much difference between us and ourselves as there is between us and other people.'[171] (Similarly, we might add, the warp of the canvas and the formlessness of the *macchie* resist, divert and lead on the brush; and the *fantasie* of the canvas may be as strange to the artist as they are to the viewer.)

In any case, if the artist's self-writing is to represent him truthfully (methektically), it must avoid the paranoia of biography, its desire to linearize the motions of the mind, to abstract them from the peripateia of the body, its unending intercourse with the local lie of the land. But there must be nothing leaden-footed or parochial about this localism. Montaigne, who glosses so well the poetics (and the politics) I associate with Giorgione, was an expert in essaying different forms, diverse figures of speech and topics. He took a pride in shifting his ground. He deprecated his changefulness, but regarded inconstancy as part of the human condition. To admit a susceptibility to outside influences might even be a virtue: the surprise of catching oneself unawares, as in a mirror, depended on one's thoughts being somewhere else. So Montaigne's mere dawdling, his caprices, his literary doodlings or grotesques, circling as it were the motion of the mind, might be a way of staying at home, of preserving a regional outlook.

A professional painter, Montaigne reflects, places his painting, 'laboured with all his skill and sufficiencie', in the 'most convenient place and middle of every wall', and then proceeds to fill up 'the empty spaces all round it with grotesques, which are fantastical paintings whose attractiveness consists merely in variety and novelty. And in truth what are these Essays if not monstrosities and grotesques botched together from a variety of limbs having no defined shape, with an order, sequence and proportion which are purely fortuitous.' Montaigne's temperamental inability to obey the laws of linear perspective, 'to undertake a richly ornate picture, polished and fashioned according to the rules of art',[172] is forced upon him by the mobile quality of his self-consciousness. It is also an exact literary analogue of the Venetian art of *macchiare*, particularly if we remember that, like Titian applying glaze after glaze to a painting, Montaigne in successive editions of the *Essais* continued revising, expanding and deepening his first sketches.

Montaigne does not free-associate, if this implies a linear progress from one thought to the next. The fortuitousness of his writings depends on his willingness to err, to depart from the high road of logic. Ideas strike him as the Venetian painter's brush strikes the canvas: they are blotches which, monstrous in themselves, radiate, suggesting bizarre connections, fantastic likenesses and capricious resonances that can never be realized within the linear perspective of formally-polished writing. Not exactly a stream of consciousness, Montaigne's essays nevertheless obey the principles of fluid dynamics; dropped into the reflective pool of his consciousness, ideas release waves that expand to the shore and, rebounding, converge on him with the sense of a knowledge environmentally derived. After all, Montaigne contends:

> The brush-strokes of my portrait do not go awry even though they do change and vary . . . I am unable to stabilise my subject: it staggers confusedly along with a natural drunkenness. I grasp it as it is now, at this moment when I am lingering over it. I am not portraying being but becoming: not the passage from one age to another (or, as the folk put it, from one seven-year period to the next) but from day to day, from minute to minute. I must adapt this account of myself to the passing hour. I shall perhaps change soon, not accidentally but intentionally. This is a register of varied and changing occurrences, of ideas which are unresolved and, when needs be, contradictory . . .'[173]

An accurate self-portrait is the trace of 'varied and changing occurrences'. It takes the form of a peripateia, a measuring-out of consciousness spatially: 'When a man is walking up and down anywhere, if his thoughts are on something else he will never fail – give an inch or so – to make the same number of equal strides; but if he goes to that place with the intention of counting and measuring his strides, he will find that he will never achieve so exactly by design what he had done naturally and by chance.'[174] 'Chance', then, is not pure chance; it corresponds to a providential arrangement of things that can only be known partially, by wandering 'off the path'. Self-knowledge is environmental; the ground where one walks provides the metre of one's thoughts. The lie of the land, its irregular stresses and *glissandi*, provides the home which makes being 'homeless' bearable.

Montaigne recognizes the temptation of a rectilinear perspective. To imagine life as a linear trajectory, the environment as a Euclidean space, has considerable attraction, aesthetically as well as morally. Complaining that 'the wind of chance events shake[s] me about as it lists,' he asks: 'What is the use of providing yourself with paints if you do not know what to paint? No man sketches out a definite plan for his life; we only determine bits of it. The bowman must first know what he is aiming at: then he has to prepare hand, bow, bow-string, arrow and his drill to that end. Our projects go astray because they are not addressed to a target. No wind is right for a seaman who has no predetermined harbour.'[175] However, the paradox for Montaigne is subtler. 'For many years now,' he writes, 'the target of my thoughts has been myself alone; I examine nothing, I study nothing, but me.'[176] It is not that the target is illusory, simply that the self is mobile, and as thc inner eye changes its point of view to see it better, so the self also changes aspect. 'Nothing has changed; but our mind contemplates the matter in a different light and sees it from another aspect: for everything has many angles and many different sheens.'[177]

But even this is too static, too cinematographic or stuttering. As the staggering bipedal back and forth of Montaigne's essays shows, such visual similes mislead. They are insufficiently processual; they suppress the connection between self-knowledge and *kinesis*, the fact that the shape of one's movement might determine what appeared. They ignore the lie of the land. The Venetian artist, say, is moved by the chance conjunction of monstrously-blotched paint and tensely-stretched canvas. If his brush is an arrow, then the broad cross-weave of the canvas is the bow-string – with this difference, that it is a bow-string in the shape of a shield. While the archer gets ready, his quarry has fled the field; no wind is right for the sailor who *does* have a predetermined harbour, and steers inflexibly for it without taking account of the tempest.

Between the pure, timeless aim of rectilinear perspective and mere drifting without a rudder, there must be another way. 'What we need,' Montaigne says, 'is topographers who would make detailed accounts of the places which they have actually been to . . . A man may well have detailed knowledge or experience of the nature of one particular river or stream, yet about all others he knows only what everyone else does.'[178] But if regional knowledge of this kind is to differ from the 'universal' knowledge of a Columbus, it has to embody a different perspective, a different conception of what constitutes knowledge. It will have to be an analogue of the process of knowing, rather than a taxonomy of places already known; and if this is to have any historical or theoretical purchase, it will have to incorporate a curvilinear perspective.

Montaigne's call for 'topographers' occurs in the same breath as he praises his servant as the best kind of observer because he is simple, and therefore unlikely to gloss over the truth with elaborate rhetorical artifice. Commenting on this appeal to an unlettered witness, Greenblatt suggests that 'discursive authority in the early literature of travel derives from a different source than it would in other forms of *poeisis* – not from an appeal to higher wisdom or social superiority but from a miming, by the elite, of the simple, direct, unfigured language of perception Montaigne and others attribute to servants.'[179] Greenblatt sees the servant *qua* unlettered witness as a go-between, mediating the difference between European and savage, breaking down the mirror symmetry of absolute self and absolute other which seemed to prevent successful communication. The servant articulates Montaigne's own desire to free himself of the rhetorical certitudes of his class, to discover himself as a foreign country which can only be described by dispossessing oneself of discursive preconceptions. This has profound historical, as well as autobiographical, implications: 'Montaigne's essay suggests that the go-between can also serve as the agent for a marvellous dispossession, a loss of the fiercely intolerant certainty that licensed unbearable cruelty.'[180]

The go-between, mercurial, ironic, enigmatic, is the ally of Hermes. He breaks down the paranoid discourse of the State, characterized by an unwillingness to entertain compromise, a tendency to react by attacking, a will to dominate and instil fear in others, intense repressed anger, a continuous state of mobilization, a lack of interest in art, a lack of humour.[181] And here we might venture a criticism of Boschini, on whose picturesque peripateia of Venice we have rather relied. It is Boschini after all who, not immune to hero-worship, likens Tintoretto to Columbus. Just as the great discoverer ignored those who said his enterprise was foolish, so il Robusti defied those who (like Vasari) failed to understand the genius of the art of *macchiare*: '*El Tentoreto ha trova le minere/Dela Pitura, col so inzegno adorno*.'[182]

Perhaps this imperial image of the artist as successful gold-prospector is harmless. Or perhaps it matters that Tintoretto, like Montaigne, saw himself as go-between, as mediator between worlds, not conqueror. Sartre took a dim view of Tintoretto's willingness to work for nothing (worse, to pay to be allowed to work).[183] But this could be construed in quite a different way, as a circumvention of property relationships under emergent capitalism. He refused to threaten; he gave where he was expected to receive. This was not naïveté; Il Robusti was no weakling in these matters, an unarmed primitive. By yielding, he inaugurated successful communication. By yielding, he gained, thus producing a double dispossession. If he was hated, it was for the same reason that Cortés's go-between La Malinche was hated: like her, he stood for the open as opposed to the closed.[184]

The question might be: what principles, what laws of attraction, will guide the 'topographers' in their peripateia? For unless the lie of the land is allowed a role in the wandering, determining the routes they take, the conjunctions and departures, their movements must continue to occur as on a level plane. Their baroque elaboration may subvert a linear interpretation of the world, but it will only mimic two-dimensionally reality's four-dimensional curvilinearity. Descartes's proposition that A produces B, B produces C, etc., as far as N, may seem unexceptionable, but it contains a contradiction. For if motion is naturally rectilinear, that is, if each moving object follows its own pre-ordained path, then it is impossible for two objects ever to meet. In order for straight lines to meet, they must deviate from their original paths – 'An event is always a knot, in which converge an infinite sequence of previous facts or events.' And Papini, who makes this comment in the context of glossing Vico's curvilinear theory of historical time, adds, 'The rectilinearity of the first [Cartesian] interpretation is cancelled out by the intrinsically curviform nature of the second, and deeper, vision of reality.'[185]

When Montaigne explains, 'There is nothing I can say about myself as a whole simply and completely, without intermingling and admixture. The most universal article of my own Logic is DISTINGUO,'[186] he defines his self-knowledge dialectically, but he provides no mechanism for this logic. What produces the collisions out of which come the opposite reactions that constitute Montaigne's identity? Perhaps Montaigne's mind behaves like the atoms of Lucretius, ceaselessly colliding with other atoms, constantly changing direction as a result of these collisions. But in that case, what is the process of accumulation whereby chance encounters assume a pattern and take on the substantiality of forms? It cannot be like Lucretius's notion of *clinamen*, a matter of chance conjunction, because it is purposeful: 'I speak about myself in diverse ways: that is because I look at myself in diverse ways.'[187]

Unless Montaigne habitually armed himself with the intellectual equivalent of mirrors, suits of armour and placidly reflective sheets of water – and in fact, Montaigne complained that his memory was notoriously unreliable – the self-appraising *controposto* this last remark implies could only be achieved choreographically, by tracing one's movements on the ground. In effect, Montaigne's stylistic will-to-spontaneity embodies an intuition of the curvilinear nature of psychological reality; ideas, sensations, memories tend to converge on one another. Thus, although 'every sort of contradiction can be found in me,' self-knowledge is still possible.[188] And to effect those points of convergence, those knots of self-knowledge, demands a novel, non-linear method of reporting.

Two verbal techniques in particular produce the deviation from previous paths that, by bringing different ideas into conjunction, creates the 'event' of self-knowledge: word association and paranomasia, 'the exploration or exposure of gaps and interstices in accepted language in a way that defies resolution or logical explanation'.[189] Paranomasia, less formally known as punning, is not simply an empty excess but a curvilinear tendency within the rectilinear cross-weave of the lexicon; it warps perspectives, dissolves boundaries, folding together conceptions that a univocal discourse ought to keep perfectly remote. Word associations blur the boundary between illegitimate cousins of sound and legitimate cousins of sense. Alliteration and assonance are not simply playful devices to subvert language's self-important monologue; the elastically echoic dialogue they improvise about the words on the page reveals 'diverse ways' in which words converge upon one another, in the process overturning the idea that the rectilinear form of writing in any way corresponds to the character of thought.

The poetic intuition informing these kinds of word-play may be akin to Leonardo's observation that 'the surface of every opaque object partakes of the colour of the adjacent object . . . no subject is ever seen entirely in its true colour.'[190] If so, we invert the Freudian insight: it is linear logic always seeking to converge on a metaphysical truth that is mystifying. Puns and other forms of verbal self-consciousness help to keep us on the surface of language, to attend to the thickening plot apparent in its material cross-ply. To explore spaces in-between, to highlight formal connections, to deepen resounding echoes is to practise in writing the art of chiaroscuro. And these stylistic propensities are not simply the *bizzarie* of an amateur philosopher; they adumbrate a new way of constructing models of reality, one that again has its cultural centre in Venice.

Montaigne's style is also a methodology or, as Feyerabend would put it, an anarchic epistemology.[191] It foreshadows the outlook of Galileo who, introducing his *Dialogue Concerning the Two Chief World Systems* – Ptolemaic and Copernican – expressed his reluctance

> . . . to compress philosophical doctrines into the most narrow kind of space and to adopt that stiff, concise and graceless manner, that manner bare of any adornment which pure geometricians call their own, not uttering a single word that has not been given to them by strict necessity . . . I do not regard it as a fault to talk about many and diverse things, even in those treatises which have only a single topic . . . for I believe that what gives grandeur, nobility, and excellence to our deeds and inventions does not lie in what is necessary – though the absence of it would be a great mistake – but in what is not . . .[192]

Feyerabend argues that the cultivation of excess illustrates the principle of 'epistemological anarchism', without which paradigm shifts in the history of science are inexplicable. He cites with approval the habit of Niels Bohr who (like Montaigne) 'would never try to outline any finished picture, but would patiently go through all the phases of a problem', and who dismissed 'the usual consideration of simplicity, elegance or even consistency with the remark that such qualities can only be properly judged after the events.'[193] Identifying with the politics of excess, Feyerabend commends the Dadaist who is 'convinced that a worthwhile life will arise only when we start taking things lightly and when we remove from our speech the profound but already putrid meanings it has accumulated over the centuries . . . A Dadaist is prepared to initiate joyful experiments even in those domains where change and experimentation seem to be out of question (example: the basic functions of language).'[194]

But perhaps the association of desire with excess can be understood less anarchically. Montaigne's will-to-spontaneity was a way of escaping from the mirror logic of mimesis and its mocking opposite, mimicry. But to effect this escape it was necessary to do more than to interpose a bewildering array of unforeseen events, chance collisions and divagations. These might obscure the clear outline, creating an illusion of freedom, but their trajectories, their little flights towards anarchic self-realization, remained predicated on a rectilinear model of motion. To escape from geometrical reductionism meant defining motion differently: as curvilinear, as a network of paths *inherently* converging upon one another. Montaigne's grotesques, and the way he elaborates them, embody methektically a solution to a philosophical impasse. Cultivating *kairos*, 'the right moment', his excesses echo 'the rhetorical practice of the sophist who allows *kairos* to figure in the invention of speech [and which] issue, then, in an endlessly proliferating style deployed according to no overarching principle of rational design.'[195]

According to Eric Charles White, 'The orator who invents on the basis of *kairos* must in fact go beyond the bounds of the "rational" to the extent that this "will-to-spontaneity" succeeds in evading the burden of the past, the repertoire of collective norms that dissemble the ambiguous, ambivalent nature of reality.'[196] And White cites Leonardo as excelling at the paradoxical 'science' of 'kaironomy': 'As he takes aim at nature's multifariously moving targets, Leonardo's remarkably quick powers of observation enable him to endow even the most fleeting sensory impressions with pleasing aesthetic form.'[197] The *macchie* of nature are pleasing to Leonardo because they offer him a passage to the unconscious of seeing, and therefore towards self-knowledge. They fire back at him inventions equal to his own inventive mind, and they do this by virtue of the innumerable mere coincidences they suggest. Freud regarded Leonardo's sketches as evidence of a mind overwhelmed by alternatives and hesitant to make a choice:[198] but Leonardo's ceaseless search for fresh angles of attack could be construed as the marksmanship of an archer whose practice was tuned to a turning world. His curvilinear inventions resemble a finger which, thrust into turbulently escaping water, can precipitate a vortex. But to close the hand on this funnel of space would be to grasp nothing. In this sense, Leonardo never hesitates.

This glosses Montaigne's poetics; it also sheds light on the politics informing it. For his curvilinear mode of composition was also an argument for *regionalism*, for exploring an open region within a closed one. Commenting on Montaigne's new space for thought 'beyond the limits and final closures of science', one scholar likens it to the new space of America – as if the Frenchman did intellectually what the Spaniards managed geographically.[199] But this is to repeat Boschini's mistake. Montaigne's temperament was anti-imperializing. Rather than conquer new territories, he wanted to dawdle where he was. The discovery of new worlds merely illuminated the ambiguous nature of what we take to be knowledge; and to understand this, it was necessary to proliferate and deepen uncertainties, rather than seek ruthlessly to clear them away.

It comes as no surprise that Montaigne, like the great Venetian apologist Paolo Sarpi, ranged himself against the territorial pretensions of the Papacy. In the attempted subjugation of America, Montaigne and Sarpi found mirrored their own situation; as objects of Papal greed, patriotic Frenchmen and Venetians might almost align themselves with the 'cannibals' – they knew at first hand the costs of heterodoxy. In the discovery of new worlds they also found an argument for their own doctrine of the relativity of judgements, their anti-Catonian advocacy of flexibility. Against the absolutism of the imperial gaze, they were able to comprehend a multitude of viewpoints; and furthermore, to understand these dialectically, as convergent upon one another, capable of making history.

When Montaigne writes of the Aztecs, 'there is nothing savage or barbarous about those peoples, but that every man calls barbarous anything he is unaccustomed to,' he is not simply urging tolerance. He invokes the other dialectically to make a point about the West's false representation of itself to itself: 'Those "savages" are only wild in the sense that we call fruits wild when they are produced by Nature in her ordinary course; whereas it is fruit which we have artificially perverted and misled from the common order which we ought to call savage.'[200] Similarly, Sarpi has in mind not only the autonomy of Venice but a different mode of representation when he reflects that, instead of calling a society disorderly or confused because it differs from ours, what we should say is that the governments, buildings and politics of the Tartars and the Indians are different ('*altro*').[201]

Again, the poetics subtends a politics; it leads logically to Sarpi's advocacy of tolerance, his respect for the relativity of judgement. He shares, for example, the Frenchman's heterodox view of Cato's legendary rectitude: 'Above all avoid that rigidity which some call virtue – such Cato-like rectitude is a pestilent vice. It is a disguise [*pretesto*] for ambition and obstinacy, but otherwise ill-adapted to human life. One cannot walk straight if one walks in folly: favour and contrive collisions [*per urtar*] as little as possible, and pass through the crowd without damage; the night-owl came home safe [*salvosi*] once as a quadruped, another time as a bird.'[202] Sarpi's right or direct motion is distinguished from an obstinately rectilinear compulsion; like a ship navigating the Lagoon (*urtar*: to collide with, run foul of, another ship), well-judged home-coming depends on a sensitivity to environmental conditions. The wisdom of Minerva's *daimon* is demonstrated by its ability sometimes to fly, sometimes to crawl; clear-headedness depends on anticipating every buffet of fortune. Against Lucretius's conception of motion as chaotic, Sarpi, with the image of the sea in mind, imagines motion as grounded in a viscous medium, itself elastic, continuous, curvilinear and, if properly navigated, ultimately supportive.

Again, the idea is that 'right' motion, the most direct progression, is parabolic because of the inherent constitution of the environment: 'If we take any two points on a smooth curved surface, such as that of a sphere or spheroid, and imagine a string stretched between them, we obtain what is known in mathematics as a "geodesic" curve. It is the shortest line which can be traced between the two points upon the surface itself, and it has always the same direction upon the surface to which it is confined; the most familiar of all cases, from which the name is derived, is that curve, or "rhumb-line", upon the earth's surface which the navigator learns to follow in the practice of "great-circle sailing," never altering his direction nor departing from his nearest road.'[203] In the case of a perfect sphere, this path proves circular. In practice, though, the passage from A to B is a parabola; and to keep to the path requires the same steadiness the archer must show lest his tensed bow wobble left or right.

Simplicio, in Galileo's *Dialogue*, asked to imagine a line drawn on the surface of the sea between Venice and Alexandretta, describes it 'not perfectly straight – or, rather, not lying in the perfect arc of a circle – but more or less fluctuating according as the vessel would now and again have rocked . . .'[204] Feyerabend interprets this and other passages that introduce the idea of relative motion, and thus serve to make the earth's motion more easily conceivable, as 'arguments in appearance only . . . psychological tricks': 'They obscure the fact that the experience on which Galileo wants to base the Copernican view is nothing but the result of his own fertile imagination, that it has been invented.'[205] But this reading takes no account of the Venetian environment, where relative motion was an 'operative concept' – one self-evident to Galileo's characters in their Venetian palace if they cared to look out of the window at the passage of vessels up, down and obliquely across the subtly fluvial and tidal Grand Canal.

Presenting his *Gramática de la lengua Castellana* to Isabella and Ferdinand in the year Columbus first crossed the Atlantic, Antonio de Nebrija commented, 'language [by which he meant speech reduced to writing, and writing reduced to grammatical and lexical order] is the perfect instrument of empire.'[206] And then, a few years later in Venice, an artist set out to paint an 'equivocal' picture: 'Dramatic though it be, the background does not set the stage. Indeed, the figures do little. They are well to the front of the landscape, encased in separate thought. It is the scenery which enacts the scene. But this is not a landscape with figures: the figures are insistent. Nevertheless, we haven't any idea who they are or why they are there. They do not belong to the landscape in the sense of shepherds, owners or husbandmen. They belong in the sense of human beings belonging to the world.'[207] Could it be that the ambiguity was strategic? Could it be that Giorgione wanted to commemorate the hour of first contact, to keep alive the possibility of another history, neither of possession nor dispossession, but of convergent belonging?

Certainly, other human trajectories, other ways of constructing meaning, were latent in, say, Columbus's first meetings with the Taino. And had Columbus gone about sketching out a common ground of understanding in the same way that Venetian artists later went about composing a painting, out of mere coincidences, some form of mutual understanding might have arisen. To judge from Columbus's First Voyage *Diário*, the first discourse of Europeans and Americans was composed largely, if not entirely, of paranomasia. How else to account for the remarkable number of homophones or near-homophones clustering around the word-sound 'ca' which are generated by Columbus's brief encounter with the Taino people? Besides Guanahani, *canibe*, *caribe* and their variants, we find *canoa*, Canarias, *canna*.[208] In due course, in accord with grammar's rectilinear expectation that each phonemic cluster pursue its own exclusive semantic trajectory, these word-sounds were associated with, respectively, an island, a people and a sea, a kind of boat etc.

But were they names, and if so, to what did they refer? To speculate, as one modern scholar does, that '*canona*', reported on 22 December 1492, is 'an error for *canoa* (canoe), probably resulting from confusion with *canoa*, Arawakan for "gold"',[209] is to ignore the dialogical and consciously convergent character of first-contact exchanges. It has been suggested that the name of the Spaniards' own country (Castille) may have had a peculiar pathos to Caribbeans; but that, if ever, was later, after the word-sounds had ceased to circulate and had retreated into mutual incomprehension and its corollary, the language of cannons.[210] In all probability, the proliferation of like-sounding words was an instance of the will to invent seeking, by way of convergent echoes, to break out of the impasse of representation's mirror logic. It was not mere mimicry but a kind of *methexis*, an attempt to incorporate and reproduce the meaningless in order to give it meaning.

Perhaps the Taino merely attempted to say back to Columbus the words most prominently on his lips: Can Grande or (pidginized) Cane Grane – a phrase that meant no more to them than the name of Venice's main artery. In a situation where no writerly script existed to pre-empt listening, phonic variability was inevitable. But in the absence of commonly shared meanings, a conscious effort was made to return the sounds with interest, subtly modified, accented, intoned. The auditory information represented by these phono-rhythmic emphases would have been no different from the blows of the painter's brush, which, differing from artist to artist, formed a unique stylistic signature. Columbus himself recognized the ease with which 'n' might be rendered as 'm', blithely remarking, 'Can Grande whom the Indians call *Cami* . . .'[211] But perhaps the ambiguity lay elsewhere: in Columbus's own authority, *Il Milione*, where on one occasion at least the Great Chan's title is spelt differently.[212]

'Cami' may be a pidginized contraction of Columbus's own words, 'Ca . . .n..e', or it may merely be a playful echo. On 1 November, the 'same' word is rendered 'Cavila',[213] a spelling again bearing witness not to an idiolectal eccentricity but to the polyphonic fertility of a word-sound as it circulated the meeting-place where two cultures, attempting to incline towards each other, reversed customary perspectives. These confusions were far from trivial; they indicated an alternative economy of exchange, where concepts and objects might circulate performatively, as indices of presence. Repeating the name Can Grande, Columbus kept on asking the Taino whether (in effect) they had read Marco Polo. For their part, the Taino returned his query with interest, explaining that they moved about in canoes. And the canoes were not simply a misunderstanding; they signified a different theory of language. In Guinea (West Africa), Columbus recalled, 'there are a thousand kinds of language and one does not understand . . .' Here, though, he reported, '[the Taino] language . . . is identical in all these islands of India, and they all understand one another and go to all their islands in their canoe.'[214]

In effect, the criss-crossing canoes thickly weaving the surface of the sea with sounds, independently converging, spreading and diffused, signified a curvilinear cultural perspective in which 'first contact', far from being relegated to the mythology of colonizing nations, was embraced as an everyday occurrence. Roger Wescott has speculated about the existence in proto-human speech of a universal phono-seme, approximated by such terms as 'kor', 'cur', 'can', corresponding roughly to the sound of growling, and signifying 'dog' – an intriguing speculation in the context of Columbus's mastiff-accompanied first exchanges with the Caribbeans.[215] But from our point of view, more significant is the identification of 'ca' with the will-to-spontaneity. The 'primitive' does not belong to prehistory; it erupts wherever dialogues are opened.

But this possibility was missed. Columbus the sign-reader was blind to the curvature of space about him. He was intent on looking through, as if whatever he came across could only be an inadequate, therefore deceitful, representation of Cathay. It was as if he could only conceive of journeys in terms of destinations; as if the curvature of the earth were nothing to him except a hypothesis of coming back, a residual nostalgia for staying at home. If, say, Columbus's ships were spears, it was as if he could attribute no value to the flight-path itself; only the scars, the landfalls and the signs signifying the proximity of land counted, for they signified history. Now Columbus's querying of the earth's sphericity takes on a new meaning. 'It is not round as they describe,' he explains in his *Narrative of the Third*

Voyage, 'but of the form of a pear, which is very round except where the stalk grows, at which part it is most prominent; or like a round ball, upon one part of which is a prominence like a woman's nipple, this protrusion being the highest and nearest the sky, situated under the equinoctial line, and at the eastern extremity of this sea.'[216]

This is not simply an awkward attempt to save mythical appearances by asserting that the naked earth revealed by Renaissance geography still retained, in the form of the mountain-top Garden of Eden, the raised scar of humankind's origins; it represents an attempt to warp the curvilinear form of the earth to fit increasingly paranoid rectilinear projections. It is as if the earth, sucked out of true by the forces of linear perspective, can no longer retain its rondure. It bulges out, pulled towards a vanishing-point at once metaphysical and ideological; for unless the asymmetry of the earth's surface can be demonstrated, there is nowhere to locate Divine Providence, setting human history in motion. And if the earth is perfectly round, symmetrical in every direction, it makes a nonsense of journeying; for what is there to discover where every horizon, endlessly changing, changes nothing?

Any historical convergence between the art of *macchiare* and the experience of Renaissance exploration must have occurred earlier, before distinctive outlines had been identified and named. It must have belonged to the exploratory phase of exploration when, as yet, phenomena had not detached themselves from their surroundings and contracted into signs; it would have corresponded to that mode of visual perception that is simultaneously passive, or unfocused, and watchful – like a hunter whose arrow is strung but who, as yet, observes nothing to fire at and lets his bow hang loosely to one side. In linguistic terms, it can be compared to what I have elsewhere called 'primary babble', associated with the earliest phases of cross-cultural contact, where 'words are not heard as units of information but as phonetic compounds . . . sounds – imitative perhaps of natural sounds or else punningly reminiscent of words in one's own language.'[217]

Floating before the eye, islands of colour were a way of perceiving the world 'auditorily', environmentally. In the order of perception, blotches of contrasting colour precede outlines. Forms with outlines are the later rationalization of images. They stabilize sensations, annexing archipelagos of impressions to known conceptual continents. Forms are colours that have been colonized and settled. So Columbus recorded that the fish in the waters off the island of Fernandina (seen on 16 October and circumnavigated the following day) 'are surprisingly unlike ours. There are some of the shape of dories and of the finest colours in the world, blue, yellow, red and every other hue and others variously flecked. The colours are so marvellous that everybody wondered and took pleasure in the sight.'[218] Columbus is often considered a poor observer of nature, perhaps because of remarks like the following (from the same 16 October entry): 'I saw no land animal at all except parrots and lizards' and, even more remarkably, of his first landfall: 'I saw no animals of any kind on this island except parrots.'[219] But, I suggest, such observations refer to the order of seeing, not the order of nature. Flying parrots and skittering lizards moved as fish moved, leaving a vivid after-image on the retina.

Again, his first sight of the people of the New World was of black and white images rising and falling towards him, rather like waves hollowing out darkness before ramping blankly on the sand: 'Some of them paint themselves black, others white or any colour they can find. Some paint their faces, some their whole bodies, some only the eyes, some only the nose.'[220] These cinematic first impressions, these *macchie* of colour resembling the early stages of a painting by a Venetian master, were valuable because, in an aqueous environment where near and far were as yet undifferentiated, they gave the European's infant eye a momentary purchase on space, a means of identifying a locality. Like the imaginary islands at the end of the world, they prevented the eye glazing over, dazzled by the glitter of nothingness.

The parrot may have entered consciousness as a shriek of colour, a coloured arc of space, a rain of feathered spears, but this moment goes unacknowledged. Visualizing conquest, historians concentrate on the after-image, on the parrot after it has been brought down and caged in signification. From the European point of view, the sighting of parrots was confirmation of a geographical hypothesis. As the Italian scholar Taviani notes: 'Parrots were the symbol of the Indies. All the medieval commentators, including Marco Polo, had included them among the marvels of the Orient. Columbus was well aware that parrots were not to be found either in Europe or around the Mediterranean.'[221] From the Taino point of view, Maldonado de Guevara hypothesized, the European interest in parrots had a completely different meaning. The Taino came to believe that the parrot was the white man's totem, the guiding spirit without which they could never have 'descended from the sky' – for the Taino seem to have insisted that the Spaniards flew rather than sailed to their islands. As de Guevara observes: 'If the early Romans could believe that, when they saw their standard fluttering at the tip of the lance, they witnessed the imperial eagle flapping its wings, it is not hard to imagine how the Taino interpreted the [scarlet] royal standards of the disembarking soldiers. They were the guiding spirits, the handsome auguries showing the whites the way; they represented, in short, the bird that guided them.'[222]

But both these accounts leave out the pre-semiotic phase, when meanings, phono-semantic lines of associations, had yet to be fixed, and the ambiguity of performative gestures was the order of the day. First meeting with the Taino on 12 October 1492, Columbus explained that 'to win their friendship . . . I gave some of them red caps and glass beads which they hung round their necks.'[223] In response, 'They came out swimming to our ships and brought us parrots, skeins of cotton thread and spears and many other things, which they exchanged with us for such objects as glass beads, hawks and bells. In fact, they very willingly traded everything they had.'[224] The next day, 'because the Indians that he had brought into the ship had understood that the Admiral wanted to have some parrots, it seems that that Indian who went with the Christians told the natives something about this, and so they brought parrots to them and gave as many as they were asked for without wanting anything for them.'[225] Evidently Columbus thought there had been a misunderstanding; he was not really interested in parrots. Perhaps on the first day Columbus had pointed out the scarlet birds, drawing his men's attention to them as good auguries. Perhaps the Indians, noticing his pointing finger, his beckoning hand and their animated speech, concluded that the parrot had a special significance for the newcomers – as, in a sense, it did. So like billiard balls, which the more they come into contact, the further they recede from one another, misunderstandings were compounded; a casual gesture rapidly became the foundation of a myth of mutual misunderstanding which, if it did not exculpate the conquistadors, explained why tragic conflict was inevitable.

As Greenblatt concludes: 'Such improvisation on the part of either Europeans or natives should not be construed as the equivalent of sympathetic understanding; it is rather what we can call appropriative mimesis, imitation in the interest of acquisition.'[226] This is indisputable once we detach the parrots from their colour; once we consider them not as *macchie* actively engaged in composing the canvas of cross-cultural contact, but as pre-fixed outlines to be moved here and there to reproduce a familiar pattern, to reinforce stereotypes. It is my contention, though, that these reductive manipulations of the other are secondary; that they presuppose a primary phase of identification when here and there, light and dark, figure and ground, have yet to be designed. This primary phase of sense construction, growing out of the mobile eye's curvilinear dialogue with its like-minded surroundings, is not appropriative but transactional, a means of travelling lightly where one is.

It may be that, approaching the end of the twentieth century, we recognize that the moral tragedy of European imperialism resides in this; that from the beginning, our culture relegated the cultivation of curvilinear space to painting and poetry, thereby excluding from historical consideration the constructive role that mere appearances might play in determining the rules of travelling, the diplomatic protocols associated not so much with crossing boundaries but with their prior definition. Boundaries could be thin or thick; they could be drawn with lines on a map; or they could evolve erotically as dark-light zones of meeting where forms interpenetrated and were lost in each other.

If this relegation is allowed, another question follows: to what end were art and poetry detached from their historical surroundings? The *trahison des clercs* is not confined to consolidating this distinction, this reduction of art to aesthetics; it extends even to those who wish to reinsert painting, poetry and music into their social, political and economic setting. These latter also assume that art's meaning is secondary, and that its primary point of reference must be located elsewhere; they never engage with the possibility that poets and painters are representing history differently, that theirs is an epistemologically distinct outlook, that their metrical construction of meaning might be a way of pacing the ground differently.

Treating an historical event semiotically helps to make historical sense of the first documented contact between white and coloured peoples in the New World, but it does so by treating both parties as if they are parrots confined in cages from which they cannot escape. I would like to give back to parrots the power of free, parabolic flight. The gifts with which Columbus opened negotiations with the Taino were not proffered naively: 'In order to win their friendship, since I knew they were a people to be converted and won to our holy faith by love and friendship rather than force . . .'[227] The exchange of gifts was a strategic deception. At the same time, the discourse of the Taino men hardly conformed to Rousseau's original language of passions and tropes. 'I have observed that they soon repeat anything that is said to them . . .' (12 October)[228] They too were going through the motions of communication. First contact depended on masquerade, on shadowing the other, on mimicking its habits, on pretending to be other than one was. To be fully present to the other side, one had to be less than fully oneself. One had to give oneself up to the present – 'these things pleased them greatly and they became marvellously friendly' (12 October)[229] – and throw off the armour of restraint. It was necessary to act as if the past and the future did not exist, as if now were a mere repetition without motive.

But this, after all, was the true genius of the parrot, which spoke in the tongues of men without understanding a word, which repeated what it heard facilely because its speech was void of memories and free of passion. The rich associations of the parrot in both Western and American cultures made it a symbol in the original sense of the term: a token that could be divided in two and the two halves used to guarantee a pledge, an undertaking given and reciprocated. In the first contact situation, it provided a means of translating contradictory ideas and intentions into an apparently common symbolic form. The parrot, combining more than one meaning, was like a figure of speech. In the absence of a common language, it provided a metaphorical form of exchange. But even this analysis does not question the structuralist logic of mutually exclusive oppositions. The parrot did not translate from one language to another. Its ability to signify many things preceded the either/or logic of national languages. Its polymorphism (if the pun may be forgiven), its protean capacity to absorb and compose the sounds around, echoed the possibility of an echoically-improvised grammar of communication. Such a language would be essentially methektic, meanings emerging dialogically, through processes of mimetic repetition predicated on the convergences inherent in a curvilinear space.

A medieval Arabic periplum reports that in Java are to be found white, yellow and red parrots 'that speak every language'.[230] But what can this mean except that everyone heard them speaking nonsense, and still they created a dazzling display? Islands in medieval and Renaissance mytho-geographic discourse played the same role: jewel-coloured, parrot-iridescent lozenges on the chart (most exquisitely in Abraham Cresques's *Catalan Atlas* of 1375) signified nothing, but provided endlessly-fertile foci of fantasy – and in the other direction, rhomb-radiating points of departure. It is one of the ironies of Columbus's enterprise that the discoverer of islands wanted to put the passages in-between back together again, to pretend that the coasts of Cuba extended to Cathay. It was as if the very passages that licensed him to travel on filled him with panic, a fear of being swallowed up; as if, unable to submit to the 'right moment' opened up by the warp and woof of the elastically-lozenged water, he longed for the stolidity of Central Asia and the stony thread of the Old Silk Road.

And again, these geographical fantasies had to do with a false or paranoid economy of desire. Perhaps these unadmitted perturbations explain why Columbus failed to visit the island of Matinino. He learned of this island, said to be inhabited solely by women, early in January 1493 (6 and 13 January). It was understood that at a certain time of the year, men from the island of Carib (ten or twelve leagues away) visited the island; if the offspring of this visit were male, they were forwarded to the men; if female, the women kept them (15 January). As Matinino was on their homeward route, Columbus was disposed to visit it himself and take away with him a number of the women (16 January), but in the end they only viewed the island on the horizon as they set their sails northwards to catch the winds back to Spain.[231]

Maldonado de Guevara predictably interpreted the intercourse of Caribes and Matuninas as a primitive myth designed to explain the enigma of sexuality. He compares the Caribes or Canibales ('dog-headed folk') with the European Centaurs, the Matininas with the antithetical warlike Amazons[232] – a connection already made in Giuliano Dati's versified narrative of Columbus's discoveries, where the women are said to carry 'bows and arrows'[233] – and draws attention to the fact that the Matininas expel all that is unlike them, as if expunging the memory of intercourse and in this way preserving their virginity. In this account, sexual intercourse is an extraordinary event, an inexplicable mingling of unlikes that resembles the violence of colonization and whose history must be suppressed. An animal necessity in the interests of survival, it is totally foreign to human nature, whose instinct is to preserve its statuesque insularity, its sovereign independence.

These may be legitimate inferences from the story as Columbus relates it, but they depend on regarding it as a rationalizing parable, not as a scientific description. It may be true that the tale seeks to explain why men and women are different, why they occupy different islands, but the narrative itself is occupied in detail not with the maintenance of separateness but with the dynamics of meeting, the ways in which differences are bridged. In any case, Columbus's brief reference to the Matininas should be compared with the much fuller account of 'How the women were separated from the men' written by Fray Ramón Pane. Fray Ramón may apologize for the confused nature of the Arawak legends he relates, explaining that, 'as these Indians have no alphabet or writing, they cannot give a coherent account of these matters,'[234] but however difficult it may be to find a unified mythic structure, the chief theme and burden of the stories is plain: the foundation myths of the Arawak invariably evoke moments of transformation – they attempt to describe the passage from one state to another.

What distinguishes the Arawak tales from Ovidian tales of metamorphosis is their vision of an in-between state which is not momentary and chaotic but which may be constitutional and correspond to the emotion of desire. One day after they had been separated from the women, the Arawaks relate that 'the men went to wash themselves; and while they were in the water, it rained hard, and they felt great desire for women; frequently when it rained they sought traces of their wives, but could not find them. However, that day, as they were washing themselves they saw falling from the trees, sliding down the branches, some creatures that were neither men nor women, and had neither male nor female genitals. They tried to catch them but they slipped away like eels.'[235] It seems that an amphibious existence did not mean loss of identity, psychic anarchy, but an enlargement of the senses.

There is a sexual desire that does not consist in getting ashore or in plunging into the deep, but which fluctuates somewhere in-between, along the littoral of desire. The fertilizing rain makes fruit-like creatures drip and run from the trees. These oneiric images, so dear to the Spanish Surrealists, may, in the Caribbean environment, have been the healthy way of looking at things.

Perhaps they intimate Giorgione's outlook as well. In contrast with Titian, Giorgione showed a lack of interest in public commissions. Where Titian sowed his experiments and reaped his triumphs in public,

Giorgione liked, it seems, to work in private.[236] Where Titian harvested one field after another, Giorgione paused in his meadow, leaning on his scythe to study the face of the oncoming storm, to ponder a genealogy of light that included the lightning's discarded skin, the gypsy's crumpled winding-cloth, the bubbling lip of water, the owl-eyed *paterae* of ancient walls suggesting the Gorgon ogre of Troy, and the whites of the eyes of a figure who, not content with circulating images, looks sturdily towards us, conducting the lightning of our gaze safely to earth.

This image of Giorgione as a lad from Castelfranco who had to work things out for himself, whose lucubrations were too slow for patrons in a hurry, may not be wholly fanciful, especially if the 'skilful rebec player' described in Aretino's dialogues is intended as a veiled allusion to the by then dead master: 'He sang of the hostility that heat has for cold, and cold for heat. He sang of why the days of summer are long and those of winter are short. He sang of the link between lightning and thunder, thunder and the flash, the flash and the cloud, the cloud and the clear sky. He sang about where the rain stays when the weather is good, and where good weather goes when it rains. He sang of hail, hoar frost, snow, and mist . . .'[237] The self-styled philosopher who, in love with dialectic, derived every effect from its opposite, finding the *poesia* of their transformations endlessly engrossing, could evidently become a bore. But the naïveté of his discourse was not necessarily naïve: in the context of a mock-Platonic dialogue on the economy, strategies, deceptions, abuses, disguises and dodges essential to profitable prostitution, the rebec player's step-by-step rule of natural attraction is embarrassing as well as humorous. His pedantic laying out plainly of the rules of attraction makes a mockery of the insignia of seduction. It suggests that signs stand for nothing; or better, that they stand in for the absence of passion, the loss of that natural conscience of incompleteness apparent to us in the partial forms that abound about us and which, though far apart, seem drawn to one another.

Constantly practising to express nature most truthfully, Giorgione might have written in more leisurely circumstances: 'I have not the magnificent richness of colouring that animates nature. Here on the edge of the river, the motifs are very plentiful; the same subject seen from a different angle gives a subject for study of the highest interest, and so varied that I think I could be occupied for months without changing my place, simply bending a little more to the right or left.'[238] In this sense, the soldier leaning to the right, the gypsy leaning to the left, were both portraits of the artist. But Giorgione added to Cezanne's preoccupation with the lie of the land a fascination with figures in a landscape. The soldier and the gypsy are treated as natural elements; like the rest of the landscape, they lean towards the centre. In contrast with the Benson Madonna, the gypsy swivels away from us. In contrast with the Castelfranco St George, the soldier's lance inclines to the centre. In the Castelfranco altarpiece Giorgione concentrated on separating forms; in the Benson *Madonna*, he may be said to have veered to the other extreme, fusing – excessively perhaps – figure and landscape.

The *Tempesta* combines these opposed but complementary developments. Let the figures stand apart, so that there is no doubt of their separate existence, let buildings, bridge and bushes half-screen them from too facile an identification with the landscape; then there is no need for babies and weapons to teeter rebelliously outwards. They may behave spontaneously, respond to their natural desires, hearken to the bend of the environment, the parabolic paths in store for them. Lastly, at a resolute distance, and in conformity with Leonardo's dictum that the further a spherical body is from the eye the more spherical it will appear,[239] let the end of space, the boss-like point where river banks converge, be the inside of a bow or shield; so that what lies round it turns to face us in every direction, its *controposto* lending the gypsy's taut pose its support, transforming it into the *ozio* we associate with being well-grounded, metrically as well as emotionally.

Following those parabolic pathways between forms, there are many routes the eye may take. But at some point sooner or later, whether it follows the soldier's gaze to the gypsy and thence, by way of tree and tower, comes to the horizon; or whether, following the inclination of the soldier's form, it passes by way of the columns to the same place, it will come to a tall, isolated tower and its lovely neighbour the dome. Gradually it will dawn on you that the painting is composed in pairs, not in like but in contrasting couples, in twosomes transformed: mother and child, soldier and lance, column and arch, column and column, lightning and breast-formed cloud. Soldier, gypsy.

And if there is a starting point for this process of composition by way of mimetic doubling-up – a process which, by re-enacting this at first appropriative mimesis, transforms it into an equitable economy of exchange (one that is not subtractive but additional) – it is the single chromatically unanswered element in the painting: the soldier's parrot-coloured jerkin and hose. This was the catalytic element which, without determining which way the eye would glance, gave it a purchase on the scene, enabling it to pass from 'passive reception' to a more finely attuned wandering across turbulent cloud, Möbius-strip bridge, waterfall lightning and foliage-plumed pool . . . and back again. Only never merely back again, as the 'enigma' of the *Tempesta* is simply its refusal to reduce space to a linear grammar.

The insular *macchie* composing the *Tempesta* are not pre-Columbian; they navigate a different surface, where different rules of attraction apply. If canoes beach easily on Bahaman keys, it is because, formally, they imitate one another, alike deriving their forms from the lie of the land – and the sea. There is no question of confusion; functions remain separate. But the curvilinear environment they commonly occupy ensures that the mimicry is constructively convergent, fertile in keeping open a common ground of communication. So it is with Giorgione; without appealing to the story that he and his mistress died together in the plague of 1510, we can truthfully say of him what Zola said of Cézanne: 'He would have invented love if it had not been an old invention.'[240]

The Venetians, it seems, inhabited their inventions. They were what they made themselves to be. Masquerading as what they were not, they became themselves. They did not look on as the entourage of Henri II outside Rouen looked on, fascinated by 'the rehearsal of cultures'; they were their own actors, their own others. They lived on the stage – which consequently could not be conceptualized theatrically. The public playhouses of Elizabethan London might be places apart, associated with sexual, political and moral incontinence,[241] but in Venice no such distinction was made. 'The chief diversion is appearing in the great square, which is called the Place of St. Mark, in all the odd habits they can invent: their faces are hid, and in short 'tis a mascarade of six weeks' continuance.'[242] And Joseph Spence adds, 'The pleasure of foreigners [there] is to see them act over their parts, for it requires a good deal more practice than we generally have had to behave so properly as they do, and the Venetians are grown the most eminent of all nations for the noble art of mimicking.'[243]

The annual Venetian *carnevale* was not an anthropological investigation of Venetian culture, but its methektic re-enactment. It was not a mere repetition of forms put on for foreigners, but the reaffirmation of a living-space. It thrived, therefore, on the ambiguity of appearances – which was not merely a matter of wearing masks but of re-orchestrating the *campi* and *calli*. Foreigners became aware of themselves as tourists when they found themselves jostled and uncertain where to stand: 'An odd blundering harlequin pushes you on one side as you are walking the streets, and while you are recovering yourself you stumble perhaps against a milkmaid who, ten to one, is a lady of the first quality.'[244]

This disordering of linear progress, this provocation of untimed encounters and illicit liaisons, is not merely playful. It signifies a return to social origins and therefore an historical opening, an occasion in which normally distinct segments of humanity – 'There are great numbers of gentlemen dressed up like country fellows, with wooden shoes . . . There are others like Turks, Indians, Sclavonians'[245] – can renegotiate their relations with one another. This is the drama *carnevale* creates: to become one with the world around or to attempt to stand aloof, to act a part or to act apart. 'The carnival seems at first a mighty foolish thing, but in eight or ten days you find it pleases you insensibly more and more, and anybody that has sense enough may easily grow as great a fool as the rest. The air is infectious, and you have nothing to do but not be too wise.'[246]

Carnevale is the diplomacy of first contact – which of course is never first contact but an improvised behaviour on a traditional ground:

> Another time there was a great fat fellow dressed up like a nurse, and one of the tallest gentlemen in Venice like an infant in swaddling-clothes; the poor child bawled out every minute as loud as it could roar for pap, and as fast as the nurse fed him sputtered it out again, very much to the diversion of the spectators. I was by him at the instant that an unfortunate English sailor, who had ventured from the port (which is just by) to the Place, stood to gape upon him, and the great child was so mischievous and aimed so well as to give him a mouthful he did not care for. My countryman took it very ill and clenched his fist very furiously at him, and I believe verily, if we had not interceded with him, would have beat the baby's teeth down his throat.[244]

This is comical enough – evidently our sailor did not recognise the parody of the *Tempesta*! – but it also captures the political intent of a mimicry that is self-empowering. Momentarily, the sailor is in the position of the native: he finds himself mocked, trapped between play-acting and punishment. Momentarily, he suffers the experience of dispossession: his historical identity is revealed as a mask, he is stripped, made ridiculous. And this is precisely because he failed to dress up, failed to wear his mask self-consciously. His reward is to come up against a baby's fist; to learn that here boundaries are as yet unfixed, and the only rule is not to gawp but to join in.

Ambiguity, the bugbear of rectilinear logic and of sailors impatient to find gold, provides the mechanism of entering into peaceful, pleasurable relations. Instead of holding up the mirror of identity, it holds half-open a doorway through which one may slip. But to embrace this invitation successfully is a matter of timing, matching one's gestures to the lie of the land. There is in this world of curvilinear trajectories no Outside where one can reflect and ponder, no Inside where the rules are already known and motion mechanically rehearsed. The masquers may move as deftly as the marionettes, which as Kleist's Herr C. explains, 'only use the ground like elves to skim it and reactivate the swinging of their limbs through an instantaneous pause; we use it to rest upon and recover from the effort of the dance – a moment that is obviously not the dance itself, and allows for nothing better than to make it disappear as much as possible';[248] but unlike the puppets, they have souls – they move because another moves, they speak to the echo, drawn along paths that both undulate and curve.

'The people here,' Charles Burney wrote, 'seem to begin to live only at midnight. Then the canals are crowded with gondolas, and St Mark's Square with company; the banks too of the canals are all peopled, and harmony prevails in every part. If two of the common people walk together, they seem to converse in song; if there is company on the water, in a gondola, it is the same; a mere melody, unaccompanied with a second part, is not to be heard in this city.'[249] So it is with Giorgione's paintings; they are the environment's spirit-double. If the eye is an arrow, then they are the bow that down parabolic paths fires it back into the world of the shadowy living. Hermes-like, they lead back into the unusual paths of time.

To avoid the other's disappearance and the institution of exclusive horizons is the office of *carnevale*. And (to repeat) it held within it, as Giorgione's *Tempesta* holds within it, a different way of imagining the culture of the West. In *Hui*, her book on Maori contact ritual, Anne Salmond describes the *Wero* or *Taki*, the series of ritual challenges that 'were once performed wherever strangers met.' There was nothing mechanical about the exchanges: 'In peace and war strangers were greeted with the same ritual forms, because an unknown group might always be planning treachery, and a display of strength could dissuade them. Early observers of these encounters remarked that it was almost impossible to distinguish peaceful overtures from warlike ones, and just to be sure, groups who are [*sic*] meeting for the first time went armed and in full strength.'[250]

In Maori society, mimicry was not a sign of submission preliminary to cultural disappearance, nor was it an indication of alienation preceding ruthless possession. The value of mimetic behaviour lay precisely in its ability to defer such either/or outcomes, to keep in play the possibility of a negotiated settlement whose result would be the perforation of boundaries without territorial forfeit. The very fact that, as one early writer reports, 'No one can possibly tell what this peaceful meeting may end in, so all are ready for action at a second's notice . . .'[251] is what defines it as an authentically historical moment. The people who take part in this mimic performance are like doubled marionettes; there is no place outside the dance where they can imagine themselves or the others standing. Their future depends on perfect timing, on ensuring that each instantaneous pose is perfectly executed, perfectly ambiguous.

It is a pity – and from the point of view of the peoples they have terrorized, a tragedy no theatre can house – that European cultures have so consistently suppressed the methektic dimension of their historical self-constitution, and have in consequence gone on as if nothing stood in their path. When Spence complains, 'Whatever the masquerading is, you find yourself dissatisfied when 'tis over, and though you don't like it perhaps at the beginning, you are sure to be sorry for the loss of it when it ends,'[252] he might be glossing the nostalgia of colonization. In the first days and weeks of violent invasion, 'inexplicable tremors and rumblings, thunderclaps out of a clear sky, distant guns,' are heard. But as the 'tortured voices' of the indigenes fade away, so do the portentous noises settle down. It is only later, when everything is quiet, that we become aware of the silence, 'the echo of our dread',[253] and wish we had at the outset paused somewhere between the lightning and the thunder's report and, hearing the child crying, like that other soldier listened.

Part Three

Light Reading

There's tempest in yon horned moon,
There's lightning in yon cloud,
Hark, hark to the music, mariners,
The wind is piping loud.
The wind is piping loud, my boys,
And the lightning flashes fire,
The hollow oak our palace is,
Our heritage the sea.

William Light, 'Notebook', c.1830[1]

Here is another soldier looking, listening:

> On the larboard a great mass is collecting and threatening something disagreeable, it moves not before the wind but seems to be coming athwart it. At 5pm weather looking very bad. At 6 sun set horribly. Took two luffs in mainsail etc. The immense black cloud on our bow approached seemingly on the water's surface. Thunder, lightning, rain, and a hurricane broke on us in an instant. In 1/2 an hour afterward our topmast and cross-tree carried away by lightning. The weather now became terrific, the darkness of the night and the quick succession of forked lightning so close with the violence of the wind and rain made one of the most horrible nights I ever experienced . . .
>
> By the light of the electric fluid which about 3 hours was one continued blaze, the surface of the sea appeared a sheet of hissing foam from the violence of the wind, it naturally strove to rise but the enormous weight of rain kept it down and we saw as it were [a] surface of boiling water with clouds of white pebbles falling on it . . .
>
> During the raging of this night's heavy storm of lightning [we] appeared for nearly four hours to be swimming in one continual blaze

> resembling a blue light and the large heavy drops of rain falling on the water was as distinctly seen as by daylight while the forked lightning dashed over the surface in appalling succession and but for the heavy rain we all imagined our little bark must have been in a blaze of fire, each clap of Thunder made our deck tremble and the wind was at every point of the compass blowing with terrific violence.[2]

The electric storm that overtook the erstwhile hero of the Peninsular War, William Light, somewhere in the Mediterranean on 25 September 1831 could be said to be as much metaphorical as meteorological. At any rate, it strangely coincided with a turbulence in the course of his personal affairs. The *Gulnare*, the yacht in which he sailed, had been purchased (with his wife's money) some four years earlier, and since then he and Mary had sailed leisurely about the eastern Mediterranean. Only now he sailed alone; while Light, flattered by the Egyptian Pasha Muhammad Ali's attention and always short of cash, agreed to undertake a trip to recruit officers and men for the Egyptian navy, Mary travelled in the other direction, up the Nile to study its antiquities.[3]

The growing emotional estrangement seems to have mimicked the widening physical distance between them. The next year, back in England, they formally separated; Mary, now pregnant by Hugh Bowen (his sister was married to John Shelley, a brother of the poet), set off for Europe with her new companion, while William pondered what to do. As Mary set about augmenting her family, reinserting herself into society, Light again found himself orphaned. It had first happened in 1792, when his father Francis Light, the 'founder of Penang', had despatched the six-year-old boy to England; Francis had died soon after, while his said-to-be Malayan mother remarried and seems to have disappeared from the historical record. Professionally, too, Light had been repeatedly unfathered: promising contracts with authority regularly ended up by thwarting the efforts of a man who, having 'neither interest nor money', had to rely on 'merit' to gain a respectable place within the complex hierarchy of the British imperium's administrative machine. His intervention in the political affairs of Spain in 1823 was a case in point; the reward for loyally fighting on behalf of the constitutional cause was imprisonment at Corunna, abandonment by his own leader.

But every cloud has a silver lining. From a biographer's point of view at least, the dark night of abandonment, reversal and disorientation provides an appropriately dramatic prelude to the hero's emergence on to the stage of history. If Light, 'the founder of Adelaide', is to be worthy of his destiny (worthy of his name), his life must evidence a dark ground or preparatory depth, a struggle perhaps between contending forces. The machinations surrounding Light's appointment as Surveyor-General to the nascent colony of South Australia only highlight the tempestuous background against which he emerged as a distinct figure, his portrait possessed of a clear outline. Even the new woman in his life, Maria Gandy, adds pathos to the picture: socially his inferior, she accompanies him as mistress, not wife. Her very consolation adds to his isolation.

In any case, when our hero reaches Kangaroo Island in late 1836 it seems to the biographer that an act of historical natural selection has occurred:

> One realises how admirably, if cruelly, Light's life had fitted him for this battle with a new environment; he had no home to long for, his friends were scattered and little seen for many years, and the woman who meant a great deal more to him than his wife was here with him in South Australia. There is sometimes a repellent ruthlessness about men who strip themselves of all ties to perform some great action; in Light, on the other hand, there is always a gentleness below the strength of feeling and purpose, that comes from an affectionate character forced into isolation.[4]

But unfortunately, Light's fateful 'battle with a new environment' did not result in a clear victory. His selection of the site of Adelaide, his town-plan and country survey did not represent an unambiguous triumph over opposing forces; they did not cancel out the memory of those humiliating reverses at sea, in Spain, in England and Egypt. Rather, things jogged on much as before. The superior timing and tactics of Hindmarsh had ensured that Light missed out on the governorship, and had to make do with a secondary position. This underlined how little merit could achieve without interest or money, but it also pointed to a psychological fact, that Light preferred to avoid decisive confrontation, to defer meeting what might prove climactic. It is true that, at the height of the storm, Light contemplated a fiery ignition, his lightning transformation into a figure of destiny; but the storm passed, the horizon cleared, the familiar in-betweens of daily life were resumed.

So in South Australia, despite the auguries of apotheosis, nothing much changed. The old resistances – class and party interests, divided and divisive administrative structures – surfaced, creating obstacles which the meticulous surveyor found more difficult to overcome than anything an unknown environment could throw up against his advance. At length, sickened by the controversy stirred up around his conduct of the survey, Light resigned, retiring to spend the last eight months of his life at 'Theberton', the cottage he had built for himself between Adelaide and the coast. Light was not averse to heroic soliloquy when it came to combating personal calumny or bureaucratic self-interest: 'The reasons that led me to fix Adelaide where it is I do not expect to be generally understood or calmly judged of at present. My enemies, however, by disputing their validity in every particular, have done me the good service of fixing the whole of the responsibility on me. I am perfectly willing to bear it; and I leave it to posterity, and not to them, to decide whether I am entitled to praise or to blame.'[5] But he was not writing his own epitaph; whatever the opinion of posterity, Light was taking his own future in hand.

Indeed, if his destiny was to die a hero's death in South Australia, Light was anxious to put it behind him. It is true that his tubercular condition finally got the better of him in October 1839, but he did not go about his affairs posthumously as it were, as if the end had been foreseen and further ambition nullified. Besides the *Brief Journal* already quoted from, and the *Last Diary* (which we shall come to), Light's extant writing in 1839 is confined to four letters. But this slender literary production is not necessarily evidence of incipient tragedy. Light was an artist before he was a writer: in his last year he produced at least five watercolours of Adelaide and its environs. During his Mediterranean years, Light had sought to augment his income by preparing albums of topographical drawings. *Sicilian Scenery* appeared in 1823 and *Views of Pompeii* in 1828, at which time, Steuart says, Light was also planning another series of sketches, entitled *Views of Genoa*.[6] Light's object was presumably the same now: by illustrating the topography and early history of the new colony, to earn himself some much-needed income.

Again, this was not the panic-stricken act of a man dying. Light had no sooner reached Kangaroo Island, some two and a half years earlier in August 1836, than he had begun sketching. His *Views of 'Rapid Bay' and 'Nepean Bay'* appeared in a booklet published in London in early 1837, while an engraving of his *A View of the Country and of the Temporary*

1 *Map of Central Australia*, compiled by R. Lewis and B. Lucas from Australian Army, ONC P–13 & P–14, AUS MAP: National Topographical Map Series 1 and Indexed Map of Aboriginal Central Australia in T. G. H. Strehlow, *Songs of Central Australia*

2 *Lutheran Church, Hermannsburg Mission*, Central Australia, 1994

3 Ewald Namatjira (attrib), *Aboriginal Tribal Country at Mt Sonder*

4 *Carl Strehlow's headstone*, Horseshoe Bend, Finke River, Central Australia, 1994

5 Giorgione, *La Tempesta*, Gallerie dell' Accademia, Venice

6 Giorgione, altarpiece, *Madonna with Saints Liberale and Francis*, Duomo, Castelfranco Veneto

9 *La Tempesta*, earlier version reconstructed according to the evidence of X-rays

OPPOSITE

7 Giorgione, *The Holy Family*, Samuel H. Kress Collection, National Gallery of Art, Washington DC

8 Lorenzo di Credi, *La Natività*, Fondazione Scientifica Querini Stampalia, Venice, Italy

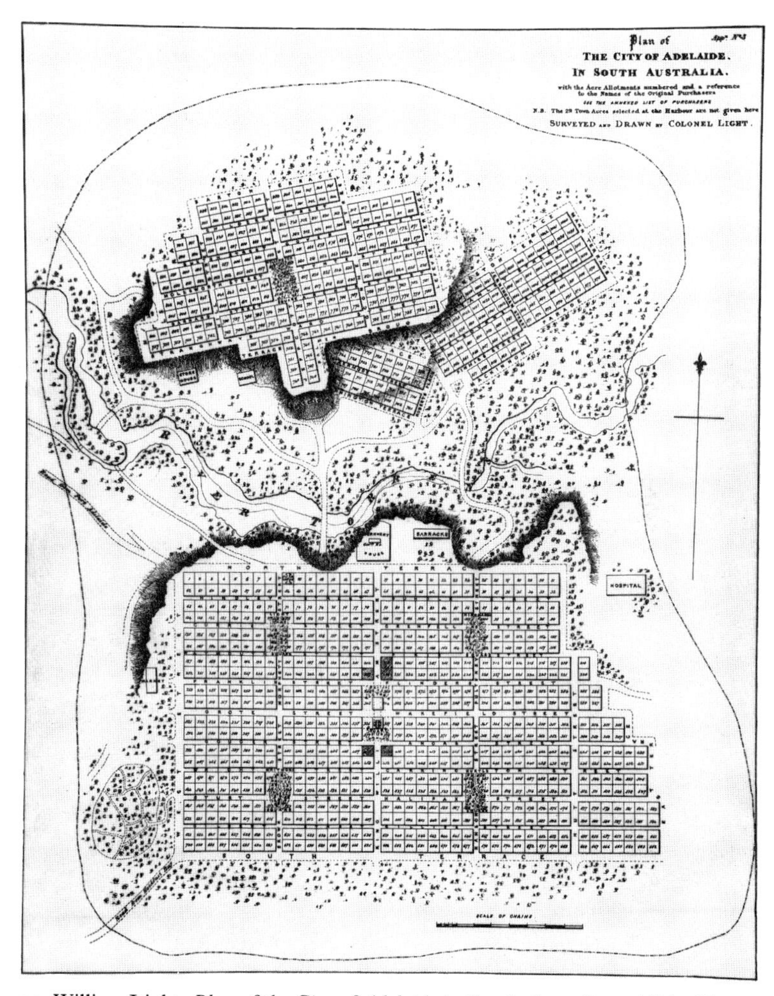

12 William Light, *Plan of the City of Adelaide in South Australia*, published by John Gliddon, South Australian Agent, 3 Austin Friars

OPPOSITE

10 William Light, *Self-Portrait*, Art Gallery of South Australia, Adelaide

11 William Light, *Sketch for Self-Portrait*, Mortlock Library, SSL:M:B16527, State Library of South Australia, Adelaide

13 *Noto, Sicily, town plan*, modified from G. Canale, *Noto – La Struttura Continua della Città Tardo-Barocca*, Palermo, 1976

14 William Light, *The Amphitheatre*, from *Views of Pompeii*, drawn on stone by J. D. Harding, after drawings by William Light, Esq, London, 1828

15 William Light, *Part of the Temple of Juno* in *Sicilian Scenery*, from drawings by P. De Wint, the original sketches by Major Light, London, 1823

16 William Light, *Landing Place, Glenelg, South Australia*, Art Gallery of South Australia, Adelaide

17 John Michael Skipper, *Holdfast Bay, S.A., 1836*, Art Gallery of South Australia, Adelaide

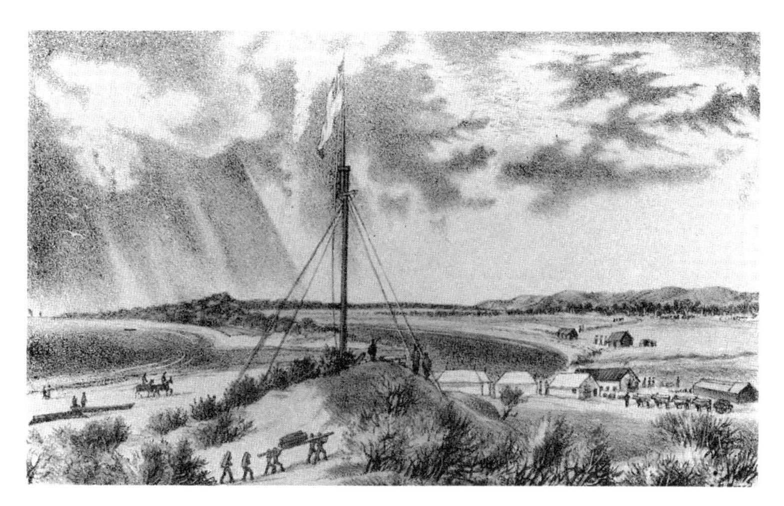

18 Alfred Scott Broad, *Glenelg, Holdfast Bay, South Australia, 1837*, Art Gallery of South Australia, Adelaide

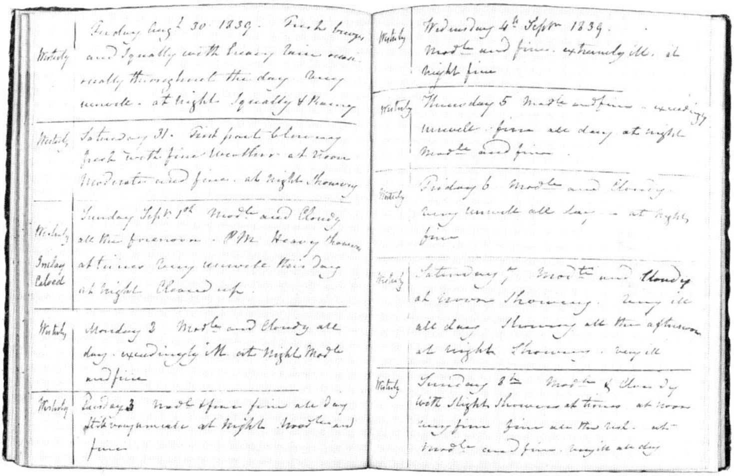

Westerly — Friday Augt 30 1839. Fresh breeze and Squally with heavy rain occasionally throughout the day. Very unwell. at night Squally & Rainy

Westerly — Saturday 31. First part blowing fresh with fine weather at noon Moderate and fine. at night Showery

Westerly / Smday Calved — Sunday Septr 1st Mod^te and Cloudy all the forenoon. P.M. Heavy showers at times Very unwell this Day at night Cleared up.

Westerly — Monday 2 Mod^te and Cloudy all day. exceedingly ill at night Mod^te and fine

Westerly — Tuesday 3 Mod^te & fine fine all day still very unwell at night Mod^te and fine

Westerly — Wednesday 4th Septr 1839. Mod^te and fine. extremely ill. at night fine

Westerly — Thursday 5 Mod^te and fine – exceedingly unwell. fine all day at night Mod^te and fine.

Westerly — Friday 6 Mod^te and Cloudy. very unwell all day – at night fine

Westerly — Saturday 7 Mod^te and Cloudy at noon Showery. Very ill all day Showery all the afternoon at night Showery. very ill

Westerly — Sunday 8th Mod^te & Cloudy with slight showers at times at noon very fine fine all the rest. at Mod^te and fine. very ill all day

19 William Light, *Last Diary*, entries August 30 – 8 September 1839, item 668 of the City of Adelaide Civic Collection

20 *Minerva with Lance and Shield*, Museo Nazionale, Naples

22 Johnny Warrangkula Tjupurrula, *Water Dreaming with Man in Cave*, 1972

OPPOSITE
21 *Papunya School Mural (Honey Ant Dreaming)*, August 1971, with (left to right) Obed Raggett, Fred Friis and Kaapa Tjampatjimpa

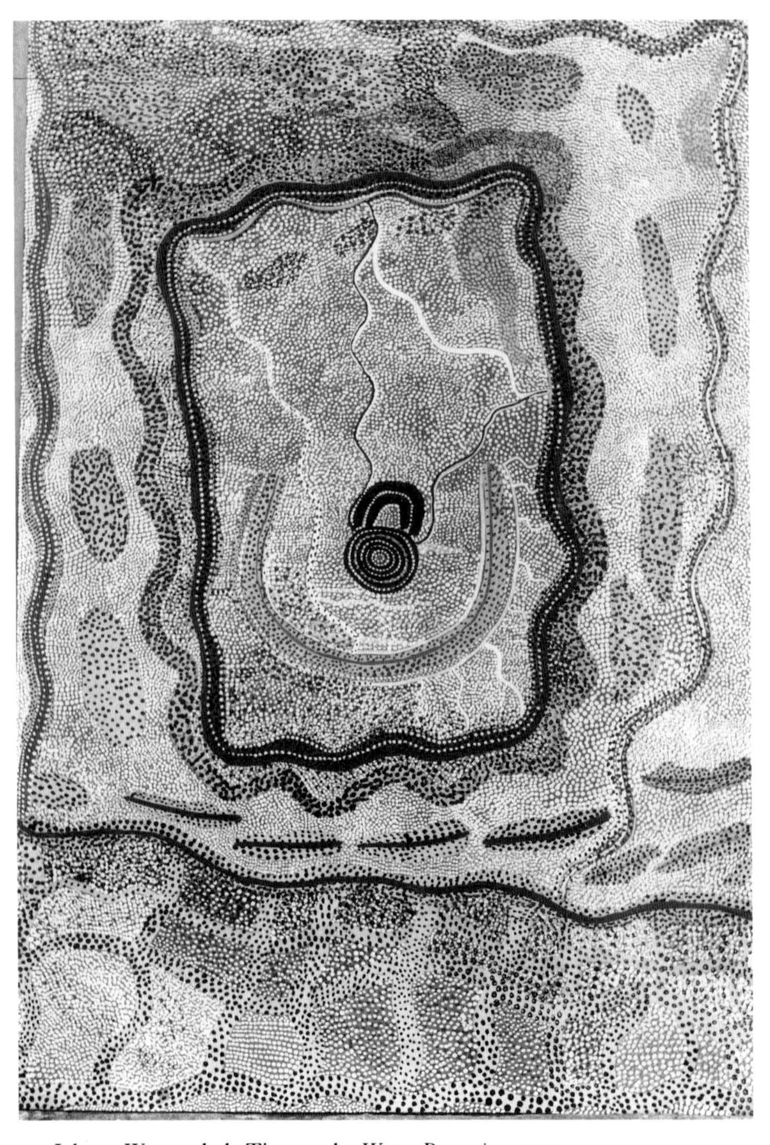

23 Johnny Warrangkula Tjupurrula, *Water Dreaming*, 1973

Erections near the Site of Adelaide was said, on its publication in London in February 1838, to be the first of a series. Elder says that no further proof of a series exists, and supposes that the failure of the print to sell made Light abandon his plans.[7] The pressure on Light to accelerate the rate of the survey and the acrimonious debate about the siting of Adelaide, which continued throughout 1838, may have held up Light's plans, but there is no reason to suppose he abandoned them. His resumption of painting with a view to working up earlier field-sketches, making them fit for sale or publication, suggests quite otherwise.

When in late February Light wrote in a letter, 'I live in perfect retirement, working as well as I am able for the support of the few years the Almighty may perhaps yet grant me for this world,' it was presumably this project that he had in mind.[8] In any case, works produced in the first half of 1839 included *Bank of South Australia, North Terrace, Adelaide*, a watercolour finished on 12 February, *The Para, about twenty-five miles North of Adelaide* (finished 22 February, from a sketch made on 13 January), *Messrs Fisher and Handcock's Station near the Gawler Range* (finished 7 March, from a sketch made on 9 January), *Mr McLaren's Party, January 11th 1839, about 14 miles North of the Para Pass* (finished 14 March 14th), *The Rapid sailing up Gulf St Vincent* (finished 20 March, and possibly representing the brig caught in a storm on 12–13 October 1836) and *The Buckinghamshire in Holdfast Bay* (after 6 April).[9]

Light wanted to avoid his destiny, to put off the ending by another means. The entrenched positions of the warring colonists had weighed him down. But Light by name was also light by nature. He wanted to move on. Swiftness, a nimble mastery of topographical advantages, was a formula for life as well as military campaigning. To stay put was to grow monumental, grave. Even though his health was poor, the phthisis he had been incubating for perhaps more than a decade making strenuous movement difficult, Light continued to harbour plans of flight. On 25 April he heard that he was 'to go home for the [South Australian] Company';[10] while 'by June he was definitely going on the *Ganges*.'[11] More actively, even while he had been engaged in the survey, Light had had his English agent open negotiations to secure him a position as captain of a new mailship planned to ply between Suez and India.[12] Most actively, Light, no longer employed publicly, offered his services as a surveyor privately; hence his two trips to Lynedoch Vale.

The biographers will have none of this. Overcome by posterity's sense of an ending, weeping in advance as it were, they find Light's efforts to put off his quietus merely pathetic. As history's Olympian gods, they know how it will finish, and as such, they are more interested in his after-life than in his life. It is his reputation whose birth they relish; and the details of his day-to-day existence cannot gloss this. They are cloudy incidentals and environmental irregularities, when what is required is a theatrical prospect, a painted sunset, a definite statue. 'There is something deeply tragic in this man turning from the settlement he had founded towards the country he had not been born in, and which had given him so little,' writes one biographer.[13]

Another, in what purports to be a work of historical geography, dreams: 'His thoughts must often have been bitter as he lay in his sweltering hut thousands of miles from "home". He had lost his inheritance, his wife lived with another man, he had been driven from office, most of his writings and sketches had been burned . . . Little wonder that Light liked to recall the freer, more expansive days of derring-do in the Peninsular Wars and dreamy wanderings round the Mediterranean. He loved to talk about famous friends and acquaintances of his military past, such as Wellington and Napier, probably contrasting them with his petty bourgeois colonial persecutors.'[14]

Is there any evidence for this? Light described himself as 'living a most retired life';[15] his friend Edward Stephens chided him, 'You must come into town, I am satisfied you are too dull where you are, ever to get better.'[16] While Light seems studiously to have avoided self-dramatization, biography insists on representing him theatrically; as if, already dead, he were ambitiously rehearsing his own apotheosis. In his last months, Keats described his 'habitual feeling of my real life having past, and that I am leading a posthumous existence',[17] and he associated this with his doctor's extraordinary prohibition on writing poems. Light's biographers too frequently write about him as if, in Keats's words, 'the knowledge of contrast, feeling for light and shade, all that information (primitive sense) necessary for a poem are great enemies to the recovery of the stomach.'[18] In order to give his life a statuesque outline and form, they ignore the subject's own power of in-forming himself, his desire to continue making sense of things, his existential awareness that consciousness, like the clouds, goes on plastically transforming itself to no end.

The biographer's urge to bring his character alive is, in this sense, a kind of historical death-wish. Making Light compose his own funeral oration, his ability to spin a different story is weakened; answering to historical demands, his art of self-preservation, which consists in giving himself up to his surroundings (to the rhythm of painting, say), is undermined. Making up a story for them, he becomes their native informant, their way of obtaining information about a country, the past, which (in truth) he does not inhabit. The colonizer becomes the colonized, characterized as an inhabitant of the land of the dead. An early description of the Kaurna people reports that 'The strangers [the Europeans] disembarked at Yertabulti (the land of sleep or death), since named Port Adelaide.'[19] This is not an ironic prophecy of the Kaurna's own fate; to read it ironically is merely to enclose these people within our predetermination of history. It refers to a cultural self-enclosure act, one that biography recapitulates when it refuses to entertain another ending.

The biographical enclosure act works, ironically, to relegate the subject's subjectivity to oblivion. When Elder summarizes Light's life under the headings 'The Boy', 'The Youth', 'The Soldier', 'The Wanderer', 'The Task', 'The Accomplishment', 'The Rift', 'The Decline' and 'The Aftermath',[20] he conceptualizes him in the same terms as Aristotle describes the tragic hero: 'For the Aristotelian grave spirit the model self was always, properly, working to purify itself of self, not only by disciplining the beast, but also by being public spirited – that is by joining the purifiers. Not to discipline the self-life by means of public service was, in essence, evil. A model self went about being good by assuming a virtuous public role as a military, political, perhaps judicial, leader in society.'[21] Aristotle views the gravitational pull of selfhood much as he views motion, as a source of instability, a dangerous and eccentric departure from what is stable and objectively known.

To write about Light's life from an Aristotelian perspective is, then, to engage in a double denial of subjectivity: psychologically, it entails narrating his life in so far as he succeeded in departing from himself; historically, it means treating his peripatetic existence as incidental to his achievement, as if his entire migratory life were a preparation for settling down. The hero that emerges from this statuesque logic is not simply a biographical fiction; he is an historical myth critical to the imperial project. Indeed, in so far as his fate is coterminous with the history he enacts, he reveals the mythic nature of Western history itself. These writers invoke what Obeyesekere has dubbed 'the "Prospero" syndrome or myth model' to which generations of imperial apologists have assimilated their culture heroes: 'The redoubtable person coming from Europe to a savage land, a harbinger of civilisation who remains immune to savage ways, maintaining his integrity and identity.'[22]

And this goes on. Strait-jacketing Light within the biographical paradigm not only creates a father-figure – and, in the colony he founded, a worthy son. It also provides a respectable genealogy for the citizens of the new country who, characteristically, understand their commitment to public service as a direct inheritance from the founding father from whom they claim direct descent. Dutton may like to speculate that Francis Light was polygamous, and congratulate the family on its lusty production of illegitimate offspring,[23] but not so Light's descendant A. F. Steuart, who dedicated much energy to showing that Light's mother was a sultan's daughter, although elsewhere he is content to say that she bore 'the Portuguese name of Martina Rozells.'[24] Nor Penelope Mayo, a lineal descendant of George Mayo, whom Maria Gandy married after Light's death, and who, in her pious memoir, makes no reference to Captain Hugh Bowen, with whom Light's second wife lived from 1834 and by whom she had two daughters, Mary (1834) and Bianca (1835). The latter of these daughters, although illegitimate herself, has played a curious minor role in Adelaide's search for a genealogy of its own.[25]

In 1901 Princess Mary visited Adelaide and talked to an old-timer who had known Light. It seemed she had once passed a summer in a Florentine palace owned by Light's daughter (*sic*) Bianca.[26] The distinctive Englishness of South Australians, their unrivalled patriotism, could, it appears, be traced back to their founder and his social connections. In 1944, Mr Justice Mayo, a grandchild of Maria Gandy, presented the Corporation of Adelaide with Bianca's sketchbook, citing it as proof that Bianca had inherited Light's artistic talent.[27] This gesture, and the earlier publication of *The Life and Letters* in 1937, drops the capstone of the nationalist genealogy into place. As far as is known, Mary Bennet's relationship with Bowen was as fecund as her marriage to Light was childless, but by repatriating Bianca in this way Adelaide's beginnings are lent a mythic logic. Light is made a father in a multiple sense, of a family, a city, an historical destiny.

The value of founding myths lies in their power to lend a community's history an allegorical dimension. Embracing the Mosaic myth of Light the father leading his people into a promised land, a 'Greater Britain', permits South Australians to be patriotic. Every mere coincidence of historical time and place can be interpreted filially, as evidence of legitimate descent. And, as Obeyesekere perceives, this way of thinking can become not merely a way of narrating the past, but the object of history itself.[28] So a book strategically published in the sesqui-centennial year of Adelaide's founding sets out to debunk the heroic myth that has grown up around Light; to show, in particular, that Light was responsible neither for Adelaide's famous town-plan nor for the selection of its site. The authors mistake Light for the myth that surrounds him, and their evidence is circumstantial at best, but the enterprise seems promising – until one discovers that their object is not to demythologize South Australia's beginnings, but to install another heroic founder: Light's assistant surveyor, G. S. Kingston. And the motivation? Not, say, a respect for spatial history, but filial piety it seems: one of the authors claims descent from Kingston. It is his own name that he seeks to clear.[29]

The Light of the biographers is a necessary hypothesis of imperial history. The white colonist – a Colonel Light, an Arthur Phillip or a Major Mitchell – overseeing a landscape in transformation from the primitive to the civilized annexes his own life to that of the imperium; an Aristotelian assimilation and redemption is effected. And to account for the appearance of the right man at the right time, the biographers, who paradoxically cling to the myth of self-determination, invoke the trope of providential coincidence. But in reality, the man who stands (whether in his own journal or in the picturesque lithographs of his contemporaries) poised between Past and Future personifies imperial history. His heroic status underlines the point that modern biography has little to do with the territory of the interior and everything to do with fantasizing the mechanisms of colonial expansion and territorial appropriation.

And for this providential convergence of the personal and the historical to work mythically, to provide an alibi of Empire, it is necessary for the biographical subject to age and die. Cook's apotheosis, say, is dependent less on the manner of his living than on the circumstances of his dying. In any case, for those servants of Empire who fail to wither, history has another remedy: forgetfulness. As the colonial functionary departs from the colony, his life peels off from that of the infant, and vigorously-growing, colony he helped to found. Back in Bath, he ceases to be heard, his days run out; and the biographer, faced with the difficulty of inventing an historically fateful ending, passes over his after-life in as few pages as is decently possible.

If the nexus sketched here between biography and imperial history is genuine, it follows that a life differently written may also be a history of colonization differently written. If, instead of focusing on the clear light of imperial identity, we attended to the daily chiaroscuro of Light's historical existence, from that more maculated surface – a surface remarkably like the topography of the tubercular lung – a different conception of living and dying might emerge. The environment, say, would no longer be a stage whereon the hero strutted his hour; its undulations, its routes and repetitions, might turn out to provide an essential context, an object of living. Even the thunderstorm might cease to mimic that great innovation of the Victorian theatre – footlights[30] – and serve instead to punctuate or 'blot' a larger atmospheric consciousness. In this light, we might be able to escape from imperialism's instant nostalgia, the impulse it feels to murder in order piously to commemorate.

But this does not mean writing another biography. It is true that a different account of Light's life would portray a very different man. It would unearth different lineages, different questions about his psychology. It would show that the deeper significance of Light's interrupted lineage – his truncated intimacy with his mother, his childless relationships with women, his own ambiguous appearance – is matriarchal; if Light was not a father-figure, but landless and dependent, in what way did he assert his power over those about him? What, indeed, was his notion of legitimacy, of continuity, of cause and effect? If the language of patriarchal authority was English, what was Light's mother tongue?

This is not simply a reminder that Light was fluent in a number of languages – as a schoolboy he was 'early noticeable for his ability in languages',[31] and he presumably had at least a relict knowledge of the tongue(s) his mother spoke – but to point to a different use of language. In so far as women depended on the patronage of men, they quickly learned to play many parts; so Light, and perhaps many men who, like him, find patriarchal poses absurd, learnt quickly to be mercurial. Slipping from one language to another, as he did in compiling his memoir of the Peninsular Campaign, his cryptography had the same effect as a woman's 'feminine charms': it intrigued and baffled the interested (presumably male) reader.

The enigmatic back-and-forth between English and Portuguese implied a model for the conduct of external dialogues. Light's conversations with his superiors would be at once deferential and non-committal, giving the impression that an innate difference or sense of pride always obliged Light to conceal or hold some part of himself in reserve, as if his vulnerability in a man's world, his dependence on patronage, were voluntary, conditional. This much is clear, and a sketch along these lines which accepted Light's own estimate that his had been 'a wandering life that precluded all advantages',[32] would undoubtedly draw attention to a mode of existence that was, after all, common in the late eighteenth and early nineteenth-century British imperial circuit (Light's father had lived similarly). It could even give us grounds for suggesting that a man without a name might, in these circumstances, take the accident of his naming seriously.

After all, it is clear that light had a highly equivocal meaning in Light's life. As a half-caste whose olive complexion stood out in white society, Light was not of the light or the dark; he had to move between them, putting on and taking off different masks as situations altered. Visiting Adelaide in 1840, Lady Jane Franklin heard that as a youth Light 'had wished to enter [the] East India Company's service, but he was refused on being halfcaste.'[33] Elsewhere, an ambiguous swarthiness might carry a different value. During the Peninsular War, Light 'was able to entertain the Spanish ladies in romantic fashion by singing to them with a guitar accompaniment, and was in turn entertained by them with music and dancing.'[34] But the same writer adds: 'His dark complexion, however, and his occasional tendency to speak in French often led to his being taken for a spy.'[35]

Light's life was consciously chiaroscuro, neither light nor dark but the drama of their dialogue. When as a fourteen-year-old Light entered the navy, he gave his birthplace as Suffolk, not Penang. Leaving the king's service at the earliest opportunity less than three years later, Light apparently spent part or all of the next six years in India.[36] From the beginning he oscillated humanly between dark and light, the sallow and the pallid, and being neither one nor the other, learned to live in between. This was how he first earned a reputation for bravery. Held up near Tarbes in March 1814, Wellington wanted an estimate of enemy numbers. Light volunteered to provide one, and riding forward 'as if he would force his way through the French skirmishers', he then 'dropt his reins and leaned back as if badly wounded.' The enemy, 'thinking him mortally hurt', allowed him to pass along the front of their light troops. Then, spurring his horse on, he galloped back behind their light troops across the French main line. 'His sudden appearance, his blue undress, his daring confidence and speed, made the French doubt if he was an enemy.' By mimicking the French in his 'blue undress', Light proved himself British; by pretending to be dead, he first came into view.[37]

Certainly, a biography along these lines would be a beginning, and it would enable us to interpret the events associated with the colonization of South Australia differently. A consciousness of Light's (and light's) ambiguity might make us see the whites, going through the motions of marking out spaces, marching here and there, erecting walls, as ghosts, men who lacked the chiaroscuro of grounded lives. The permanent shadows cast by their solid walls were proof of their insecurity, their ungroundedness – their determination to divide the light from the dark. This evidenced a discomfort as much metaphysical as physical. When an early South Australian colonist remarks, of an Aboriginal boy whose behaviour 'evinces some notion of a future state', that this 'would seem to show that they are not altogether without "light"',[38] he illustrates that metaphysical prejudice. Associating aliveness to the parrot-colours of this world with a blindness to the unseeable light of the next, he also described the price of enlightenment: voluntary burial of the physical shadow, resurrection as light.

But while this inversion of the rhetoric of binary oppositions is seductive, it does not escape from the enclosure act it purports to expose. To assimilate Light to the other side of the colonial argument, to portray him as the secret agent of a post-colonial sensibility, a figure with a natural, because historically-shaped, sympathy with South Australia's native peoples, is not simply to ignore the inconvenient fact of Light's quite conventional assessment of the Kaurna as a degraded race fit only to provide the colonists with servants.[39] Under the aegis of metaphor, it is to continue to treat him biographically; to have Light personify a different historical narrative which, although it may appease white consciences, does nothing to help us out of the fundamental enclosure act it presupposes.

Whether Light is the willing or unwilling agent of Empire, it makes little difference to how, for example, we read the document referred to earlier, Light's so-called *Last Diary*, kept between 22 January and 9

September 1839. Begun on the day that most of Light's personal papers – his charts, sketches, diaries, letters and notebooks – were destroyed by fire, the *Last Diary* might be expected to have a special place in the biographer's artillery. Instead, its value proves negative, serving only to confirm the impression of a hero tragically worn down. 'The diary is,' according to its modern editor, 'a sad document, revealing . . . the decline of the invalid until his death.' He summarizes it as 'an increasing number of references to ill health . . . and querulous comments on heat and mosquitoes.'[40]

And indeed, what can one do with entries like these?

> *Wednesday 27 February* – Dark gloomy weather and very disagreeable. Very unwell all day. Took medicine in the middle of the day. Very squally, rainy, and cold from 5 p.m. throughout the night. (Variable and light).
>
> *Monday 1 July* – Moderate and fine. At 9 a.m. long arched cloud extended from south to north nearly over the whole arch, indicating a change of weather. Pleasant air most part of the day. At 4 p.m. very cold. I felt rather better this day . . . (Light and variable).
>
> *Monday 2 September* – Moderate and cloudy all day. Exceedingly ill. At night moderate and fine (Westerly).[41]

Instead of incisive pen-sketches of people and places, wry observations and sentimental reminiscence, complacent judgements, or backward glances over travelled roads; instead of a conventional invocation of Providence and a determination to resign oneself to God's will, there is only this – an increasing number of references to ill-health, etc.

It is as if the man behind the handwriting has already evaporated. Instead of a settled character, we have a record of clouds; instead of a man, a troubled breathing. As a document to annex to the swelling theme of South Australian colonization, the *Last Diary* is of negligible value; but it is equally resistant to a revisionist interpreter. The latter needs 'facts' to make out his case. He is interested in debunking myths: Light's poverty, for example, is refuted by John Tregenza, who shows that 'Theberton', far from being a peasant's cottage, was a comfortable house that more than adequately reflected Light's military rank and public position. Far from expiring in penury, Light died a relatively wealthy man, leaving to Maria Gandy (and her future husband) substantial assets in the form of land.[42]

Light's self-righteous *Brief Journal* is better construed as a semi-official report, designed to commend him to colonial authorities in London, than as a final testament.

And so on . . . but the *Last Diary* can throw no light on such matters. It evinces no interest in them. Even more telling, it proceeds as if unaware of biographical convention. The environment of Light's little narrative is not the predicate of an autobiographical 'I'; if anything, their relationship is reversed. The 'I' of the *Last Diary* is the predicate of its surroundings, and is continuously reconstituted by the changes in the weather. It does not represent a fixed position, an historical personality, whether heroic or anti-heroic, simply a sequence of textual 'dots' which, linked one to another by a pattern of breathing, add up to a kind of 'printout' of Light's physical condition. The *Last Diary* may not represent any significant idea, but it can be said to mimic a life going on. As mimesis, the dramatic expression of a tragic destiny, it may be paltry; as *methexis*, though, the re-enactment of the primary scene, the exchange between life and death, its value might be very different.

But to appreciate this, it is not enough to assert the *Last Diary*'s poetic power. To detach Light from the pageant of colonization – as if his subjectivity had simply been overlooked, and could be recovered by an empathetic attention to eccentric details (the weather, say) that others in their haste to create a clear outline had overlooked – would only continue the mystification. Light's *Last Diary* is an historical document; not just because, say, it reflects a view, current in Light's day, that there was a correlation between climate and the causes, course and cure of phthisis, but because its very negativity, its refusal to anticipate and prepare for an ending, point to a counter-intuition of time and space – one in which the lie of the land, as the support of a man lying down at a particular angle to a particular window, disclosed a meaning, the possibility of a different ending or beginning. And this was an intuition as much historical as poetic; for it resisted the ideological enclosure acts that had come to bound both poetry and history, fitting them for the task of imperial expansion. In effect, it kept alive the idea of the ground.

This somewhat grandiose rhetoric needs itself to be grounded, and we might begin with a justification of the meanings I have been ascribing to the term 'enclosure act'. For the Enclosure Acts which transformed the appearance of parts of England in the eighteenth century, and which, by accelerating advances in the art of practical surveying, set the scene for the rational colonization of South Australia, were not simply physical encroachments on the land with far-reaching social, political and economic implications. They were part and parcel of a much larger process of philosophical and poetic closure, whose primary supposition was a neutralization of the ground, and whose most potent consequence was a theory of colonization as a clarifying return to origins; as a journey which, being circular and played out on a level, markless plain, left no historical trace. Finally, for us, interested in punning as a mechanism of causation, the enclosure acts of Enlightenment thinking had their consequences for the interpretation of light.

That biography recapitulates history is implicit in the writings of John Locke, whose theory of mind is analogous to his theory of the state. If at first after the Fall, man's 'only inherent property was the labour of his body', this property nevertheless 'gave man the means to acquire more'; or, as Locke explained, '*As much Land* as a Man Tills, Plants, Improves, Cultivates, and can use the Product of, so much is his Property. He by his Labour does, as it were, inclose it from the Common.'[43] It is the distinction between 'the Common' and land profitably enclosed that lies behind the doctrine of *terra nullius*; as Alan Frost writes, 'in European eyes the Aborigines had not subdued and cultivated the Earth so as to obtain "dominion" over it. In Locke's description, New South Wales was one of those "*great tracts of Ground* . . . which (the Inhabitants thereof not having joyned with the rest of Mankind, in the consent of the Use of their common Money) *lie waste*, and are more than the People, who dwell on it, do, or can make use of, and so still lie in common." '[44]

'Clearing' then, at least as it applies to the process of colonization, involves a double enclosure act. It means a physical division of the land; but before that, it entails a prior conceptual enclosure act in which the 'Ground' is subsumed within the category of 'Land'. The clearing-away of obstacles – tree stumps, obstinate slopes, rocks inconveniently scattered in one's path, dense passages of bush – masquerades as the disclosure of a land for all; it seems to increase the quantity of space available for settlement. But the impression of an extended ground, the revelation, say, of a topography, is illusory; 'occupation means clearing', as one settler succinctly remarks,[45] because to clear is to neutralize the lie of the land and, by minimizing local differences, to prepare the way for linear inscription and division. Colonial history begins when and wherever the 'Governor marked out the Lines for the Encampment.'[46] Denying the charge of a common ground, clearing neutralizes the lie of the land; producing the ideological enclosure act essential to colonization's self-legitimation, it gives historical significance to that ambiguous phrase's other connotation.

But this passage from ground to land equally describes the biographical colonization of subjectivity, its determination to set the ego against its environment. Locke's picture of the unformed mind as a *tabula rasa* corresponds to the colonist's vision of an unenclosed ground open for occupation but originally (at birth) undifferentiated and held in common. In this context, the object of biography becomes plain: as a history of the mind's development, it is a narrative of successive enclosure acts – those processes of intellectual planting, tillage and improvement – through which the individual came to distinguish himself from those about him. But for this process of annexation, this extension of 'his Property, which another had no Title to, nor could without injury take from him,'[47] there would be no individual, and therefore no biography to relate.

Selfhood as a personal property is also a critical *a priori* in engineering the ground's disappearance. The process can be described in simple terms: how could the 'I' of biography or autobiography lay claim to a distinct identity if he could not stand erect, clear-cut against the landscape (as he might appear in Gainsborough's full-length portraits)? It is true that the land falls away around and behind him; but he is merely 'stuck on' to the ground. In order for him to possess a statuesque and imperturbable uprightness, resembling that of an oak tree, he must inhabit a park-like world where the lie of the land has been recomposed as a flat combination of pathways and prospects. The ability to stride forth confidently is associated, by authors as diverse as Svevo and Sacks, with psychic integration.[48] On the contrary, resting on a prior smoothing-away of obstacles, a sub-military gait corresponds to James Hillman's concept of paranoid communication[49] – in which the subject, afraid of genuine contact and dialogue, talks without listening, walks without looking where he puts his feet.

If this relationship between the biographical 'I' and a particular mode of standing erect seems merely 'poetic', it is perhaps because insights of this kind – where identifications rather than identities are described – are precisely what biography's enclosure act seeks to exclude from the realm of selfhood. Light may be another of biography's victims. One of my own biographical interests is the late eighteenth-century poet Henry James Pye, and there is a passage in his prospect poem *Faringdon Hill* whose didactic flatness allows a surveyor-like triangulation between the emergence of the biographical 'I', the differentiated land of the Enclosure Acts, and the psycho-physical properties of light. The opening lines of the poem make a little-frequented way into the historical landscape of the picturesque – a key term in the rhetorical artillery of colonization – but here our gaze is focused in the opposite direction, on the internal landscape the poem reveals.

Climbing the eminence which lies adjacent to his country seat, Pye finds not only the landscape of Oxfordshire, Gloucestershire and Berkshire coming into view, but also the countryside of childhood. What is more, the spatial organization of the landscape is structurally analogous to the mechanism of memory. Pye is at first baffled:

> Large, and more large extends the spacious scene;
> Till on the verdant top our labour crown'd,
> The wide Horizon is our only bound.

An undifferentiated view of this kind might be another Australia; its 'glare' offers no point of access to the classifying eye. However, this first impression is immediately contradicted. In fact, it is a picturesque excess, not a wilderness monotone, that overwhelms the bard:

> What various objects scatter'd round us lie,
> And charm on every side the curious eye!
> Amidst such ample stores, how shall the Muse
> Know where to turn her sight, and which to choose?[50]

In this sense, the local prospect is antipodal to that described by the likes of Barron Field. If in Australia the aesthetic gaze felt the vertigo of absolute liberty,[51] in eighteenth-century England it was too hemmed-in to wander.

Despite his rhetorical question, Pye sets out to mobilize language, to catalogue his surroundings:

> Here lofty mountains lift their azure heads;
> There it's (*sic*) green lap the grassy meadow spreads;
> Enclosures here the sylvan scene divide;
> There plains extended spread their harvests wide;

Here oaks, their mossy limbs wide stretching, meet
And form impervious thickets at our feet;
Through aromatic heaps of ripening hay,
There silver Isis wins her winding way;
And many a tower, and many a spire between,
Shoots from the groves, and cheers the rural scene.

But now an odd thing happens: not content to contemplate the picturesquely historical landscape on every side:

Still, as I look, fresh objects seem to rise;
And lovelier pictures strike my raptur'd eyes,
As young remembrance paints each sylvan glade,
Where full of glee my careless childhood stray'd.

A new, inner landscape emerges; as Pye explains:

When in Memory's fond mirror shewn,
The country smiles with beauties not it's (*sic*) own;
Her fair reflection new delight supplies;
And every floweret blooms with deeper dyes;
The landscape seems to brighten while I gaze,
And Phoebus shines with more than summer rays . . .[52]

Reading this, one is tempted to backdate 'the passage from outer to inner travelling,' which Richard Holmes sees as a 'vital transformation or watershed in the history of Romanticism'. Here, long before de Nerval, is an imagination 'doubled back on itself'. In Pye's 'fond mirror', rivers and mountains at least have become 'a purely internal landscape.' This comparison is forced, but it is not wholly false; de Nerval's inward turn had, as Holmes notes, a technological context – the invention of photography.[53] Similarly, Pye compares the operations of memory to the behaviour of light in the 'fond mirror' of the Claude glass, 'a tinted convex mirror often carried by tourists and artists, which gave the landscape the ideal qualities of a Claude painting.'[54] The picturesque writer William Gilpin described landscapes viewed in a Claude glass as 'like the visions of the imagination; or the brilliant landscapes of a dream. Forms, and colours in brightest array, fleet before us; and if the transient glance of a good composition happen to unite with them, we should give any price to fix and appropriate the scene.'[55]

Unlike de Nerval, though, Pye observes a near-perfect, and therefore self-fulfilling (in more than one sense), coincidence between perception and memory. The mechanism of this equivalence is a light conceived of in Newtonian terms, as a principle of association, as a catalyst that joins objects in the eye of the beholder whilst itself remaining unbent, unimplicated, by these meetings. In this sense, as a mental principle, light is always more than light, a source of illumination and insight as well as a condition of sight. On Faringdon Hill, the horizon is not, despite what Pye says, the 'only bound' but simply the outermost of many. The 'Enclosures [that] here the sylvan scene divide' are metonymic of a mental as much as a physical landscape; they intimate a mode of seeing that corresponds to the process whereby consciousness becomes aware of its own operations. To understand the view, to 'possess' it, is to grasp the principles of its division, which are evidently as much logical and rhetorical as spatial. Only after the land has been enclosed in this way can it be grasped as a whole, as a picturesque prospect; the compositional equivalent of this double process of deconstruction and reconstruction are Pye's rhymes, emphasizing likeness in difference, and his tentative enjambments, reintroducing a sinuous obscurity into what has been laid bare.

This exercise in topographical analysis, whereby wholes are divided into fragmentary parts with the sole object of bringing them rhetorically, picturesquely, closer together, is analogous to the operation of the mind itself, which is not simply a mirror held up to nature but, like the Claude glass, arranges what it holds into harmonious forms. The faculty which, operating upon fragments it has detached from the whole, sets about joining them together according to the principles of association is what Hume called 'imagination'. And he saw a direct connection between these mental powers of associative grouping and enclosure and the cultivated landscape of Pye which, presided over by a network of landowners and propertied interests, was a physical expression of the way in which society went about constituting itself. As he wrote, 'the mind has a natural propensity to join relations, especially resembling ones, and finds a kind of fitness and uniformity in such an union. From this propensity are derived these laws of nature, that upon the formation of society, property always follows the present possession; and afterwards, that it arises from first or from long possession.'[56]

Applied to Pye's landscape, Hume's 'Newtonian' psychology finds a precise analogue in the multiplication of hedges and fences, as these are the essential mechanism of association. Joining 'two closely related objects', they both divide and bring into a closer relation. Hume's psychology explains why Pye's 'Enclosures' are bound to multiply. If the principle of mental association obeys the same laws as govern physical motion, it will seek to join related objects rectilinearly, rather than by serpentine or parabolic lines. This rationalization of the enclosure process should not be seen as a forfeit of liberty; from the point of view of human progress, it signifies an access of self-possession. To survey a countryside enclosed and cultivated is to behold a history of the mind.

And if we ask what the hedges, bringing all parts into communication with one another, correspond to in Newton's theory, then the answer is clearly light, whose rectilinear propagation made feasible the Claude glass and the camera obscura. It is light as a principle of mental organization that explains why, in Pye's poem, the coincidence between the landscape of memory and the landscape of the present is not complete; the second Phoebus of the imagination adds to the visible landscape a unifying order and compositional harmony which the outer light of day cannot match. This is why a serene summer's day only brings the past more sharply into relief: the very clarity of its light, its ethereal transparency, conjures up by association a light that, while it cannot be seen, may be imagined; and in that imagining, the spatial outlay of the land is made to represent the origins, the ground, of the biographical subject's self-constitution. As if, but for the many recollections of his former life which it harbours, it would be a wilderness, an Australia.

This prehistory of the Enlightenment of light bears directly on the progress of colonization; we could say that it provided an analogue of the doctrine of a return to origins. For a ubiquitous light was, by definition, one incapable of casting shadows; shining everywhere with equal intensity, it flattened out every difference. It treated the ground, say, as if it were planar, as if it already laid itself out before the gaze as a plain. So that when, in his biography of William Light, Geoffrey Dutton writes, apparently without irony, 'If Adelaide is lacking in mystery, so is the light that beats upon it and the plain that bears it,'[57] he unconsciously bears witness to the double enclosure act on which 'Adelaide', capital and symbol of a rationally-planned colony, was founded. The mystery of the city's historical coming into being is cancelled out by establishing an equivalence between the character of the light and the lie of the land. It is from their association, their providential mimicry of each other, that Adelaide springs; as if, even before it was built, the city was already invisibly there, and its colonial consolidation commemorated not its novelty but the longevity of its connection with the site.

Such a providentially smiling country could be said to glow with an inner light. It was ready for colonization; it seemed to wink like a diffused lighthouse to the newcomer intent on identifying resemblances – eyes in the landscape that answered his glittering gaze. Light of this kind, steady, diffused, invisible, lent the land a face, even an inviting sheen. We can say that it masked the ground. In any case, its purer light suggested the existence of a whiter Albion, a state of mind and being that lay as much in the virginal past as the redeemed future. And this, perhaps, provided a spiritual reason for the land's further levelling: the proliferation of sightlines which clearing facilitated not only signified the surveyor at his work; they answered to the colonist's desire to create a light house. Exposed bedrock shone; permanent pools and docilely-flowing brooks glittered; even the temporary flanks of bell-tents lent the military operation a festive appearance. It was if they were uncovering the uppermost layers of a buried city, and in sinking foundations recapitulated their own culture's beginnings.

The power to perceive inner light, spiritual gold, to discern the invisible within the visible, provides the invader with his metaphysical justification: he is being drawn magnetically home. Biographically, the possession of this insight marks the culmination of the subject's journey towards self-knowledge. Historically, or perhaps mythically, it shows that Haeckel's principle acts in the psychic as well as the physical sphere: the stages of the individual's inner life recapitulate the stages in the life of his tribe, whereby it has ascended the gradual path from darkness into light. To see the light is to see the justification for colonization. The dreamlike aspect of the white strangers, so often noted by indigenous witnesses, was not merely a satirical comment on their automata-like approach to walking; it described the fact that the newcomers were, indeed, focused on *tableaux vivants* of their own inflamed imaginations. To colonize was to substitute for the subtly-breathing earth an oneiric landscape of remembered museums or their literary counterparts. It was to inhabit a Romantic stage-set of abysses and broken columns – without ever once losing one's footing.

In a chapter of his autobiography entitled 'Psychical', Rider Haggard reports a series of 'imaginings' or 'dream-pictures' or (most tellingly) '*tableaux vivants*' which have come to him 'between sleeping and waking'. The five scenes, in all of which Haggard appears, seem to recapitulate the earliest days of mankind; generically, they recall nothing so much as museum dioramas, glimpses of remote places and times minutely reconstructed in miniature. The first scene features a clearing in the wood, a rough hut made of poles, a skin-clad woman cooking over a fire, 'I, standing by, a youngish man', children playing round. The second suggests a South African setting: a round hut surrounded by a fence, a black woman within, 'myself there also, a black man,' and a spear attack 'where I fall into the arms of the woman and die.' In the third scene, 'Myself, a man of about thirty' occupies a splendid chamber in a palace 'built in the Egyptian style', where a beautiful woman throws herself straight into his arms. In the fourth, the same beautiful woman is translated to the north, to the interior of a timber-built hall, where she sits, 'her elbow resting on her knee, her chin in her hand, and stares hopelessly into the fire'; 'myself, wearing armour' enters, and she throws herself on his breast. In the final tableau, the only one Haggard interprets, the setting appears to be Cyprus; the man and woman of the previous scenes are discovered in 'the mouth of a tunnel or mine-adit running into a bare hillside', where they eke out a miserable existence as miners, having been 'reduced to slavery by some invading and more powerful race.'[58]

When Haggard described these scenes to Sir Oliver Lodge, student of communication with the dead (and theorist of the modern radio receiver), Lodge showed little interest, excusing himself by saying that 'he lacked imagination.'[59] Haggard seems to have believed that his pictures provided evidence of transmigration or metempsychosis, or that they were 'racial memories of events that happened to forefathers.'[60] In any case, Lodge's remark is very much to the point: Haggard's dream-scenes might have been plucked from his own romances; far from evidencing a profound insight into early human history, they were Victorian cultural clichés. It was their clarity, their verisimilitude, that impressed Haggard; it was their photographic precision, their light, that persuaded him of their hidden significance. It was precisely Haggard's lack of an environmentally-attuned imagination that made him find them real.

Inner light of this kind, illuminating ancient times, was the agent of Empire. The past, dematerialized of its darkness, uniformly illuminated, was theatricalized as a sequence of dumb-shows demonstrating the drama of human progress. It might seem innocent to dabble with distant ghosts, but as von Rezzori recalls in his biographical novel *My Brother Abel*, spiritualization of the light had, from the point of view of those historical subjects it so one-sidedly illuminated, only one end. Devout theosophers, von Rezzori's aunts 'had but one sole wish, to dematerialise more and more and finally become pure spirit and unite with God'; Hitler, they explained, was 'spiritualizing the Germans and cleansing Germany of the low, materialistic Jews.'[61] But light that is Fascist, racist, can be traced back even to Humphry Davy. In the *Consolations*, which Christopher Lawrence characterizes as 'a florid example of the historical-evolutionary thought of the early nineteenth century,' Davy maintains that it is the '"intellectual power" of the "Caucasian stock" and those "powers . . . acquired by cultivation" [both of which Davy identifies with light] which are the source of European superiority. In time the narrator says this civilising process will lead to the extinction of the "negro race, and the red men" as the Caucasians absorb the "power belonging to a ruder tribe".'[62]

Noting that Davy was part of a social and political order based on division and exploitation, Lawrence finds it unsurprising that the famous Davy lamp, 'far from saving lives . . . was used to effect the exploration of deeper and more dangerous seams which in turn resulted in an increased death toll.'[63] And we might take this further; thinking of Charles Wesley's earnest addresses to the coal-miners of Bristol, the light his lamp cast into the darkness was analogous to the light of conversion trickling down the collier's begrimed cheek. It enclosed the savage workman within the dialectic of a progress predicated on the absolute opposition of light and dark; it preached the banishment of shadows, of the earth's down-to-earth chiaroscuro. Attaching the light to his brow, the miner advanced towards a light he could never reach; he saw ever more clearly into the heart of darkness – standing in the light thrown out by his mate behind, he saw his own outline metamorphosed into a diminishing cone of shadow, the imminence of his own rectilinear reduction and eclipse.

Conquest of the underground, whether psychic or telluric, is cognate with acts of colonization in so far as it depends on conceptualizing the environment of activity passively or theatrically. Before it can be penetrated, the ground must be compacted into a solid surface; the land, say, that can support the tread of feet. But this process of compaction – and the corresponding tirade by settlers against grounds that belie their most promising appearance on the map by being steep, marshy, intertidal, speluncar – not only provides a surface over which to advance; in its preternatural solidity, even in its glassy shimmer, it provides the transparency of the overground, that upper state ideally occupied by the far-seeing surveyor – not to mention the biographical subject keen to achieve intellectual self-possession. In this sense, the painfully tunnelled-out galleries of the mine embody the same impulse to headlong flight that the open plain harbours. Even if the coefficients of resistance they encounter are markedly different, the rider and the miner share the same ambition to enter the light.

'"Ennui" is not the inhabitant of a new colony,' Napier explained in *Colonisation*, a treatise he wrote to explain why, despite his personal enthusiasm for Light, he was declining the invitation to become South Australia's first governor:

> In England, a man is like a bird in an aviary; in Australia, he regains the woods and glades, and exchanges sameness for variety; the dulness of repetition, and *con*finement, and *re*finement, for the constant change of scenes, for freedom and the happy feel, which belongs to that state, "When wild in woods the noble savage ran," possessing as many of the advantages of civilisation as are required for social enjoyment, but which, in England, we are pushing, perhaps, beyond that point. Mr. Babbage's powerful genius seems to have found out, how to make us even *think* by machinery; and we may live to see "Frankenstein" no longer a romance! but my writing is as wild as the places I describe; led away by the recollection of those beautiful and lonely scenes, which I have seen on my pilgrimage through many countries; all crying aloud for *people*: everywhere regions without people! and yet in despite of this we huddle together in towns . . .[64]

This is an escapist fantasy: 'We rise, filled with curiosity, we half shave, half wash, half dress, and then half mad, with high and joyous spirits, we jump on our horses, (our breakfast half swallowed,) and away we go, the beast as wild as ourselves, crossing the country as we please. We mount a new hill, and a new country spreads far and wide before us . . .'[65] But it is also a method of possession and self-possession; self-knowledge may depend on escape from the aviary of refinement, but this flight from the conventional conveniently coincides with the occupation of new countries. The associationist logic, 'as wild as the places I describe', makes explicit the connection between self-writing and colonization; the imaginative movement from topic to topic proper to biography applies equally to traversing unknown lands. Where the ground is 'common', only the links that the mind makes can serve to differentiate it; his linear narrative is no different from the explorer's running survey which, ignoring their location on the surface of the earth, defines the position of objects in relation to his own line of passage.

Napier may resist Babbage's conception of the mind as a calculating machine; in the same vein, he expresses reservations about Wakefield's plan for the rational colonization of South Australia. But this difference, profound as its resonances are within, say, the history of science (and perhaps for a theory of human movements, if we had one), is superficial in the context of our enquiry. If the Enlightenment philosophers (including the visionary Wakefield and even the flat-footed Pye) inherit the Aristotelian suspicion of movement, the Romantics react by predicating knowledge on endless movement. If the former understand Progress as a calculated and incremental self-replication over the surface of the globe, as an expansion that leaves no gaps, the latter understand it as a long, Odyssean return to origins. Napier's rhapsody, like Rider Haggard's dioramas, is romantic in this sense. But although Charles Napier's Byronic desire to 'revisit those beautiful and lonely scenes, which I have seen on my pilgrimage through many countries,' differs from Pye's complacent contemplation of 'lovelier pictures' all about him, and suggests contrasting attitudes towards the relationship between self and environment, the differences may be more technical than philosophical.

Napier increases the distance between himself and the country that answers his dreams, but only in order to entertain more rapid ways of getting there. His Pegasus aspires, in short, to the condition of flight; he would like instantaneously to connect the remotest, loneliest regions, holding them together in the palm of his hand. The linear divisions he makes, in his fantasy 'crossing the country as we please', no longer resemble steadily-advancing lines of hedges; they are dreamlike precursors of the telegraph wire and the electricity cable. The colonization that Napier imagines, where peoples and places currently fragmented and isolated from one another are reconstituted in another country, is technological. It substitutes near-infinite speed for an accelerated rate of movement. If, in the associationist imagination, 'kindred objects kindred thoughts inspire,/ As summer-clouds flash forth electric fire,'[66] Napier's vision circulates the globe at the speed of light.

*

The history of light throws light on Light; or better, it introduces a complicating chiaroscuro retarding Light's too-easy biographical enclosure. And if, as von Humboldt maintained, history is a landscape of clouds, these magnifications of background details normally considered too remote from the human subject to have any value may even have a historical usefulness. For example, the stand-off between Romantic and pre-Romantic modes of knowing (and travelling), while undoubtedly overdrawn, contains in-between, as it were, a passage towards a Light who is not annexed to one historical movement rather than another, but whose subjectivity comes into existence precisely in his managing to hold his place on the curving line between their respective positions. And in navigating this course, refusing to be a founding hero, Light simultaneously avoids the enclosure acts of biography and imperial history. And this enigmatic refusal to have his portrait taken raises the question: where, on what ground, does he then claim to stand?

Take Light's conduct of the survey, and his subsequent defence of it contained in his *Brief Journal.* The science of surveying might be supposed to go hand in hand with a policy of organized colonization. Certainly, it was the essential *techne* of scientific land enclosure. And as Alfred Wallace saw, it could be a tool of social and political control as effective at home as abroad. It was Wallace's early experience as an apprentice surveyor, employed to implement parliamentary legislation for the enclosure of common ground along the Welsh Marches, that helped to turn him into a passionate advocate of land nationalization. Arbitrary land enclosure was as foreign to the principle of 'natural selection' as Lamarck's theory of the inheritance of acquired traits; agrarian Lamarckism could not produce a modification (improved yield, say) that could benefit future generations. Wallace was of the view that 'the only method of advance for us, as for the lower animals, is some form of natural selection . . . the only mode of natural selection that can act alike on physical, mental and moral qualities will come into play under a social system which gives equal opportunities of culture, training, leisure, and happiness to every individual.'[67]

But this phrase illustrates the fragility of Wallace's reasoning, its ungroundedness. It was just such an equitable social system that Wakefield thought could be achieved through close settlement based on the equal division and enclosure of the land. From our perspective, this apparent paradox is easily resolved; as neither party takes account of the lie of the land, but premises their social vision on an even, planar extension, they are logically bound to arrive at the same two-dimensional patterning of the surface. Wallace may envisage the process of enclosure centrifugally, as a means whereby indigenous but nucleated groups put themselves, cell-like, into contact with their neighbours, thus building up an increasingly complex social organism. Wakefield may view the matter centripetally, imagining the surveyor's chequerboard as a rationally attractive grid drawing in productive forces from without. But both assume that the surveyor's task is to flatten out the ground, to eradicate it of an uneven, even shadowy history.

And both, more importantly, fail to take account of the survey as a process which, whatever its ultimate outcome, entails in the first instance a going over the ground and a disclosure of locally-distinctive irregularities. The word 'survey' is said to have carried a double threat for the poet John Clare: 'On the one hand, scientific surveyors were enclosing the landscape of his boyhood; on the other, topographical artists and poets "overlooked" what made his life and landscape meaningful.'[68] Clare's vision, by contrast, was ground-level and magnified details at the expense of the whole; it was filled with a kaleidoscopic array of *macchie* – small birds, nuts, snails, tufts of grass. 'His eye does not pan the view as on a tripod; it zigzags from object to object like a gadfly, it has no resting place or focal point around which to frame a design.'[69] Clare 'begins anywhere and stops anywhere'; 'he is nearly always in motion, walking through a landscape which is itself in the process of continual seasonal and atmospheric change.'[70] But it would be a mistake to identify Light with the surveyors and 'overlookers' simply because he was South Australia's first Surveyor-General. In many respects, his vision resembled that of Clare, with its insect-eye attention to minutiae, its preoccupation with the local lie of the ground rather than with general prospects.

Accused by a Lieutenant Dawson (a London 'expert' consulted by the South Australian Commissioners) of not carrying the survey of the country sections forward swiftly enough, Light responded in his *Brief Journal*: 'Lieut. Dawson has reckoned as if this survey should be made in England or Ireland, where every facility is given by roads, carriages, provisions, lodgings, etc.; he could never have considered the difficulty of moving tents, provisions, and even water over a country without roads and without proper conveyances.'[71] To borrow a distinction made elsewhere, Light was not going over the ground again. His activity was not a diegetical narration of events, 'the redrawing of a line already drawn'; his task was 'to draw the line for the first time, to give space a narrative form and hence the possibility of a future history, a history that will subdivide, and even efface, [the explorers'] own narratives in the interest of a thousand domestic plots.'[72] In this sense, and bearing in mind the petty, malicious self-interest that seemed to animate his employers, Light would have been sympathetic with Clare's description of enclosure as the fencing-in of 'little parcels little minds to please.'[73]

'Lieut. Dawson seems to have overlooked entirely . . . the difficulty of passing over high hills without a path, or going through long grass reaching nearly to one's chin, nor does Mr. Hill or Lieut. Dawson consider that in surveying signals or some mark at different stations are absolutely necessary, and that in fixing these it takes sometimes a whole week for one party without doing any other work (not in England or Ireland where very often church steeples, chimnies, and various objects are stations already fixed for triangulations) . . .' Opposing the cursory running survey advocated by some impatient settlers, Light refused to join the facile overlookers. He would not pretend to see what he could not see: 'in many cases the parties have not been able to see one hundred yards before them.'[74] At least for a time, Light studied the lie of the land as Constable studied the clouds, carefully recording in his provisional, open-ended charts and sketches, 'the chiaroscuro of nature'.[75] And this approach carried over to the way he organised the *Brief Journal* in which he defended his actions.

Kant remarked that they say of someone 'whose mind has stepped over the border' that 'he has crossed the line'; and the philosopher commented, 'Just as if a man who crosses the equator for the first time were in danger of losing his understanding.'[76] The *Brief Journal* is, in this context, not simply a forensic display; its odd structure, the emotional chiaroscuro of its prose, embody a struggle to avoid the loss of 'understanding' – or a literary strategy for grounding understanding differently, as a gradual process of coasting rather than as a decisive but idealized coastline drawn on a chart. In criticizing Light's choice of site for Adelaide, George Stevenson, the Governor's Private Secretary, and his associates were not only questioning Light's knowledge of the ground; they were casting doubt on the grounds of his knowledge. But how, in the absence of a comprehensive survey of the entire coastline and its hinterland from Encounter Bay to Port Lincoln, could Light ground his reasoning more solidly?

Instead of reacting to the criticism in an equal and opposite fashion, Light seeks to deepen the conflict, to lend starkly-articulated differences a moody, dramatic chiaroscuro. His opponents appeal to universal economic and geographical principles which should determine the siting of capitals; Light responds by emphasizing the impossibility of generalization. More important than this suspension of panoptic judgement, though, is his counter-strategy of rehearsing the sequence of provisional steps which led to his eventual decision; by reprinting the journal he kept while engaged in surveying as much of Spencer Gulf as time permitted, he ties the process of reasoning to the route of his voyage. Rather than sum up and rationalize the results of his survey, he emphasizes the open-ended uncertainty of the process, including in his 'report' such apparently indecisive data as 'Sept. 1st [1836] – Fresh breezes and squally; went on shore to take some angles, but owing to the weather could effect nothing. Sept. 2nd – Too hazy for observations. Sept. 3rd – Bad weather all day, and nothing done. Sept. 4th – Sunday.'[77]

Light's reasoning is profoundly meteorological. Weather-patterns determine the content of his report, with its emphasis on the pathways and likely precipitation points of clouds, and also its form: its hesitations, back-tracking and states of in-between indolence. This is not to say that the variability of the weather – its open-ended motion towards no end, its cyclic but non-circular stability in change – corresponds to Light's character; this would be to indulge in the sentimentality of biography, and again to imagine Light as if he moved apart from the environment in which he acted. Nor did the offshore depths and shallows, the rack of the clouds and the mutable appearance of the lie of the land 'produce' Light. The local environment did, however, lend his movement the chiaroscuro of a deepening knowledge, one composed in equal measure of light and shadow; and this absorption in and of his surroundings surfaces, not in a table of wind and rain, but as a history of fleeting impressions.

On 20 November, Light reports, 'I observed something like a rock on the starboard quarter about half a mile from the beach, and apparently about two miles from ourselves; as I had not seen this before, I took the glass to examine it – it then appeared something like the hull of a ship in a haze, and in a few seconds, masts, yards, and rigging, were seen, and in a very few minutes after, the two ships at Holdfast Bay, full 12 miles from us, were distinctly made out, with the projecting land beyond them, and in less than ten minutes more nothing but sky and water was to be seen in that direction.'[78] Perhaps the 'extraordinary refraction' reflected on Light's skills as an observer; it was not the kind of information hungry land investors sought. By including ephemeral impressions in the historical record, Light kept alive the possibility that Adelaide might be grounded differently, as the product, not denial, of movement.

Motion produced emotion. Anxieties associated with fixing a site to settle were associated with balance of mind, with keeping an even keel; how, at sea, did one navigate between cloudy alternatives, how adjudicate between levels of uncertainty and probability? On 8 September, landing and discovering 'a fine stream of fresh water', Light's hopes 'were now raised to a pitch I cannot describe.'[79] On 12 October, 'we all felt in high spirits, the air had a freshness quite exhilerating (*sic*).'[80] By 6 November though, dealing with disgruntled emigrants, 'I had to undergo a little torment.'[81] A few days later, his spirits have once more soared: 'It is impossible to describe my feelings on this occasion – seeing three English vessels, on a lee shore, riding safely at the roadstead.'[82] But a day later his mood again plummets: 'I felt again quite broken with such repeated bad weather.'[83]

Light's 'repeated' is not simply an expression of impatience. It marks a momentary retreat into mechanistic solipsism; as if the weather is banked up against him, as if it conspires to defeat him. For the essence of his enterprise depends on the weather not repeating itself but extending to him dappled interludes where, with the assurance of the archer aiming his arrow at a gap in the trees, he can break out of the circular motion of the colonizers' cant. Unless he can demonstrate certain unrepeatable effects with an evolutionary logic of their own, there can be no way forward, no understanding of the nature of the new colony's groundedness. Unless the process of filling in the historical environment with impressions can continually add to the complexity and density of appearances, the whole colony must end as it began: a Utopia symmetrical with its dreaming half a world away.

This preoccupation with provisional appearances needs to be distinguished from a tendency to mistake appearances for reality. After all, the Wakefieldists, building their first houses in the parklands around Adelaide, could say that they were only proceeding 'as if' at home, and that they fully expected to shift camp as more knowledge of the country's true properties and prospects became available. But where the little capitalists understood their temporary settlements as an awkward hiatus in the grand return to origins, Light, one surmises, saw them as historically constitutional. In any case, a question of poetics, and not simply politics, was at stake here, one analogous to the distinction between the compositional practice of Giovanni Bellini and that of Giorgione. Did stability, at once psychic and social, depend on a linear stabilizing of boundaries, an arrest of unpredictable movement? Or did it reside in a choreography of the ground, a device for circulating to no end, much as ordinary dialogue does, or the walker who deepens certain paths in order to stay where he is?

The men who invested in Wakefield's Plan shared Kant's (and Aristotle's) prejudice against movement. They accepted the necessity of travelling to a new world in order to put their Utopian economics into operation, but they saw no virtue in the journey itself. People on the move, who were in between, were a threat to social order. From the village perspective (which even the colonist was supposed to possess), the traveller was always suspect: 'no one knew where wandering men had their homes or their origin; and how was a man to be explained unless you at least knew somebody who knew his father and mother . . . even a settler, if he came from distant parts, hardly ever ceased to be viewed with a remnant of distrust . . . especially if he had any reputation for knowledge, or showed any skill in handicraft.'[84] And if systematically to imagine oneself somewhere else represented 'positive unreason', or 'Vesania' as Kant called it,[85] their suspicions were no doubt well-grounded.

Wakefield's plan for the colonization of South Australia sought to create an 'as if' society: a community that behaved *as if* independent of the mother country, trading, building and legislating for itself as if autonomously constituted and self-regulating. But this pretence of sturdy self-determination was in reality proof of its continuing subjection to imperial authority; in asserting its internal efficiency, it mimicked and flattered the patriarchal gaze which liked to see in it a likeness of itself. Its movement was in this sense purposeful and circular, like the pistons of the steam engine or the pendulum of the clock. And again, this enclosure of motion within the ideology of an eternal return served to reinforce a theory of colonization whose implications were as much poetic as political. Hans Vaihinger's once-popular neo-Kantian vision of a scientific progress occurring by way of a staircase of 'as if' hypotheses usefully glosses these ideas.

'The psyche,' Vaihinger wrote, 'is a machine that is continually improving itself, and whose purpose is to perform as safely, expeditiously and with the minimum expenditure of energy, the movements necessary for the preservation of the organism; movements in the broadest sense of the word, as the ultimate objectives of all our acts.'[86] But movements have no value in themselves; they must be manipulated by 'psychical levers' in order to give 'the movement of thought . . . a definite and fixed direction.'[87] Similarly with the clarification of 'general ideas': they serve as 'pulleys . . . that allow particular sensation-complexes to be connected with one another and to interact.' Ever more purposeful and rapid movement depends on the 'formation of fixed nuclei by means of categories and of fixed centres by means of general ideas.'[88] These nuclei and centres are 'fictions': 'the only object of these centres is to facilitate and accelerate the comparison of particular sensations . . . the centre of equality can in the end serve only as a point of transition for movement, so that the essential interest is only in the reciprocal movement of the particular sensations themselves.'[89]

Vaihinger's mental levers and pulleys may not explain much, but his mechanistic metaphors eloquently gloss the mythic mind-set of the nineteenth-century colonist who, as an economic rationalist, aspired to a condition where the movement of capital, and the interest earned on it, were cognate with the movements of the mind, and the interest that thereby accrued: 'the object of the world of ideas as a whole is not the portrayal of reality . . . but rather to provide us with an instrument for finding our way about more easily in this world.'[90] And 'we could compare the logical or thought-process with the organic creative process . . . In the course of its growth, it creates its organs of its own accord in virtue of its adaptable constitution, but only when stimulated from without, and adapts them to external circumstances.'[91] A law of natural selection governs psychic as well as organic phenomena, and it follows that the culture that can find its way about more easily in this world, that can minimise the resistance of the world to its movement, will inevitably be the culture best fitted to dominate.

The historical embodiment of Vaihinger's psychic machine, ever more efficiently traversing inner space with the help of fictional 'similarity centres', is the purposive movement of people to colonies, places which (for both rhetorical and ideological purposes) are represented as similar to the places from which the colonists come. Rational colonization of the kind Wakefield proposed does not mean an aimless, open-ended movement away from the old country; rather, it facilitates movement (of goods, of manpower, of capital) to the advantage and profit of the 'machine' (in this case the British race) as a whole. In Vaihinger's terminology, the colony is a 'fiction'; the colonists live in their new surroundings 'as if' they lived at home, but they are conscious that this is only a pretence, that the culture of the colony is only a makeshift or stand-in, that its sole justification lies in the fact that it is progressing towards somewhere else.

And if a colony conceives of itself as involved in a progressively more efficient journey, it will not only regard its buildings and the layout of its cities, but even the land they occupy, as instrumental fictions. As levers and pulleys accelerating a larger movement, they will be seen as catalysts of return in a double sense. The surveyor's role is clear: by chequerboarding the land, to prepare it for economic tillage; by finding the lines of least resistance, by levelling unprofitable differences, to maximize the circulation of goods, in this manner preparing the ground for world domination. And this implies a poetic as well as a spatial practice; in giving names to local phenomena, the object will not be to articulate their uniquenesses and differences, but to assimilate them to the discourse of the imperial machine. Keats, with his usual perspicacity, understood this function of poetry when (paraphrasing Hazlitt) he wrote that 'the language of poetry naturally falls in with the language of power', as it 'reconciles us in fact to the triumphant progress of the conquerors and mighty Hunters of mankind, who come to stop the shepherd's pipe upon the mountains and sweep away his listening flock.'[92] Vaihinger inadvertently gives us an insight into the mechanisms of this poetic imperialism.

The oddity, the ungroundedness, of these patriarchal myths of origin and purpose are obvious. They offer a cultural equivalent of asexual reproduction. Rigorously denying any intercourse between a mind, a people, and its human and natural surroundings, they are obliged to posit a reason for the movement of one towards the other. But it is the paradox of patriarchy, with its fear of the other (whether the feminine, the indigene or even the uncertain weather), that it suspects its own sons of treachery. The process of fission whereby the All-Father scatters his power over the world induces in him a paranoid suspicion that his parts (his self-replicating colonial offspring) have conspired to bring about his destruction. These contradictions within patriarchal ideology touched Light directly; for the survey, and the different attitudes it might harbour towards the land, recapitulated tensions at the heart of the colonial enterprise itself.

Biographers recognize that the controversy which dogged Light stemmed from the fact that authority in the colony was divided between the governor (representing the imperial government) and the resident commissioner (representing the interests of the Colonial Commission). The 'collateral association' or commercial arm of the Commission, the South Australian Company, constituted a third interest whose demands had to be met. These different interests, and the necessity to refer every dispute back to London, paralysed the local exercise of power; they undermined political authority, they eroded confidence, they provoked panic (among emigrants) and demagoguery (among journalists). Little wonder that Light resigned; showing an authority that transcended self-interest, firmly keeping hold of the reins of his own destiny, even if this cost him his salary, Light by his resignation delivered a stinging moral rebuke to those 'authorities' who put factional self-interest above the public good.[93]

This is the biographical myth: the Aristotelian hero who transcends himself in order to become worthy of a place in history, a founding father-figure. But it fails to recognize that, described in this way, Light's salvation (of himself, his reputation and Adelaide's future) only encloses him more firmly than ever within the self-destructive terms of patriarchal reference. What use is it to become a figure of authority, when authority is clearly a source of division? Would it not be better to find a different mode of cultural self-reproduction, one which was not marked by the lumbering installation of statues but took account instead of the lie of the land and its endless peripateia? Even within the conventions of patrilinear descent, and its injunction to the son to exhibit filial piety, Light had good reason to hold a heterodox view. Francis Light not only fathered William, but a colony, Penang. Questions of authority attended both events: the British government took control of Penang away from Francis;[94] death, and the dissipation of his estate, removed Francis from his son. The question for Light might always have been: in whose name to act? To whom to look for orders? And, having received them, how to interpret them? Did identity mean mimicking authority, becoming oneself a figure of authority? Or did it mean self-division, splitting off from the old order, striking out on a course of one's own? Might not filial insubordination be the sincerest form of flattery, mirroring the manliness said to have characterized the father in his youth?

In any case, systematic colonization attempted to suspend such questions. Wakefield attributed the political and economic stagnation of existing colonies to 'the unsatisfactory nature of colonial government resulting from the lack of local control. Where there was no representative assembly, the colonial government was altogether in the hands of a close oligarchy of officials appointed by Downing Street.'[95] In a telling comparison, Wakefield said that such officials 'resemble the official class in British India, which exclusively governs, but does not settle, and which regards the natives as a race only fit to be governed by a superior race.'[96] But his advocacy of colonial self-government was not preliminary to secession and independence; he understood it, like emigration, medicinally, as a means of bringing Britain back to a former state of political and social well-being. In establishing its own government, the colony would replicate the British Constitution: 'they might frame their own laws, in a Colonial Assembly, under the eye of a viceroy, incapable of wrong, and possessing a veto like the king of England, but whose secretaries, like the ministers of England, should be responsible to the people.'[97] Far from representing a threat to imperial power, such a development would serve to reinforce its authority – and by removing the possibility of its corruption, it might even serve a therapeutic function.

This explains why, when the Colonial Office objected to the amount of self-government allowed for under his South Australian proposal, Wakefield could shelve this part of his plan without compromising its social and economic scope. Wakefield's plan was, in his own word, 'imperial': it was meant to bring about 'a progressive enlargement, partly domestic, and partly colonial, of the field for employing capital and labour'; the colonies were 'no longer to be new societies, barbarous and uncivilised, but were to be "extensions of old societies".'[98] Such 'enlargement' would increase the empire's productive power without disturbing its essential constitution. Ensuring the orderly transfer of human energy, it would also improve the efficiency of the imperial machine.

Indeed, the similarity between Wakefield's system and, say, James Watt's steam engine is striking. Mills sums up Wakefield's self-regulating model of colonization: 'The sufficient price [of land] would produce revenue, which, best applied to emigration, would introduce labour into a colony. With the consequent extension of industry, capital would be accumulated, and more land bought both by capitalists and by labourers who had completed their term of service. These new land-sales would yield money for fresh emigration, and the process would begin again.'[99] So coal produces steam power; steam power drives pistons; and soon the locomotive, thus driven, can run to the pit-head and, transporting more coal, enlarge its own field of activity.

In the same spirit, Colonel Torrens, promoter of the South Australian scheme, noted that the system offered '"a geometrical principle of progression", which would, in the mother-country, operate in precisely the opposite direction to that of Malthus.'[100] In Wakefield's theory, land suffers a double enclosure: it is not merely enclosed in Locke's sense, differentiated from the commons and regarded as a personal property, it is stripped of any local character it might possess and treated wholly as a unit of social and economic regulation whose monetary value is subject to variations in exchange rate: 'The sufficient price, "the groundwork of the system", is imposed for one object only, and bears no relation whatever to the value of the land, or to the cost of an emigrant's passage . . . it is to be somewhat arbitrarily fixed, and constantly adjusted to the fluctuations in the supply of labour.'[101] Land acts as a regulator, which can be set higher or lower according to the prevailing input-output ratio of the imperial engine. The premonition of Vaihinger's 'fictional centres' designed to encourage circulation is remarkable.

So much, then, for a survey that aimed to preserve the lie of the land. Napier, with whose views Light is likely to have sympathized, objected to the Malthusian cast of Wakefield's theorizing on grounds that might at first seem merely sentimental. In reality though, he was objecting to the mimetic mode of self-reproduction that Wakefield's system entailed. More broadly, he was airing a temperamental aversion to an asexual theory of cultural and historical production. By unlocking lands abroad, Wakefield might pose as the saviour of natural increase in wedlock, but his assimilation of reproduction to the needs of production was parthenogenetic. The authorities might represent colonization as a fulfilment of the injunction to go forth and multiply (Wakefield certainly did); but the multiplication intended is arithmetical, a replication of identical images, all of which, like coins, bear the profile of the father.

These reflections on the 'as if' state of the new colony add to our historical understanding of light: authority was associated with environmental transparency. Whatever resisted translation defied it and must be removed; the cloudy sky, the shadowy body of earth that recalled the baffling curvature of the pregnant mother, must be made to submit to reason, the order of lines. Light's attention to undulating ground, to an accommodation between the rectilinear and the lie of the land, and an at-first baffling reluctance to site the city on the sea, may have been part of the survey's process; but they could easily be interpreted as impiety, as a rebellious desire to undermine authority. For where the ground could only be construed as a deception, it must be hurriedly covered over, interred as it were beneath a mantle of streets and roads. Only thus could the patriarchal mirror state be preserved, with its power to create colonies which, mimicking the authority of the centre, contributed to its self-centredness.

But there were, as we have seen in connection with Strehlow, at least two modes of mimicry, or two valencies that it might bear. There is the internal mimicry of patriarchy whereby, expanding outwards, the imperial machine remained stationary and impervious to change, ever more repressive; which suggests an interesting modification to Homi Bhabha's account of 'the ambivalence of mimicry as a problematic of colonial subjection.'[102] It is not only the native who is forced to ape the manners of the foreigner; those foreigners themselves, the emigrants subject to officials representing the Colonial Office, are also mimicking what may be foreign to them. Bhabha's conception of mimicry as 'a difference that is almost nothing but not quite' evokes the situation of the educated Indian, the loyal servant of the British Crown, who found nevertheless that his efforts to disavow his otherness only drew attention to it – and who, unable to escape his enclosure within a racist representation, articulates 'the problematic of colonial subjection.' But Wakefield's description of colonial authority suggests that 'the official class in British India, which exclusively governs' not only lords it over 'the natives as a race only fit to be governed by a superior race,' but over the European settlers.

This is the mimicry of authority that Light could not bear, because he saw in it only trumped-up officials going through the motions of public office, playing roles that were evidently not second nature to them. But there was also the mimicry of the indigenes, which the colonists, assuming it was motivated by the same social forces that determined their own borrowed antics, took as a sign of the natives' suitability to become colonial subjects. Kaurna men who adopted the names of the leading colonists as their own sobriquets were in no danger of being mistaken for 'Governor Gawler' or 'Captain Mitchell'. Their 'extraordinary' 'powers of mimicry' serve to mark them out from Europeans; these powers could even turn the tables, placing the colonizer in the uneasy position of seeming to repeat his own questions, to be his own mimic: 'After an interchange of signs, I succeeded in making him understand that I wished to know the names of certain things in his own language; and at last obtained a few dozen words. The greatest difficulty arose from his propensity to mimicking, which led him to repeat every word that I uttered, and the correctness with which he did this was surprising.'[103] But above all, a gift of mimicry suggests filial tractability. 'They are very observing and attentive,' Gouger noted, and as if one led to the other, 'They are, moreover, very obliging, and they very willingly perform works for those settlers of whom they form a good opinion.'[104]

Here was a folk who slipped on the role of servant and peasant as if it were second nature. In this role, mimicry changed its valency: it became proof of a capacity to advance, to leave the degraded self behind. It proved their gravity, their recognition of a future outside their control. Within the system which identified power with the coinage of identical images, the ability to ape one's superior might make the Aborigine more 'white' – closer to the light – than his moral look-alike, the white savage who abused the system. The Colonial Commissioners opined, using the argument that Columbus used to justify his invasion of Carib territory: 'The colonisation of South Australia by industrious and virtuous settlers, so far from being an invasion of the rights of the aborigines, is a necessary preliminary to the displacement of the lawless squatters, the abandoned sailors, the runaway convicts, the pirates, the worse-than-savages, that now infest the coast and islands along that extensive portion of New Holland, and perpetrate against the defenceless natives crimes at which humanity revolts.'[105]

These, it must be stressed, were the ordinary modes of constructing meaning in the colony. Mere coincidences, mirror-images (gestural, rhetorical and logical), were the means whereby the invaders wrote themselves over the land. No wonder the new South Australians could only imagine the Kaurna in their own image, as exiles from their native culture. Of the language spoken by the Adelaide people, Gouger said: 'There is every reason to believe that it is of Malay origin, the similarity of some words being almost complete. For instance the Malays of Dampier's Straits call water "owey", and the sun "tindoo". The aborigines of Glenelg call water "cowey", and the sun "tindook".'[106] Leigh, another early visitor, supposed that the custom of circumcision was 'most undoubtedly borrowed from the Malays, who, some time or other, must have touched here.'[107] As to 'the Australians' religion,' Leigh's view was 'that there are among them the remains of Mahomedanism, derived, perhaps, from the Malays.'[108]

Whatever evidence of a culture the Adelaide Aborigines possess – language, arts, religion – they have, it seems, copied it from another people; they have all along been mimics. Furthermore, in so far as these relics of an older, more advanced culture lie half-buried in the everyday behaviour of the Aborigine, they suggest the latter's decadence, his falling-off from an earlier excellence. It is further possible that this degeneration has been caused, in part at least, by intercourse with those 'more-than-savages'; early inter-racial conflict was less over land than over outrages by white sealers against Aboriginal women.[109] It seems unlikely that Wilhelm von Humboldt's view, that the ancient sacred language of Java was the type and original of all human languages, was on the lips of most colonists; although Stephens's remark that 'the native language (*sic*) of the southern tribes is not difficult of acquirement, being neither sonorous nor guttural,'[110] might suggest an acquaintance with Humboldt's dictum that a fully-articulate language depends not on 'the wealth of sounds' but on 'a chaste restriction to the sounds necessary for speech, and [on] the proper balance between them.'[111] What matters, though, is that the indigenous people can be fitted out with a lineage.

The ambiguities of this lineage reflect the ambiguities at the heart of a system of patriarchal descent. For just as it is an imponderable question as to when culturally, not biologically, the son becomes a father, and the father, stripped Lear-like of power, a child, so it is difficult to decide if the Kaurna are originals, preserving in its purest form the first impressions of patriarchy, or whether they are primitive in a pejorative sense, mere children orphaned by time and space. Alfred Wallace found in the Aru a human society perfectly in harmony with the organic balance operating in the Malay archipelago's geographically-insulated natural system: 'What are the finest Grecian statues to the living, moving breathing men I saw daily around me?', he writes. In comparison with this original world, where a natural relationship exists between man and land (as it exists between the fauna and flora and the region where they uniquely occur), '"thickly populated England", full of proprietors, is still in a "state of social barbarism . . . as regards true social science".'[112]

To come into contact with the Aru and the Dyak bespeaks, on the one hand, a nostalgia for a society purer than the Greek; on the other, it means that society's degradation and extinction. The same ambivalent colonial discourse characterizes the colonization of South Australia: the Aborigines seem to share with the Utopian emigrants a desire to better themselves; at the same time, their mingling with the Europeans is fraught with danger. 'In those first months of the settlement two white men were tried for stealing weapons from a hut on the Glenelg, the first which the natives had built in imitation of the settlers.'[113] Thus 'civilization' produces barbarism: building themselves a shelter, the Aborigines enclose themselves within a double darkness, that of the 'light' and the light-fingered. At the very point where they press forward, hoping to become civilized, they are reduced to a childlike vulnerability.

Where did the Malay hypothesis originate? Gouger says that the linguistic coincidences were noticed by a Mr Donovan, chief officer of the emigrant ship *Katherine Stewart Forbes* which first arrived in the colony on 16 October 1837.[114] But Leigh, who saw traces of Malayan influence in the circumcision rite, had been to the colony and gone again before that date.[115] Is it possible that it came from Light himself, that Light heard in their voices the whispers of his mother's speech? Leigh reports how, kangaroo-hunting one day on Kangaroo Island and 'almost dying of heat', he 'had the satisfaction of hearing the well-known "coo-ee!" a native word signifying "ahoy!".'[116] Presumably Light would have heard this differently, not as a sound in-between, the *lingua franca* of Australian first contact, but as the distant echo of the Malay word for 'water'.[117] Such are the everyday ambiguities of living in a new country.

The patriarchal enclosure acts which ensured that the Kaurna could only be seen in terms of the colonists' intense, and solipsistic, interest in the affirmation of their own identity, the legitimacy of their origins and aspirations – whether this had the effect of ennobling them or degrading them – places Light's indifference to the 'natives' in a different perspective. Light's very refusal to project on to the Kaurna his own genealogical fantasies becomes a sign of his refusal to assimilate himself to the central myth of imperial expansion: that everywhere the colonist goes, he will find, hidden in the heart of light, under the mask of blackness, an image of himself. Not of one complexion or the other, Light was free of their nostalgia perhaps. His double identity inoculated him against the fiction of a fixed centre. Psychically, and perhaps physically, he was disposed to a different kind of movement.

Perhaps this is the underlying significance of Light's enigmatic *Self-Portrait* (Plate 10). Or perhaps it conceals nothing. Perhaps its double perspective, its evidence of an evolving, but still provisional, self-knowledge, reveals everything. The biographers, ignoring the first draft as an upside-down aberration, focus exclusively on the dominant hemisphere of the picture plane, where Light's self-image provides ample scope for romantic speculation. Assuming that the second portrait is finished, they interpret it as a backward glance over travelled roads. But it is evidently unfinished; or better, its state of unfinish itself signifies not least perhaps Light's own desire to defer the ending. Even if we were to dispute the significance of this, of the cloudy chiaroscuro about the dominant image where it melts away into the surface, it is indisputable that Light chose not to cover over his first effort; we cannot even say that one succeeded the other. Perhaps Light always intended a double portrait, and worked alternately on the images.

John Tregenza has suggested that the *Self-Portrait* dates from Light's last illness: the flushed cheeks, the pearl-white iris, the impression of nervous energy barely mastered, are symptoms of TB.[118] His hypothesis may be right; a portrait of the tuberculous Shelley shows the same staring eyes.[119] But on the other hand, the non-tuberculous Claire Clairmont receives a similar treatment in her portrait.[120] The pallor of Light's portrait may simply be a symptom of the painting's unfinished state; the oddly lightless eyes may indicate life departing, or they may indicate nothing more than the fact that no highlights have been added to the pupils. Judging from the least worked parts of the canvas, along the left shoulder and collar, Light was building up his portrait from an almost white ground; the appearance of a man possessed by a terrifying vision, pupils dilated, the whites of the eyes lightning-blanched, may reveal nothing more than a preliminary light and dark, lacking the supplementary depths an art of chiaroscuro would bring.

Suppose we accept the hypothesis that Light commenced his *Self-Portrait* by painting the figure whose upside-down, half-effaced head can still be made out in the bottom right-hand corner of the present painting; that he became dissatisfied with the way that figure was developing and decided to begin again. Admitting this order of events, what was it about the earlier version that dissatisfied him? If we compare both versions with the (presumably earlier) pen-and-ink sketch on which the oil painting is obviously based (Plate 11), it appears that the second version follows the sketch much more closely than the first, abandoned version. In the sketch and in the later version, Light looks directly into the onlooker's eyes. Both sketch and later version also preserve Light's high cheekbone and the finely-chiselled outline of jaw and chin; indeed, in the oil version the chin is further refined, any hint of a prognathous underhang being entirely eliminated. By contrast, the first oil version depicts a man distinctly flabby in the cheeks, lacking a prominent cheekbone, heavy in the jaw and close to possessing a double chin.

Perhaps even more significant psychologically is the fact that the eyes of the first version do not meet our gaze, but stare away to the left. The result is to suggest a figure who is altogether more at home with the world, who seems snugly housed in his flesh, sure of his point of view. A figure, in short, resembling a father. Returning to the sketch, determined to copy it more exactly, Light turned his back on a self-portrait that was in danger of becoming parodic. Self-portraits, like biographical sketches, had a habit of becoming tricks of self-authoring; there was a temptation to see oneself as others might see one – as a father-figure, say. To counteract this, it was not enough to depict oneself photographically. It was perhaps necessary to sculpt one's features differently, to dramatize a certain reluctance to fulfil the expected role; the in-drawn cheeks, the listening stare, the restrained *controposto* suggest one who will only be met on his own terms – one who authorizes.

The portrait that meets the viewer's gaze refuses to become the spectator's subject. The dialectic is subtle: the figure which gazes regally past you, his attention apparently fixed on a distant object unknown to you, represents the idea of command, authority. He is the surveyor of all he sees; you, the spectator, are located within his field of vision but are not its focus; you are one of many subjects his space accommodates. This is what the indirect gaze represents, a character free of ordinary restraint. But the very fact that the artist enables you to grasp this inverts the hierarchy of the gaze; seeing who he is, grasping his superiority in his own domain, the spectator nevertheless encloses him, subjects him to biographical reduction.

But by staring back, meeting your look, this dialectic is refused. The painted subject makes of you a looking-glass; it is as if he is looking into a surface that reflects his own image. Or it is as if you are looking at your own portrait. In any case, the effect is to transfer attention from the statuesque pose associated with biographical enclosure to the moment of first contact when, across a divide of time and space, one first catches the other's eye and becomes implicated in a history whose outcome is unforeseen. This is the effect of the unaverted gaze: to refuse history's theatrical enclosure, to insist on time's performance, on a present continually renewing itself. The eyes that regard you do not 'look back', but insist on an equality in difference; and if, as yet, they seem to stare at nothing, at least they have not foreclosed on what might appear.

The later *Self-Portrait* does not supersede the first. It is not more 'accurate' than the first; the two heads taken together are better understood as a double portrait depicting, seeking to resolve, the contradictions of self-identification under the aegis of patriarchy. They also suggest the connection between these problems of self-authoring and the ideological underpinning that informs the figure of the 'artist'. In representing himself, the artist both fathers himself and becomes the subject, the offspring, of his own gaze. While the doctrine of the frame (the metaphysical as well as physical condition of representation *qua* mimesis) goes unchallenged, there is no way out of this self-enclosure act – the same that the autobiographer uses when he describes himself in the third person, as a figure belonging to the past.

And it is true: as the portrait comes down to us, Light carries his older mask like a Medusa's head on his breast, as a mimic image, the *impresa* of lightning, as a persona that might easily be donned. There is no escape from its stench; a black wind sweeps like a scarf across the upper man's neck, but it also serves to place the faded under-face into a ghostly light relief. The two faces are life and death; the soul of one gives body to the other. So we might say. But we might also say that Light finds a way of dealing with his dilemma by representing both figures as orphaned, and the whole as an amphisboena monster that can only hold its place by continually melting into another. His is a portrait without a background, one that makes its own construction its ground. From the point of view of representation, this may mean that it looks 'unfinished', insufficiently framed, lacking a stably picturesque ground. But from another angle, that of *methexis* say, it accurately evokes a state of becoming, embodying a process actively designed to avoid the enclosure of patriarchal homecoming.

This oscillation between states as an end in itself enables Light, we might hypothesize, to hold his place in the slipstream of history, hovering there like a falcon. The pre-Romantic colonist takes a linear view of history, treating the journey as the fulfilment of a line already laid out in the mind. The Romantic seems to differ, conceiving the journey as a circle. A writer like Napier might agree with the poet Kleist that 'We must make a journey round the world and see whether it may not be open at the back,' but this *frisson* of eccentricity remains instrumental: to effect a return to simplicity. As Hölderlin explained: 'The eccentric way by which mankind, in general and individually, passes from one point (that of more or less simplicity) to the other (that of more or less cultivation) shows itself to be the same in its essential direction.'[121] But Light is neither one nor the other. He is interested in a return that is also a going-on, a way of proceeding that resembles a banner of silk being folded up from one end backwards and forwards over itself until it grows compact and deep, ready to be stored.

This interest is discernible in Light's celebrated town-plan (Plate 12). Perhaps the layout was influenced by the old Roman camp plan, but this is a generic form of town-plan hardly of much critical value in negotiating the local lie of the land.[122] 'Light's plan is, in the end, entirely original,' Dutton considers, by which he appears to mean entirely pragmatic: 'It is intimately related to local circumstance. Light had neither time, the men nor the equipment to lay out a plan more complicated than the rectangular one he devised.'[123] Robert Cheesman takes the opposite view. According to him, Light's plan is entirely *unoriginal*, an involuntary synthesis of the types of rationally laid-out colonial settlements favoured by Robert Owen and Jeremy Bentham, 'of self-containment, concentric land use and common land. But above all there prevailed the conventional wisdom as pattern imagery, the topical layout . . . with its squares, gridded streets, north-south orientation, axial regularity and continuous perimeter of common land.'[124]

The difficulty with these views, which ultimately collapse into each other, is that they simply fail to describe the city Light designed; one that in no way followed the generic outlines of the Hippodamian grid, and which conspicuously took account of the lie of the land. Furthermore, in so far as his plan *did* embody the conventional rectilinear principles of colonial towns, it interpreted these differently, subverting their overly-reductive rationalism. Some of the most imaginative provincial town-plans in Australia, those devised by Sir Thomas Mitchell, are said to have been inspired by the hill-towns of Spain and Portugal; a similar provenance might plausibly be suggested for Light's plan. At any rate, even though it occupied a 'plain', it went out of its way to articulate the land's relief rather than to smooth it away.

The Hippodamian grid of the ancient Roman camp is a knot located at the meeting-place of roads originating from the four points of the compass; it provides an efficient point of departure, a centre of dispersion. In theory, its grid can be extended indefinitely in all directions; it is a machine for building on the move. If this is the classic form of invasion, then Light's Adelaide seems to be conceived as a machine of anti-invasion. Instead of encouraging 'spread', it seems designed to tangle up and frustrate outward expansion; at the same time, though, it avoids implosion by 'staggering' lines of attraction likely to encourage centripetal concentration. Further, this sense of a space designed to defer arrival is not only articulated spatially but temporally. That is, the town-plan suggests a city in a state of evolution or perhaps of decay. It implies the possibility of different rates of progress; more menacingly, it suggests that the halcyon days of civic order and virtue may already be past. Either way, its rationalism is baroque, recognizing that a commanding visual impression is more telling in establishing social order than any appeal to a common tradition.

Spatially, Light's Adelaide is not a unified master-grid; it is more like a 'collage' of four fragmentary grids. Indeed, the ground-plan recalls an ancient city in a state of partial excavation. The irregularly-stepped blocks of land to the east of South Adelaide and to the west of North Adelaide suggest that more streets and buildings still lie interred. Light arranges the parts of his city like so many tectonic plates, sliding into one another or breaking away at the edges where they press up against the surrounding plain. The effect is to suggest depth, successive phases of occupation. At their north-western corner, the allotments that are centred assymetrically on Jerningham Street appear to slide under the larger mass of North

Adelaide proper, as if the latter had been built later, by a race ignorant of the site's earlier history. The stepped edges of North and South Adelaide suggest a topography to be reckoned with, the lie of the land.

By these spatial means, Light seeks to articulate a social and political organization. He does not simply make visible a hidden order; his is not the bringing to light of an invisible light (of order and reason). Rather, in the manner of the Sicilian baroque town-planners, he seeks to create rhetorically a framework for a society that, in view of the theocratic rhetoric of some of its founders, must successfully negotiate a stable balance between secular and sacred government. So Light sets aside a precinct for the headquarters of government, and locates it ambiguously in between the two main halves of the city, at once outside and inside. Perhaps more significantly, he recommends a prominent position for the '*chiesa madre*', which in the spirit of toleration (or more probably, his own agnosticism) he conceives as inter-denominational; only he also ensures that its position, while appearing pivotal, is marginal, standing at the head of a street that leads nowhere, beckoning across the river to a people that cannot (directly) reach it, even though they can hear its summons.

Perhaps mindful of Wakefield's insistence on the advantages of 'concentration', Light conceives of his city as a bringing-together of diverse elements. At the same time, the concentration is not mindless: the approach of the parts to one another is oblique, deferred. In Light's original plan, none of the main north-south thoroughfares south of the Torrens connect with streets to the north. Instead, Light projects southwards North Adelaide's main avenue (Jeffcott Street) to where it intersects with South Adelaide's North Terrace. This same principle of blocking easy passage, of maximizing the resistance to rectilinear progress which a rectilinear grid might be supposed to harbour, also governs the angular street connections made between the three blocks of North Adelaide. In this context, the symmetrical layout of squares can be interpreted either as the survival of a former, more highly-civilized, culture whose spatial ideals are now in the process of barbarous pidginization and decay; or as the emergent form of a new society, determined to overcome the inadvertent lie of the land, with its irrational declivities and time-wasting periphrases.

If precedents for Light's plan are to be found, they will have to demonstrate their interest in inculcating a comparable form of movement or social intercourse. A physically similar layout will not necessarily produce a similar social, economic, political and even emotional circulation; to create this, the blockages it introduces to slow up and divert a too linear progress will be quite as significant as its rhetoric of straight and parallel streets. Because the object of Light's plan is not to clear away differences, but to introduce them. Taking advantage of the smallest rises and falls the plain affords him, Light endows these with a historical significance. It is as if he is refounding a city and conceives the ground as the ruins of a former place, which he must both build over and mimic. The old plan cannot be replicated but it can show through, and as it does so, it will encourage the nomadic colonist to gravitate and slow down. The sense it projects of former habitation will encourage him to think of himself as a citizen with civic responsibilities.

In this light – and if we have to father Adelaide on another – two Mediterranean towns well-known to Light assume some significance: New Noto in south-eastern Sicily (Plate 13), and the partially-excavated ruins of Pompeii. Light's acquaintance with Noto was passing: the plate of the town subsequently collected in *Sicilian Scenery* (1823) carries the date 1 May 1821, although Elder believes that 'Light almost certainly made his sketches in 1818.' Pompeii he presumably knew intimately: 'From the diary covering his travels on the continent in 1825–26 it is learned that Light was in Pompeii in April 1826 and he recorded making three or four sketches a day. (No doubt in his usual manner he made rough sketches which he used later to work upon his finished drawings.)'[125] In any case, Light's *Views*, engraved by J. D. Harding, appeared in 1828.

After Noto Antico was shaken to the ground in 1694, it was decided to replan and relocate the city. Noto Nuovo is, in this sense, a colonial city, albeit located within a few kilometres of its builders' first home. The new town did not replicate the old urban design. Built on the side of a hill, New Noto was planned on two levels: a monumental centre straddling the east-west axis of the Corso Vittorio Emmanuele, and to its north, above a steeply-rising rampart of rock, the popular residential area known as Pianazzo, an informal grid of streets at whose centre lies the Piazza IV Aprile. In this process of refoundation, the public buildings underwent a transformation: political hegemony, formerly symbolized by the medieval castle, passed to the Casa Senatoria located at the 'town centre'; churches no longer nestled within their parishes but occupied visually commanding vantage points. The political dialectic between Church and State split open to recognize a third force, the middle class. In New Noto, the location of the cathedral and the Casa Senatoria on opposite sides of the main piazza is no more significant than the character of the space that opens up between them: an amphitheatre-like piazza traversed by a main street leading in both directions to the city gates and beyond into the country. The Enlightenment's Utopian project of integrating 'man' into 'society' and of creating a 'culture' in harmony with the laws of nature is here succinctly realized.[126]

Light may not have copied Noto in planning the future Adelaide – although the formal resemblance is striking, even extending to a parallel between the irregularly laid-out complex of streets lying at an angle south-east of the Pianazzo and the Jerningham Street complex to the south-east of North Adelaide. But he appears to have recognized the applicability of its reformist spirit to his own situation; a scenographic representation of society did not translate into a political programme, but it did signify an ambition to control one's own affairs. Habsburg monarchists were afraid of rationally planned cities like Noto harbouring republican ambitions; a century later, the British government suspected Wakefield and his dissenting followers of wanting to secede from the Crown. Bentham suggested calling the new colony 'Utopia'.[127] Even moderate emigrants hoped the settlement would furnish a model 'by which to correct our system of Colonial Government.'[128]

Light's plan was not politically programmatic; it may even have been deliberately cloudy. If we imagine it as a further rationalization of the Enlightenment Utopia – New Noto laid out in a plain – its scope becomes clearer: to transcend the analytic spirit of such places, to create a synthetic model for the colony's development. Noto and its ilk were planned statically. But Adelaide is imagined evolutionarily, as cellular structures in the process of morphogenesis; its future is conceived in terms of the discovery and progressive articulation of internal lines of communication not as yet apparent. The unity of the colony, the synthesis of parts, is yet to be achieved. Unlike Hoddle's Melbourne,[129] Light's Adelaide suggests an unresolved history, a future that cannot repeat the past. In a colony which has no past, and is determined to make its mark on 'history', historical consciousness may express itself differently. It may be that the future cannot help but be the recovery of a forgotten past, of a past that up until now has not come to pass. In the absence of any previous attachment to the site, this is perhaps the only way in which a colony can ground itself: by regarding the gridded lie of the land as the ruins of a former state, which, rebuilt, will surely provide the foundations of the future.

That these ironies were grasped by contemporaries is evident from the curiously urgent and perplexed comment of W.H.Leigh who, walking over the recently laid-out site of Adelaide in July 1837, was disappointed to find English reports of the city's rapid advance decidedly false: 'I strained my eyes in vain, to see either square, terrace, street, house, or even anything to lead me to the conclusion of there ever having been any. There was no volcanic matter; not even a stone could be found to indulge in the benevolent propensity of throwing it at a dog; and two or three people were jogging along together, talking calmly of bullocks, when one would have expected to have beheld them at public thanksgiving for their own preservation from the mighty earthquake which had, doubtless, suddenly swallowed up the once noble city of Adelaide.'[130]

Leigh's comments, his prevision of a city in ruin, destroyed, utterly effaced by earthquake and volcanic eruption, also intimate what may have been the ambiguous appeal to Light of Pompeii, a city which had to be buried and lost in order never to grow old; a city whose second foundation dated from the mid-1770s when, after eighteen hundred years asleep, its ruins began to be excavated, to reveal a city half-built, still unfinished, awaiting completion now in the speculative minds of savants, scholars – and novelists. Or perhaps further dissolution awaited it: this was Pompeii's ambiguity, to be poised between one destruction and the next, its foundations in danger of a second burial at the hands of the excavators.

But even this oversimplifies matters. It is sometimes forgotten that the town gradually uncovered during the nineteenth century was, at the time of the AD 79 eruption, already in partial ruin as a result of an earthquake seventeen years earlier. 'The earthquake of A.D. 62 was a cataclysm. We see its havoc all over the city – in the mountains of debris, in the buildings cleared of all fallen masonry but still unrepaired . . . in the buildings hurriedly put back in working shape.'[131] The picture was further confused by the fact that the earthquake had stimulated the Pompeians to embark on an ambitious urban renovation and public building programme: 'At the time of the eruption of Vesuvius in A.D. 79 Pompeii was a patchwork of the newest in architectural forms and engineering interwoven with layers, often ruined, of past grandeur and juxtaposed with the ramshackle domestic arrangements of those less well-off, poor but determined to overcome an almost unbelievable catastrophe.'[132]

Now this detail of ancient history – the fact that Pompeii (somewhat like Light's *Self-Portrait*) was at the time of its burial in a process of self-renewal, and had internalized, as it were, its future as a city poised between foundation and ruin – directly illuminates the difference of Light's approach, his anti-Romantic determination to stay with the shifting appearance of things. It is not difficult to make a superficial case for linking Pompeii to Adelaide. From the first, the climate of Adelaide and Naples were recognized as similar; some enthusiasts went so far as to dub Adelaide the Naples of the South,[133] and geographical and topographical pretexts exist to support the argument that Light modelled Adelaide's site directly on the setting of Pompeii. Investigator Strait and the Gulf of St Vincent, flanked north and west by Yorke Peninsula, south and east by the Fleurieu Peninsula and Kangaroo Island, crudely reproduce the shape of the Bay of Naples, protected on its north and west by Cape Misenum and the adjacent islands of Procida and Ischia, on its south and west by the Sorrento peninsula and the island of Capri. To complete the comparison: in the direction that Vesuvius lies behind Pompeii, Mount Lofty rises beyond Adelaide.

And so on. But to speculate that Light sought to resurrect Pompeii in the south is to miss the point. In Light's day, scientists, travellers, poets and novelists were all interested in resurrecting Pompeii. The important question was not an archaeological one but an historical one: what did the unearthing of Pompeii have to say about the representation of the past? Here, in the excavation of an average Roman seaside town, the historical past was made palpably present; yet paradoxically, there was nothing lively to see or hear. In this odd situation, two choices existed: to respect the indefiniteness of the position, the curiousness of the site's new conjunction with present time going on, its refusal to shape itself into a story with a definite end or perspective. Or to repress these sensations and, in an act of conscious over-compensation, to conjure up the world of Pompeii as it never was, as a phantasmagoric display of archetypal scenes and passions. The first approach abided by the natural light of reason, or at least acknowledged the fleecy clouds passing over to no end. The second turned history into theatre, and by representing the past as present, temporarily at least suggested nothing had changed – or the historical validity of La Place's dictum that, with enough data, we could not only predict the future but retrodict every event that had ever occurred in the past.[134]

To appreciate this difference, it is useful to compare Light's album *Views of Pompeii* with the almost exactly contemporary literary portrait of the town created by Edward Bulwer-Lytton. Like Gibbon Wakefield, Bulwer-Lytton first drew attention to himself by undertaking a spectacular and scarcely respectable marriage. Rather intriguingly, a relative of his, H. Lytton Bulwer, was among the nineteen members of the House of Commons on the committee of the South Australian Association formed in 1834, the year after Bulwer-Lytton's Pompeian romance was published. It might be interesting to explore the patriarchal tensions which metaphorically surfaced in Bulwer-Lytton's vision of the irresistible volcano immolating a decadent society; as if only a transcendent patriarch could overthrow a corruptly patriarchal society. In any case, his historical romance *The Last Days of Pompeii* makes an odd foil to Light's way of representing things.

Bulwer-Lytton, invoking a kind of historical catastrophism, depicts a culture fatally succumbing to an ancient prophecy of its doom: decadent, effeminate, amoral. As the hour of its destruction draws near, the Pompeians seem to have exhausted their own historical imagination. They have lost the will to sympathize, to represent themselves as they might be. They have even lost the power to distinguish between mimesis and *methexis*, apparently mistaking the latter for a repetition of the original bloody act itself, rather than a Pythagorean identification with its human meaning. Their retreat into barbarism is illustrated by the gruesome spectacles put on in the amphitheatre: 'a vast theatre, rising row upon row, and swarming with human beings, from fifteen to eighteen thousand in number, intent upon no fictitious representation – no tragedy of the stage – but the actual victory or defeat, the exultant life or the bloody death, of each and all who entered the arena!'[135]

In terms recalling the apocalyptic sublime of the English artist James Ward – not to mention the fiery works of such other Vesuvius-enthusiasts as Pietro Fabris, De Loutherbourg and Joseph Wright[136] – the gradual immolation of the gladiators, the audience and the whole of the city is represented, not simply as the death of a city, but as the ending of the world, of history itself. The chief symbol of this historical process is 'the cloud'; a fact that conveniently brings into focus the difference of Light, and the historical meaning of that difference. Bulwer-Lytton's cloud is not of the type that inhabits Light's *Brief Journal* or his *Last Diary*. It is not even the storm cloud of that Mediterranean night when death was foreglimpsed, for even there it was its natural indifference that most impressed. The cloud o'erhanging Pompeii is theatrical, it is there as an agent of the action: 'The cloud, which had scattered so deep a murkiness over the day, had now settled into a solid and impenetrable mass,' resembling 'the close and dark blindness of some narrow room.'[137]

Such a self-conscious agent of nemesis has no time for the subtle mediations of chiaroscuro. Its obscurity is a cannon-barrel unleashing its opposite, a surreal and hellish light. 'The lightnings around Vesuvius' increased 'their vivid and scorching glare . . . now brightly blue as the most azure depth of a southern sky – now of a livid and snakelike green, darting restlessly to and fro as the folds of an enormous serpent – now of a lurid and intolerable crimson, gushing forth through the columns of smoke, far and wide, and lighting up the whole city from arch to arch, – then suddenly dying down into a sickly paleness, like the ghost of their own life!'[138] As for the cloud, it 'appeared to break from its solid mass, and, by the lightning, to assume quaint and vast mimicries of human or of monster shapes, striding across the gloom, hurtling one upon the other, and vanishing swiftly into the turbulent abyss of shade . . .'[139]

Compare this cinematic vision of the amphitheatre's dying moments with 'The Amphitheatre' (Plate 14), the penultimate plate in Light's *Views of Pompeii*. The contrast is not merely generic – Bulwer-Lytton is straining to produce a melodramatic historical romance, while Colonel Light, temperamentally opposed to displays of emotion, is content to translate his impressions into a topographical sketchbook – but also historical. If Bulwer-Lytton subscribes to a theatrical view of history, imagining the past as a sequence of tableaux that can be revisited at will (or at least with the help of the novelist's imagination), Light conspicuously refuses to speculate, presenting instead a building void of sound and fury, bereft of every vestige of 'history' – and which, for this reason, captures the ambiguity of 'the past'.

The incomplete symmetry of the amphitheatre in Light's drawing looks both ways, towards construction, towards destruction. It is difficult to tell whether the inner walls peeping over the outer ramparts are falling down or are in the process of erection; if this Utopian structure belongs to the remotest past or to the visionary future, whether it models the *omphalos* of a world over which the sun sets for the last time, or whether it symbolizes renewal, the Orphic egg about to hatch, the dawning of a new generation. These ambiguities are formal, but they are also historical. They depend on Light acknowledging his own presence in the picture, on his making the monument his own contemporary.

At the building's vanishing-point, an arch of light frames a diminutive figure. There is no question about his identity: he is not the *larva* of an ancient gladiator, but a gentleman tourist, a Bulwer-Lytton perhaps. In any case, the implication is clear: can the modern visitor who seeks to absorb the 'atmosphere' of the place, to absent himself from himself, and who fails to take account of his own viewpoint, the interpretative distance between himself and the history he seeks to relive, ever achieve a truly historical consciousness? The proto-photographic framing of the subject, the mere coincidence of modern and ancient viewpoints, mimics knowledge of the past theatrically. To understand history methektically, it is necessary to enter into the contingency of its temporal processes.

Light's Pompeian sketches are generally ambiguous. Looking at the almost-deserted streets with their broken pediments, their half-stuccoed walls and undressed arches, it is hard to tell whether this is a graveyard or a building site. The plaster on the arch at the entrance to the Forum is flaking away; is the cross-hatched cement still damp, or anciently stiff and powder-dry? Elsewhere, a Doric capital has just been lifted on to the fluted column . . . There at last is the long-expected thunderous sky and chiaroscuro cloudscape after Rosa, hovering predictably over the Tragic and Comic Theatres; but for the rest, the air is curiously unemphatic, the skies vacant.

Similarly, Adelaide was a palimpsest of past and future, presenting at once the most primitive and the most refined of prospects. Squatting on their allotments, inside 'dwellings . . . composed of mud and grass', in a 'semi-savage state of life', emigrants could see all about them parklands whose beautiful drives were reminiscent of 'the Boulevards of Paris'.[140] But already it was a case of clearing away debris as much as building; Stephens reports that 'temporary dwellings' built on the green belt surrounding the town site 'have assumed the appearance of one long straggling village'; 'the time will soon come, when the park-land will be cleared of temporary erections.'[141] And that clearance could not help, it seems, but be the beginning of the end. If the land was to be returned to its Arcadian past, it was going to be necessary to depopulate it, not populate it. The Kaurna, going about their former business alongside the settlers putting up their temporary shelters, could hardly foresee that the diplomatic mimicry all about them was feigned, and that shortly it must lead to trouble. 'There is hardly an hour in the day they are not either lopping down branches or burning some tree and it is in vain speaking to them,' complained Light.[142] And it was true that, to preserve the illusion of a common ground, they would have to leave.

In the colony, it seems, even the provision of a common depended on an enclosure act. Adelaide's famous parklands could only be shared if no one was allowed to live there. As quickly as possible, we might say, the ground had to be covered (perhaps in a double sense). A primarily kinaesthetic sense of the unfolding ground was replaced by a primarily visual apprehension of the land as a picturesque prospect. In this sense, it was as if the colonists retreated from the land rather than entering into it. In any case, instead of a deepening emplacement, a substitute for displacement had to come into view – the panoptic fantasy of the entire region as a theatrical backdrop to progress in the foreground. It was as if everywhere the land closed around the newcomers and, appearing to centre on their point of view, lent their artful enclosures the appearance of nature.

An early exercise in real-estate puffery has Adelaide:

> Situated on gently rising ground on both banks of a pretty stream reaching down to the sea, over which the south west breezes blow nine months out of the twelve, with invigorating freshness. At the back is a beautifully wooded country, which extends for about six miles to the base of the first range of hills which are capped by a high wooded one called by Sturt, Mount Lofty, 2,400 feet above the level of the sea. To the left the hills gently curve around and trend down to the coast at about nine miles from the town, enclosing a plain country in some places open, in others wooded, having a few small streams and freshwater lakes. To the right the hills run in a N. and E. direction, continuing for 30 or 40 miles, where they appear to sink into a plain. The country along their base is well timbered, nearer the coast it is open and level.[143]

Here is a picture where successive enclosures harmonize with one another so picturesquely that we might miss the cultural and perhaps spatial paranoia it represents. It corresponds to no possible viewpoint except possibly that of the museum diorama. In this, its refusal to allow the gradual curvature of the ground to put things out of sight, resides its mental and physical balance. Kant, no doubt, would have found nothing exceptionable about its mid-air rhetoric, but in fact the author of this passage, and the Home Counties readership able to translate it into a smiling investment, suffer from *vesania*, that condition in which, according to Kant, 'the soul is transferred to a quite different standpoint, so to speak, and from it sees all objects differently. It is displaced from the *Sensorio communi* that is required for the unity of (animal) life, to a point far removed from it [ ] just as a mountainous landscape sketched from an aerial perspective calls forth a quite different judgement about the region than when it is viewed from the plain.'[144]

The strongest proof of *vesania* is that the sufferer is unaware of his derangement: 'It is true that the soul does not see or feel itself in another place (for it cannot perceive itself as situated in space without committing a contradiction, since it would then intuit itself as an object of outer sense, whereas it can be only the object of inner sense); but this is how we account, as best we can, for the so-called displacement.' Further, the out-of-body experience is a particularly subtle and dangerous form of self-division because, according to Kant, it manifests itself as a form of stability. The sufferer from *vesania* appears to himself perfectly centred, although from the point of view of those around him his outlook is utterly eccentric: 'He is the calmest inmate of the hospital and, because of his self-enclosed speculation, the furthest removed from raving; for, with complete self-satisfaction, he shuts his eyes to all the difficulties of his research. This fourth kind of madness could be called *systematic*.'[145]

Whatever the condition to which Kant refers, his interpretation of it is also clearly pathological, embodying the paranoia of a culture philosophically committed to defining the world in terms of permanent properties and hierarchically-stable relationships. Perfectly circular motion can be countenanced because, continually returning, changing nothing, it represents accurately the paradoxical union of space and time in a system universally uniform, eternally changeless. But a motion that insists on being recognized as motion gives the lie to this equilibrium. The parabolic or cometary wanderer does not orbit neo-Platonically, his mind on other matters; his mind is his movement. Against the dogma of mimesis, where apparent change represents a fundamental changeless-ness, he embodies a methektic principle, inventing space and time as he goes.

So Light also suffers from *vesania*, being 'perfectly centred' and 'utterly eccentric'. But while his view may at times coincide with the interests of the smallholder colonists financing the South Australian experiment, it at best mimics their outlook. We can put it another way: the description of Adelaide's situation superficially suggests a principle of reversed perspective at work, as if an engraving of the scene would show the same bunching of sight-lines witnessed in Jacopo de' Barbari's great view of Venice. In fact, the sense of convergence rhetorically achieved corresponds most exactly to the window-frame of linear perspective. It does not arise from, and respect, the radiating lie of the land; rather, it negates that tendency to fold away and disappear, determined to hold every part up to view and inspection. Drawn in reversed perspective, standing on the ground, the subtle rises and falls of the environment would be foregrounded, not backgrounded, and it would not be necessary to substitute picturesque contrasts for the continuous chiaroscuro of the ground's cloud-shadow – or *its* shadow, the wind in grass.

Besides, to characterize his aerial perspective as an off-the-ground or out-of-body experience is to adopt the plains-dweller's point of view. It is to judge movement with a sedentary prejudice, to insist on the traveller's eccentric behaviour. But the bird-like view of the estranged soul is not strictly comparable with the mole-like attitude of the plains-dweller. It is not two places that are being compared (two perspectivally-equivalent positions or points of view), but two differing attitudes towards seeing the world. While the plains-dweller is immobile, the aerialist is necessarily 'on the wing', inebriated with the breezes. From the point of view of the plains-dweller, the mountains, perhaps noticed for the first time, signify the futility of travel. From the point of view of the migratory soul, however, it is the plains that, as Lyotard puts it, suggest a 'burrow in which it is impossible to see anything, impossible to breathe.'[146]

I am even tempted to say that the 'different standpoint' so deprecated by Kant is close cousin to the point of view Giorgione evolves in the *Tempesta*. What characterizes it is a sense of imminent change, of rigid boundaries dissolving, of atmospheric phenomena; where 'a column of beautiful crimson . . . seen right up and down with well defined edges',[147] such as Light reports on 6 September 1836, might have more substance than a Utopian dream of colonnaded fora and courtyards. The nursing mother of the *Tempesta* is also 'the homeless woman suckling her babe at the roadside,' observed by Walter Pater's peripatetic Gaston de Latour: a sign of modernity, with its civil strife, its recrudescent barbarism, its newly 'moral' sullenness of sky.[148] It is no accident that these phenomena preface Gaston's visit to 'the abode of Monsieur Michel de Montaigne', whose boast it was that 'throughout those invasive times his house had lain open to all comers.'[149] Montaigne has responded to the darkening skies of the new age by grounding his thought mobilely, in the eventfulness of things: 'He was at his best, his happiest, amid the magnetic contacts of easy conversation.' Montaigne, 'constantly, gratefully, announcing his contact . . . with forces full of beauty in their vigour, like lightning, the sea, the torrents,' had learned 'to base virtue on low, safe ground.' But this ground had a mobile physiognomy: 'In the presence of this indefatigable analyst of act and motive all fixed outlines seemed to vanish away. The healthful pleasure of motion, of thoughts in motion! – Yes! Gaston felt them, the oldest of them, moving, as he listened, under and away from his feet, as if with the ground he stood on.'[150]

Montaigne's habitation, open to all, refusing to take sides, to exclude points of view, recalls the attitude of the Aborigine described by the German missionary C. G. Teichelmann in his *Aborigines of South Australia*. Told to desist from his totemic rituals – 'we endeavoured to show them the foolishness of this practice, and spoke to them of Jehovah . . .' – he protests: 'Why do you charge us with a lie, i.e. reject our opinion, we do not charge you with lies; what you believe and speak of Jehovah is good, and what we believe is good.' But the obstinately purblind Teichelmann reports, 'We replied that only on one side the truth could be, and that was on our side.'[151] Perhaps this was why the Europeans hastened to erect houses for themselves: they could not bear to see the other side.

This was the paranoia, the historical tragedy, associated with the doctrine that a man who dares to step over the line is in risk of losing his understanding. Light of necessity moved differently, navigating a medium, the sea, neither bound by circular horizons nor planar as a table. He moved as Gaston moved, the surface he ploughed continually streaming out into the wake, as if his personal history only surfaced in a lightning-streak and as quickly melted away, absorbed back into the general rise and fall. What was the point of talking about meridians of madness where the world was continually coming into view and passing out of sight? Not that Light was a 'useless' wanderer, or even secretly aimed to undermine the colonial programme. His life signifies a counter-current within that imperial enterprise, the presence of a contrapuntal movement prolonging in-between conditions where going forward and going back were doubtfully distinguished, and there was as yet no need to clear and enclose the ground, to erect walls to keep out the enemy – to sublimate the growing nostalgia.

To approach, then, the issue of Light's subjectivity and its historical meaning by way of clouds, and more broadly by way of an attention to that least monumental of sciences, meteorology, is not to extract him entirely from the patriarchal matrix of dutiful deeds, tragic poses and posthumous fame. The clouds themselves had a history, a fact illustrated by the fate of Light's own sketches. If the skies of the Pompeian album are relatively restrained, those of the earlier *Sicilian Scenery* almost constitute an inventory of symbolic atmospheres. Peter de Wint's drawings, although derived from Light's sketches, fit out the different Sicilian views with cloud forms presumably felt to harmonize with the subject's topographical, historical and even mythological associations. Distant prospects of plains, bays or seaside cities, viewed from an elevated point, usually come with high bands of cirrus or distant scrolls of incipient cumulus. Rural and rustic genre scenes inspire a measured, benevolent cumulus, casting a light that is dissipated, undramatic, while mountain scenes invariably attract cumulus accumulating, broken up, incubating a deepening chiaroscuro. It is over classical ruins, however, that thunder-heads mostly brood: at Girgenti, jagged light slashes through angry black billows – except where the Temple of Juno is foregrounded, its noble presence seeming to conjure a sky likewise serene, all passion spent (Plate 15).

This associative cloud grammar lent the landscape an air of drama. As such, it could also be mobilized on behalf of a history conceived theatrically. As agents of change, the clouds could, for example, be the prologues of Empire, although equally they could be prophets of doom. Bulwer-Lytton might associate them with civilization's ending; in the First Fleet journals, they have a greater, because more ambiguous, interest: '"Heavily in clouds came on the day" which ushered in our arrival. To us it was "a great, an important day", though I hope the foundation, not the fall, of an empire will be dated from it', wrote Watkin Tench of the First Fleet's arrival in Botany Bay, quoting from Joseph Addison's play *Cato.*[152]

Tench's theatrical image suggests a theatrical vision of history. One thinks of the Prologue to Goldsmith's play *Zobeide*, put on in the year Cook first sighted the eastern coast of Australia, in which the playwright compared exploration itself to a theatrical production. The author who puts on his play is like the navigator fitting 'his little frigate for adventures.' The audience is like an unknown country:

> This seems a barren and a dangerous coast.
> Lord, what a sultry climate am I under!
> Yon ill-foreboding cloud seems big with thunder.
> (*Upper Gallery*) There mangroves spread, and larger than I've seen 'em – (*Pit*).

Eliciting no applause, indeed producing no reaction from the different sections of the audience, our Prologue elaborates the comparison: 'The place is uninhabited, I fear', but a snake-like hissing suggests otherwise: 'O there the natives are – a dreadful race! . . . No doubt they're all barbarians . . . I'll try to make palaver with them though . . .'[153]

The wit of this depends on a tradition of visualizing colonial encounters theatrically, as pantomimes whose ulterior motive is apparent to the colonizers, while remaining hidden from the 'Good savages'. The London audience enjoys the joke because, although cast in the role of savage, it shares the Prologue's point of view, and thus understands the intended enclosure act. The humour consists in Goldsmith's ability to assimilate every sign the audience makes to what he, the actor, wants to see and hear. As for the audience, amused to be cast as mimic savages, unable to communicate what they want to say, able to appreciate the joke, they find their understanding subtly flattered. They are drawn into the Prologue's point of view; not to share it, not to connive in his fiction, would indeed be to behave like 'barbarians'. As for the real 'natives', they are consigned to a double darkness: rhetorical points of reference, they serve merely to illuminate the act of cultural self-enclosure represented by the symbiosis of actor and audience.

This is not to say that a weather conceived theatrically could not produce genuine historical effects. The same associative logic governed its moods; indeed, the link between different skies and different phases in the life and times of a society ensured that the alternations of dark and light were immediately comprehensible as signs. The pale cloudscapes of Light's last watercolours might be pre-semiotic, in that they did not foreshadow a definite end, and looked as if they could go either way, building up or evaporating. But the storms and fine spells attending, say, the foundation of a white settlement at Sydney Cove were semiotically enclosed, always dramatic, signifying this or that vicissitude within the great pageant of colonization.

Thunder and lighting in particular could be interpreted, like the lie of the land, as a malevolent *genius loci* bent on resisting civilization. As the First Fleeter Ralph Clark wrote in July 1788:

> The country is over run with large trees not one Acre of clear ground to be Seen nor is ther one tree out of fifty but what is burnt with the lightning nor nothing in it fitt for the Subsistance of man what with Earthquakes, thunder and lightning it is to be sure a Sweet Country – the Tunder and Lightning is the most Terrible I ever herd, it is the oppinion of every body here that Goverment [*sic*] will remove the Settlement to Some other place for if it remains here this country will not be able to maintain its self in one hundred Years for with all the Marines and Convicts here we have not been able to clear more Ground than what we are now putting in as fast as possible – the Convicts behave very bad . . .[154]

Clark's associative rambling may suggest a man of weakish character, but it also evokes a paranoid state where, under the necessity to have things signify unequivocally, the ambiguity of appearances upsets the balance of the mind. Where no panoptic survey is possible, he can only wander on from point to point, like one lost in the bush who is only lost because everywhere he finds signs of former occupation, indications, that is, of a prior invasion, a home he cannot return to; the ground is 'over run' by trees. Where it is unclear what the causes of phenomena are, what their history is, the writer can only proceed by frantically scanning left and right in search of something familiar. So Clark staggers between light and dark, between staying and going, between order and disorder. This is dramatic, but the drama is internal to the plot of colonization, the result of attempting to enclose the environment within the linear logic of an imperial history.

If clear and settled skies were associated with Progress, with political order and clear-sightedness, then storms signified the breakdown of order and rebellion: 'The Men Convicts got to them very soon after they landed, & it is beyond my abilities to give a just discription of the Scene of Debauchery & Riot that ensued during the night. They had not been landed more than an hour before they had all got their Tents pitched or anything in order to receive them, but there came on the most violent storm of thunder, lighteng. & rain I ever saw. The lighteng. was incessant during the whole night & I never heard it rain faster.'[155] So Arthur Bowes Smyth reported the notorious rape of female convicts that occurred on 6 February 1788 upon disembarkation at Sydney Cove.

Stormy weather precipitated the breakdown of character. Social divisions grew ragged and haemorrhaged. What had been enclosed was disclosed; what imprisoned, released. The accumulation of clouds aroused superstitious fears, raised questions about power and control. It reminded the settlers of their vulnerability and nakedness. It was like a return of the primitive. Ordinary seamen and illiterate petty criminals brought with them, no doubt, their fair share of superstitious weather lore. They too were on the lookout for signs, irregularities of the sky, sea and land surface where they might secrete themselves, where (like clouds) they might change identity and come back as another person, or pass out of reach to another country.

After 'two of the women Shot at today by the Centinells because they would not come back when they were cald,' Clark remarked, 'I never Saw a Skiy look So revengful as it dose now.'[156] Now who was being superstitious? While 'it came on to blow Remarkable hard . . . I was very much frightened . . . and thunder . . . made a Terrible Sound close to our Markee – there was a most darring Robbery committed by taking away 18 Bottles of wine out of a Tent beloning to the Contractor.'[157] The convicts were, it seems, rationalists when it came to exploiting irrational fears. Under cover of turbulent darkness, they went about their light-fingered work, clearing away what had accumulated in the wrong places, relocating it, letting it resettle.

Stormy weather had a bearing on cross-cultural, as well as class, relations within the colony. Elizabeth Macarthur expressed a widespread view when she wrote about the Sydney area Aborigines in 1791: 'It is not discover'd that they Worship the Sun, or any of the heavenly Bodies, and yet they say all who die, go up to the Clouds.'[158] But in the context of the clouds' symbolic significance in the white narrative of colonization, this is evidently not simply an ethnographic datum. At the very least, it implied a convergence of interests. Less benignly, a common interest in clouds was a way of finding a place for the Eora and neighbouring peoples within a European conception of history. The First Fleeters linearized what their informants told them; or in view of the intimacy that existed between them and their informants in the second year of occupation, it may be that the latter consciously pidginized their religious conceptions, simplifying them for foreign consumption.

Tench, recalling the reaction of the Aboriginal girl Abaroo to unsettled weather, assimilates it to his own picturesque conception of the clouds as portents of historical change: 'I remember Abaroo running into the room, where a company was assembled, and uttering frightful exclamations of impending mischiefs, about to light on her and her countrymen. When questioned on the cause of her agitation, she went to the door, and pointed to the skies, saying, that whenever the stars wore that appearance, misfortunes to the natives always followed. The night was cloudy, and the air disturbed by meteors.'[159]

Similarly, David Collins, asking Bennelong about his beliefs, frames his questions in genealogical terms. Observing that 'the white men here come from England', 'I then asked him where the black men (or Eora) came from? He hesitated. – Did they come from any island? His answer was, that he knew of none: they came from the clouds (alluding perhaps to the aborigines of the country); and when they died, they returned to the clouds (*boo-row-e*).'[160] The colon in this passage is eloquent. It is like a caesura, marking both a point of arrest and a sudden leap forwards, as if, pulled up short by Collins's nonsensical question about islands, Bennilong at length finds a way out of the conversational impasse. But Collins finds Bennelong's talk of clouds equally unintelligible.

Under another name, Wolare-warre, Bennelong, with considerably more wit 'once asked the judge-advocate, if the white men went to the clouds also,'[161] a question that strongly suggests Wolare-warre was merely saying back to his white interlocutor what the latter had formerly said about him. Which is not to pretend that this mutual mimicry was without substance. It is hard to imagine a more succinct or poetic statement of the differences between European and indigenous conceptions of historical time than their respective comparison of it to an island slipping away or coming into view along the horizon, and to a cloud which, never having gone, never needs to come back, but continually reforms itself on the spot where it casts its varying shadow.

Although less fully-documented, similarly theatrical enclosure acts overtook the weather in South Australia. For instance, some time after 16 June 1837 William Light painted a panoramic watercolour of 'The Landing Place, Glenelg' (Plate 16). As settlers had been disembarking along this beach since November of the previous year, Light's painting was already a representation of history, taking for granted (for example) its own settled and commanding point of view. Still, the hazy cloud-cover, broken here and there by pale blue embrasures (a cloud formation combining, dare one say, altocumulus and stratocumulus characteristics), seems carefully chosen, and to judge from other, more circumstantial, watercolours and from entries in the *Last Diary*, evokes those weather conditions – 'Cloudy, sultry, with very warm air' – which Light seemed to find typical of the Adelaide Plain.

However, by the time J. M. Skipper came to represent the same scene, using Light's composition in a watercolour of his own (Plate 17), the sky has become decidedly more eventful. A flotilla of fleecy cumulus clouds gathers expectantly offshore, both threatening and benevolent. And when, later still, Alfred Scott Broad returns to the scene, preparing a hand-coloured lithograph, the tonally neutral coastline is dramatically transfigured (Plate 18). Thunder-heads (nimbostratus) and their ragged avant-garde make a ghostly negative of the sun's rays. Light struggles with dark, and out of the fruitful conflict are pressed the first drops of longed-for rain turning the wilderness into a garden. The Union Jack, listless in Light's version, flutters in a rising breeze; permanent depots have sprung up where Light sketched the barest outline of a tent-frame.

Rain not only brings the history of the weather to a triumphant denouement, enclosing its rhythms within the one-way pattern of colonial progress; it encourages, even licenses, the enclosure of the land. And it may be that this double enclosure act dispossessed the Kaurna spiritually in ways quite as catastrophic as those associated with the unlawful usurpation of their land. Shelters – walls and roofs – can be justified in the first instance as a response to the weather. Bad weather may hamper getting ashore, but it also provides a reason for organizing the business of surveying the land, felling timber, sewing canvas and baking bricks. But for the enclosure of the sky, there would be no reason to chequerboard the subtly-undulating ground with little houses, whose tiny eyes, while looking out at the framed view, testify to the tunnel vision accommodated inside. Bark-roofed huts were designed for rain; they were like beseeching palms spread wide. At the same time, their slopes drained off rain's power; now it could come when it liked and make no difference.

But what of the indigenous people who until then had been unconscious of living outside, assuming the insides of the world extended infinitely in all directions? They suddenly found themselves exposed to the Europeans' rain. Physically dispossessed, they also found themselves spiritually undressed and vulnerable. Somehow, one imagines, the new dialectic between interior and exterior, fundamentally altered their relationship to their environment. They knew blindness, the deception of walls. Out of step with their surroundings, they were liable to get caught out in the wet. Perhaps it is the traumatically altered logic of the environment that contributes as much as anything else to their depression, their sense of metaphysical imprisonment.

As one Kaurna informant remarks, enigmatically but dismally: 'All my moveables become wet by the rain, which could enter into the house. Did it not rain, I should still be sitting in the house; had no rain come, I was sitting warm in the house. I could not foresee the coming rain whilst in the house – now I am outside, the rain just comes.'[162] It is no accident that this passage occurs in Teichelmann and Schurmann's *Outlines of a Grammar*, where it is a translation of a passage in the language of the Adelaide Tribe designed to illustrate their manner of forming verb tenses. Grammatical paradigms, and the ethnographic impulse they fuel to attempt to conduct and contain dialogues within their grid of persons and suffixes, are the linguistic equivalent of a Wakefield Plan for the enclosure of the land.

The pathos of ethnolinguistic data from the colonial period often resides in its syntactical strait-jacketing of sentiment, the linearization of contradictory feelings. Dialogue becomes a machine for the production of sentences, just as the open pages of the settlers' roofs were rain-charms. What they had in common was their exclusion of *affect* from the transaction. The native might be starving, he might be shivering with cold, but what counted was his ability to answer grammatically, to represent his feelings objectively. Within this world-view, mimicry was not proof of sympathy but a sign of obstinate ignorance: 'Do you not know the word (or, what has been told?) – I do not know it.'[163]

Similarly, colonizers interrogated clouds for what they could tell, not for any tendency to mock the observer. In 1836, with less than two months to survey Spencer Gulf and locate the best position for South Australia's capital, Light was keener than any to make the clouds eloquent. His *Brief Journal* makes it clear that meteorology, rather than geography, determined his site selection: 'My previous observations . . . were that all the vapours from the prevalent south-westerly winds would rest on the mountains here, and that we should, if we could locate this side of the gulf, be never in dread of those droughts so often experienced on the east coast of Australia. And I was now fully persuaded by the evidence here shown, as well as the repeated collection of clouds, and rain falling on the hills even at this season.'[164]

Colonial clouds were useful in so far as they revealed an environmental grammar, providing a way of translating the landscape into a plan of regulated occupation. It may well be that one object of Light's *Last Diary* was simply to furnish himself with a more adequate history of the weather of the Adelaide district. In view of the hostile criticism his choice of site was receiving, it was necessary to have all the facts at his finger-tips. Light needed to substantiate his prediction of rain-bearing clouds from the south-west. The presence of cooling sea-breezes, combined with, say, a record of storms that might have proved costly had Adelaide been sited beside the sea; these were data which, if accumulated over a long enough period, formed significant patterns, wearing all the solid appearance of scientific fact.

But this is largely guesswork, the result of reading between the lines of the *Last Diary*. Besides, the weather data there are too subjective and sketchy to have much historical value. Temperatures, barometric pressures, even the picturesque descriptions of light-effects found in the *Brief Journal*, are missing. The rationalization of the *Last Diary* as a public document also fails to take account of the 'increasingly querulous' elements in it, in particular its record of Light's fluctuating health. Perhaps most significant of all, in the context of a desire to disclose rather than enclose his historical subjectivity, the explanation of the *Last Diary* as another document in the rhetorical edifice of colonial foundation ignores its open form. Somewhere between a diary and a notebook, Light's *Last Diary* records a 'series of uniformity'[165] only in so far as it departs from repetitions to suggest a *tourbillon* of atmospheric eventfulness.

Light's *Last Diary* is not 'scientific', if this means an attachment to the statistical demonstration of the repetition of patterns. But it may be scientific in another sense, in documenting (as we have suggested) a correlation between the state of Light's health and the altering states of the air, and more importantly, in understanding that the interest of both lies in the open-ended, non-self-repeating forms both took. At the very least, we can say that Light's lack of eloquence, whatever it may say about his state of mind, also expresses a desire not to enclose passing events theatrically, to represent them as being more fateful than they are. The aim might be to trace a continually evolving curve corresponding to the continuous transformation of wind, cloud and light. The entries in the *Diary*, which are so unsatisfactory as the representation of a life, might have something of the quality of *macchie*, dabs or blotches serving to deepen rather than define.

There were precedents in the meteorological literature for this equivocation. As has often been pointed out, Luke Howard's system of cloud classification (first published in 1803) allowed the formation of clouds to be conceptualized as a narrative. The metamorphosis of cirrus into cumulus, and of cumulus into stratus, was temporally as well as formally structured. But the narrative was evolutionary rather than linear, a fact recognized in the later description of Howard's three cloud-types as 'genera', each with its own species. Even the evolutionary analogy, with its image of growing differentiation, is too prescriptive; in cloud taxonomy, identical species could reappear in different genera. The genus cirrus included the species fibratus, uncinus, spissatus and castellanus, but this was no reason why genera such as altocumulus and stratocumulus might not also claim castellanus amongst their species.[166]

These oddities of taxonomy pointed to the nature of clouds. They also implied the limitations of genealogical narratives incapable of comprehending the simultaneous coexistence of convergent forms, and the possibility of a non-linear taxonomy founded on mere coincidences, repetitions and mimicry. And leaving these classificatory difficulties aside, there was still the question of what tale the newly gestaltic clouds told: what did the history of the storm signify? Was it to be understood as a representation, a kind of allegory? Or was it to be appreciated as the revelation of a process without ulterior motive? Did it conform to the conventions of mimesis? Or did it display the nature of *methexis*?

In 1812, Thomas Forster, paraphrasing Howard's system, offered a summary which, especially in the context of our exploration of the symbolic significance of the Venetian blot technique, can be interpreted not only as the description of methektic process but as the evocation of a different kind of history.

> After a continuance of clear weather, the cirrus is frequently the first cloud which is seen. In this case it often looks like a fine whitish thread pencilled, as Mr. Howard expresses it, on the clear blue sky . . . the lines frequently extend quite across the welkin, while their ends, being lost in either horizon, appear, from a well-known optical deception, to converge into one point . . . sometimes transverse lines are formed, which intersecting the others at right angles, give to the sky the appearance of being covered with a beautiful network . . .[167]

The terms Forster uses recall the early stages in the evolution of a painting by Giorgione and Titian. There is an engagement with the thickening cross-ply of the canvas, a dabbing of the coloured ground with blotches that are at first insular but which soon join up to form suggestive images: 'Cumulus [at] its first appearance is generally a small irregular spot, which becomes the nucleus on which it forms. This increases in size . . . Cumuli vary in shape and dimensions, according to peculiarities in the operation of the causes which produce them. Sometimes they are pretty well defined hemispherical masses; at others they rise into mountains, ranged in one plane, their silvery summits presenting a beautiful appearance.'[168] Giorgione's storm clouds, in which a perfect hemisphere nestles, capture a stage in the clouds' formal evolution. They register chromatic effects, and what is more, recapitulate the widespread view that these are associated with impending and tumultuous change: 'The cirrostratus . . . is remarkable for exhibiting a great variety of beautiful colours, according to its variation in density.' Forster remarks that 'modern meteorologists have corroborated the speculative notions of the ancients, and have observed the prevalence of the cirrostratus to be usually followed by bad weather . . .'[169]

'The change of the cumulus into the cumulostratus is effected in the following manner: The cumulus, losing its hemispherical figure, increases irregularly upward, grows more dense and overhangs its base in uneven or rugged folds . . . Cumulistrati frequently remain in this state for a long time, and constitute very picturesque skies . . .' This might be said of Giovanni Bellini, but hardly of Giorgione, where, borrowing Forster's words, we might say 'the processes are more rapid', and the red-jerkined soldier with his lance and lightning-conducting glance seems drawn to the sky: 'Before thunderstorms it seems frequently reddish, which some people have imagined to arise from its being highly charged with the electric fluid . . . The best time for viewing the progress of nimbification is in stormy weather [when] the whole phenomenon [cumulostrati permeated with long strata of cirrostratus] has the appearance of a range of mountains, transfixed by the mighty shafts of giants.'[170]

In effect, 'nimbification' corresponds to the art of chiaroscuro, except that instead of producing a deeper identity in difference, it leads (at least in Forster's narrative) to a climactic denouement and curtains: 'After having existed some while in this form, they become large and irregular, and they get darker by intensity, till all seems concentrated in a dense black mass, with a cirrose crown extending from the top, and ragged cumuli entering from below; and eventually the whole resolves itself into rain.'[171] In other words, even within the emergent science of meteorology, emphasis might be placed upon the process of metamorphosis, rather than on the cataloguing of cloud gestalts and their cinematic succession. True, both led to one end, cathartic precipitation, but for Forster at least the process rather than the progress matters. It is those in-between states where ambiguous images are born and proliferate that engage his pen most poetically, because there, where irregular blotches spread their fingers, where outlines grow ragged, where colours multiply, the forces at work can be visualized, and what is observed is not a picturesque representation of them but their physical trace.

An analogous respect for the environment of phenomena characterized Goethe's ambition to prove (against Newton) the ultimate and original unity of white light. It was by focusing on in-between or boundary states, by attending to the chiaroscuro of nature, exemplified by the changing colours of the setting sun, that Goethe reckoned to detect the *Urphänomen* of colour. He considered the sun's transition from nearly white to yellow, orange and red, and the corresponding change of the sky's colour from bright blue to indigo, as 'chromatically "Urphänomenal" encounters of light and darkness (the interaction of matter and light produced the warm colours red and yellow by the "darkening" of light, the cool colours blue and violet by the "lightening" of darkness).'[172] And his light experiments were equally sensitive to the environment of seeing: 'Rather than perform just a single prismatic experiment with rigidly fixed circumstances, Goethe would vary the distance of the screen, adjust the aperture to control the quantity of light, substitute prisms with different angles (he sometimes used a hinged water prism for genuinely continuous change) or made of differently dispersive materials, and so forth. Goethe's method thus aimed not at isolating particular experiments but rather at carefully controlling and varying their circumstances and noting the correlation between these circumstances and the continuously developing result.'[173]

In any case, within this context of a growing attention to the environment of events, we can begin to glimpse the (anti-) biographical import of the *Last Diary*, a document that throws light on Light because it renounces any ambition to enclose a life within a theatrical plot, and emphasizes instead the endless variations that can be played on the ordinary rhythms of everyday life. But while the changing patterns of the weather provided an analogue of these patterns, they could hardly supply their subject-matter, their human interest. The *Last Diary* might be a minimalist record of wind directions, recurrent cool changes and occasional rain, but its subject was the state of the writer's lungs. And what brought these inner and outer events into correlation, making the relationship between wind patterns and breath patterns significant, was the unspoken presence of tuberculosis. Indeed, it is a triangulation between TB (or in Light's day, 'phthisis'), light and the weather that discloses the personal history, the obvious but unspoken lie of the land, that the *Last Diary* contains.

Of course, peremptorily to relocate the central drama of Light's life in an illness might be to indulge in another biographical stratagem. There is circumstantial evidence for saying that Light became aware of his condition during a visit to Rome in the mid-1820s, and a sketch he did of Sta. Trinità dei Monti and the Spanish Steps, presumably at that time,[174] might well bring a flush to the cheek of the sentimental biographer anxious to lend Light's aimless wanderings a fateful pattern. But to invoke consumption theatrically, as the biographers have, as another dramatic device lending pathos to a self-sacrificing history, as if it deepened an already completed outline, is to miss the point: that Light's awareness of his condition may have obliged him to conceptualize life differently, as a condition of his subjectivity that could not be taken for granted, but must be carefully shaped and drawn out.

However, even to recognize that Light may have spun his own life out of himself, out of 'that information (primitive sense) necessary for a poem',[175] as Keats put it, is not of course to escape biography's enclosure act. It may simply be to substitute for providence, or family, or native genius, a different cause of his life's course. Romancing of this kind is lent at least a superficial plausibility by the fact that in Light's day the causes of phthisis or consumption or pulmonary tuberculosis were unknown. Some held that it was hereditary, others that it was environmental, yet others that it was contracted by direct contact with a phthisis sufferer. Now while this multiplicity of hypotheses testified to a scientific ambition to reduce the condition to order, to fit it out with a plausible linear biography, the resistance of the illness to this kind of explanation also undermined the authority of genealogical approaches. The sufferer from consumption was most likely to die; this much was clear. But if he asked himself how he had come to this point, by what means his fate had overtaken him, he remained completely in the dark. The victim of consumption who wanted to understand the meaning of his life, a life whose end was now fast approaching, was at liberty to explain the origins of his illness – and so of his individual mortality – in any way he liked.[176]

Perhaps Light inherited a tubercular predisposition from his father, who died at the same age as William from unspecified causes. Or perhaps Light acquired his fatal condition while (let us imagine) nursing his first wife – who, it appears, died a lingering death. This would explain Light's silence. The popular conviction that tuberculosis was contagious – a belief strong in Italy, not least among the porters, nurses, hotel-keepers and servants on whose services wealthy foreigners depended – would have rendered inconvenient in the extreme the kind of existence Light and his second wife enjoyed.[177] Perhaps the invisible germs of tuberculosis were borne on the air. This would explain Light's sea-going, his longing for light, unpolluted breezes . . .

A picture is certainly beginning to form. Is it chance that amongst the fragmentary records surviving the January 1839 fire is the account of a sailor's death at sea on 5 July 18–: 'He complained towards evening of a chilling tho' the day was very hot.' From the remedies prescribed – apart from an emetic, 'a dose of bark' taken as often as thirteen times a day – the man was evidently in the last stages of consumption. He appeared to rally, but a week later, 'it was a dreadful day to all hands nearby. The wind blew very strong from the eastwards and a hot pestilential air all around. The

Capt. was seized with an excruciating headache, I was myself very ill.'[178] From this day, the sailor's decline proved irreversible.

Evidently, Light had not only died before he died, he had witnessed how it was going to be, been present at its dress rehearsal. This explains no doubt Light's interest in visiting Lerici in 1828: 'It was here that poor Percy Bysshe Shelley was residing with his wife when he was unfortunately drowned.'[179] In Shelley's death, the themes of thunder and lightning and consumption oddly converged. It has been pointed out that the romantic melancholy of Shelley's *Ode to the West Wind* perfectly expresses the consumptive's awareness of his own fragile hold on life. But perhaps the poem is something more: a biography of tuberculosis, an attempt to lend the death it brings a meaning, and by prophecying a resurrection and return, to redeem its life. Perhaps Shelley voluntarily steered into the heart of the storm, and perhaps this is the inner sense of Light's own tempest poem quoted at the beginning of this section: 'The darkness of the night and the quick succession of forked lightning so close with the violence of the wind and rain made one of the most horrible nights I ever experienced.'[180]

Seizing on such incidents, investing them with symbolic value, a pathology of Light's life might be constructed, a genealogy of symptomatic events leading inevitably to his end. But they would have no necessary connection with Light, with the man nothing is known about. Did he smoke a pipe? Did he speak through his chest? Did he practice self-auscultation? Was his hearing equally good in both ears? Could he tell pus from mucus? (Was he familiar with Doctor Darwin's method?) Did he long for the old days when a *tussis* was still a *tussicula*, and he had seriously entertained the idea that 'a severe blow received upon the chest, or a wound of the lungs from the sword, a bullet' might cure him? Did he liken the whites of his eyes to pearls, and wonder whether the 'pearls' in his finger-nails had the same origin? (Could an etymology of puns provide a better diagnosis than the quack's?) Was he aware of matter resembling brick-dust suspended in his urine? Where did he obtain his supplies of ipecacuanha? Did he cultivate foxgloves for medicinal reasons?[181]

Instead of answers to these questions, we have the biographical equivalent of cures. Just as the remedies for phthisis were legion, so the psychological surmises of biography are numberless. And again, in Light's day they mimicked each other. If, as one Dr Carmichael Smyth maintained, 'mere motion is much superior to any exercise', and the continuous up and down of a vessel at sea superior to any other kind of motion,[182] the cause of Light's addiction to ships becomes obvious. It can account for other kinds of restlessness too. The three expeditions Light made to Lynedoch Vale (11–17 December 1837, 8–21 January 1839, 1–9 June 1839), for example, were reconnaissance trips, but they were also symptomatic of an illness that notoriously mimicked a return to health: 'They in general entertain sanguine (*sic*) hopes of a speedy recovery; and during the severity of the paroxysm, they are often observed to have a peculiar flow of spirits, and uncommon quickness of genius.'[183]

Each time, Light's health fluctuated rapidly, bouts of energetic activity alternating with periods of breathless fatigue. And each time, coming closer to whatever little Xanadu he hoped to find for himself or the settlers, he was obliged to turn back. In his account of it, Lynedoch Vale acquires something of the same hectic air. If the landscape of the first visit is bland, flat, 'very beautiful',[184] that of the second is eventful, changeable, atmospheric: 'Open with here and there some patches of wood. It's undulating and the soil much the same as the rest. At night some heavy showers with thunder and lightning.'[185] But the pattern of sudden reversal is the same, and is repeated with variations in Light's account of the final expedition in June, where a change in the weather on the sixth produces simultaneously an improvement in health and a positive assessment of the lie of the land: 'Pools of excellent water and very fine soil and grass and well wooded with green trees. At night fine with cold air.'[186]

And so on . . . If nothing else, a forensic narrative of this kind underlines the point that biography is a form of literary tuberculosis. It attempts to enclose the life within a mythic genealogy of causes and effects, held together not by any grounding in the 'continued blaze' of living, but by a reductively associationist logic. And if TB itself can be enlisted in support of this form of life-writing, all to the good. The convergence between two myths of causation is so complete that each seems to provide evidence of the truthfulness of the other. The truth is, of course, that biography's recapitulation of the tubercular discourse merely illustrates another application of Susan Sontag's thesis: it is not only the way TB was conceptualized, theorized medically and mythologized socially that served to objectivize the sufferer, and to discount the reality of his experience, but also biography, which long after TB's 'cure' tries to explain the life in terms of symptoms.

But this, as I said, is but one way of interpreting a tubercular history. To dwell, as Sontag does, on the historical construction of consumption, and to notice its similarity to the biographical construction of a life, is to imply that the explanations of TB in Light's day were purely ideological, had no purchase on reality, and for this reason ruthlessly repressed historical subjectivity. The difficulty with this is that it seems based on a naïve view of the nature of diseases and their cures. As cultural parasites, they do not go away when properly named or explained. Diseases operate historically not only to suppress human potentialities, but also to force their expression, not least by obliging the sufferer to construct his and her life within and against a new idea of ageing and dying. One consequence of this may be to focus attention away from those biographically-privileged moments of extraordinary achievement or insight and, using the symptomatology to hand, to devise a genuinely liberatory life story, one that is, for instance, anti-colonial in its willingness to go on as it is, to remain at sea, like the sea breathing in and out deeply, regularly. And such a story might be a way of linking together phenomena that, from a biographical standpoint, were inaudible and invisible, but nevertheless pressed on the historical subject constantly and continuously – like the weather, say, or the chiaroscuro of night and day.

Especially in the Romantic period, a disposition to tuberculosis was, as is well-known, associated with genius. For Sontag, the association is fanciful, an ultimately cruel metaphor: 'By validating so many possibly subversive longings and turning them into cultural pieties, the TB myth survived irrefutable human experience and accumulating human knowledge for nearly two hundred years.'[187] But the association may have been less irresponsible than she supposes. In the eighteenth century, the body of the air and the patient's body were conceptualized in similar ways. Medical practitioners conceived disease in what Foucault calls 'a space of projection without depth, of coincidence without development.' 'Disease appears in the "space" of the human body as in a space without character, flat; the different locations in this space do not affect the disease,' and Feldman, the American historian of science, comments: 'Just so, meteorologists perceived the space of the earth's surface as characterless . . . Just as space, of itself, did not affect the weather, so "there is no process of evolution in which duration [i.e. time] introduces new events of itself"'.[188]

The correlations that eighteenth-century scientists made between weather and diseases exemplified the 'classical' episteme, as Foucault defined it; they were superficial, failing to penetrate 'to the interior forces that govern their interactions.' Feldman contrasts them with Humboldt's notion of a climatic system, 'a region in which the different factors of climate vary in a continuous manner, so that in specifying for example the mean annual temperature one has fixed by implication the range of other climatic factors such as winter and summer temperature.'[189] This shift has a double significance in relation to the biographical interpretation of the *Last Diary*. The new meteorology seeks to understand the weather historically, and this means regionalizing phenomena both spatially and temporally, translating them into a narrative. To disclose the 'character' of the weather means enclosing it, localizing it. So with the 'self'; it comes into existence as an interior force at the point where it is seen to exhibit a distinctive pattern.

Biography and meteorology do not necessarily retreat from each other at this point, pursuing their structurally-parallel courses. The theory of a propulsive self, capable of steering a unique life-path, is analogous to the search within weather studies for a unifying physical principle determining climatic regimes. A direct link between the two fields occurs through the medium of electricity. That thunderstorms were due to a difference in electrical charge between sky and earth had been known since the 1750s, but nearly a century later electricity itself remained mysterious. Harris described it, in terms that recall Newton's conception of the Ether, as 'some elementary or primordial principle in nature everywhere present, and intimately associated with the particles of common matter according to some general law.'[190] In any case, if lightning signified the swift resolution of a disorderly state, a return to health, then perhaps human illness was to be understood similarly. Rejecting the old theory of humours, Forster speculated: 'It appears to me that it is not heat or cold, dampness or drought of the air, which is chiefly concerned in producing disorders, nor the sudden transition from one to another of those states; but that it is some inexplicable peculiarity in the electric state.'[191] If this is true, then the appearance of the sky might be directly correlated with the interior condition of the patient. Thunderous skies might be a direct analogue, say, of haemmorhaging occurring in the lungs or of other kinds of unhealthy discharge.

'When medical practitioners have spoken of the general ill-health of their patients,' Forster continues, 'I have remarked circumstances which appeared to denote an irregular distribution of the atmospheric electricity. The manner of the distribution, and the continual and multiform changes of the cirrus cloud, ramifying about and extending its fibres in every direction . . .' Weather which is 'remarkably unwholesome is characterised by all the clouds having confused indefinite edges.' Forster further speculates: 'Atmospheric peculiarities . . . may deprive persons, already weak, of a portion of their electricity, and thus the energies of the brain and nervous system may be diminished: or the atmospheric electricity, being unequally distributed in the air, or propagated downwards at intervals, it may occasion an irregular distribution of it in our bodies, and produce an irregularity of function.'[192]

Humphry Davy saw more than a correlation between external and internal states. It might be true, as Harris later cautioned, that 'an essential distinction exists between the light of lightning, for which, as Franklin observes, we want an appropriate term, and the presence of the electrical agency itself,'[193] but this did not prevent Davy identifying light with human perception and volition. Oxygen, which Davy called 'phosoxygen', is composed of two parts, oxygen (the gas) and light; during respiration, this substance enters the blood and is dissociated, the light 'then fuelling the sensibility of the nerves'. 'Thus essential then is light to perceptive existence.'[194] In 1806, Davy used electricity to decompose water into 'oxygene and hydrogene'; this might have suggested an analogy with the dissociation of elements said to occur in respiration. In one of his dialogues, Davy's characters speculate about the nature of life. One conjectures that 'during respiration "some sensible matter" reaches the blood and stimulates the vital property of sensibility. Sensibility, and at a higher level intellectual activity, were not to be explained simply as the product of organised matter – the optic nerve and the brain "are but the instruments of a power which has nothing in common with them". This power, the sentient principle or monad, is connected to the body "by kinds of ethereal matter" . . .'[195]

This description suggests that the power in question was electricity. In this context, Samuel Rogers's image, 'Thus kindred objects kindred thoughts inspire,/ As summer-clouds flash forth electric fire,'[196] was not fancifully poetic; it embodied a seriously entertained scientific hypothesis. If consciousness was electrical, it followed that self-consciousness was the power to reproduce electricity, to transform its energy into intellectual light. Humboldt strapping electrodes to his back and suffering an electric current to pass between them, Davy ecstatic on nervous gas, reproduced experimentally the operations of genius; they used electricity to produce knowledge.[197]

Romantic identification of the life-force with the 'electric fluid' bears on the description and treatment of TB, whose symptoms were interpreted as a disordering of the blood. Pulmonary bleeding suggested locally high blood-pressure tearing the artery walls. The withdrawal of the blood from the capillaries in the whites of the eyes, giving them 'very much the colour and appearance of pearl,' and later, the development of a hectic fever when there frequently occurred 'a peculiar glowing heat in the face . . . attended with manifest flushing of the countenance',[198] could be similarly accounted for, as a tempestuous disequilibrium within the bloodstream likely, unless safely discharged, to burst the heart's reticulated banks and flood the body cavity. To bleed the patient was to provide a timely and therapeutic lightning conductor; by drawing off the disorderly 'effluvium', to forestall the body's self-consumption.

If, then, the blood was an alchemical medium capable of transmuting light into genius, a particular volatility of the bloodstream might reasonably be associated with an unusual quickness of mind. Keats's image, 'Physician Nature! let my spirit blood!/ O ease my heart of verse and let me rest,'[199] is bitterly ironic, but it is not fanciful. It was on the assumption that Keats's metaphor was medically valid that his doctor maintained 'that the cure lay in rest – in avoiding any excitement and (after he learned more of Keats's life) any work on poetry.'[200]

So to return to Sontag's thesis. The association of TB may have been wrong, but it was hardly gratuitous, mischievous or ideologically cynical. Furthermore, it provided ways of thinking about illness which were liberating, if only because they allowed the possibility of conceiving one's life non-biographically, in terms of an environment that history at least regularly ignored. The difficulty with Sontag's thesis is that it seems predicated on the possibility of naming a disease non-metaphorically. If we could call TB (and cancer) by their true names, this would not only bear witness to our success in curing them; it would also cure us of our falsifying, victimizing metaphors. The politics of this is, of course, admirable, but the poetics more doubtful: medical hypotheses, as well as Fascist demagogues, depend on metaphorical modes of description.

Koch's cure for TB did not deliver us from metaphors; it simply provoked a new one which, framed in the absence of any knowledge of the body's immune system, was also metaphorical.

Light was not simply named by his illness, he was not only the victim of the social construction of his malady. He also, one supposes, named himself, making in whatever way he could his TB part of his own narrative. The myths about TB limited the stories he could elaborate about the origins of his illness, its meaning and his destiny, but they did not wholly predetermine what could be said. The burgeoning literature devoted to cataloguing symptoms, treatments, cures, made a study of TB somewhat analogous to a survey taking account of the lie of the land. One could as well fathom the wellsprings of character as determine precisely the causes of consumption. From the sufferer's point of view, TB avoided flattening out the mental prospect, introducing unpredictable folds, grooves and sidetracks into the process of memorialization.

Without demanding that he choose one route over another, TB invited him to think about his life environmentally, in terms of circumstantially-convergent phenomena. It obviously enclosed the mind, but it also disclosed a possible pattern, a genealogy of events that, like the weather, could be regionalized and which, even if they could not be predicted, displayed the chiaroscuro of statistical probabilities. It could even suggest a release from the imprisoning tendency to survey one's life panoptically, to suppose that knowledge must resemble a map. Perhaps it was musical instead, so that in order to see who one was, it was necessary to listen. And not to listen to the too-eloquent fictions of forensic oratory, but to the voice itself and its pre-semiotic vocalizations, which nevertheless accurately 'read out' the climatic changes occurring within the body.

Furthermore, what was intuited aurally, as a physical vibration across the differently-tuned membranes of the body, might find its exact analogue outside in the undulations, now *agitato*, now *arioso*, of the sky's airy substance. There would be no representations in this world, only trails of phenomena winding round and through one another methektically, and as their turbulent passages magnified or miniaturized them, and they seemed to identify with one another, events registered as memorable sensations.

'TB,' Sontag writes, 'makes the body transparent. The X-rays, which are the standard diagnostic tool, permit one, often for the first time, to see one's inside – to become transparent to oneself.'[201] But this was later: in Light's day, the inside of the body remained cloudy. And the metaphor is used advisedly. I think it is quite likely that certain 'atmospheric peculiarities' – notably 'multiform changes of the cirrus cloud, ramifying about and extending its fibres in every direction' – were interpreted methektically, as externalizations of the physical rupturings of blood-vessels, and the subsequent seeping of blood by capillary action throughout the lungs. Watching clouds, Light did not merely look for signs; he saw his own disease backlit against the sky.

In a metaphorically elaborate (but scientifically precise) description of cirrus in a state of 'great disturbance' evolving into cumulus – a description which might usefully be compared with contemporary descriptions of TB's successive phases – Forster lists the appearance successively of 'Comoid tufts, like bushes of hair . . . angular flexures; streaks; reticular intersections of them . . . cyphon shaped curves, and lines with pendulous or erect fringes . . .' and, as cirrus becomes cirrocumulus, 'fleeces of wool, or myriads of small specks; of long tapering columns, like the tail of the great manis, or of mackerel back skies, or of *striae*, like the grains of wood.' At the conclusion of the transformation, 'Cumuli have not now their hemispherical figure; tuberculated, or fleecy; elevated and flimsy, or heavily sailing along like scud, they appear operated on by an unusual condition of their causes.'[202]

As the sky grew stormier, as light clouds solidified into dark and brooding lumps, it was a magnification of tubercles growing, ramifying and taking hold of the body that was cinematically witnessed. And if a direct relationship existed between the inflammatory state of the blood and the prevalence of 'electric fluid' in the atmosphere in a state of disequilibrium, then the resemblance was not simply metaphorical. One produced the other, or more exactly, by a process analogous to magnetic induction, reproduced itself, bodily symptoms physically imitating atmospheric ones.

Davy's supposition that light was breathed in can be traced back to Homer. According to Onians, 'In actual seeing, something – what is received through the eyes – is "breathed" from the objects seen. What is received is "breath".' The Homeric verb meaning 'I perceive', usually referring to hearing but also embracing seeing, is the same as the verb signifying 'I breathe in'. The Aeolic verb 'to breathe at' means to 'to look at', 'the eyes being in fact not only passive and recipient like the ears, but also active outwardly.'[203] But while the ears may be passive, the body, through the office of breathing, is acoustically active: it produces sounds. Air that inhales and exhales light also resonates.

René Laennec's discovery of mediate auscultation – listening to the internal sounds of the body with the help of a stethoscope originally improvised out of a rolled-up quire of paper – provided, in this sense, an acoustic X-ray. The different sounds emitted by the different parts of the tuberculous chest enabled Laennec to 'see' the distribution, size and density of the tubercles afflicting the patient. Light may not have been able to see inside himself, but he could, in theory, illuminate the darkness inside him by listening. Inhaling deeply, critically examining the pitch, timbre and frequency of his cough, he became aware of a voice within the body addressing him in a language far more eloquent than English.

Laennec was surprised to hear through his stethoscope the voice coming directly out of the chest. He found that the variabilities in its distribution there, its resonance and strength, were diagnostic. The voice that avoided intellectual translation, emerging from the mouth as speech, retained its physical chiaroscuro, providing a shadowy map of the lungs' diseased topography. The voice vibrating in the chest cavity grew primitive. Laennec referred collectively to the sounds 'caused by the passage of air through the fluids of bronchia or lungs or by its transmission through any of the air passages partially contracted' as *râle*, a term borrowed from the call of the land rail or corncrake. Towards the end, the voice was transformed into a death rattle or *rhonchus*, a sound that could be compared with a frog croaking.[204]

Light dies, is reborn as sound. Musicologist F. Joseph Smith, advancing the philosophical claims of sound, says we should not talk of the image or *eidos* but of 'musical *tonos* or of a fundamental *echos*, that describes things not only as seen but as felt and heard. For *echos*, as sound, takes in everything from the tumultuous roar of the ocean and the grandeur of a summer cloudburst to the specifically musical *tonos* of Greek music, the *tonus* of medieval music, and the tonal/atonal systems of modern history. In short, *echos* takes in what we call the primordial world, as it sounds and swells all about us and within us, as we are borne aloft on the crest of life.'[205] This is emotive and attractive, and using an auditory analogy, rather than a visual or geometrical one, we can imagine a life being narrated, perhaps notated, in terms not of ends and outcomes, but of regular or altering pulses: breathing, the rise and fall of waves, walking, the regular but never repetitive cycles of weather.

> *Tuesday, 22 January, 1839* – Moderate breezes and fine. At 2 p.m. while finishing our dinner a rumbling noise was heard, and looking out we discovered Fisher's house to be on fire. At the same time, the breeze freshening up, the destruction to both houses became inevitable. In less than ten minutes both houses were burnt to the ground, mine catching fire at the roof by a lighted piece from Fisher's. We saved nothing of value.[206]

At the same time, Smith's somewhat Wagnerian image of the life-process seems curiously insulated from space and time. A kinaesthetic synthesis is evoked – but only in the opera house or concert hall. It is the unexpected noises of the everyday that provide Light with his index of fateful change: noises that are symptomatic but address the hearer in a language he cannot fathom, and which as a consequence remain attached to their physical loci, auditory traces signifying nothing but the air vibrating analogously with a physical event. Noises are in this sense grounded, localized; they cannot be notated or easily translated. They do not add up.

> *Saturday, 16 February* – One of the most horrible, suffocating days I ever felt. Hot winds and dust till about 7 p.m., when we had a shower of rain. At 8.30 p.m. it was again very warm, but got cool during the night. (Northerly. Westerly.)'[207]

Likewise, the *Last Diary* is not composed of lightning and thunder, nor even marked by a conscious patterning or grouping of temporal phenomena. It could be characterized as a ship's log kept on land; the weather phrases are identical with those used in the surviving fragments of the *Gulnare* Log. It certainly did not mark any kind of self-conscious literary debut. Though precipitated by a fire in which, according to George Gawler, 'the whole of his valuable portfolios of drawings executed during his residence in Egypt and in the Peninsula' as well as 'the private journal he has diligently kept for the last thirty years' were lost,[208] Light carried on exactly as before – as if merely extending the cursory notes kept during his survey (and reproduced in the *Brief Journal*).

One day vanishes to be replaced by another, but no magical transformation is involved. The mere succession of days does away with the need to order the diary entries associatively. A fresh entry does not supersede or interpret or revise the one previous to it; it does not close it off. Rather, it nearly repeats it, again disclosing the open aspect of the world. But the disclosure is not revelatory. It is not that diaries dissociate one experience from another, picturesquely breaking up the expectation of a linear narrative, an emerging 'I'. They lack the momentum associated with moving from one point to the next, and the related ambition to survey the path taken and the road ahead. Instead, they find their reason vertically, in the simple contingency of writing itself, of continuing to occupy a portion of the earth's surface. The transition from one day to the next is a measure of endurance, a means of staying where one is.

> *Friday, 8 March* – Early part strong breezes and heavy rain. At 9 a.m. cleared up with very cold air. Cold the whole day. Employed all day in accounts and writing . . .[209]

A sense of being grounded is not 'associated' or likened to the changing states of the winds and clouds. Rather, meteorology and the anti-autobiographical condition evoked here participate in the same spatio-temporal reality, employing the same 'infinitesimal calculus' of change. A mechanistic psychology cannot illuminate it; the psyche, like the skies, does not have an aetiology. It does not 'repress' its feelings, or seek climactic release. Its unpredictabilities, turbulent occasions, side-tracks, its disappearances and self-renewals require no other explanation than that implicit in the partial patterns they make on the surface – a surface complicit in their formation. The history that describes such phenomena adequately would be consonant with what occurs when 'the physics of falling, of repetition, of rigorous concatenation is replaced by the creative science of change and circumstances.'[210]

> *Tuesday, 26 March* – Early part calm and fine. At 8.30 a.m as the day got warm I felt myself very unwell again. P.m., at 2 Woodford and his wife came here. More ease this afternoon. This day has been extremely hot. At night cool and pleasant. (Calm. Unwell with dysentery.)

> *Wednesday, 27 March* – Early part calm and fine. At 8 a.m. very warm. At noon very hot disagreeable weather . . . Very unwell all day . . .

Tuesday, 28 March – Moderate and cloudy with cool air. At noon breeze increasing and weather looking like a change. At midnight blowing very strong and rainy.[211]

A history of Light which can begin to see him as other than history's theatrical creation needs to essay a psychology of 'change and circumstances'. It avoids recourse to Freudian neurotic nosogenesis. But, under the influence of auditory analogies, it does not seek to emulate Henri Bergson's 'true empiricism .. which proposes to get as near to the original itself as possible, to search deeply into its life and so, by a kind of intellectual auscultation, to feel the throbbings of its soul.'[212] Instead of seeking to re-present the absent one, it participates in the disappearance, drawing inspiration from the patterned discontinuity of the life record, the gaps between entries, and the meaning of these preliminary endings which death eventually discloses. It contents itself with analysing the remains as they are, not seeking to fill in the gaps but, if anything, determined to preserve them, respecting the environment they leave out. This is not to deny that their hidden ground needs interpretation, but it is to say that its elucidation does not depend on a talent for cryptography.

Tuesday, 9 April – Light airs and variable. Very unwell all day. Attempted to draw, but could not. At night fine and cool.'[213]

Cryptography is not a shorthand but a longhand, a way of delaying the end. It aims to put off the final reading, where the truth 'comes to light'. It is a kind of writing designed to baffle reading, a biography biographers cannot paraphrase. Sciascia writes of the novelist Stendhal that he consciously delayed his precocity as a writer, preferring to doodle with his pen in the oddest places, and he concludes: 'His graphomania is thus a way of extending in space a life he feels is threatened by brevity in time – a way of leaving "signs of life" on whatever space is available (most moving, among the objects in the Bucci Foundation now in Milan, is the powder or tobacco case, the lining of which is entirely covered with writing). And his cryptography is a trick to make such signs obvious by concealing them . . .'[214]

In this sense, Light's *Last Diary* is cryptographic, a sign of life that discloses its meaning by hiding its end. It is a record of disappearance, and to arrest and reverse its process, not merely bringing Light back to life but monumentalizing him, is to subvert the intention of his own biographical record, to deny his precocious knowledge of death and its corollary: a desire to circle as long as possible the centre of his fate, and by participating in the light's daily ending, to put off the time when the light should go out.

> *Saturday, 18 May* – Very light airs and variable. Fine all day. Felt a little better this day. At night fine.[215]

Sciascia's allusion to Stendhal occurs in 'The Mystery of Majorana', an essay that makes its point of departure the antithesis of the biographical *mise en scène*: not the story of a man's rise to prominence and fame, but the opposite, his complete disappearance. Sciascia senses that the mystery of the famous Sicilian scientist is not to be explained positively, by psychological or political hypotheses, but negatively, in terms of Majorana's voluntary renunciation of a name, his determination to take control of his fate by fading overnight from the public record. Evidently then, the writer interested in finding out 'what happened' has, if he is to succeed in uncovering the biographical truth, to preserve the subject's absence. He has to decipher the equivocal signs of life – the fragmentary official records, private letters, memories of friends – not with a view to putting the missing man back together again, but in order to map, as it were, the terrain of his anonymity.

The aim is, biographically, to transfer attention from Majorana's inner life, his intuited motivations, towards the environment of his life, the social, political and geographical lie of the land. This is not intended as a casuistical attack on doctrines of presence, it shows how the act of disappearance is a sign of presence that implicates an entire society. 'In all things,' Sciascia writes, 'there is a "rational" mystery of essences and correspondences, a tight, uninterrupted network of almost imperceptible, almost inexpressible significances linking one point to another, one thing to another, one being to another.'[216] This 'network' does not lie beneath the surface; it is all about us if we know where to look. It is not a matter of one thing leading to another; the very chanciness of their arrangement may hold the key to the story.

> *Monday, 10 June* – Early part sharp frost and calm. Towards noon a disagreeable sirocco fell with light variable airs and strong appearance of change. At 5 very cold indeed. I felt very unwell the

> whole day. At night I turned in early with a high fever. Calm and cold all night.[217]

(And earlier, Light's London publisher, James Carpenter, forwarded him four volumes of 'light reading which has the recommendation of cheapness,' and advised him, 'you desire some light reading . . . modern novels are very dear and most of them worthless, all Captain Marryat's novels with Cooper's and many of the best romances are printed cheap such volumes containing an entire work. I send you a number of the Athenaeum on the back of which you will find a list of "the standard works".'[218])

Apropos of chanciness, is it mere coincidence that Sciascia illustrates his argument by reference to the novelist Savinio's superstitious conviction 'that the ruins Schliemann excavated must be those of ancient Troy, because during the First World War the British destroyer *Agamemnon* had bombarded them. If,' Savinio averred, 'the British sailors had not been inspired by the unspent fury of Agamemnon, why should they have fired at ruins in a wilderness? Names are more than a definition of things: they are the thing itself.'[219] An unnoticed local force-field draws the guns to their target, and ensures they cannot miss their mark; it is the hill of Hisarlik itself that puckers the ground and grooves the air. Whatever the status of these subliminal attractions, they are cognate with the agglutinative grammar of the Aranda hunter who, even as he unleashes the spear from its shuttle-like woomera, never lets go but follows its flight with an expanding envelope of words that, properly naming its flight, ensure its success. They belong to the same curvilinear universe that draws the soldier's lance to the hemispherical cloud in Giorgione's *Tempesta*, confident that a meteorological lineage links them.

Is it merely coincidence that Light bore the name he did? Or to put it another way, is a more economical account of his life possible? Perhaps the methektic relationship between the pattern of his life and the character of light, the theories of its nature, propagation and transformation, means nothing. Or else, not seeking to enclose a life, to lay the foundations of another myth, but seizing instead on the chance coincidence of names, perhaps another history is disclosed, a network of correspondences so obvious as to slip, like air, through history's hedges, those logical enclosure acts that smooth away the ground in the interests of plain law and order. This is not to say that the mystery of Light's subjectivity is not a historical question, but it is to suggest a history that history leaves out, that of the rainbows, say.

> *Monday, 1 July* – Moderate and fine. At 9 a.m. long arched cloud extending from south to north nearly over the whole arch, indicating a change of weather. Pleasant air most part of the day. At 4 p.m. very cold. I felt rather better this day, but terribly annoyed with some visitors. At night dark and cold, towards midnight blowing fresh. (Light and var.)[220]

To rewrite history is not to turn back the clock. It is to find a mode of writing that does not, however anxiously it aims to occupy the moral high ground, repeat the enclosure acts associated with imperial history. It is to inaugurate a post-colonial history on other grounds than those of ideology. It is to dispense with the myth of progress, the idea that the future entails leaving the past behind. The common ground that would emerge from this recognition would show how the Kaurna were right: going to the clouds was a preliminary to returning – not as ghosts (the foolish interpretation of the whites, who could only, it seems, conceive of binary oppositions), but as presences rendered palpable, resident in the land, by their decision to absent themselves. Death is never for the first time, and never ends.

At any rate, recognizing the meteorology of Light's life, we can see why he died. Up until the end of July 1839, every change in the weather corresponded to a change in Light's condition. On Wednesday 31 July, for instance, after a week of being 'very ill', he notes, 'At p.m. some appearance of change. At night fine. Felt a little better.'; and the following day, 'Light airs and cloudy. At 9 a.m. rain. Rain all day. At 5 p.m. blowing fresh. At 7 blowing fresh and rainy. Much better this day. At night squally and rainy. (Northerly)'[221]

This was the last time, though, that the expected, even longed-for, correlation occurred. After a relapse on 4 August ('At noon cloudy with sharp air. Between 5 and 6 taken very ill with spasms near the heart'[222]), the advent of another change became a matter of urgency. Throughout the next week of cold, showery weather, Light continued weak; on the 12th he thought it was 'looking like a change',[223] but nothing came of it, the light airs and fine weather persisting until the 16th.

Over the next two days, the wind swung round from north-west to west, bringing heavy rain and a predictable improvement in Light's health: 'Sunday, 18 August – Heavy squalls with rain. At noon cleared up. Moderate and cloudy with pleasant weather all the afternoon. Miss Jacob came to see me. Very well indeed today . . .'[224] But no less predictable was his relapse, once the change had passed through and the fresh breezes died away again. And as his breathing grew shallower, so his style became staccato: 'Tuesday, 20 August – Light airs and fine all day. Very unwell indeed today. At night fine. Unwell at night, and no sleep (Var).'[225]

Again, and perhaps with greater anxiety, Light looked forward to a change in the weather. On 24 August the wind strengthened and backed easterly ('strong gusts of wind all night [ ] Opened Morphett's brandy'), and over the 26–27th, the wind direction rapidly reversing, another cool change swept in: 'Towards evening heavy clouds with thunder and lightning . . .' And the following day, 'At night much thunder and lightning with much rain.'[226] Only now it was a change that brought no change.

On 29 August, after failing to mention his health for three days, Light noted 'Very unwell all day.'[227] The expected improvement in his breathing had apparently not happened, and although the fresh west wind continued blowing, bringing with it showers that lasted into the night of 1 September, Light remained unable to respond. Now, if not before, it was clear what form his death would take. It would simply be an unravelling of his breathing from the breath of the skies; it would be a retreat from that 'conversation' with his surroundings; it would be the slumping of the undulatory line, rising and falling symbiotically with changes in temperature and atmospheric pressure, its regression to a straight line incapable of any sympathetic deviation.

Or perhaps, settling into a stable pattern, continuing the same day after day, the weather remained in sympathy with Light to the very end. If so, the very constancy of the light, its clarity, was the clearest proof of death's impending presence. The air did not abound with cryptic messages; the mere fact of its staying on, its lack of perturbation, implied that the house was by now scarcely breathing. Perhaps the endlessly-altering winds, with the scarcely-discernible chiaroscuro they induced in the sounds reaching Light's ears, modelled the parts of his *Last Diary* and their composition. At any rate, by juggling conventional phrases, recombining them, even merely repeating them more emphatically, it was possible he might activate a hidden system of correspondences, and by a form of sympathetic magic, harmonizing his breathing to the curtain-wafting coming and going of the winds, bring about a change, a return to health. If the theory was wrong, or if this attempt at environmental attunement failed – if writing became merely biographical, uselessly cryptic – at least they would ride on to the shore together.

> *Monday, 2 September* – Moderate and cloudy all day. Exceedingly ill. At night moderate and fine. (Westerly.)
>
> *Tuesday, 3 September* – Moderate and fine. Fine all day. Still very unwell. At night moderate and fine. (Westerly.)
>
> *Wednesday, 4 September* – Moderate and fine. Extremely ill. At night fine. (Westerly.)
>
> *Thursday, 5 September* – Moderate and fine. Exceedingly unwell. Fine all day. At night moderate and fine. (Westerly.)
>
> *Friday, 6 September* – Moderate and cloudy. Very unwell all day. At night fine. (Westerly.)[228]

Within the interstices of colonialism's rhetorical and territorial enclosure acts, Light kept alive a different subjectivity. At Theberton, his house symbolically located in between the city he had laid out and the sea, marginal to either sphere of interest, he returned TB's deadly compliment, and preying on it biographically transformed it into something life-giving. And when the end of writing came, its indecisiveness – so like the ragged edge of electrically-charged clouds or the fibrous thickening in the linings of the pulmonary cavity – attested to an experience of dying in life, a process of ageing that needed no epitaph: no statues, no heroic stances, no parentages and no colonial prospects. The last utterance seemed designed to sound out the hollowness of a history that, in the interests of a posthumous fame, had suppressed the eloquence of the body's breathing.

> *Saturday, 7 September* – Moderate and cloudy. At noon showery. Very ill all day. Showery all the afternoon. At night showery. Very ill. (Westerly.)

Sunday, 8 September – Moderate and cloudy with slight showers at times. At noon very fine. Fine all the rest. At night moderate and fine. Very ill all day. (Westerly.)

Monday, 9 September – Moderate and fine. (Westerly.)[229]

Part Four
Drift Lanes

The nomad is perfect
but the pure motion which has no track is
utterly lost

J. H. Prynne, 'The Common Gain, Reverted'[1]

In an illustrative aside in his essay 'Poetry and Abstract Thought', Valéry remarks: 'The state of mind of a man dancing is not that of a man advancing through difficult country of which he is making a topographical survey or a geological prospectus.'[2] Valéry is elaborating his familiar point that poetry and prose are fundamentally different. If poetry's symmetry of sound and sense resembles the dance in 'creating, maintaining, and exalting a certain state, by a periodic movement that can be executed on the spot', prose resembles walking, in being 'an act directed at something we wish to reach'.[3] Taken at its word, the corollary of Valéry's remark is that poetry or art of any kind is, in the colonial context, almost unthinkable. A society engaged with clearing the ground, in danger of tripping over the unthinkable and the unnameable, is hardly able to internalize movement and transform it into a self-sustaining dance.

Valéry's aside can be interpreted differently, though. If the man dancing can enjoy a certain 'state of mind', an absorption in his own movement, it is because of the prior activities of the explorer and the surveyor. After all, without their labours in discovering or creating a clearing, levelling its irregularities and removing its obstacles, the figures of the dancer could hardly be performed. Logically, and perhaps historically, the colonizing explorer precedes the pirouetting dancer. The surveyor's prior reconnaissance and survey of the folded ground creates the conditions for the emergence of the planar ground occupied by the dancer – and by extension, the poet, the orator and the actor. The metaphysical ground that Western art assumes – planar, linear, firm – presupposes the mobile, asymmetrical, variably-resistant ground of 'difficult country'.

Valéry's magisterial opposition recapitulates an act of suppression characteristic of Western mimesis. The rules of representation arise in part because the environment which might have determined and directed poetic form has, by an enclosure act at once conceptual and architectural, been neutralized. We might say that the plots of the drama, the progressive forms of both epic and lyric – indeed, the Western sense of an ending – spring directly from this preliminary displacement. To some extent, the closure of Western poetic forms grows from a sense of occupying a stage rather than a radiating ground. The art of the West is a conditional one: it inhabits the realm of the 'as if' or 'once upon a time'. In this sense, our art's preoccupation with the journey, its profound formal assumption of transporting the audience from one place to another, springs from a deep nostalgia. Once upon a time (before the once upon a time of the wandering bard), there was a ground that did not slip away.

It might be thought that this is reading too much into what was intended as a purely rhetorical comparison, but the casualness of the great poet's figure of speech may be exactly what defines its significance for our thesis. For Valéry, it is as if no two activities could be more antithetical than walking and dancing. The unspoken assumption is that, but for the mere coincidence of both employing the human body, they have nothing in common. But this dissociation, and the construction of their relationship in terms of mere coincidence, defines the ideological enclosure act implicit in Valéry's poetics. Activities that might superficially resemble each other – dancing and walking, prose-writing and verse-writing – are rigorously distinguished; indeed, remembering Valéry's disparagement of the value of history's truth,[4] the insights of the former may even be said to be deceptive in comparison with the higher revelation the latter allows.

Our thesis begins from the opposite position: that in defining the poetics of colonization, mere coincidences have been both fateful and fruitful. They obviously help to determine the dynamics of cross-cultural exchange. The fortuitous resemblance of Aranda *kalla* and English 'colour', the equally under-motivated sound-alike of 'Canibali' and 'Can Grande', belong to the realm of the curvilinear, and furnish obvious instances. Look-alikes can be equally foundational: Adelaide is a city in ruins before it is a city, and the fantasy of ruination may, it seems, be critical in mobilizing history, in bringing the seasonally self-adjusting land under the aegis of a linear temporality. Mimicry, far from being a source of self-congratulation – proof of the colonizing power's superior faculties of discriminating between true and false – is a primary mechanism for the institution of differences that make a difference. Without these casual convergences – without which, as Vico recognized, there could be no 'events'[5] – colonial representations must remain signifiers of nothing.

The treatment of mere coincidences as 'mere', whether they prove fateful or ephemeral, may spring from the same conceptual enclosure act that opposes the 'difficult country' of the topographer to the cleared level occupied by the dancer. A linear space where objects are at rest, or else move linearly on independent paths, encourages the view that meetings are always collisions and exceptions to the rule that need to be explained. By contrast, in the difficult country of the everyday, where space is experienced parabolically as a folded ground projecting a labyrinth of convergences and departures, coincidences will constitute the normal reason of appearances, the mechanism that binds them together. If, to adapt Gibson's argument, the environment is experienced 'ecologically' and there is a correlation between the 'pick-ups' we make – the coincidences or convergences we are sensible of – and the 'affordances' which the environment extends to us[6] – the intentional and unintentional gestures, surfaces, faces and the like that turn to meet us – then 'mere' coincidences are always motivated.

Gibson's critique of empiricist theories of vision, with their Cartesian hypothesis of the static and disembodied monocular observer, insulated from the environment his camera-eye records, also has implications for the logic of historical causation. We could say that the problem of historical causality is directly associated with the theatricalization of the ground and its corollary, the treatment of historical figures as actors, masks whose movements, lacking external or environmental motivation, must be explained by the psychological equivalent of Newtonian laws of motion. Where these laws fail, the convergences embedded in the historical records must be written off as motiveless or purely coincidental.

Interpretation along these lines is always semiotically-motivated. It assumes that mere coincidences must signify something, shadowing forth some hidden motivation, trend or direction. Only if they stand in for a historical process, if they can flesh out a narrative, are they to be regarded as historically significant. And this is true whether the bias of the historical method is synchronic, revealing the underlying structures of a historical period, or diachronic, establishing a genealogy for it. Both approaches presuppose the planar emptiness of historical space, and the necessity to treat whatever occurs there semiotically.

Thus, for example, Max Müller, the great champion of the genealogical analysis of languages, recognized that structural resemblances and genealogical resemblances between words were but two aspects of one theory of meaning. Kant's conception of the General and the Special was, he considered, fulfilled in Darwinian evolution: 'And what has the theory of evolution really done for them? It has safely brought them back to their original meaning.'[7] Darwin, he says, has reinforced the validity of the Kantian distinction between the genealogically-defined *gens* or kin and the structurally-defined *eidos* or species. 'It has shown us,' Müller says, 'that we can conceive . . . or generalise or speak in two ways only – either by common descent (genealogically) or by common appearance (morphologically). Difference of form is nothing if we classify genealogically, and difference of descent is nothing if we classify morphologically.'[8]

As a natural consequence of this binary logic, Müller makes a distinction between two kinds of coincidence. There are, he points out, especially in the Indo-Aryan languages, many apparent coincidences between words in different languages that turn out on closer inspection to be evidence of a common genealogy; there are others, though, that are mere coincidence: 'The Samoyedes . . . when they are smitten with love . . . say that they are *amuru*, while the French . . . say *amoureux*'.[9] These coincidences 'between languages not held together by any organic relationship' are, he says, 'signposts' that head 'the explorer into a barren desert'; and in a significant image, he contrasts these false leads with those other coincidences that lead to the 'rich Eldorados' of genuine knowledge.[10]

But our choice never lies between the El Dorado of pure recognition and the Desert of pure non-recognition; that is a semiotic myth. As mere coincidences occur within a world where knowledge is attained by movement, whether linear ('ambulatory') or circular ('ambient'),[11] where the ground is never neutral, but always implies convergence and divergence, they are always motivated. From the perspective of spatial history, they are prominent facts, not dangerous mistakes, and if they have a signification, it is a twofold, methodological one. Firstly, that difference of form need not be negated by genealogical reductionism – a form is not explained (away) by identifying its father, that of which it is a sign. And secondly, that common appearance does not negate difference of descent – because phenomena resemble each other, it does not prove common origins. If their formal convergence signifies anything, it is the fact of cultural and historical difference, and the possibility of 'mere coincidence'.

To take account of the lie of the land is not simply to seek to ground historical knowing differently; it is to break down the opposition between history and poetry. What if, say, the manner of going over the ground were itself a poetic act, and not merely a prosaic means of getting from one place to another? Giorgione's processual mode of painting, Light's 'atmospheric knowledge', his habitual remaining at sea, Strehlow's elastically-inclusive musical phrase; these embody a different relationship with the environment, in which the making of marks is understood to be simultaneously historical and poetic. Furthermore, the marking process has been conceptualized differently, not as a breaking-through, as a penetration and destruction of the other, but as a dimpling or grooving of the surface, comparable with the breeze billowing a sail or the miniature stilts of Braille script stippling the fingertips. It is in this cloudy, kinaesthetic realm that historical events turn out to obey a spatial poetics, and that poetry, the making of marks, turns out to be performative and historically implicated.

It is doubtful whether Valéry would have had much sympathy with this view. For him, the poetic symmetry of sound and sense is an off-the-ground experience. To be inspired, say, is to float above the earth, to feel all resistances to passage negated. When Valéry recalls one day being 'suddenly gripped by a rhythm which took possession of me and soon gave me the impression of some force outside myself,' it is as if walking disclosed the possibility of a complex dance. And he explains his state of mind by saying that 'the person who knows he cannot fly has not yet become active in the man who dreams he is flying'.[12] Walking becomes its opposite, an intuition of flight of the kind familiar to Valéry's hero Leonardo da Vinci. In any case, inspiration, the state of complete integration of psychic and physical being, which he describes as a transformation into a 'living machine', depends on the transcendence of external resistances.

While Valéry can surmise that 'a reciprocal modification is possible between a form of action which is purely muscular and a varied production of images, judgements, and reasonings' and even 'a very subtle system of rhythms', he does not countenance the possibility of another reciprocal modification: between walker and environment, between mode of movement and the lie of the land. Valéry's state of rhythmic possession occurs one day 'as I went along the street where I live'. It is his familiarity with his surroundings that ensures that it offers a minimal psychic resistance. Presumably the same is true physically: the pavement's swept chequerboard allows him to walk without looking, to transfer the exploratory charge of the occasion from the environmental to the poetic, from the desire to get somewhere to the desire to experience a liberating state of psycho-physical animation. When 'the magic suddenly vanished, leaving me on the bank of the Seine',[13] it is because the lie of the land has intruded itself upon his thoughts.

Evidently, Valéry's poetics not only implicate the dance, but architecture and even urban design; they presuppose the regulated, open spaces characteristic of imperial centres. Within the prosaic landscape, the poetic edifice stands out as sharply and as proudly as Heidegger's type of Greek thought, the Doric temple crowning the cliff, its level, imperturbable stylobate supporting a steady beat of fluted columns.[14] The dance, and the architectural enclosure act that provides its precinct, does not forget Nature, but it locates it picturesquely in the background – as 'Nature'. The old dialectic between group and place, embodied in methektic ritual, yields to the representative drama. This is the story according to Harrison and Cornford, and it is from this historical clearing of the ground that Valéry's poetics, no less than Heidegger's philosophy, stem.

Even within the sources available to the Cambridge Hellenists, a different account of the spatial *mise-en-scène* of Western mimesis could have been found. As J. C. Lawson, who descried in modern Greek folk dance 'the rudiments of ancient drama', explained: 'Often, as is only natural in so mountainous and rugged a country, the only level dancing-place which a village possesses is a stone-paved threshing floor hewn out of the hill-side.' Here the dancers perform, and 'here too a small booth or tent, still called *skene*, is often rigged up, to which they can retire for rest or refreshment, while on the slopes above are ranged the spectators. The circular threshing floor is the *orchestra*, the hill-side provides its tiers of seats, the dancers, who always sing while they dance, are the *chorus* . . .'[15] Equally suggestive of an alignment between the lie of the land and the composite form of the danced chant is the illustration facing this passage, in which two boys, a pace apart on different steps, serenade a black-clad matron who stands a further pace above them, on the massive stone threshold of her dwelling, looking down at them, listening.

Perhaps it was the steepness of that environment, its division into uneven steps, that first inspired the peripatetic chant. The mastery of feet would not have been simply a poetic or musical matter, a question of shaping speech rhythmically; it would have entailed understanding the cobbled streets choreographically, letting the white stones that lipped the sloping street at intervals – suggesting the beginnings of a tiered arrangement – serve as rhythmic marks, incipient bar-lines; or, as they were irregular, corresponding to the lie of the land, as actively creating groupings of feet, breath and gesture. In this sense, the physical form of the village was the outcome of this peripateia, and the threshing-floor, which Western poetics made art's exclusive focus, was a kind of vanishing-point where the ground, swallowed up in the vortex of an unnatural, unintervalled flatness, could only be seen as something else – a waiting room, a before in search of an after.

One can imagine, then, an in-between state where, by attending to the lie of the land, the walker's steps are metricalized, the dancer's steps rendered exploratory. This is not to whitewash the history of colonization; if anything, it is to deepen its implications. The explorer-surveyor who, like Light, traverses difficult country does so not only instrumentally – on behalf of settlers bent on profit – but also poetically, through the very mode of his progression. He constructs the appearances he wants to find. Similarly, Giorgione's exploration of painterly passages occurs in the context of a complex set of negotiations within Venetian and Spanish imperialism. Strehlow may preach a new, poetically-grounded localism, but his ideas, as we have seen, are founded ultimately on a notion of territory that is essentially colonial.

But it is to say that only by imagining an in-between movement of this kind can we make sense of the spatial history of colonization – a history which is not exhausted by a catalogue of conquest, whether told as a one-sided pageant of progress or as an inventory of cruel disaster, but persists as a mode of negotiation across difference. The significance of the counter-histories unfolded in this book resides partly in the fact that they evolve close to the core of the patriarchal vortex, serving to reveal structural contradictions at the heart of the imperial project. It was not poetic whim that induced Giorgione to paint as he did; or if it was, then the whim was a communal one, extending to the whole of Venetian culture. Light cannot foreshorten the survey, any more than he is temperamentally capable of representing Pompeii in a dramatic chiaroscuro. Strehlow can only stay where he is – can only avoid becoming an exile at home, like Columbus returning to Spain – by detaching himself from the fatherland.

But the image of the vortex, together with the baby counter-vortices its spinning produces, is not simply ornamental. In a way, it has to be taken as an accurate description of historical force-fields. The persistent contrast made between linear and non-linear space-time conceptions not only points up a psycho-physical fact, that our environment is perceived as what Flocon calls a curvilinear space;[16] it also intimates a contradictory pattern that grows directly out of the West's attempt to linearize thought. It is the linear thrust itself, as it penetrates the 'other', that creates these counter-patterns rolling back from the lip of the hole. And these unwinding arabesques, while they may be eccentric, are not marginal, constituting in fact a fundamental dialectic within which the teleological project of the West can be measured.

Within the history of Western poetics, the contrast between the Venetian absorption in a peripatetic, curvilinear construction of cultural space, and the Florentine cultivation of the all-seeing observer enthroned in his architectural lighthouse, is only one expression of a fundamental modality. It is almost predictable that Valéry's classicism will stimulate the unwinding of its other, the 'open' form of musical compositions by Boulez, Berio and Stockhausen, say. Eco associates these with the baroque sensibility, where 'it is precisely the static and unquestionable definitiveness of the classical Renaissance form which is denied: the canons of space extended round a central axis, closed in by symmetrical lines and shut angles which cajole the eye toward the centre in such a way as to suggest an idea of "essential" eternity rather than movement. Baroque form is dynamic; it tends to an indeterminacy of effect (in its play of solid and void, light and darkness, with its curvature, its broken surfaces, its widely diversified angles of inclination); it conveys the idea of space being progressively dilated.'[17]

But even this eloquent definition may be too static, failing to suggest how the anti-representational spirit of the baroque implies the dissolution of the distinction between the observer and the art-work, and their mutual convergence and transformation in the act of performance; a methektic process that is not chaotic, although it mimics the dynamics of the whirlwind, but corresponds to turbulent movement's alinear logic of composition and decomposition. '*Les mots et les idées s'y organisent selon des lignes de forces biologiques ou cosmiques, s'y developpent par bourgeonnement ou par épanouissement, en suivant les méandres aquatiques d'un flux d'idées ou les règles centrifuges d'une spirale ou d'un tourbillon. La composition se réfère a un ordre biologique qu'a un ordre rationnel.*'[18] It might be maintained that these lines of force are in origin rectilinear, but this speculation is academic. As they operate about the curvilinear zone of the earth's surface, their effects, the forms they take, are bound to be curved. And this is just as true microcosmically as macrocosmically. As D'Arcy Thompson reported, the 'intrinsic powers of growth' of the microscopic spicule might be linear, but 'its line of growth will be geodesic to the surface of the cell. And if the cell be an imperfect sphere, or a more or less regular ellipsoid, the spicule will tend to grow into one or other of three forms: either a plane curve of nearly circular arc; or, more commonly, a plane curve which is a portion of an ellipse; or, most commonly of all, a curve which is a portion of a spiral in space.'[19]

The baroque describes, then, the poetics of the storm, but its logic is environmentally attuned in another sense, accurately capturing the performative rituals of cross-cultural first contact, whether these are located on the shores of the Caribbean or in the multilingual backyards and streets of Newtown and Carlton. The Italian novelist Antonio Tabucchi shares my fascination with '*Malintesi, incertezze, comprensioni tardive, inutile rimpianti, ricordi forse ingannevoli, errori schiocchi e irremediabili*,' and compares his taste with that of the artists of the baroque period, who also cultivated '*gli equivoci*'.[20] These breakdowns of common sense do not belong simply to a Second Baroque school of writing, as I have called it;[21] they create a space where the tactics of colonization (temporarily at least) fail, where for a while irremediable differences communicate without ceding ground. Here, the tracks – of echoic words, gestures and movements – still improvise environmentally-localized co-ordinates of communication; syntax and the survey have yet to settle differences, and one-sidedly to settle down.

In any case, this 'search for kinetic excitement and illusory effect [which] induces the spectator to shift his position continuously in order to see the work in constantly new aspects, as if it were in a state of perpetual transformation'[22] could equally be called 'Venetian': an epithet that would have the advantage of indicating that the 'baroque' may be anti-baroque in its economy of means. Umberto Eco contrasts the self-consistency and closure of Dante's poetic and philosophical *oeuvre* with the 'open form' of the baroque; but along another axis, the anti-Dantesque poetry of Dante's first poetic mentor, Guido Cavalcanti, is 'baroque', focusing on the psycho-kinetic construction of desire as sentient, but invisible *spiritelli* dart back and forth between lover and beloved. Unlike Dante, Cavalcanti does not represent ideas theatrically; his thought moves as his verse moves. This was what Pound meant by '"absolute rhythm", a rhythm, that is, in poetry which corresponds exactly to the emotion or shade of emotion to be expressed.'[23]

Pound's one-time acolyte Adrian Stokes completed the triangulation of poetic cultures by identifying the same spirit with the historical environment of Venice: 'It is one thing to walk past a building, another to glide past, to slip slowly in a continuous movement. The hesitancy of water reveals architectural immobility.'[24] Evidently, the Bergsonian sense of becoming evoked here belongs as much to the poetics of Modernism as it does to Venice. So it comes as no surprise that, while Stokes praises la Serenissima for its avoidance of 'stuck-on' effect, its disdain for baroque ornament, the historian of science Paul Feyerabend, writing in a decidedly post-Modernist environment, can, as we have seen, characterize the poetics of Venetian culture in almost antithetical terms. But Feyerabend's Galileo is not only close kin to Michel de Montaigne, and his peripatic mode of creativity not only finds its literary counterparts in Boschini's *El Navegar* or Marco Polo's *Il Milione*: when the composer Luciano Berio sets about composing a work, it is, he says, like 'deciding to go on a journey, say to China.'[25]

From Berio's description of the compositional process, it is evident that the poetics of the open work recapitulate the anastomosing pattern of Marco Polo's journey, with its endless divagations, reversals, redirections, zig-zags and creeping circuits: 'In the course of realizing a global project and defining its details . . . it may happen that the discovery and proliferation of unforeseen elements becomes so important that it effectively alters the project. When this happens I follow the opposite path: from the details that I had worked out and put together I move on to a different project.'[26] This Galilean excess is not ornamental, but essential to the work's emerging structure; it means that the 'end' is implicit in the 'beginning', and both, through the process of 'perpetual transformation', exist simultaneously. But there is no other place, outside the frame of the work, where they can be glimpsed separately. It is precisely the enclosure act that allows an overview which this mode of composition refuses. Likewise with the author of *Il Milione*; even if he had imagined providing a summary of where he had been, the proliferation of unforeseen details obliged him to take a different path.

These oscillations within the Western tradition of representation are important. Without the evidence of this continuing internal dialectic, it would make no sense to seek some form of common ground with non-Western poetic systems, which are anti-monumental, performative and obey a poetics of *methexis* rather than mimesis. The early history of the Papunya Tula dot-and-circle painting movement, for example, so uncannily predicted by Strehlow, appears to occur historically and conceptually at a point of convergence between the Modernists' privileging of the kinaesthetic over the photographic and the Aranda and Pintupi's transference of the art of ground and body marking to the blank and planar surface of the painting board.[27]

To repeat, these modalities within the Western tradition are not emptily formal or structural; they imply different ways of occupying land and governing its peoples. They fuel historical hypotheses as well as poetic compositions. Heidegger's deep aversion to the 'Romanization' of Greek thought finds its British equivalent in the cult of the Celt. The ancient Celt and the Aranda have more in common than the fact that they have both been the victims of ruthless colonization. They share, it seems, similar conceptions of land and social organization. The Celtic village is not the 'English' village; instead of the market-place at the crossroads, it is a network of paths symbolic of a circulatory rather than an accumulative economy.[28] On a larger, pan-European scale, Doughty at least compares the ancient Celtic confederacy of tribes favourably with the repressive, centralized rule of the Roman *imperium*. Strehlow's Aranda were, it seems, Celts *avant la lettre*.

Against this colonial background, where an anti- or post-colonial cultural vision is directly associated with a different politics and poetics of the ground, we can for example make much better sense of *The White*

Stones, the remarkable volume of poems published by the English poet Jeremy Prynne in 1968. Prynne's sentiment that:

> In any street the pattern
> of inheritance is laid down, the truth is for our
> time in cats-eyes, white markings, gravel
> left from the last fall of snow[29]

remarkably parallels the Aranda mode of reading the country. But in its evocation of the local environment in terms of a perpetually self-transforming *pointillisme*, it also recalls Cavalcanti's troubled contemplation of floating-down snowflakes. But the genealogy of Prynne's poetic perception is also historical and political. Thus, the historical roots of his walking poems are in the aura attributed to the pre-colonial British landscape, whose topography once provided a fully poetic environment; and as our epigraph intimates, this directly implicates an environmental practice, a politics of the ground. Prynne's nomad is not a disciple of the contemporary science of nomadology, he is not an expert in territorial disintegration and reformulation. He aligns his movement to the lie of the land; the trackless transcendence that Valéry's muse experiences is, for him, to be 'utterly lost'.

It will be necessary to come back to Prynne's poems, to come back to the early months of the Papunya Tula painting movement; but it will not exactly be to return. The historical divagations that have characterized the opening of this section have, as it were, taken place on levelled ground. They have traced connections between poetic events that history usually holds far apart. But the connections have been like the patterns made by the ice-skater's boot, baroque elaborations on an uninspected ground. The very idea of return is, as we have seen, dependent on this primary forgetfulness. We have invoked movement over the ground metaphorically, as a way of illuminating a counter-tradition within Western reason, and we have suggested that this counter-tradition is intimately implicated in the poetics of colonization – and thus, perhaps, in the continuing critique of Western *Logos* that will characterize the emergence of a post-colonial polity and poetry.

But the movement itself remains mystified. Marco Polo's zig-zag may be aesthetically pleasing, but it remains linear; even its arabesques are imagined within the two-dimensional plane of the chart. Stokes's 'continuous movement' may acknowledge the minute up-and-down of small waves, but the 'hesitancy' these flutterings under the hull induce is undeveloped; perhaps it corresponds to the goldsmith's hammer dimpling the tractable metal into a shining mask. Prynne comes closer when, in his English way, he reinstates walking as a major mode of philosophizing, and understands that movement is physically projective. Just as the Stoics maintained that seeing was produced by a fire emanating from the eyeball, so Prynne understands:

> They are
> said to trudge when in fact their empty thoughts
> unroll like a crimson carpet before their
> gentle & delicate pace.[30]

But even this image seems to suppress the curvilinear nature of movement, the spring and fall of the foot, the parabolic path described by the walker's centre of gravity, and the larger curvature of air, earth and path in which these participate.

To transfer attention from the footfall to the track in-between, and to understand that track not as a line laid out across a surface, but as a surfaceless vector whose trajectory constitutes its own ground; this requires something more than the rhetorical asides, back-trackings and footnotes of literary discourse. It requires, as has been intimated earlier, a conceptualization of space that is as much auditory as visual – or which, to be more accurate, borrows from the facts of auditory perception in order to rescue seeing from the reductionist cast of 'visualist' thinking, reinserting it into its naturally mobile setting. But even this, while it can give back to sight its cloudily ambient indeterminacy, reiterates the dialectic already described. Linear space may be opposed rhetorically to curvilinear space, but the question remains: how to unhoop the latter, to lift it off the ground of the linear, not so that it appears like the portent of some promised poetic land, but so that it can constitute its own ground, a mechanism of movement that is 'groundless' and therefore not 'utterly lost'.

'The ecological approach to visual perception,' Gibson writes, 'begins with the flowing array of the observer who walks from one vista to the next, moves around an object of interest, and can approach it for scrutiny, thus exploring the invariants that underlie the changing perspective structure and seeing the connections between the hidden and unhidden surfaces.'[31] Reinserting seeing into the physical environment, and into the physical body of the person seeing, Gibson was able to reconceptualize the space of visual perception in a way that drew it close to the space of auditory perception. Just as in listening no sound is detached from another, or loses its character as it dies away, so in seeing we inhabit an environment without perspective. 'It is obvious that a motionless observer can see the world from a single fixed point of observation and can thus notice the perspectives of things. It is not so obvious but it is true that an observer who is moving about sees the world at no point of observation and thus, strictly speaking, cannot notice the perspectives of things . . . The arrested image is only necessary for a photographic camera. An observer who is getting around in the course of daily life sees from what I will call a path of observation.'[32]

This leads to what is in many ways Gibson's climactic assertion, that we normally see what is hidden, that we 'protend' and 'retain' visually as well as auditorily: 'An occluding edge is seen as such . . . the persistence of a hidden surface is seen . . . the connection of the hidden with the unhidden is perceived.' This fact that, even visually, the world is folded, containing the unseen within the seen, leads Gibson to the conclusion that 'the doctrine that all awareness is memory except that of the present moment of time must be abandoned. So must the theory of depth perception. The importance of the fixed point of view in vision is reduced. But a new theory of orientation, of way-finding, and of place-learning in the environment becomes possible.'[33] Auditorily speaking, the fold is the echo. The echo coexists with the sound that produces it; sound and echo are not simultaneous, they overlap one another. The physical condition of this occurrence is a folded ground. 'With the experience of echo, auditory space is opened up . . . mountains and valleys reveal their distances to me auditorily as my voice re-sounds in the time which belongs so essentially to all auditory spatial significations.'[34]

So far, so good then, and we can add that the 'echo' is not only an environmental phenomenon. Our linear habits of thought and expression encourage us to think of it as a secondary or posterior event. However, speaking and hearing coexist; as F. Joseph Smith comments: 'We think "contrapuntally", as is our common experience; but grammarians force us into expressing ourselves in monolinear fashion.'[35] To hold out the promise of going back, then, is to forget that we carry the history of our memories, our reading, forward, letting them accumulate, transform and even, as clouds will, disperse. In this situation, all we can do is, like the Venetian painter, attempt to bring all the parts of the composition forward simultaneously.

Be that as it may, Gibson's visual ecology, combined with the new phenomenology of listening, offers a reasonably solid theoretical basis for considering curvilinear, echoic modes of thought as intellectually respectable; and the off-the-ground nature of sound – the fact that, like the weather, it is primarily available to us through the movement of air – appears to give us some licence for attending to the environment, the turbulent behaviour of the medium of transmission, rather than concentrating too single-mindedly on the objects propelled through it, and the line drawn between their points of origin and arrival. In short, it makes plain that to bring the environment and the figure moving in it into a significant relationship, not only a poetics is needed but a theory of ballistics. Otherwise, our spatial metaphors will remain just that: metaphorical, merely ornamental.

Without a feeling for the natural tracks of things, movement from one place to another remains penetrative, violent. Instead of marking the ground lightly, the passage of feet flattens and obscures the land's lie. The land, instead of being composed of potential proximities, folding in and out of sight, becomes a landscape pinned to the distance. As a matter of fact, it is precisely this transition from a conception of the ground where, as Prynne puts it, 'The way is of course speech/ and a tectonic emplacement,'[36] to a view in which the ground, rendered pathless, is theatricalized as a void, a *tabula rasa* available for imperial over-writing, that may be said to mark the inauguration of Western poetry; and the poetic tradition descending from Homer at least can, in this sense, be said to represent not only the triumph of mimesis over *methexis*, but the linearization of flight – a transition in which, with what Jane Harrison would have regarded as a typically Olympian sleight of hand, Pallas Athene's nature is utterly changed.

In the twenty-second book of the *Iliad*, the gods withdraw their support from Trojan Hector, and Pallas Athene, descending from Olympus, sets about sealing his fate. She flies to Achilles to forewarn him that the sack of Troy is imminent. She disguises herself as Deiphobus, son of the king of Troy, and persuades Hector to confront Achilles. When Hector dodges Achilles's first lance, she plucks it from the ground and, 'unseen of

Hector', returns it to Achilles's hand. When Hector hurls his far-shadowing spear, she makes it rebound harmlessly from Achilles's shield. And when Hector, seeing Achilles brandishing a second spear, turns to Deiphobus to borrow his spear, she arranges it that Deiphobus has vanished into thin air. And then Hector understands: 'Athene hath beguiled me.'[37]

In Homer's interpretation, Athene's power lies in her ability to manipulate events theatrically. She can disguise herself; she can cancel out events; she can reverse them, rehearse them; she can neutralize the everyday contingencies of time and space. Her power is technological: to have invented a superior machinery of fate. Zeus and his family are the first stage directors. Their offspring include the Sicilian puppeteer's unseen hand manipulating the duels of Orlando and Rinaldo; the extravagant stage machines of Bernini and Inigo Jones; the 'little world' that Phillip de Loutherbourg 'so manipulated it was a perfect picture of reality.'[38]

Indeed, the theatricalization of space personified in Pallas Athene is not only a magic device within the poem, but defines Homer's narrative technique, which is one of cinematographic visualization. It is no surprise that when the first-century AD Greek geometer and inventor Hero of Alexander invented his miniature mechanical theatre of moving figures, he demonstrated its capacity to create convincing illusions using a typically Homeric scenario: Nauplios's shipwreck of the Greeks off Euboia on their way home from Troy, in revenge for their murder of his son. In episode four, Athene appears alongside Nauplios and 'the man and the goddess join in the same act of vengeance.'[39] But in effect, Athene has already become a theatrical puppet in the *Iliad*, personifying the poet's own unseen hand.

In this context, Hector's tragedy is poetic in a double sense: he stands his ground, and he adheres to a conception of song which, like the flight of the spear, cannot be divorced from the site of its utterance. In Hector's philosophy, it is impossible that a spear, once avoided, once lodged quivering in the distant sand, should return to the hand of the thrower. In his world, no strings attach to physical events; they do not represent the hidden hand of fate, they are not symbolic gestures. There is nothing rhetorical about a spear in flight. A flying spear is neither seen nor unseen. It glitters briefly as a firework, an image, a metaphor, rapidly contracting the space in-between; and the man who would stand his ground must match its mobility and duck and weave.

Hector 'looking steadily at him, avoided it; for he was aware of it in time and crouched, and the spear of bronze flew over, and fixed itself in the earth.'[40] It might have been thought that Hector derived his kinetic foresight from the goddess herself. In another guise, Plutarch reports, the name Athene is said to signify 'I came from myself, which indicates self-impelled movement', a quality Plutarch associates with magnetism.[41] But in Homer, Athene operates under a different (but still her own) aegis, that of the Gorgon. The Gorgon's head is a pre-photographic camera: whatever it sees, it fixes for ever. And Achaean Athene has no patience with the natural, sprawling motion of things. She prefers to fix, to neutralize, the uncertain phenomena of nature in order to make a space for history, the unseen hand of fate. She wants to re-create Nature as theatrical setting, and to this end institutes a self-divisive dialectic between the mobile and the static, between the lance and the shield (Plate 20).

Through Pallas Athene, let us say, Homer inaugurates mimesis: the representation of far-off events. The force of mimesis lies less in its power to conjure up what is absent, than in its conception of what is absent as a sequence of events, lineally related one to another, each bounded by a beginning and an ending; history as a sequence of episodes loosely sewn together distinguishes mimesis from *methexis*. Lindsay, like many before him, tries to illuminate Homeric time-consciousness by reference to the Australian Aranda, for whom 'time has a rhythmic aspect; it is a circling rhythm with an organic pattern.' But even he is obliged to admit that Homeric time is, at the very least, spiralling rather than circular: 'Homer's method is appositional: that is, one word or phrase links with another, extending meaning but not moving forward in a linear way.'[42] Lindsay argues for a direct parallel between Homeric and Aranda time: 'We might say that what happens is the obliteration of one circle by the next; the old one completes itself and closes up; the new one appears on the same ground . . .'[43]

There seems to be a subtle but important confusion here. Aranda song and dance does not merely continue 'on the same ground'; it is the living re-inscription of that ground. By contrast, Homeric ground is theatrical, a proto-agora where anyone may stand and speak of anything. It may be true that the structure of Homeric narrative retains traces of the oral tradition, where the bard might recite successive episodes on sucessive nights – always to the same audience, in the same mead-hall. But this returning to the same subject, going over the same ground differently, is purely illusionistic and implies no daimonic connection between the poet and the place where he recites. In no way does the poet sacralize the ground where he sings: it is flat, a floor within a building, its topographical charge already negated. He occupies a theatrical place, and it is precisely its emptiness, and the silence that crowds in on every side, that obliges him to raise his voice and defiantly sing of other places, other far-off times – without whose memory the loneliness of the migrant condition might be intolerable.

In this guise, Athene, as the mistress of representation, is Odyssean, a specialist in false representations. She advances the plot by dressing up, by assuming successive false *personae*. She speaks in voices not her own; she borrows clothes, arms, make-up; she telescopes distances, superimposing Thessaly on Ephesus; she deals in lies. In her hands, Odysseus becomes a robot: he is likened to a statue 'of silver overlaid with gold.'[44] Thus endowed, he is irresistible; not being himself, he is free to go where he likes. Athene's automaton, his passage is both secured and demanded, for he is exiled by his guile and can never settle down. Despite his claim to be homecoming, Odysseus is the prototypical colonist, advancing his interests by stealth, with the aid of technology's magic and by the improvisation of false genealogies.[45] His armoured appearance to Nausicaa remarkably presages Columbus's landfall in the West Indies. For just as his movement is lent superhuman authority, so the ground he walks is smoothly characterless, a repetition of theatrical spaces which, but for the events they serve to represent, are indistinguishable from one another. In this sense, he does not lie; for the veritable wanderer, every port is a homecoming, every circuit leads to another.

If Athene's lance symbolizes self-impelled movement, her shield represents the territory whose circuit it enlarges and defends. According to Vico, the first 'shields' were the fields; they were round because the first cultivated clearings represented for their inhabitants the first *orbes terrarum*.[46] Plato associates Athene with the founding of republics generally, whose *logos* is reflected in their Hippodamian layout: 'Instead of a city of the archaic type, similar to our medieval cities, with a maze of streets tumbling untidily down the slopes of a hill, he [Hippodamus of Miletus] chose a fine open space, made a grid of straight streets intersecting at right angles, and created a town resembling a chequerboard, entirely centred round the open space of the agora.'[47]

If pre-Homeric space is non-homologous, asymmetrical, non-reversible and mobile, the new space is static; or better, founded on an opposition between stasis and movement – an opposition symbolized, says Vernant, by the opposed but complementary roles of Hestia and Hermes. 'Because her fate is to reign, forever immobile, at the centre of the domestic sphere, Hestia implies, as her complement and contrast, the swift-footed god who rules the realm of the traveller.'[48] And Vernant detects in this opposition the same rival conceptions of space symbolized by Athene's lance and the shield: 'Space requires a centre, a nodal point, with a special value, from which all directions, all different qualitatively, may be channelled and defined; yet at the same time space appears as the medium of movement implying the possibility of transition and passage from any point to any other.'[49] And this new physical arrangement, the archetype of the colonial town, encourages a new, distinctively Western polity as well as polis. So according to Vernant, the Athenian agora has its origins in the assembly of warriors on an equal footing, which 'creates a circular space with a centre in which each man can freely say whatever suits him'. Via a series of economic and social transformations, it comes to embody public as opposed to private space, 'a society where one's main relationship with another is conceived in terms of identity, symmetry, reversibility.'[50]

In this view, Athene's double nature models the self-fulfilling dialectic of European imperialism. Conceived theatrically, outward movement neutralizes the ground; it refuses to grant authority to anything except its own representations. In this way, local topographies become picturesque backdrops, easily dominated. At the same time, the actors of their own epic do not see it like this. No sooner are they out of sight of land than all their talk is of homecoming, and the further they depart from the centre, the more they mutter of return. This is the magnetic power of the agora: to reverse the centrifugal charge, transforming it into centripetal nostalgia. Movement is deferred stasis, and who can blame lonely soldiers for massacring natives when they stand in their path, holding them up on their way home? What is more irritating to an actor than an unforeseen obstacle or distraction? It is axiomatic in the theatre that everything be arranged to facilitate the action. No wonder, then, that the indigenes are in the way.

What *should* have met the circumnavigators on the beach was none other than Pallas Athene, for if new land reared up on the horizon, it was due entirely to her power to manipulate the stage machinery convincingly. So when, in his fifteenth-century Latin epic *Hesperides*, loosely modelled on the *Odyssey*, Sigismondo Malatesta's court poet Basinio describes the Lord of Rimini's voyage to Spain to seek military aid for his Italian campaigns, what could be more natural, more appropriate, than the anticipation of his journey by Minerva who, while she awaits him, gathers seashells in the guise of a poor peasant girl?[51] And if Athene accompanied Europe's imperial armies as she formerly shadowed Odysseus, it accounts perhaps for the European habit of beguiling the natives with mirrors. These mirrors were, mythologically at least, none other than souvenir reproductions of Minerva's shield:

> *Scudo di cristal, là donde viva*
> *Vedease entro la testa de Medusa,*
> *Che per spavento la sua boca apriva.*[52]

Even in the primitive state of late fifteenth-century ballistic theory, it was well known that a stationary target was easier to hit than a moving one.

All this, then, may be said to derive from the magical manipulation of Achilles's spear, and the patriarchal appropriation of Pallas Athene it represents. The former deity of movement who, as David Jones's Celtic Rhiannon, commanded the flight of the spear as if it were a slim shuttle, the air its woof, becomes the figurehead of stasis, signified by her Gorgon-embossed shield.[53] She continues to be associated with movement as the goddess of crafts, overseeing the circular motion of the potter's wheel[54] – and it is true that the circle has cosmic connotations in Greek science, alluding to the dance of the heavenly bodies.[55] But the Dionysian huntress and All-Mother – 'Athena is the real Kourotrophos ["Rearer of Sons"], but for patrilinear purposes she is turned into a diagram of motherless birth'[56] – forfeits her independence of action. She presides over a theatrical world of smooth floors and gliding deceptions, a culture of mimesis which can colonize, even masquerade as, the other, but never mingle with him, seeing as he sees, moving as he moves.

At the same time, though, it would be a mistake to presume that the opposition established between the territorially-stable shield and the magically-murderous missile – an opposition that characterized all but circular, self-negating movement as eccentric and lawless – is absolute or irrevocable. Jack Lindsay's remarkable study *Blast Power and Ballistics* shows the gradual ascendancy of mechanistic concepts of force and energy in Western physics as an ideological enclosure act, reflective of Greece's and later Renaissance Europe's increasing organization of its social and economic relations in capitalistic or imperializing ways, in terms of class interests promoted and defended by a technology more and more designed to manipulate and control gunpowder, or 'blast power'; a process he finds epitomized in the changing symbolic value attached to 'the supreme form of power which human endeavours have sought to master and imitate' – the thunderstorm.[57]

But as we have already seen, the imperial significance of the storm does not exhaust its historical meaning. Lightning and thunder can also be understood cyclically, as a manifestation of the inter-relatedness of things, and of the curvature of lived time and space that ensures their transformation and renewal. Lindsay notes that Newtonian mechanics 'omits all reference to a definite (that is, real) coordinate system,' and 'as soon as we connect a material coordinate system with any body large or small, the first condition of the law of inertia ceases to be fulfilled: the condition of freedom from external influences. For at once there occurs a mutual gravitational effect of the bodies.'[58]

The same mutual effect is expressed in the relationship between the lightning bolt and the soldier's lance in Giorgione's *Tempesta*, and it subtends, as its complementary other, the gypsy's shield-like breast and the bosom-cloud. It also characterizes the atmospheric reciprocity to which Light, as a student of breath, attends, attributing value not to decisive discharges, but to in-between states of rising and falling pressure. The same spatio-temporal in-folding appeals to Strehlow, who finds within it a principle of creativity free of patriarchal constraint, whose 'spears' of rain do not so much inseminate a passive, maternal earth as – like the *spiritelli* of Cavalcanti – make manifest the circulatory pathways of desire.

Awareness of an environmentally interactive 'coordinate system' does not disappear because technology treats it as operationally insignificant. It surfaces, for example, wherever the ideology of the force-neutralized, planar ground comes in contact with spaces and histories that retain their environmental charge, continuing to allow, as Hector did, an ontological value to the lie of the land. As William Wales, astronomer and meteorologist on Cook's second Pacific voyage (1772–5) observed in Vanuatu:

> I have been often lead to think of the Feats which Homer represents his heros as performing with their Spears a little too much of the Marvellous to be admitted into an Heroic Poem, I mean when confined within the straight Stays of Aristotle . . . But since I have seen what these People can do with their wooden ones; and them badly pointed and not of a very hard nature either, I have not the least exception to any one Passage in that Great Poet on this Account . . . he has I think scarce an Action circumstance or discription of any kind whatsoever relating to a Spear, which I have not seen & recognised amongst these People as their whirling motion & whistling noise as they fly. Their quivering motion as they Stick in the Ground when they fall. Their meditating their aim when they are going to throw & their shaking them in their Hand as they go along . . .[59]

In this passage Wales recognizes a theatre which yet is not theatre, in the Aristotelian sense of obeying the proto-Newtonian unities of time and place. Its space is not an empty stage, but a dense, finely-tuned, finely-striated force-field, a pneuma which, as the Stoics generalized it, comprised not simply air and fire but 'the physical field which is the carrier of all specific properties of material bodies.'[60] This performative space is acoustic, kinetic; it vibrates. In fact, these three properties are aspects of each other. The spear agitates the air because of the way it is moved; the air vibrates before the resounding earth, and the reactive spear vibrates and quivers.

This is a world where actor and action are tuned to one another, where actions are not represented but gone through in real time, where historical events and their dramatic re-enaction converge and coalesce into a single performative moment. Ritualized, this movement is also improvised; not in a spirit of wilful invention, but from necessity, because the ballistic ground-rules demand it. Such exhibitions of skill are simultaneously poetic and political in import. Like border disputes or trade exchanges, they rehearse well-known movements but are not themselves rehearsed. In a culture where the ground retains its spatial charge, the Western notion of rehearsal is perhaps unthinkable, for it supposes the existence of non-places, grounds without physiognomies. But by the same token, improvisation as the will to invent is also unthinkable. The *rhapsode* who is inspired is not taken out of himself, as Valéry is; he is put back in touch with his body. Or better, like Light, he is made conscious of his body as the house of pneuma, as an orchestra that accompanies the long bow of the breath scraping back and forth across the vocal chords with many other instruments: the heart, the dancing measure of the foot, the glancing eye, the quivering thigh, the arm raised, tense, to throw.

Another colonial observer, John Macgillivray, comments of a staged battle he witnessed at Cape York, northern Australia: 'The precision with which the spears were thrown was not less remarkable than the dexterity with which they were avoided. In nearly every case the person thrown at would, apparently, have been struck had he stood still, but, his keenness of sight enabled him to escape by springing aside as required, variously inclining the body, or sometimes merely lifting up a leg to allow the spear to pass by, and had two been thrown at one person at the same moment he could scarcely have escaped, but this I observed was never attempted, as it would have been in war.'[61]

This report might be augmented by an account of an Aboriginal 'tournament' in Queensland witnessed towards the end of the last century: 'A really fine-looking man, hideously painted, dashed a spear at a Maryborough warrior. The precision and strength with which that spear was thrown was something to remember. We watched it go straight at the Maryboroughite, who received it cleverly on his shield, and with a sudden, almost imperceptible, twist of the shield, broke it off, leaving the point buried in the shield. As quick as thought he then hurled a spear at his opponent, with a yell of defiance, who watched its direction for an instant and then slipped on one side to avoid it. This was the signal for general action . . .' The author adds the fascinating observation that, amid the mêlée, 'during the hottest part of the engagement, we observed three or four men, unarmed, coolly walking backwards and forwards a few paces in front of each line of fighting men, engaged in collecting the spears and other weapons lying on the ground, and taking them to the rear.'[62]

Although serving secular or non-site-specific diplomatic purposes, these events, like the Aranda songs and dances, employ a principle of *methexis* rather than mimesis. There is no question here of *pretending* to dodge a spear. At the same time, though, the warriors are not free to throw and parry as they wish. They are bound by the conventions of the ground and the physics of the missiles' flight to pass their spears through certain prescribed tunnels. What is mimicked as they fight in earnest is the lie of the land, the invisible conditions of air, light, gradient and interval which determine the meaning of the spears in flight, the way they are to be read. And mimicked in this way, the ground is inscribed historically, not as a place 'with a history' but as a space of *poiesis*, as a grooved interval that sings.

If spatial rituals of this kind are primarily poetic in nature, acts commemorative of the lie of the land, it follows that a poetic breakdown of law and order might have as its corollary the suspension of the ordinary rules governing ballistics. The bushman and Jindyworobak poet Roland Robinson describes an uncanny occasion when, as a socially-isolated farm-hand on an outback station some time in the 1930s, he was hunting in the bush and came upon an 'old man' kangaroo. However many times he shot at it, he kept on missing: 'The kangaroo just sat there. I remember getting closer and this time resting the rifle on a dead, fallen wilga tree. I took careful aim. I squeezed the trigger slowly so as to not move the rifle in its sight. Had I missed? What was the matter?' Robinson relates this experience to one told him by Kianoo Tjeemairie of the Murinbata Tribe, who one day similarly found himself unable to strike down an emu with his spear: 'Like a man in a spear fight, the emu danced and dodged the spear again. Kianoo used up all his spears on the emu but could not spear it. The emu then raced away.' The emu, an old man back at camp explains, was 'a friend of mine, who was coming to see me on secret business. When he saw you, he changed into his totemic form of an emu. That's why he dodged your spears.'[63]

Stories in which a colonized, oppressed people develops the power to pass from one place to another while remaining invisible to the colonizer are common. But Robinson's experience is self-consciously different. He is an outsider (an 'Irish-Pommy-Australian') and an in-betweener ('a white Black').[64] As a Jindyworobak, he is preoccupied with developing an indigenous Australian poetic tradition, which, like Strehlow, he believes will belong to all post-colonial Australians. He shares Doughty's prejudices, identifying himself with the oral bards of ancient Greece, Anglo-Saxon England and Ireland. Furthermore, Robinson is on the way to identifying himself with the autochthonous people of the country, conceiving his destiny in terms of the mandates of a *daimon* or spirit of place, 'Like Ankotarinja, the great ancestral being of the Aranda tribe, whose country I stood in, my Demon sank down again into the soft soil of the watercourse,'[65] he writes in his autobiography, referring to the resolution of a poetic and personal crisis.

In this context of spiritual reaffiliation, the incident with the 'old man' kangaroo assumes a poetic import. A warp in time-space which succeeds in baffling the flight of his bullets symbolizes a blockage in other areas, an inability to align himself with 'the drift of things', the phrase that supplies Robinson with the title of his autobiography. In the erotic realm, it manifests itself as premature ejaculation.[66] Poetically, it is associated with the difficulty of making words strike home; with those questions of metre, vocabulary, metaphor that also preoccupied Strehlow. Robinson understands instantly that the quality of his poems will depend directly on the quality of his wandering the land.

The culmination of his poetic life (as opposed to his poetic output) might have been a day in Katherine Gorge: 'I was thin and spare then and I could run through the bush like an Aboriginal. I ran ahead of the truck, quickly picking out a clear way as I ran.'[67] Against this light-footedness, the parallel Robinson draws between Kianoo's encounter with the emu and his own confrontation with the kangaroo is less telling than the difference. While Kianoo's daimon dances elastically from side to side, sure of its footing, Robinson's kangaroo sits leadenly still, like an artist's model, like a Grecian statue; as if to say, where the non-Aborigine looks and points, the ground loses its spring and petrifies.

Within the Western tradition, the limitations of mimesis, a mode of seeing that freezes what the eye strikes, were also, of course, well known. We might say that it was the daily experience of the foot-soldier, not to mention the hunter or the *discobolus*. After all, blind Homer, the Peripatetics, and even Florentine princes, did not inhabit a Newtonian world where notions of inertia and linear motion were well-accepted physical principles. In Aristotle's physics, the cause of an object's movement was external; objects could not move by themselves, and to continue to move they must continue to be acted upon externally. According to this view, a lance or javelin, while grasped by the hand, received its forward propulsion from the hand. But once it left the hand, something else must take over the hand's propulsive role. Aristotle thought that 'the thrower's hand imparts to the air the marvellous power of being an unmoved mover, or at least a no-longer-moved mover. In fact there is a series of pockets of air behind the projectile which acquire this power in turn, and they move the projectile on.'[68]

Philoponus successfully ridiculed this argument in the fifth century

AD, but his ideas did not become widely available in the West until the early fourteenth century, when Jean Buridan of the University of Paris 'used the term impetus for the imparted velocity that would carry on indefinitely . . . as long as no opposing force slowed or halted the moving body.'[69] The concept of *impetus* or impressed motion helped to bridge the gap between ballistic theory and the foot-soldier's everyday experience, but so long as it was subsumed within Aristotelian mechanics, it suggested no way of accounting for the spear or the arrow's parabolic flight path. 'Aristotle held that only two sorts of simple movement exist: the *circular* (movement of rotation) and the *rectilinear* (movement of translation) . . .[consequently] Aristotelians, considering the fall of a stone cast up by a sling, could only describe the trajectory as made up of two straight lines joined by a circular arc.'[70]

Empirical observation refuted this description daily, yet it persisted, even in what purported to be practical artillery manuals, well into the sixteenth century. Niccolò Tartaglia's *La Nova Scientia* (1537) explained that 'a heavy body when projected by a force moves for a space in violent [rectilinear, at an oblique angle to the earth] motion gradually diminishing in velocity, and then falls into a natural motion [rectilinear, perpendicular to the earth]'[71] In between these two rectilinear paths, the projectile described an arc of circle. Mathematical comprehension of the projectile's parabolic flight path had to wait until Newton replaced the idea of impressed motion with that of inertia: 'The idea of inertia was unificatory, because it showed how rotation related to rectilinear motion. It was no different in principle from accelerated or decelerated rectilinear motion.'[72]

From this point of view, Athene's theatricality assumes a quite different significance. Where objects are naturally at rest or shortly to come to rest, theatrical space, it might be argued, tries to keep them in motion. What is more, it represents them as moving of their own volition. But as they can have no internal volition of their own, it follows that the heroic enlargement of their sphere of action depends directly on the continuous presence of external forces – the puppeteer gods – who do not simply oversee the action from a distance, or mischievously manipulate it, but between them keep the theatrical space open. Hero's mechanical theatre creates the illusion of figures and elements moving. From a Newtonian perspective, his theatre models the principle that objects continue in a state of uniform rectilinear motion unless acted upon by external forces; they behave like industrial automata. But from a pre-Newtonian position, Hero's illusion of self-impelled movement, created by an elaborate system of balances, counterbalances, cogs and ratchets, subscribes to the opposite intuition: that nothing goes on moving unless continuously acted upon by an external (if unseen) force.[73]

Pallas Athene's self-impelled motion is not prophetically Newtonian. It is eccentric and magical; as a motion of attraction or repulsion, it still implies an external force. And Athene's role, when she retrieves Achilles's spear, is similarly intimate and binary. In letting go of his weapon, Achilles does not relinquish control of it; his hand flies with it – otherwise, how would it move forward? As this drawing close to Hector, this puckering-up of space as if it were the mouth of a purse pulled tight, cannot be done by Achilles in person, it must be his theatrical *persona* who communicates his intention by other means, lending it her tutelary propulsion. In the same way, Hector does not merely dodge a flying spear, whether it flies straight or curvedly; he directly outwits Achilles' protension – and pretension. Until Newton's laws of motion emptied it of aura, theatrical space was a machine for making things move, for giving people an internal momentum, an illusion of choice. The ground may not have been smooth and neutral. If, in Homer, time, and especially fateful time, is said to approach from behind[74] – not as it does now, advancing down the road to meet us[75] – Hector's turning back to find and not find Deiphobus is the directest expression of theatre as spatial history. At this culminating moment where Hector meets his fate, the plot is no different from the lie of the land.

In short, as part of a mythic apparatus useful in negotiating a post-colonial poetics, Athene's dual nature needs to be recognized, not suppressed. It must be freed from the kind of binary thinking that identifies her true nature either with the shield of stasis or the lance of self-impelled movement, for the theatrical space she engenders has no inertia, no architectural autonomy. It cannot stand apart from the manifold competing forces that constitute the theatrical action; and these forces are not imparted directly to bodies, but to the air behind and around them. They are expelled words as much as lance-gripping hands, and they do not take the form of sharp, infinitely-fine needles goading the fat air. They are better thought of as currents of wind, fluid layers, plumes with wakes which, as they press forward, peel back a hundred counter-turning vortices and perturbations within a continuous medium.

In this context, the flight of the lance is not assured because the arm is skilful, the target stationary. Much depends on the right timing, on grasping the propitious moment when the nebulous medium of air parts to reveal the swift and sure passage. And even then, having thrown the spear into this furrow in space, much depends on the weapon's torque, its flexibility and internal balance. For the spear is like the keel of a boat, fashioning about itself a cocoon of conformable liquid, whose perturbations have been combed out and temporarily align themselves with the missile's direction. The lance does not savage a cold, untempered emptiness. Nor does it unzip a well-tempered Euclidean net. It moves fatly through cloudy country, absorbing the jars and twists of the surface, unpredictably veering to left and right. And the same applies to the shield-bearer, who cannot calculate the lance's landing-place from the moment it leaves the thrower's hand, but must monitor the missile's oceanic path minutely, lest a local crest in the medium of transmission swell up and break over the shield's border, and he find himself wounded to the heart.

Lindsay speculates that Athene's power to transfix with her shield-stare 'was one of vivifying rather than of magically binding.'[76] As a craft-goddess associated with that microcosm of the turning heavens, the potter's wheel, 'the apotropaic mask, guarding organic life or craft-process at a critical moment, may be said to embody both the attacking and the defending forces . . . it expresses both the terrible energies of uncontrolled nature and the human domination of these energies which makes of them the core of the creative process.'[77] This may cast Athene as a typically Western *techne* goddess; were nature's self-control recognized, there might be no reason to dominate it. But applied to the lance and the shield, the notion of the 'critical moment' is useful. Taken together, they symbolize a movement that is well-timed, trajectories that find their target.

In seizing opportunities, in opening up propitious passages and threading them, Athene personifies *kairos* – which Eric Charles White, paraphrasing R. B. Onians, succinctly defines as 'an ancient Greek word that means "the right moment" or "the opportune". The two meanings of the word apparently come from two different sources. In archery, it refers to an opening or "opportunity" or, more precisely, a long tunnel-like aperture through which the archer's bow has to pass. Successful passage of a *kairos* requires, therefore, that the archer's arrow be fired not only accurately but with enough power for it to penetrate. The second meaning of *kairos* traces to the art of weaving. There it is the "critical time" when the weaver must draw the yarn through a gap that momentarily opens in the warp of the cloth being woven.'[78] White characterises *kairos* as 'a principle of invention . . . [it] establishes the living present as point of departure or inspiration for a purely circumstantial activity of invention.'[79] Noting the importance of *kairos* in the theory of rhetoric of the Greek sophist Gorgias of Leontini, White argues that the power to improvise on the spur of the moment, to respond to circumstantial contingencies as one speaks, to continue to begin again, represents an attempt to overcome the epistemological impasse that opens up between Plato and Aristotle, for whom truth is associated with the constant, the static, and Heraclitus, according to whom 'everything gives way and nothing stays fixed.'[80]

The agile warrior and the light-footed orator share a capacity to respond creatively, one might say baroquely, to historical contingencies; the well-armed goddess of eloquence is appropriately associated with them both. In the will to invent, in the gift of improvisation perhaps, lies a key to the creation of Strehlow's new Australian poetry. If so, it will be the gifts of spontaneous free association that will be privileged in the new poetry, as poets of different linguistic and cultural heritages engage each other in post-colonial *tensons*, energetically modulating their own voices to each other. The meaningless or too-meaningful pun will dominate these latter day *jocs de flors* . . . But before running ahead like this, and in the process identifying rhetorical ingenuity with poetic inspiration, we need to be aware how much it presumes a Newtonian world-view. What, for example, can it mean to talk about wilful inventiveness in a world *not* governed by notions of equal and opposite forces and a space that is neutral, empty? Where motion is either 'natural' or 'unnatural', where objects (including words and concepts) swim in a fluid medium, unpredictable departures, dialogically-induced ricochets, are difficult to imagine.

To bounce off a surface, to react quickly to an uttered word, to strike out creatively in another, totally unexpected direction, implies inertia. Without this, the will to invent remains powerless, and the bewildering Brownian motion of apparent invention remains only a mechanical description of the physics of fluids. And besides, while it may be true that the weaver has to time the passage of the arrow-headed shuttle with the woof to ensure it finds the warp's gap, the critical moment originates outside, and the successful weaver is he who aligns himself completely with its movement. In this context, improvisation would not be a sign of mastery but of forgetfulness; as if space were not a manifold of vortices, openings and closing, as if the ground were not an infinity of holes held together by well-timed feet.

Perhaps, as regards rhetoric, this does not matter. The conventions of forensic oratory are said to have had their origins in the difficulties that exiles returning to Syracuse found in proving land title. Unable to show their right to the land directly – by a knowledge, say, of the local lie of the land – they had to construct persuasive arguments on other grounds.[81] Perhaps rhetoric thrives best where all trace of former occupation has been bulldozed away, and where every groove and stress-line, every raised-vein foundation, has been flattened. There, the orator can strut his finest hour without fear of interruption. But the space of poetry is different: it is airy, consequently folded, grooved, vortical. Its words do not fly direct. They not only lose velocity on their way from the speaker's tongue to the hearer's ear; they flutter, stagger, soar, change direction according to the circumstances. But these changes do not signify a will to invent, simply an ability to ride the wind. As pneuma, as soul-speech originating in the double movement of the lungs, winged words are not only picturesquely like birds; they imitate avian flight. Plato likened the mind to a cage full of birds,[82] and even though Onians rejects the suggestion that the epithet 'winged' should be understood as feathered like an arrow,[83] it is clear that poetic understanding, although transported over the ground, is not off the ground but responds to its lie.

The uncertainty of flight, its infinitesimally self-correcting parabolic nature, seems to have been ignored not only because it was hard to model theoretically, but because in practice it was not held to be of critical importance. The theatres of classical and medieval warfare were remarkably intimate. One has the sense that the reversed perspective of medieval Byzantine mosaics, with their besieged towers leaning over and their arrows bending doubly under the representation of gravity and the curvature of the cupola's own inner surface, intuitively capture the closeness of ancient combat conditions. Marsden reckons that a large Roman stone-thrower 'had to stand within 150 yards of a wall to be effective, the machine being forced to shoot at a very low angle of elevation so that its shot would have the maximum possible forward momentum.' The maximum effective range of a composite bow or *gastraphetes* was probably little more.[84]

Even in the seventeenth century, 'warfare was still an affair of closely concentrated groups of men scarcely separated by a stone's throw, battering each other with the smallest refinement.'[85] A good musket was not reliable (when it fired at all) beyond 600 to 800 feet; and at sea, as late as Nelson's time only a broadside fired at point-blank range was felt to be effective.[86] Generally, archers and gunners were interested in flight paths in so far as they approximated to straight lines drawn parallel to the ground. Missiles that either climbed or began to fall to earth had lost their striking power. And besides, by this stage they were almost certain to have veered widely from their target; experimenting with musket-balls in the 1730s, Benjamin Robins found that 'at a range of 800 yards the ball he used diverged as much 100 yards to the right or left of the line of fire.'[87]

In this context, the medieval representation of the divine afflatus as a dotted line descending from the clouds, finding its way undeviatingly to the waiting saint's ear, assumes a different significance: here was a mode of communication that was definitely an exception to the rule. In general, words, feathered or unfeathered, missed their mark, got dispersed. If the Word was difficult to hear, it was not because the Lord had withdrawn to an intolerable distance, or that His bow was tired, but because the wind continued to blow laterally across the earth; the auditory conjunction of Heaven and Earth was bound to be hit and miss.

Perhaps this technologically-reinforced tradition of thinking in straight lines contributed to a deficiency in Western poetics. Words, like bullets, were deemed effective in so far as they found their target, which was always construed metaphysically as the listener's understanding. Their meaning was never considered to be tied up in the manner of their flight. Consequently, there never grew up in the West a body of poetic ballistics, devoted to elucidating the rules of behaviour governing the flight of words and their representation. Words were spoken or written: they were not danced; they were certainly not written on the ground. As for the space they plied across, perhaps it was inconceivable that it should have a poetic grammar of its own, that it might be tuned and resemble a topographically-strung musical instrument which the cross-play of sounds merely plucked into self-naming.

But then again, the recognition of Pallas Athene's double nature, of the fact that, although assimilated to the role of *mater patriae*, she retained the power to direct inertia, to trace out certain fateful historical grooves, suggests that a less pessimistic view is warranted. So Cavalcanti's difference from Dante, for example, is not only a matter of poetics but reflects a very different conception of ballistics. Cavalcanti's famous comparison of his lady to '*aria serena quand' apar l'albore / e bianca neve scender senza venti*',[88] was intended as a perceptually-accurate description of his state of mind. As many commentators have remarked, it was 'visualized' and rendered picturesquely theatrical by Dante: '*Piovean di foco dilatate falde, / Come di neve in alpe senza vento*.'[89] More than this though, Cavalcanti's sensation of embodied blots of light dimpling the surface of the eye, comparable to the way in which Giorgione's brush later fell upon the canvas, is replaced by a fascinated horror in contemplating a diabolically graceful, dance-like motion occurring on a stage over there.

The contrast between Cavalcanti's conception of light as a force-field governed by the same laws of attraction and repulsion as human desire and Dante's respect for it as the (sometimes deceptive) representative of angelic insight and human wisdom is a poetic difference over the flight-lines taken by 'winged words'. For if words do not represent concepts but participate in their generation, transmission and reception, then there is no or little room for similes of the kind Dante deploys. Words strike the inner sense apparitionally and correspond, like the Venetian *macchie*, to the fluctuating rain of sensations beating on the sentient surfaces of eye and ear. If so, the intermediate paths described by the gravitational units of desire are as critical to an understanding of their meaning as their origin and end. The weaving, never quite returning, folding and unfolding drift-lanes of the snowflakes will not represent a deferral of truth, but the very form of its continuously self-transforming becoming.

So it is that sparrowhawks who miss their quarry 'soar about in the air with outstretched but apparently motionless wings. On these occasions they seem to be taking a rest . . .'[90] The Syrian pigeon 'in the course of its usual flight forward suddenly turns over two or three times as if it were bewildered, and then resumes its usual course. We do not know why it does this – perhaps because of good spirits and cheerfulness . . .'[91] It may be no accident that the Emperor Frederick II of Hohenstaufen, the great Maecenas of courtly love-poets, was also a keen falconer and author of an encyclopaedic *Art of Falconry*. Falconry, it may be surmised, offered a welcome release from the leaden-footed business of warfare, where the flight of balls and arrows offered so little sport, so little scope for invention or ingenuity: 'In the days when there were only feeble and clumsy guns, or none at all, the only chance of bringing down birds which flew out of the range of arrows was to send falcons after them.' [92]

Perhaps the struggles of peregrines and sakers to overcome and bring down their flying quarry also suggested a different way of thinking about territories, their occupation and defence. Falcons were trained to prey on birds of passage – cranes, ducks and herons migrating from one clime to another. The successful falconer had to identify with the migrant's needs: 'Once begun, their migration is to birds always the most important object in their lives, and to its successful completion, in spite of fatigue, hunger, and headwinds, they bend all their energies. They come to earth only when contrary winds force them to rest from excessive fatigue and restore their strength, or when food becomes essential. Influenced by this hereditary or family experience they fly from one point to another, from island to island, until they reach the haven they have selected for winter quarters.'[93]

Frederick's remarkably modern understanding of avian migration was probably the result of observations made during his own extraterritorial expeditions to North Africa and the Middle East. Able to island-hop himself, he had no difficulty in understanding that other species could change their homes. In any case, to hunt these nomads it was necessary to improvise a comparably light and mobile *modus operandi.* Falconry modelled a kind of guerilla warfare where rival insurgents might cross each other's tracks without disturbing the larger part of the civilian (passerine) population; or it might foreshadow indigenous tactics in retiring to the hills in order to pick off the invaders as they trailed slowly through the apparently deserted valleys.

Be this as it may, the thrill of the chase did not consist in the easy slaughter of noble birds, but in the balancing of chance. Three of the six books of *De Arte Venandi* are devoted to the difficulties of bringing the hawk to its prey. Open plains, hillsides, breezes, winds, the combination of these and the position the falconer takes up in relation to all of these, and in relation to the quarry; all this has to be calculated. It is as if the object is to open a tunnel in a dense environment, to find a way through a cloudy manifold of scents, sounds, distracting flight-patterns and views, so that, albeit momentarily, the falcon sees a way through where it can fly unimpeded.

The falconer's art consists in so deciphering the lie of the land that he successfully exploits its *kairos*, the opportunity it occasionally and fleetingly affords him to find a way through. The beauty of his art is the strength of the line the falcon describes; and this, of course, will not be a straight line to where the cranes stand quietly feeding, for there is no sport in this. It will be the parabolic path the falcon describes as it steers towards where the long-legged birds are creakily climbing upwards and obliquely away; and where, as the two lines converge, once again everything becomes unpredictable, subject to local contingencies which even the best calculations of the falconer are powerless to predict.

Falconry was a way of thinking about the physical properties of the space in-between. The improvisatory behaviour of the slipped hawk, ringing up then stooping, enacted an alternative, non-rectilinear model of movement. Frederick, and even Leonardo two centuries later, believed that it was the constant beating of their wings that kept birds aloft.[94] This may have been a mistaken view, arising from the absence of a fully-developed concept of momentum, but it reinforced the sense that birds sculpted the air, that the motion of their wings directly tunnelled a way through chaotic country. They suggested the intellectual and aesthetic challenge of spaces in-between.

In this way, they also suggested common ground between ballistics and poetry. Giacomo da Lentini, who was a notary at the court of Frederick II as well as a poet, relies heavily on the Ovidian cliché of Cupid's arrow in describing the lover 'wounded' by his lady's glance. But he adopts the imagery critically, even sceptically. His sonnets resemble miniature scientific hypotheses designed to resolve obvious contradictions in the classical terminology of love and its theatrical representation. How, for example, is it possible for love to pierce the glass of the eye without shattering it?[95] How can the full-size figure of the beloved pass through the eye which is so small?[96] Lentini rehearses the idea that the faculty of sight consists of fiery rays of light which the seer projects towards the object he looks at.[97] He is interested in what might be called the meteorology of love: how is it that, just as rain has been known to fall from a clear sky and dark thunderclouds produce lightning, so Love produces contrary effects?[98] He wants to understand why certain sights affect him like the stare of the basilisk.[99] He wants to know how she concentrates within her gaze more light than the multi-faceted diamond.[100]

In short, Sicilian Lentini, together with certain Tuscan practitioners of *il dolce stil nuovo*, may be said to lay the groundwork for Guido Cavalcanti, whose unique achievement it was to create a ballistic theory of love, which was also a fully-fledged theory of poetry. The relationship between Cavalcanti's conception of love and his intuition of a non-rectilinear geometry is made conveniently plain in an early exchange of sonnets with the poet Guido Orlandi, who had accused him of 'losing the thread through excessive subtlety.'[101] Cavalcanti answers: 'Because you know how to string a crossbow and hit a large target at right angles, have read some tales of Ovid, can fire an arrow and make a false rhyme, your understanding cannot come where Love plainly and subtly explains her nature.' Love, Cavalcanti explains, is not something you hold in your hand, and he advises Orlandi: 'Love has manufactured what I polish.' To which Orlandi, missing the point, replies unabashed: 'Friend, I well know that you know how to polish chain-mail with a blunt file, to fly from post to bower like a bird, to turn in a confined space with great ingenuity . . .'[102]

Cavalcanti's point is both philosophical and poetic. Orlandi misunderstands love because he employs the wrong metaphors; or better, he fails to think through the relationship between vehicle and tenor, metaphor and metaphrand[103] – which, for Cavalcanti, cannot be dissociated. In taking the conventional imagery of love too literally, Orlandi is not only poetically like the archer who fires at point-blank range; his philosophy of love is equally childish. Orlandi and the love-poets generally employ the metaphor of Love's bow and arrow without once thinking what it means, what psychokinetic experience it is meant to illuminate metaphorically. Because of this philosophical failure, they cannot create a metaphorical discourse with any truth-value.

Orlandi's sarcastic reply inadvertently hits the mark. The futility of trying to pierce and polish the interstices of chain-mail with a blunt file may not illuminate Cavalcanti's poetic method, but it well describes the contradictions implicit in his own. By contrast, Cavalcanti, like Lentini, is interested in the physical laws governing the flight of Love's arrow: how it pierces the lover's defences, how it continually transforms its own nature. It is clear to him that analogies from medieval warfare cannot help. A different ballistic theory is needed, one which understands that the random flight of the bird is never random but obeys curvilinear, environmental principles. But this is also a different kind of poetry, one that reintegrates vehicle and tenor, revealing the obliquity of metaphorical discourse as something other than rhetorical artifice designed to dazzle – as the only, and most direct, way of imitating Love's transformational kinetics.

This is not simply a polemical view. Many commentators have appreciated that Cavalcanti develops what might be called a verbal algebra to explore the psychokinetic phenomenon of Love. His minimalist vocabulary (*donna, occhi, amore, cor, figura, spirito*) is used repetitively, even monotonously, as if to map a network of significant points which constantly redefine their positions in relation to one another as the lover pursues his journey through Love's dolorous landscape;[104] so that the poems might almost be thought of as a set of rhythmic diagrams or musical geometries mapping Love's various figures or manifestations. If they are the biography of a lover, they are also an emotional topography.

But this digitalization of emotion, splitting Love's magnetic field, the space between and encompassing lover and beloved, into clearly-distinguishable foci – points of arrival (*occhi, cor*) and departure (*occhi, dolor*) – cannot merely describe Love. Nor should it be interpreted technically, mechanically, as if the poems were treatises on the art of poetry, displaying the power of concrete images to produce abstract knowledge – rather than to be what they are in Dante's *Divine Comedy*, the concrete representations of abstract principles. Digital knowledge is always an analogue for something else. Cavalcanti's poems, like the poetics Pound bases on them, are about something beyond themselves; something we may identify ultimately with the lie of the land.

To articulate the folded space of desire, Cavalcanti improvises his own vocabulary. The *spiriti* or *spiritelli* which inhabit his love poems, and are fired back and forth between his and his beloved's eyes, are not simply figures of speech, ways of rendering the invisible visible; they are psychokinetic hypotheses intended to correspond to spatial realities. They obey laws of attraction and repulsion as precise as those obeyed by the spear and the arrow. As the medium of emotional transfer, they have, as it were, their own fixed mass and ballistic properties; it is merely their charge which changes as they pass between lover and beloved. So, coming from her to him as the spirit of Love, they enter his eyes and wound his heart. His heart is a citadel they invest and enter, with the result that his own *spiriti* are forced to flee, going via his eyes to her. Evacuated of vital spirits, the lover feels himself draw near to death. At the same time he welcomes Love's negative, as he knows that his own spirit, in abandoning him, has returned to its true home, which is her face, her *figura*. The *spiritelli* are a hypothesis explaining the mystery of asymmetrical desire. They suggest how one can love without being loved, and yet communicate that distress. They are a way of defining a space of desire that is at once subjective and objective, visible and invisible.[105]

Cavalcanti's difficulty, as his exchange with Guido Orlandi illustrates, and as his philosophical canzone *Donna me prega* explains, was to evolve a poetic (that is, scientific) discourse capable of dissolving the philosophical distinction between substances and accidents, between metaphysical concepts and physical appearances, the one static and changeless, the other mobile and fleeting. Unlike Dante, who continually elaborates a vertical hierarchy of meanings, so that the *donna* progressively becomes Beatrice, Philosophia, the principle of Truth,[106] Cavalcanti stays on the ground, continuing to stare, as it were, into the heart of light, refusing to allegorize his experience, keeping alive its essential mobility:

L'essere è quando – lo voler è tanto
ch'oltra misura – di natura – torna
poi non s'adorna – di riposo mai.[107]

The *spiriti* enable him to preserve the mobility of his experience by advancing a different, non-rectilinear theory of light's propagation, one curiously anticipating later particle models of light's transmission. The one '*che fa tremar di chiaritate l'are*'[108] is not simply a woman; she is an embodiment of light. But even this is too Platonic, for the light does not exist apart from her coming towards him. It is '*un lume pien di spiriti d'amore*',[109] a psycho-kinetic energy that elsewhere 'rains' upon him; as if numberless photons dashed through the air, their friction producing a tremulous light. The air, galvanized by the gaze of desire, is a force-field. The same psycho-kinetic sensation is evoked in the line '*e bianca neve scender senza venti*' where, of their own volition, flakes of light fall, palpable, errant, quickly melting.

Critics frequently comment on the theatricality of Cavalcanti's *mise en scène*,[110] but I think this obscures a more fundamental aspect: its awareness of space's historical contingency. The subject of Cavalcanti's poem is not a static target, fired at and struck by every passing woman's amorous gaze; he is himself on the move. And far from promiscuously answering every glance, he is blind to the visual temptations of his surroundings. And then, unexpectedly, a sensation more than visual tunnels its way through the normally-slack air and catches him. And from this invasion there is no turning back. He is trapped, his free-will arrested, a sensation Cavalcanti frequently dramatizes by imagining himself outside himself looking on.

The space Cavalcanti delineates is the same that Homer's Hector occupies; there are no magic reversals of fate available, no side-alleys. The opening line of his famous ballad '*Perch'i'no spero di tornar giammai*'[111] is not, I suggest, an exile's self-pity; it summarizes Cavalcanti's life-situation, one where he has no choice but to go forward, but where by going forward to meet his fate (his life) he knows he must inevitably experience defeat, disablement, death – where the lie of the land, the unpredictability of the human vicissitudes it harbours, becomes the occasion of the poet's anguish, his need obsessively to go back over the same emotional ground.

The flight of the spear is the poetic word by another name. It does not arc over an empty space. Rather, it denominates a common ground, knitting its topography together, reuniting it in an event. So with the poetic word: it does not originate on one side or the other, but in the measure of the poetic exchange. A word that finds its target means nothing unless it elicits an equally passionate reply. But the answer that strikes home is not improvised according to no rules. It can be likened to the echo which gives back to the caller his voice modified by the lie of the land, the dimensions, forms and textures of the environment. It originates outside itself, just as the meaning of the thrown spear, its direction, originates outside the thrower – in the future it intends.

But this analogy may still seem forced, merely poetic. The temptation is always to interpret aerial weapon-play in terms of its most bloody outcomes, to assume that the real object of the exercise is territorial domination, unification under the banner of the most powerful. Ours is not a poetics of curved paths; metaphors reinforce the rectilinear rhetoric of classical ballistics. We regard departures from the straight and narrow as deviations; or if we do allow their legitimacy, we interpret them pyschoanalytically as the divagations of Eros seeking to put off the end, the inevitable coming to the citadel of Thanatos. Was it not Heraclitus who said puningly, 'The name of the bow [*biós*] is life [*bíos*] but its work is death'?[112]

It is on these grounds that Daniel Dennett has criticized the phenomenologists' notion of *intentionality*. Quoting Elizabeth Anscombe to the effect that the term ' "comes by metaphor" from the Latin *intendere arcum in*, which means to aim a bow and arrow at (something)', Dennett fears that this way of conceptualizing consciousness fails to achieve its objective of breaking down the old Cartesian division between perceiving ego and perceived world. Its stress on aboutness, on the primary nature of the relationship between perceiver and what is perceived, may seem to combat successfully the idea of an observer unimplicated in his surroundings; but in Dennett's view, philosophers 'have traded in the complex process of aiming a real arrow for a mere "logical" arrow, a foundational or primitive relation, made all the more mysterious by its supposed simplicity.'[113]

Dennett would like us to focus instead on 'the actual business of aiming at something, "keeping it in the crosshairs" '. 'The best way to keep in touch with something,' he maintains, 'is, literally, to keep in touch with it – to grab it and not let it get away, so that you can examine it to your heart's content, in your own good time. The next best way is to keep in touch with it figuratively, by tracking it with your eyes (and the rest of your body), never letting it out of your sight.'[114] But Dennett's critique of the philosophers applies equally to his own argument: it takes for granted the rectilinear nature of the arrow's path. In reality, the hunter never aims at his target. To make contact, he must always fire somewhere else. If the quarry stands still, then he must fire his arrow or hurl his spear upwards towards a point somewhat above it. Only by this oblique route, following the logic of the parabola, will it find its mark. To aim directly would be to guarantee its falling short. When the target moves, horizontal deviation is as important as vertical displacement; the hunter who lets fly at the fleeing beast aims in front of it. The animal that is struck down runs to meet its death; it advances from its own side into the flight path of arrow or spear. The archer who fires directly at what he sees is bound to miss it.

Dennett perpetuates a Cartesian misconception in supposing that our visual tracking of objects is no different from the way we track them kinetically; or better, he ignores the fact that seeing is not simply a matter of grasping and holding but of anticipating, foreseeing. The hunter's skill does not depend on his visual acuity, his ability to observe and interpret signs that others overlook. It does not even reside in his athletic agility in keeping his quarry in view. Primarily, it consists in the prediction of converging flight paths, in aligning himself to the lie of the land. Nothing is gained by following in the animal's path. He must be tracked obliquely, as if the hunter were going somewhere else, towards the place his prey has not reached yet, where in the near future they will meet.

Dennett is right to think in terms of 'tracking', but he seems to conceive of this process digitally, as a process of continual readjustment, as if the observer needed at every moment to recalculate his own trajectory. But the process is an analogue one. The observer does not move across a bare surface, but occupies a ground he shares with his quarry; his is always a motion more or less towards, and the paths taken by hunter and prey are like the drawstrings of a purse which, as they are shortened, pucker the surface along their convergent and curvilinear lengths. 'People with Parkinson's disease,' Madeline Gins notes, 'unable to move unless they throw something out in front of themselves . . . need to get a specific perceptual traction on something that they can then pull themselves towards. Or they can find nothing within or about them that would be their movement until they find to where it is to go.'[115]

This condition, where a normally analogue function has been digitalized, grown jerky and shuddered to a halt, would be normal if the ground were genuinely trackless. In reality, it extends an invitation, a 'carpet' that draws us on, not according to any linear calculation of the motionless eye but kinaesthetically. And as Gins notes, this is not merely a description of physical movement through 'space' – not simply instructions to a hunter – but applies intimately to the making of art. Of the Japanese-American artist Arakawa's *Separated Continuums* (1964), she writes, 'The forms I harken to are schemas of what might be there (and will be again) and of what has happened to me. They are pictures of schemas of pictures. I break my head against the images that don't form every time. To be transitive is to have a carry-over onto something else. Thinking, I find, works as a field that is all transitive. So thought commands a voice all spread out in transitivity.' Which meditation provokes another authorial *persona* to comment, 'The best way to draw a line is to do it with your eyes closed.'[116]

But 'transitive' perhaps conveys the wrong impression if it suggests an imperializing ambition to inscribe blank space with certain preconceptions of one's own. If the essence of the transitive is a 'carry-over onto something else', a return that is not a return, the process of composition would seem to answer closely to Strehlow's conception of the 'additive' nature of Aranda song, grammar and social organization, which embodies a non-linear space-time perception – one that may be inherent not merely, as Gins shows, amongst blind people, but wherever language is experienced auditorily and not visually. As F. Joseph Smith comments, 'regarded as linear, language is "syn-tactical", that is, it is "put together", in that something is predicated of a subject. Regarded as an audial phenomenon, that is, as actually spoken, statements need not be described in linear manner. Rather they are heard as audial phenomena. Words do not come out in ready-made statements; rather they come one-after-the-other in an "additive" manner, thus not syntactically, but "paratactically". This applies particularly to musical rhythm; but it is obvious also in the observation of speech rhythm.'[117]

Following Husserl, Smith contends that the 'building of form' involves what he calls 'passive synthesis', an attitude that entails simultaneously giving and receiving, and he compares this to the middle ground between active and passive as embodied in the Greek middle voice. 'The middle voice emphasizes the *subject* acting either for itself or for others, we might say, intersubjectively. This self-action is expressed in modern languages by means of the reflexive form.'[118] Thus, he writes, when listening to music, 'something "happens to me", is constituted for me as a unified and structured happening. Musical sounds fall together or pull themselves together for me in synthetic patterns,' and he notes that the putting-together of notes is a 'process of continuing becoming.'[119] The middle voice may be described as folding time in the sense that it dissolves the subject-object relation, grounding each in the other, continuously redefining both in terms of each other, so that the two sides exist echoically or simultaneously.

This description of musical (or auditory) experience as additive – phenomena continually bunching and rebunching themselves synthetically through the act of listening – suggests the folded landscape gradually, but never completely, disclosing itself to the walker. But it also suggests a psychological attitude. Thus, White makes a sharp distinction between the self-regarding and fixing narcissism he associates with the reflexive voice and the 'self that goes out into the world to become what it is not, so that even as it repeats itself, it makes a difference.' When White writes, 'such a self would lead a fugitive existence, always on the move from one newly constituted version of itself to another. The middle voice suggests not a fixed and abiding selfhood but a sequence of discontinuous partial selves, or the self as historical process,'[120] he evokes the historical personality I attribute to Light. But he also describes any art that makes its subject the process of its own grounding.

Such an art will, it seems, mobilize what we may call an environmental poetics. The good archer – but it might equally be 'a man advancing through difficult country' – knows how to read the winds. As Ascham implies, this sensitivity to an element 'so fyne, and subtile' that 'To se the winde, with a man his eyes, it is unpossible', is constitutional. Unless he takes proper account of the wind's whirlwinds, as they reveal themselves chasing across the bended grass, or agitating the leaves of a tree or chivying the river's surface, he cannot shoot true. To shoot directly, trusting to the sharpness of his arrow to cleave the air immaculately, risks disaster: 'But seynge that a Master of a shyp, be he never so cunnynge, by the uncertaynte of the wynde, leeseth many tymes both lyfe and goodes, surelye it is no wonder, though a ryght good Archer, by the self same wynde so variable in hys owne nature, so unsensyble to oure nature, leese manye a shoote and game.'[121]

It is the master of the middle voice who rides the wind of becoming, who understands its curvilinear motions as a mode of composition. Ascham recalls a winter's day between Topcliffe-upon-Swale and Borowe Bridge. Snow had fallen, and now 'the winde was whistelinge a loft':

> Sometyme the wynd would be not past two yeardes brode, and so it would carie the snowe as far as I could se. An other tyme the snow woulde blowe over halfe the felde at ones. Sometyme the snowe would tomble softly, by and by it would flye wonderfull fast. And thys I perceyved also that ye wind goeth by streames & not hole togither. For I should se one streame wyth in a Score on me, that the space of two score no snow would stirre, but after so much quantitie of grounde, an other streame of snow at the same very time should be caryed lykewyse, but not equally. For the one would stand styll when the other flew a pace, and so contynewe somtyme swiftlyer sometime slowlyer, sometime broder, sometime narrower, as far as I coulde se. Nor it flewe not streight, but sometyme it crooked thys waye sometyme that waye, and somtyme it ran round aboute in a compase. And sometyme the snowe wold be lyft clene from the ground up in the ayre, and by & by it would be al clapt to the grounde as though there had bene no winde at all, streightway it woulde rise and flye

> agayne. And that whych was the moost mervayle of al, at one tyme two driftes of snowe flewe, the one out of the West into ye East, the other out of the North into ye East: And I saw two windes by reason of ye snow the one crosse over the other, as it had bene two hye wayes.[122]

Ascham not only bears witness to the character of the wind; he participates in its mode of movement, its restless going back over an ever-changing ground. His paratactic sentence structure assembles impressions on a common ground; it is a way of halting phenomena from passing away without denying their motion. His is an 'audial' mode of description, one that (even in its unstable spelling of words) imitates the echoic nature of a knowledge assembled environmentally. All of what he describes occurs at once; there are multiple observers, a multiplicity of threads being woven, unwoven. There is no viewpoint, no view. But in compensation, there is the kind of knowledge Leonardo tried to replicate in his drawings of the storm: a braid of force-lines, an orchestration of environmental 'tones'. Evidently this is the world of Cavalcanti and Giorgione, who impute to these airy structures an ontological value, making of them the ground of their poetic practice.

Likewise, Strehlow's hunter can only describe a ground that remains as it continually transforms itself because he has to hand, at least in Strehlow's methektic recreation, a medium of expression that is analogous to the art of *macchiare* available to the Venetian painter. By this process of continuous transformation, the hunter is able to stay where he is. His movement is genuine because it is grounded, because it carries embedded within it the history of its coming into being; a pattern of syllables, like the first blotch, is continually returned to, added to and modified until it becomes not the representation of a history but its methektic enactment. But this we owe to Strehlow as much as to the Aranda language. Like Ascham, Strehlow writes poetically as well as scientifically; do we not 'see' the mountain kangaroo differently now? Not as an image but as a moving trace, a physically-inscribed history which comes into being because of the hunter's interest. And just as Ascham implicitly juxtaposes his account with one that would, all unseeing, assume the wind to resemble a white wall, so Strehlow, in his English paraphrase, grooves and striates its movement so that, slowed down, English is licensed to do what the linear electrification of its syntax seldom permits: to idle about the resonating phonic centres of our language, its whirlpools and odd, illuminating patterns of likeness.

In effect Strehlow's description of Aranda directly inverts or contradicts Benjamin Whorf's thesis, that cultures are bound in their outlooks by the languages they use. True, Aranda exhibits a poverty of numerals, its shortage of abstract terms, its lack of capacity to express hypothetical states, but this merely proves that the Aranda culture had no need of such concepts;[123] the post-contact ability of Aranda people to adapt and expand their language underlines this point dramatically. Strehlow's Aranda are not the puppets of a theatrical grammar that they are powerless to modify; quite the contrary, they produce (just as the totemic ancestors are said to have done) the ground of their being out of themselves; or more exactly out of their primary movement over the ground.

And this movement cannot be linear. It is in fact a curved line, one that continually calculates the changing balance between what has been passed and what lies ahead, and as it leans progressively one way or the other, continually modifies its direction. It is a curve that desires to return, but which never loses sight of the shape of the curve itself. It is not that self-negating curve, the circle. It is parabolic, and this in two dimensions, rising and falling with the lie of the land, swerving outwards to left and right and arcing back again towards the point of origin. Further, being conceived as a relationship, it is always timely, a matter of seeing, opening up and seizing upon a coincidence, as the hunter does when he catches sight of his prey and aims to bring him home. Such a curve, always gravitating towards an end as if for the first time, originary, is in my terms performative.[124]

Strehlow cited with approval Spengler's contention that the Aborigines possessed 'a mathematical instinct . . . that as regards the interpretation of pure space is far superior to that of the Greeks. Their discovery of the boomerang can only be attributed to their having a sure feeling for numbers of a class that we should refer to the higher geometry.' Spengler continues, '*Accordingly* – we shall justify the adverb later – they possess an extraordinarily complicated ceremonial and, for expressing degrees of affinity, such fine shades of language as not even the higher Cultures themselves show.'[125] Obviously this formulation is motivated; in our sense, ungrounded. By reducing the boomerang to an intellectual exercise in applied infinitesimal calculus, it serves Spengler's thesis of civilization's decline. Nevertheless, we can extract from it a valid poetic insight: the infinitely-subtle curve of the boomerang's flight as, degree by degree, its revolving form performs more and more elaborate arabesques returning to the thrower's hand is analogous to the process of verbal agglutination employed by the hunter which, rather than identify binary oppositions (subject and object), expresses incremental differences as 'degrees of affinity'.

In this context, we can go back to the episode where Odysseus, that great seizer of opportunities, seizes the greatest of opportunities, his own bow, 'drew the bow-string and the notched arrow even from the chair where he sat, and let fly the shaft with sure aim, and did not miss the end of the handle of one of the axes, but clean through and out at the end passed the arrow . . .'[126] Leaving aside the vexed question of the shape and arrangement of the axes, it is clear that this definitive, and from a narrative point of view, climactic, act is achieved against almost all the odds. The space Odysseus inhabits is secularized, we might almost say slack; in order to evidence the existence of a higher geometry, a mechanical installation of axes has to be devised, modelling a curvilinear path. But these, located within a time-space that is linear, dissipative, individualized, merely bear witness to the oddity of curvilinear space in a newly-linearizing age.

This is not simply to suggest that Homeric *kairos* is a secondary intuition, that it marks the disappearance of that older time-space consciousness where the hunter, psycho-kinetically identified with the lie of the land, could not miss. It is also to explain the form of the *Odyssey*: the idea of a narrative composed of successive delays, divagations, near-misses and supernatural coincidences depends on a notion of space-time analogous to that embodied in the row of axes where, unless one shoots true, one is bound to miss. In such a world, where the ground is no longer grooved, no longer bears witness to a curvilinear space-time manifold cradling the human being from birth to death, hitting the target will always be a matter of chance or superhuman skill. The hero does not merely pit himself against other heroes; collectively, all heroes pit themselves against the lie of the land, against the (now-dishonoured) fable that the ground once had a mind of its own. No longer worshipped or lightly footed, it must be dyked and subdued.

Mimesis is in a mythic sense associated with migration; it arises from the experience of displacement. But as we have seen, the derogatory associations of migration – the assumption that movement from one place to another is eccentric and marks a form of cultural impoverishment –

arise from a political agenda, from the centralist ambitions of the Athenian *polis* and its apologists. The challenge, at least for a post-colonial poetics, is to see in what way migration might entail a form of emplacement, might in fact be constitutional and signify a mode of being at home in the world. Is the history of Western culture simply a sequence of ever more abstract scientific and technological enclosure acts progressively divorcing us from contact with the ground, and characterizing physical motion as primitive? Or is there within that sequence a counter-tradition, a form of wandering that constitutes a ground-marking? Can Pallas Athene ever again take command of the storm?

This in effect glosses Prynne's ambition in his significantly titled collection of poems *The White Stones* (1968), where the stones may be boundary markers, signifying the advent of the *polis* and territorial closure, or path markers, stippling the uneven ground. Prynne writes:

> As I walked up the hill this evening and felt
> the rise bend up gently against me I knew
> that the void was gripped with concentration.
> Not mine indeed but the sequence of fact,
> the lives spread out, it is a very wild and
> distant resort that keeps a man, wandering
> at night, more or less in his place.[127]

In defining that 'very wild and/ distant resort' the possibility of a grounded poetics may reside. So Prynne is preoccupied with retracing the earliest history of Western civilization. Like Lindsay's, his is a materialist account, directly correlating the emergence of new cultural patterns with technological developments arising from a growing power over the earth (reflected particularly in an ever more sophisticated metallurgical knowledge). But it is also a poetic account, as Prynne recognizes that, preceding the emergence of the Marxist division between use-value and exchange value, there must be a primary shift from property as 'substance' to property as 'quality'.

'Until this stage [the early Bronze Age],' he writes, 'weight was the most specific carrier for the inherence of power, and weight was and is a mixed condition, related locally to exertion. The focus of this condition is typically stone . . . Whereas with copper, tin (and perhaps antimony), weight coincides with other possible conditions which are less mixed and specific: brightness, hardness, ductility and general ease of working . . . And through the agency of the most ostensive control of force, namely fire, sword-blades or spear-heads could be forged into a strength infinitely more abstract than the flaking of high-quality flint or the hardening of wooden points . . . The new quality of spiritual transfer was concentrated in these most durable forms of leading edge, seen especially in the flattened motive of ornament, and the history of substance (stone) shifts with complex social implication into the theory of power (metal).'[128]

The history of stone is also a history of the ground. With the 'theorising of quality, with its control over weaponry and tillage', stone became admired for its self-consistency, 'as the zone of being in which the condition was also the limit: the interior knowledge of dying.'[129] The white stones also signify headstones. The important point is that this first reconceptualization of stone represents, Prynne speculates, 'an exilic theory of substance', and he acutely notes that, in due course, a second enclosure of the ground occurs: 'The rapid advance of metallurgy, shifting from the transfer of life as power (hunting) into the more settled expectation of reaping what you have already sown; this itself produces the idea of *place* as the chief local fact, which makes mining and the whole extractive industry possible from then.' The Sumerian settlement is an instance of this process: here, 'the innovations of metallurgy, and these abstractions of substance were in turn the basis for a politics of wealth: the concentration of theoretic power by iconic displacement of substance.'[130]

According to this account, a growing knowledge of the processes of smelting and beating inaugurates a sequence of metaphorical manoeuvres: quantity (weight) is replaced by quality (durability, sharpness); ground (stone, including the 'cultic inside: the cave') is replaced by 'place', the theatrical locus for the production of wealth. Associated with migration or exile from what Prynne elsewhere calls the 'common world',[131] a succession of displacements occur which not only shape the fate of Western civilization but also adumbrate a theory of poetry: is the poet's *techne* bound to parallel these developments? Is he to be a forger of metaphors, a technologist of words twisting them to new forms and uses? Is his alchemy an apology for theirs? Or must he sing the processes of ungrounding themselves, adumbrating reactively 'an exilic (left-wing) history of substance.'[132] Is he to resist the metallurgical urge to probe beneath the surface of appearances and instead to ground his analysis in the lie of the land?

'The Common Gain, Reverted' should be read in conjunction with 'Thoughts on the Esterhazy Court Uniform', whose opening phrase, 'I walk on up the hill', obviously echoes the passage already quoted. These poems seek to ground being in the world differently, to construct a life that does not consist in a sequence of displacements and their consequence, a sense of irremediable loss. To this end, they meditate a methektic conception of movement, which sacralizes the act of walking by making it a recovery of the ground. Recovery entails a sense of direction and a sense of rhythm. A sense of direction depends on apprehending the ground beneath one's feet as tracked, as a vectorial rather than scalar history of movement. Thus, 'The nomad is perfect/ but the pure motion which has no track is/ utterly lost.'

This perception has the effect of transforming the meaning of movement. Instead of being construed as a means of getting from one place to another, it becomes a rehearsal of the surface, a means of staying 'more or less' in one place. The markings of the surface signify a history; the borders of the track signify a direction. And yet these guides are not there in advance: they unfold, as it were, from the direction of one's feet – which are themselves the offspring of one's thoughts, or of the two motions becoming one. Progress in this terrain may be likened to the act of speaking which, although never original, making use of age-old markers (words), has subjectively the sense of a performance occurring as if for the first time:

> Those who walk heavily
> carry their needs, or lack
> of them, by keeping their
> eyes directed at the ground
> before their feet. They are
> said to trudge when in fact their empty thoughts
> unroll like a crimson carpet before their
> gentle & delicate pace. In any street the pattern
> of inheritance is laid down, the truth is for our
> time in cats-eyes, white markings, gravel
> left from the last fall of snow. We proceed
> down it in dreams, from house to house which
> spill nothing on to the track, only light on the
> edge of the garden. The way is of course speech

and a tectonic emplacement, as gradient it
moves easily, like a void . . .[133]

Prynne appears to understand the 'void' positively, as what is left when our being in the world, our 'presence', is relieved of its onerous inheritance of logical and psychological categories that displace it from itself; the primary displacement consisting perhaps in the identification of memory with place, and the consequent nostalgia that accrues when every journey has to be a kind of return and must be evaluated qualitatively as it oscillates queasily between sentimental nostalgia (the hope of arrival) and romantic despair (the narcissism of homelessness). 'Empty thoughts', in this context, are precisely those which, because they do not evaluate, have 'substance'; they give weight to the fact of their own embodiment as walking. They gravitate towards the ground, they have a 'presence', not in the solipsistic sense of regarding themselves, but by attending to the 'pace' of the ground. The passage quoted above continues:

It is now at this
time the one presence
of fact, our maze
through which we
read the shadow or
at midday pace
level beneath our own.

'Thoughts on the Esterhazy Court Uniform' takes this observation one step further, as it were, attempting to define the process of 'emplacement' not simply as a reading of the ground but as a rate of exchange, as the 'pace' itself. The difficulty Prynne explores is the same we encountered in Aristotle's conception of motion: how to give movement a meaning apart from its promise of return and the resumption of stasis? How, for example, to avoid mythologizing that 'gentle & delicate pace', seeing it as a form of exile or as a preliminary to homecoming. Prynne explores this dilemma through the analogy of music; for music gives the impression of getting from one place to another but always in the form of a return. But this occurs at the cost of losing contact with the 'fact' of the surface. Music composes movement but its structure suggests a 'hidden purpose', a meaning to be extracted:

> I walk on up the hill, in the warm
> sun and we do not return, the place is
> entirely musical. No person can live there
> & what is similar is the deeper resource, the
> now hidden purpose. I refer directly to my
> own need, since to advance in the now fresh &
> sprouting world must take on some musical
> sense. Literally, the grace & hesitation of
> modal descent, the rhyme unbearable, the
> coming down through the prepared delay and
> once again we are there, beholding the
> complete elation of our end.[134]

This, then, is music's 'hidden purpose': to enclose movement within the prospect of return, to make that prospect deliciously picturesque, to mimic temporarily its inaccessibility, then to resolve the difficulty. But to what end? For the place returned to, not corresponding to the course of the journey itself, can only signify a loss:

> Each move
> into the home world is that same loss; we
> do mimic the return and the pulse very
> slightly quickens, as our motives flare in
> the warm hearth.

This may be admitted, but even if we accept that the return journey is qualitatively different from the outward route – 'we go more slowly as we come back' – the ultimate intent of this return is clear: to negate movement. 'Soon one would live in a sovereign point', Prynne goes on, 'and still we don't return, not really, we look back.' In other words, return imagined modally, as a return to the home key, promises the recovery of full presence while in fact institutionalizing loss as the natural condition of being in the world. It musicalizes the world, making it literally 'unspeakable', and it sacralizes the distant 'place', whilst negating the local lie of the land:

> To our unspeakable loss; we make
> sacred what we cannot see without coming
> back to where we were.

If the consequence is to constitute self-consciousness from the beginning elegiacally, as a mode of regret for the road not taken or the home forfeited, the challenge is to give back to movement its gravity, to be assured that each step is neither a repetition nor an admission of loss:

> How can I straighten the sure fact that
> we do *not* do it, as we regret, trust, look
> forward to, etc? Since each time what
> we have is increasingly the recall, not
> the subject to which we come. Our chief
> loss is ourselves; that's where I am, the
> sacral link in a profane world, we each do
> this by the pantheon of hallowed times.
> Our music the past tense:
> if it would only
> level out into some complete migration of
> sound, I could then leave unnoticed, bring nothing
> with me, allow the world free of its displace-
> ment. Then I myself would be the
> complete stranger, not watching jealously
> over names. And yet home is easily our
> idea of it, the music of decent and proper
> order, it's this we must leave in some quite
> specific place if we are not to carry it
> everywhere with us.[135]

'Music,' Prynne very properly realizes, 'is truly the / sound of our time, since it is how we most/ deeply recognise the home we may not/ have.' And the corollary is evident: a regrounding of ourselves factually, in the world, will mean amongst other things escaping from the false promise inherent in modal music. Our homesickness, our inheritance of displacements, renders us incapable of living where we are, of 'wandering/ at night, more or less in [our] place.'

A 'world free of its displace-/ment' is one characterized by 'some complete migration of sound.' These are sounds that are not necessarily modally-related or tonally-centred but which must have a shape, if only in order to be 'complete'. These sounds do not fly past us on their way from one place to another – we cannot stand to one side of them – hearing rather than seeing obliges us to stand at the centre of their continuously-fluctuating passage as they whirl round us, an auditory envelope resembling perhaps a murmuration of starlings wheeling over a winter field. 'The vortex in this case is the "whirlwind" of reality. Music can indeed be forced into the linear dimension; but it is legitimate to ask whether the raw musical experience is not rather "vortical", emerging from a veritable whirlwind of the creative activity of the artist subject.'[136]

This is the storm which does not imperialize, or provide colonization with its picturesquely-redemptive frame, but which, as long as we live, swarms about us. It is the auditory apprehension which reveals that time is not simply linear: it is a whole network or tissue of experience that thrusts ahead or pro-tends itself and leaves a trail of after-shadows. Thus the experience retains itself and each given new-point stands not in isolation but in the pattern of thrust and trail, almost in the manner of a comet. But the musical tone is the best example, and Husserl describes retention as a 'musical tail', or as a series of after-echoes exemplified in the flight of a bird. As 'the forward thrust of musical time builds a horizon of expectations and possibilities for the composer and for the listener; and, as the musical tone unfolds in its forward movement of "protension", it leaves in its wake a whole series of tonal shadows (*Abschattungen*), that spread out in ever diminishing diagonal lines behind it.'[137]

But this image of auditory time is not quite exact. It retains a linear bias. Sound is produced when air encountering an obstacle (a reed, a string) causes it to vibrate. The encounter not only changes the obstacle's state, it alters the calm and steady flow of the air: 'When the wind or a blast of air encounters a small obstacle, little whirlwinds are formed which are the exact counterparts of the whirlpools which are formed when a stream of water strikes a rock. There is a steady flow of air in front of the obstacle, and a steady train of whirlwinds behind it. These whirlwinds are formed on the two sides of the obstacle alternately; as soon as one comes into existence, it begins to drift away in the general current of air, thus making place for others which are formed in turn behind it.'[138] A recognizably 'musical' note is produced by the transformation of the current of air as it passes over the obstacle's leading edge into a rapid sequence of pulses (the whirlpools): 'If the wind blows in a continuous steady stream, these shocks are given to the air at perfectly regular intervals. We may then hear a musical note – it is what is often described as "whistling of the wind", or the "wind whistle". Its pitch is of course determined by the frequency of the shocks to the air, and this is the number of whirlwinds formed per second.'[139]

In other words, the migration of sounds imprints itself on the air as a trail of alternating eddies – a model that has informed the structuring of this book. The 'quality' given to the air, that is, its musical note or pitch, can be likened to a trail of revolving pressure-systems continually unwinding. Another of Prynne's poems is titled 'Quality in that Case as Pressure', a proposition that the poem's opening lines gloss:

> Presence in this condition is quality
> which can be transformed & is subject
> even to paroxysm – but it is not
> *lapse*: that is my chief point. As I
> move with my weight there is collusion,
> with the sight of how we would rise
> or fall or on the level. How *much* we
> see is how far we desire change, which
> is transformation from the ridge and fore-
> land *inverted* – with all the clouds
> over the shore.[140]

To move over the ground is not simply to align oneself with the lie of the land; it is to be aware of a leading edge (the cone of sight) introducing perturbations into the environment. I think that the 'ridge and fore-/land inverted' can reasonably be likened to the alternating eddies forming behind the 'obstacle' – divisive vision itself. But the key point is that these impressions are produced by one's own motivated movement, the desire of change. And whatever we may see in the sky, it is an echo of the impression left on the ground 'As I/ move with my weight.' If we ask what form 'the one presence/ of fact, our maze/ through which we/ read the shadow or/ at midday pace/ level beneath our own' may take, the answer appears to be: the form of the whirlwind.

With this conclusion we can begin to spiral inwards towards our own conclusion, as we do so drawing together some of the book's threads. With the advent of smelting, Prynne maintains, 'The new quality of spiritual transfer was concentrated in these most durable forms of leading edge . . . and the history of substance (stone) shifts with complex social implication into the theory of power (metal).' This may be described as the first displacement of Western civilization: 'The North American Indians developed no real metallurgy at all.'[141] But Prynne's object is to see what can be recuperated from this history, how else it might be told, how a history of displacement might disclose a shadow history of substantive emplacements – which, though continually effaced, provide the hidden ground, the *gravitas* of progress.

If the term 'spiritual transfer' is used ambiguously, suggesting being's mystification as it comes to be represented materially, aiding the identification of *poiesis* with *techne*, the power to command and change, it also implies what needs to be relocated: the flight of the spirit as living breath. This is to be found along 'the leading edge', but not in its quality of sharpness, the spear's power to penetrate armour, the arrow's swiftness to bring down the bird. The emplacement of the spirit in the new technological order is located in the wave-front that the propelled edge produces as it climbs through the air. It is the undulating pattern of tiny *tourbillons* that stream out in its wake that shows where the living breath is. As Jeans notes, these perturbations have an influence on the 'obstacle', causing it to vibrate differently, to wobble and twist.

The wise archer propels his missile into a cloudy medium, conscious of looking for the passages in between contending vortices. The arrow 'sings' when its natural period of vibration coincides with the forced vibrations set up by the wind. The warrior is a musician, tuning his instrument to the elements. In turn, the phenomenon of 'edge tones', 'produced when a stream of air or gas strikes the sharp edge of a wedge of metal or other hard substance' is in effect a wind-tunnel where the hunter might study his weapons and learn to tune them.[142] Organs, which mechanize the production of edge tones, may be said to harmonize the flight of myriad leading edges, to be machines for the representation of curvilinear flight.

The concept of the wave-front also illuminates our understanding of *kairos*. Onians argues that *kairós*, meaning 'opportune', 'timely', is the same word as *kaíros*, a term in weaving referring apparently to the parting of the warp-threads 'making in the warp a triangular opening, a series of triangles, together forming a passage for the woof.'[143] If this definition is correct, 'Through the opening, the passage through the warp, should be the path of the shuttle with the woof, as the proper path for the arrow was through the series of apertures in the axes. The analogy is even closer. Arrow-shaped and arrow-named spindles were used as spools . . . and the casting of the spool or shuttle thus through the opening between the warp-threads is still known as a "shot", a single woof-thread thus cast is a "shoot".'[144]

Odysseus, then, understands archery as a form of air-weaving. His skill in shooting is the same he exhibited as master of a ship (whom only the direct intervention of the gods could prevent from coming swiftly home). It is a Leonardo-like ability to read the vortices of wind and water, and to steer his vessel along their revolving edges – and where vortices slide into one another, to judge the direction and strength of the resulting current and to ride it. It is a power of kinetic tuning, of keeping his balance in a constantly-altering environment. Odysseus hits the mark not because he is a better murderer, but because he is a superior musician, alone able to make his bow sing. Odysseus does not see where to fire; he hears a space open up. And when he hits the mark, what has been demonstrated in the stunned silence following is the complete migration of sound.

As F. Joseph Smith explains, 'The word *tonos* . . . has to do exclusively with an audial experience. It is directly related to the tuning of the Greek *kithara* . . . tuning had to do with various degrees of the tenseness of strings, as every string player knows through his fingers. Thus the tablature, though mediated through the eye, was really a contact between the fingers and what I would like to call a musical *tensor*. And thus the performing subject was in direct touch with the very heart of music: with musical "tensility", and thus with musical "space".'[145] This elucidates the poetic meaning of Penelope's twenty-year-long weaving and unweaving of her father-in-law's burial shroud. As the activity of the blind Fates illustrates, weaving is primarily a haptic, not a visual, art. The good weaver tells with her fingers whether the proper tension of warp and woof is being maintained. Penelope, making and unmaking a pattern on a ground, does not display helplessness in a world controlled by male desire; she does not 'wait' for twenty years. Refusing to submit herself to a linear conception of time, she cultivates, in the limitations of evanescent time, union with Eternity.

Her practice directly recalls that of the sand-artists of the Western Desert. Geoffrey Bardon recalls that one of the foremost painters at Papunya, Tim Leura, 'said to me that he thought that the paintings on board or canvas were toys. He also said that the idea of a permanent artefact was the white man's.' And Bardon comments, 'The corroboree was only an ephemeral event and after the ceremony the sand mosaics were allowed to blow away. The idea, however, and the form within which the particular Dreaming were comprehended, were eternal.'[146] What we may have in the written-down poems of Homer are 'toys' – artefacts of a blind bard's performance, once chanted, as Strehlow notes, 'to the accompaniment of a lyre.'[147] To ground Homer differently, to find how he is not simply the apologist of Olympian patriarchy and colonialism, we would need to attend less to the linear narrative than to the retarding devices, those eddies in the story's smooth current which, transferring value from the tale told to the act of telling, helped to define the narrative space performatively, as a temporarily-shared common ground, rather than theatrically, as a spectacle over there, music in 'the past tense.'

Air-weaving takes place where the leading edge becomes a tongue ululating in the wind. The obstacle, whether an arrow or a vibrating string, is considered not simply as a triumph of quality over substance. It is valued for its resonance, its quality of transforming its own substance into a pattern of vibrations that resonate well. By this means, *techne* remains in contact with *poeisis*; the making of things consisting in the tuning of substance, the discovery of its *tonos* serving to discover the centre of its gravity. In this mutually-reinforcing exchange between vibrating edge and perturbed surrounding medium, a pattern of pulsions or waves is created that, without going anywhere, never exactly repeats itself, continuing to evolve about the trembling, quivering centre.

Air-weaving is directly related to the 'word-weaving' which, according to Strehlow, distinguishes Aranda songs. 'One or two bare verses would have sufficed to achieve the practical purpose of the magician. Instead of this we find songs in which couplet has been strung upon couplet, and ornament added to ornament, in order to achieve verse which is not merely efficacious but, to native ears, thrilling, stimulating, and beautiful.'[148] And in an audio-visual comparison rare in *Songs of Central Australia*, Strehlow adds in a footnote: 'The same love of decoration can be seen in the patterns engraved upon the *tjurunga* slabs, in the body markings of the ceremonial actors, and in the designs cut into shields and spearthrowers. In these patterns the circles, curves, lines, and dots are all intended to signify the impressions left by human figures or animals on and around a camp site, or shadows thrown by trees and the spaces occupied by fires on the ground of the mythical centre. Single circles and half-circles and straight lines would have served adequately to indicate these impressions on a sketch map. But the native craftsmen, like the verse-composers, always loved repetition and variation in their art. Consequently the single lines and curves were generally trebled and quadrupled, and circles were turned into highly elaborated figures containing from five to twenty five (and even more) spirals.'[149]

Evidently the Aranda understood the poetics of the storm. Their composite art-forms reproduced the lines of force that were constitutional of their environment. In these revolving shapes, a mere coincidence between the patterns of cosmic movement associated with the creation of the land and the patterns of human movement deriving from men's biological endowment was established. And the mere coincidence was performative: it depended on tunnelling out methektically a space-time manifold where the movement of the foot imprinting the ground was also the movement of the ground giving impulse to the puppet-mover. In this ambiguously kinetic environment, the cleared, carefully-grooved performance space was magnetized, a force-field fraught with the equivocations of creation. Because nothing was here, monumentally and deceptively present, nothing could be absent. To be present was not to be a spectator –it was to participate in the process of re-creation.

These considerations bear directly on the early history of the Papunya Tula painting movement, a phenomenon which uncannily fulfilled Strehlow's prophecy that 'in two or three generations' time – perhaps sooner – young aboriginal artists may begin to use again spirals, lines, and circles in a new, geometrical form of abstract art.'[150] According to Geoffrey Bardon, who as a schoolteacher at Papunya in 1971 was the catalyst of the new movement, Strehlow was both right and wrong. He was right in the sense that the art did become decoratively 'abstract'; from around 1979, 'the painters seem to have omitted the hieroglyphs which spoke to what was being done, and often simply covered an area with an intense patterning, brightly coloured and symmetrically right.'[151] But that was later; in the early days the artists worked differently. The designs they had once made in the sand or on each other's bodies, and which they now transferred to the permanent medium of paint on board, had what Bardon calls a 'hieroglyphic' power.[152]

It was not simply that, in contradiction to Strehlow's gloomy prognostications, the men gathered at Papunya retained a knowledge of their traditional stories and the designs expressive of them. What happened in 1971 was not a fulfilment of Strehlow's return to the 'elementary', an act of historical amnesia in which the Aranda and Pintupi men fulfilled the whitefella's nostalgia to discover a primitive other. Rather, to judge from Bardon's account, the significance of the new work resided in the fact that it actively set out to create a provisional space where a different kind of cultural transaction might begin to occur. The space was poetic, fulfilling Strehlow's desire for an 'Australian' art – although hardly in the form that he imagined it. The space was also political, the physical site of the Painting Room at Papunya providing a breathing-space within the architecturally-reinforced discourse of assimilation where another kind of colonial negotiation could be inaugurated.

The novelty of this was that it was contained in the hieroglyphic manner of the painting itself. The haptic engagement the paintings evidenced did not submissively mimic traditional forms; but nor did it exploit them decoratively. Rather, it 'deepened' their grooves, lending them a baroque elaborateness that might signify, on the one hand, a 'pidginization' of motifs for external consumption, but on the other hand could be seen as a way of informing them methektically, performatively, with an additional historical meaning. And at the heart of this process, it seems, was the role that Bardon played; not exactly as a catalyst, as this implies an external agent of change who remains unchanged himself, but as a participant in the creative act. Without his willingness to be seen to see, their efforts must have remained representative; but by entering into the process of the paintings' production, Bardon helped create a different kind of space, one of localized becoming rather than abstract being.

In this context, the circumstances in which the Papunya Tula movement began matter, not because of any (Western) preoccupation with chronology – and its art-historical sibling preoccupations, Genealogy and Originality – but because they establish the asymmetrically-folded nature of the historical ground; the fact not simply that what unfolded there depended on a circling mimicry, a tactical biculturalism, traditional in Central Australian Aranda culture (at least since Carl Strehlow's day), but that the coming-together of these cultural vortices through the mere coincidence of Bardon's provocative presence depended on a performative conception of the ground. In short, the art of Papunya embodied a different conception of history, one in which the opening and maintenance of a space in-between might occur, where impending cultural genocide could be held at arm's length, and room for an alternative destiny set aside.

In Bardon's published accounts of the *Honey Ant Dreaming* mural, whose painting on a schoolyard wall may be said to have inaugurated the painting movement (Plate 21), he mentions Obed Raggett only in passing. But Raggett's position in the Papunya community, as a gentle diplomat of the in-between, seems to have been critical to the initiation of the Papunya painting movement. 'From the Lutheran records he was technically a three quarter cast Aboriginal Aranda person from Hermannsburg, his grandfather having been Fred Raggett.' Raggett was multilingual, and a Christian: 'Obed said grace in Pintupi for the entire school every lunch time . . . All his training came from Hermannsburg and the Lutheran movement.' At the same time, he respected his own people's beliefs: 'Although he was a Christian, he could also be thought of as a fringe tribal person.' His in-betweenness was reflected in his occupation of one of 'the grotesque transitional houses' which the white authorities, in their assimilationist wisdom, had erected at Papunya.[153]

These barn-like sheds, their curvilinear corrugated-iron roofs suspended far above the ground on spindly stilts, half-walled, concrete-slabbed, would make a worthwhile study in themselves. Permanently, and so dysfunctionally, directional, unlike a temporary Aranda shelter; shadowing an undifferentiated space, its floor of uninscribable hardness, something like the burnt-out ruin of an old Community Hall, they are the architectural embodiment of the assimilationist fallacy. The common ground they created was off the ground, placeless, pointless, uninhabitable. Nevertheless, 'Obed had made particular improvements to his accommodation . . . He had built windbreaks of corrugated iron around the verandah perimeter and within the verandah and this was quite different from what I recall of the other families.'[154]

In any case, Obed Raggett became Bardon's 'translator and classroom assistant in 1971 during my very first days at Papunya. He became an integral part of my art teaching, had duties such as calling the roll and collecting lunch money from the Pintupi children.' Bardon notes, 'I was the only one of fourteen staff to use a translator':

> On the famous occasion of the making of the murals, Obed's participation was like this: I said to him, "Would you like to help me make a mural?" and he said, "Yes". I have not previously gone into the detail of it but the making of the mural was in three stages. Firstly, Obed and I made some imaginary Aboriginal designs on large pieces of paper on the floor of the classroom in which I taught, after I had

removed all the tables and chairs from the room and the children had gone. These designs were zig-zags, spirals and some of the dotting seen by me on the *Tjurungas*. The designs were, as I said, imaginary, and Obed made no comment upon them other than to assist me, with great warmth. After we did the designs on the floor of the classroom on the paper, we went downstairs under the school and again painted these designs and variants of them onto the rough cement which was quite unenclosed.

The making of the designs on the exposed cement floor in the school and in the classroom took days of work. After I had completed the work with Obed on the ground, it occurred to me to draw the same motifs on the walls which were quite nearby the rough ground. I had said to Obed, "We will paint these classroom pictures on the wall and make them flash." He would simply nod and continue working as I asked him to. It was at this moment, after the work was completed on the floor underneath the school, that our activities had become known to the yardmen, including Long Jack and the others, and at the moment when I began to apply the designs to the wall, the yardmen then approached me. I spoke to Obed at all times in English since my Pintupi was not sufficiently fluent at that time. The yardmen, I recall, after they had begun talking among themselves, talked to Obed and not to me at first, so that Obed was the intermediary, most significantly so at that moment. The rest of the story about the murals follows on from my other narratives.[155]

There, Bardon has explained how, after a series of negotiations, the group of Pintupi men took over the painting operation, producing under the direction of Kaapa Tjampatjinta, an Anmatjira Aranda man, five further murals, including the well-known and much-reproduced *Honey Ant Dreaming*. This success encouraged other men to want to paint; Bardon provided materials, and before long five or six groups of men joined in what he refers to as 'the sudden blossoming of their traditional art.'[156] In Bardon's view, the painting movement consequently went through three phases. In the first, the artists used mainly small boards to represent sacred objects, the *tjurungas*, 'bullroarers' and the like. In the second, they no longer represented these sacred objects but transferred their designs directly to the painting boards themselves. This is the phase where, to use Bardon's terminology, the Western Desert painters harnessed a 'graphic vocabulary [that can] accurately be seen as hieroglyphic': 'The painters appear to understand space as an emotional idea, or form, or hieroglyph,' and he adds, 'their capacity to feel the hieroglyph seems often to exclude any need to visualise what is represented.'[157] In the third phase, already referred to, hieroglyphs were omitted.

This is a conveniently linear history of the Papunya movement, but its rise and fall pattern hardly does justice to the facts. It is not simply that an artist like Clifford Possum Tjapaltjarri continued throughout the 1980s to produce large-scale works of astonishing compositional integrity and poetic power.[158] It inadequately suggests the performative nature of the art movement in its early stages, the sense that the distinctive style it evolved was a response to the invitation that Bardon and Raggett extended (which was equally extended to them) to enter an in-between space where social relationships would be renegotiated performatively, where the painters and their white 'teacher' improvised a creative dialogue. So, for example, Bardon distinguishes between a *Water Dreaming* painted by Johnny Warrangkula Tjupurrula in the School Room in 1972 (Plate 22) and a painting of the same subject requested by Bardon fifteen months later (Plate 23). The latter painting shows an advance in painting technique combined with a decline in haptic expressiveness. Superior in terms of finish, meticulousness of in-fill, compositional symmetry and decorative allure, it lacks the emotional quality of the earlier painting, where the 'dotting' of the surface is highly-accented, irregular and incomplete.

In fact, the earlier painting is not dotted. Rather, the marks that later contract to mechanically-replicated fields of dots are in this earlier work *macchie* in the Venetian sense, haptic gestalts corresponding directly to the artist's state of mind and body. As I interpret it, Vivien Johnson misunderstands Bardon when she attributes to him the claim that dotted infilling originated with Tjupurrula; as she points out, 'dotting' was traditional in Central Australian body-decoration,[159] and indeed it features widely in rock-painting and petroglyphs. But Bardon's point was different. As he writes, 'dots in Vivien Johnson's sense did not temporarily disappear in the Papunya painting room. They were a stylistic device used by Johnny Warrangkula. They became small haptic "splashes" during my time perhaps because of the intensity of my relationship with Johnny.' And Bardon comments: 'The word splash is perhaps inappropriate. An appropriate description is an elongated dot, or hatching with overdotting creating a tremulous illusion, at his best.'[160]

In short, the traditional dotting has become intensified, coming to resemble (technically) the Venetian art of *macchiare*; coming to look like the tremulous light experienced by Cavalcanti. And just as this sense of light-pummelled air is for the Florentine poet a kinaesthetic writing or glyph of the intensity of his relationship with the other, so for Bardon it is born of the closeness of his rapport and identification with the Loritja master. Dotting might have been traditional, but it was Warrangkula's distinction to give it a new hieroglyphic status, and Bardon notes that numerous paintings from the first eight months of the movement (before Tim Leura or Clifford Possum chose to become involved) 'have no dotting. They simply stand with the hieroglyphics, the graphic power of the image.'[161]

Bardon has explained his use of the term 'hieroglyph' as an attempt to encapsulate the world-view of the Western Desert painters: 'The painters appear to understand space as an emotional idea, or form, or hieroglyph, and their capacity to feel the hieroglyph seems often to exclude any need to visualise what is represented. The painters have given emotional coherence to the idea of space by assuming something that has been lost to other cultures for millenia: that one sees in relation to an existing social organisation.'[162] In this culture, the landscape is not seen, it is narrated; it is not static, but endlessly mobile. As Bardon writes: 'In the original sand paintings the painters could, in an instant and at will, change a hieroglyph, making it neither exclusive nor permanent. The same story could be rearranged into endless variants of hieroglyph clusters. There is no sense of words being read simultaneously with an image, for the word and the image are the same. It is as though the entire landscape were made up of a lexicon in which visual "words", in their apparently inexhaustible interrelationships, dynamically create and recreate the landscape apprehended by the painters.'[163]

But this brilliant description still fails to explain why, in Bardon's estimate, the hieroglyphic phase of the Papunya Tula school was precipitated by, and largely coincided with, his own residency. The retreat into decorativeness, a non-essential abstraction, had to do partly with disputes within the Aboriginal community regarding the ownership of designs and the propriety of their being exhibited and sold. It also reflected the inherently conservative nature of the white art-market. But these negative factors hardly account for the positive fact: the miraculous outpouring of paintings, as remarkable for quality as quantity, associated with Bardon's eighteen-month spell as a teacher. 'In the painting room,' he writes, 'there was usually an absorbed silence, broken occasionally by chanting or pleased laughter. Often the painters used secret/sacred designs but abandoned them when they realised that they might cause controversy. They were amused because I did not want to know any of their secrets behind such designs, but all I wanted was for them to paint non-controversial designs that would earn them good money . . . I did not want [their graphic symbols and motifs] to be changed and advised against "whitefellow" elements.'[164]

Bardon was evidently smart ahead of his time. He foresaw that difficulties would arise from the use of sacred material, so he directed the artists unsentimentally towards sales. But still, this combination of diplomatic and entrepreneurial skills hardly explains the emotional energy that produced the hieroglyphic painting. From my conversations with Bardon, it is clear that his advice against using '"whitefellow" elements' did not occur in a social or, for that matter, political void. It was one element in his characterization of the painting-sessions as performances, as consciously improvised acts of self-empowerment which he not only oversaw but actively directed and channelled. When Bardon urged the men to 'paint it flash, cheeky, strong, happy' and told them, using cattleman's pidgin, 'we gotta catch that man' (i.e. that customer), he addressed the men as he would have addressed children, coaxing, criticizing, praising; but with this crucial difference, that with the men he transparently *mimicked himself*, entering into the performance by playing his whitefellow role.

Bardon has described warm-up sessions with the men. Before they settled down to painting, he would throw a ball to them one by one. 'I throw,' he would say; and they would reply – I take it good-humouredly, banteringly, signifying their willingness to enter into a two-way transaction – 'I catch'. Bardon has emphasized that both inside and outside the painting room he organized his transactions with the men formally, even ritualistically. His respect for their culture avoided being patronizing because he predicated it on his own vulnerability, on his request that they respect his status as a teacher. Within this improvised social framework, things loosened up.

Bardon did not so much verbalize as choreograph his teacherly role. As he walked about from one group of painters to another, he would reward particularly slow or mechanical progress by pretending to fall asleep and snoring loudly. Another painter, progressing too obsessively, too quickly, would find Bardon at his shoulder, leaning over him, whispering, never loudly, 'Stop there.' And laughing. Pulling a face. It was as if Bardon was regrounding that room, taking his cues from the progress of the painting; and in return, drawing the painters to perform for him in a style, and with an intensity, that had no precedent. Elaborating on his published account, Bardon recalls: 'While the men were painting they certainly hummed. They chatted, sang boisterously, they whistled and there was a great deal of laughter. The atmosphere was dynamic. I often clowned for the Aboriginal men and I am quite a good mimic. For example, I would pretend to snore for Shorty Lungkata. There was a great deal of humour in my relationship with the painters; there was a loving relationship between myself and the painters. There was conversation but the priority to all of us was the painting purpose.'[165]

In this mimetically-exuberant situation, the hieroglyph assumed a new significance. It became the embodiment of the situation's creative flexibility, its power to draw those involved into a new relationship with one another and with their surroundings. The motifs were traditional, but they were not reproduced by traditional means or in a traditional context. They were invoked out of context to create a new context, as acts of diplomacy, as methods of improvising a new grounding of black-white relations under colonialism. It is in this context of autonomous evolution that Bardon can describe the hieroglyph in terms that recall the linguistic theories of the Russian Modernists: 'The hieroglyph is a gestural word, a thing in itself, and the painters' ideographic vocabulary is a systematic use of the environment to form meaning clusters or "words". The paintings are calligraphic, austerely linear visualisations. The originality of the late painting of May to July 1972 seemed to me to arise in part because this vocabulary was retained, and the sand did talk, and also in part because the gestural, hieroglyphic articulations were expanded by abstract yet highly Aboriginal figurations of animals, birds and men.'[166]

In short, the creative, additive flexibility of the hieroglyph furnished the Papunya painters with a gestural grammar that could ground the history of colonization differently. But in so far as this development was inseparable from Bardon's willingness to step out of his white *persona* and, without any literal desire to identify with their condition, to don the mask of the clown or the joker, it also inaugurated the possibility of a post-colonial poetics. Briefly, a community was created whose economy of exchange was based on the circulation of the gift, on the performance of giving. A right to the land was asserted, but it was asserted in terms of the re-inscription of the no man's land of the Painting Room, as a place where people could live.

The power released there, at once poetic and political, to ground the future differently remains potential. Fearfulness saw that the school was later pulled down; the same fearfulness will, in a misplaced spirit of piety, I predict, see to it that the school is one day rebuilt to commemorate what happened there. But the grounding of a society adumbrated there fell outside these bleak, architecturally-imagined historical enclosure acts. It was intended to institute a different mode of exchange, one that acknowledged the coexistence simultaneously of many stories on a shared but not owned ground. The irony that this group empowerment depended on their powerlessness as individuals was inescapable; double vision was integral to their stance. Imagining the ground, they were anti-fundamentalist. They turned the outward mimicry of colonial oppression into an inward mimicry. They insisted that the planar surfaces that surrounded them were folded, full of sounds.

Bardon has written of the 'simultaneity' of the Papunya Tula paintings: 'As simultaneity is pre-eminently a symbolic way of reducing all understanding to space, the hieroglyph becomes idiomatic, contingent, provisional, qualified by its dynamic relationship with other hieroglyphs.'[167] This may gloss the middle voice in which, as it were, these works are made, but the notion of 'simultaneity' may be misleading. The practice of the Western Desert painters can, Bardon says, be compared with the way in which Robert Delaunay used the concept of simultaneity, interpreting the picture-frame critically as suggesting a fourth dimension, inviting the viewer to become peripatetic, to walk round the picture plane, imaginatively at least to view the painting from every side at once. But the simultaneities cultivated by the Orphists, no less than the Cubists, the Futurists and the Suprematists, presupposed what Gibson calls the aperture perspective of Western linear logic. They presented themselves as a poetic trick, an historically-transcendent *trompe-l'oeil*. As one Apollinaire scholar writes: 'Paradoxically, simultaneity is itself a fiction: two points of view or a multiplicity of aspects cannot be perceived simultaneously, but only sequentially.'[168]

By contrast, Bardon's account of the Papunya-Tula movement's beginnings suggests the opposite: that in those weeks and months, the artists and their teacher felt themselves reinserted into history. Of his posting to Papunya, Bardon has said, 'I believe I was set up by some destiny.'[169] And witnessing a communal manifestation of the human spirit that seemed to him, even at the time, little short of miraculous, he remembers, 'I prayed to be worthy of my high responsibility.'[170] These remarks recall the self-justifying rhetoric of the pioneer South Australian Lutheran missionaries almost a century earlier; but, to repeat, Bardon had no desire either to negate or to transcend differences. He wanted to deepen them, to keep alive a folded ground where different histories could surface and coexist – where simultaneities could endure. This was why he eschewed curiosity about the paintings' mythological significance. It was a necessary pose if he were to prevent their disappearance into the realm of representation and its semiotics of profit and loss.

In *Life Among the Aborigines*, Bill Harney reports wryly on his time as a patrol officer with the Northern Territory Department of Native Affairs. It fell to Harney, an inveterate drifter himself, to attempt to control the movement of Aborigines from one place to another. As he explained: 'The disruption of a tribe brings about migration, and the routes the migrating tribes travel along are called Drift lanes. Drift can come in by many methods, such as "footwalk", "motor", ship or canoe. The carrying of natives by ship and motor can be controlled by an ordinance that lays down that permits must be granted for anyone to remove natives from one district to another, but in spite of these laws drift did occur to swell the Karamalal tribe. So the Branch decided to establish settlements for the drifters, and at the same time control the drift.'[171] Needless to say, the initiative meets with little success; as an early colonial official in New South Wales once remarked, one might as well try 'to confine a flock of birds by tracing a circle round the place on which they have accidentally alighted.'[172] A judgement with which Harney would have heartily agreed.

It is against enclosure acts of this kind that this book is written. Ours is not a history of movement, not even of the directed and regulated movement associated with colonization. Instead, it draws attention to certain drift-lanes or counter-movements that these acts of linear oppression precipitate. As Harney makes plain, the drift is not random; it may tunnel a historical space in-between, but that should not be construed (in planar terms) as, say, occupation of a no man's land. Rather, it occurs down ancient routes or 'lanes' which, by this enforced movement, are re-grooved. The image of birds may be appropriate, as their migration is not linear, from one displacement to another, but consists of a slow oscillation up and down certain roads. Marked out is a history of spiralling returns that never quite come back to the beginning. The white administrators cannot see this, because they are indifferent to the lie of the land. Had they drawn the circle in accord with the dictates of the ground, understanding ground-marking performatively, there is no reason why their patterns might not have worked. Instead of an enclosure act, something might have been disclosed.

This was the significance of 'reversed perspective', which was not simply a continuation of the 'traditional' Byzantine style of depth-representation, but a reaction to it precipitated by the imperializing culture of the Florentines. It was a way of finding a place for the cloudy intermediate environment, of preserving the passage between foreground and background, between the architecturally-bordered grid of the piazza and the picturesquely-stacked woods and cliffs of the remote distance, that linear perspective could not accommodate. The newly-rationalized space of Alberti could not evoke our sense of the ground spreading out like a carpet; it could not entertain the possibility that the object of composing a landscape might be to represent the process of passage, the continuity in transformation linking us to our surroundings – and that the *piano nobile* prospects of a Baldovinetti or a Piero were, apart from their class interests, perversions of the naturally-mobile order of seeing.

In effect, 'reversed perspective' is not only an alternative space conception but embodies a refusal to rationalize the ground as flat. The art of *macchiare*, which makes all parts of the composition (near and far) stand up and forward, so that they enter into an endlessly-spiralling, even musical, dialogue with one another, is the equivalent of an auditory conception of mountainous echoes. In effect, the Venetian artists, unlike their Florentine brethren, continue to treat 'space' as a physical rather than a metaphysical idea. Space for them is always an embodied, multiplanar surface rather than a theatrical vacancy to be composed. It is processual, peripatetic, the equilibrium of palpitating light and shade evenly distributed across the surface corresponding to the easy lope of the walker's left-right.

Perhaps in this style of painting there is a reminiscence of walking, where the swing of left and right arm balances the swing of right and left legs; for in that balanced rhythm, one is not merely reminded of four-legged animal motion but of a correspondence between the two axes of our space – the horizontal and the vertical. The rise and fall of arms, which mimic the thrust and draw of the painter's brush, are timed to the march, the meander, the wandering line of feet on the ground; the ground, 'the table' that comes between the painter and his subject, which blocks the field for walking in order that it may be painted, is the earth's surface symbolically mapped, its topography represented as an ever-deepening impression of paint, of dark and light 'passages' in both senses of the word. Venetian space is not 'space' in the abstract Western sense of an accommodating emptiness. Mountainous, echoic, it recognizes the ground as simultaneously the foundation of the painting and its subject; and just as the ground of the painting is subsequently valleyed and mountained with chiaroscuro, so the environment it portrays is similarly pocked, rounded, folded, pierced and caverned.

The enclosure acts of colonizing history produce their counter-acts, the emergence of drift-lanes. To resist the planarization of time and space is not to set oneself up as a trackless nomad; desert nomadism of this kind is a projection of the West's own nostalgia for a less highly-regulated form of movement – but it takes for granted a cleared and trackless field of operation. Rather, it is to refuse to adopt the off-the-ground perspective that makes possible the identification of ground-grooving with the process of exclusive enclosure and dispossession. From another perspective, the enhanced heights and depths of the land might disclose the natural containments of the earth's surface, and their topological continuities as they tip over from one incline into another, rearing and falling, folding and unfolding.

To conceive of enclosures as arbitrary delimitations is already to visualize them in a particular way, as marks on the ground whose significance lies outside them. The fence, the fosse, the dyke, even the hidden ha-ha, may be robustly physical, unlike the drawn line that represents them, but they are not constructed with a respect for their environmental proportions. They are not construed as folds facilitating curvilinear progress across a transforming earth, but as obstacles to movement. Blocking our passage, they rule out the need to represent drift-lanes, those pathways that respect the lie of the land. The new hedges correspond to the curtain walls that in Giorgione's *Madonna and Saints* or Masaccio's Brancacci frescoes conveniently divide foreground from background, and thus preserve the illusion of flatness. They are like steps, non-places in the landscape that nevertheless serve to define that landscape as a cinematographic succession of prospects. But the effect of this process of digitalization is to outlaw the analogue motion on whose experience their interpretation depends.

Edges, being lines of sorts, imply a motion, an impetus or momentum. They are the aggregation of footsteps, and correspond to the Aranda artist's recognition that no dot exists in isolation but is always on its way to becoming a ring. So with footsteps: they presuppose an earlier step, they project a future step, being constituted essentially as a rhythmic measure. This, incidentally, is the fateful obscenity of Robinson Crusoe's discovering a single footprint on the shore; the relationship between colonizer and colonized, between master and slave, is always conducted as if between monopods. No common measure is permitted to emerge. The slightly ridged and sloping sand is not recognized as a carpet projecting many figures. Instead, it is mined to build walls – against which the previously-hesitant fluctuations of the waves now beat with servile aggression.

Footsteps make a discontinuous line. As a trace of movement, they are read for their elemental properties of depth, irregular pressure, direction, and for the drift of weather across them. Footsteps move and have no edges; they do not cut across or edge along but maintain a balanced rhythm with the ground. Compare this intuition of the track with our highroad or pavement. It might be thought that these formalize the conditions of walking by providing a flat surface, one where the risk of tripping or falling is minimized. But this is not so; these planes, which retain no trace of the foot or imagine motion as a continuous sliding across (like a wheel's rim, or the blade of the skate, or even the stylus in the old record groove), are a negation of the way in which we move upon the earth. They set the foot at sea; they take away from it the motive for stepping out, which is to determine a way over the ground. On these asphalt expanses, the foot appears to enjoy a new freedom; it is no longer bound by the danger of potholes, inclines and declines. But this appearance of liberation disguises a real enclosure.

For surfacing the earth in this way, negating the charge of the lie of the land, that discontinuous, or folded, surface to which our way of footing it is adapted, has the effect of rendering our walking a largely symbolic activity. No longer can the peripateia be exploratory or constitutional;

walking not on the ground but on the negation of ground, our motion can only be construed as a sign of something else – an intention, an emotion. We come to think of walking as we think of other lines, including hedges and their 'other', the highroad, as purely mental or psychological states, as passages from one 'place' to another. Pavements drag the foot down, although admittedly their depressive quality depends on the materials out of which they are built. Pavements which retain something of the quality of stepping-stones have, for me at least, a springiness that is enlivening. The nature of this 'spring' can be defined, and derives from the subtle contouring of the (usually) limestone slabs – a quality of weathering which creates concentric rings, puddles, a sense of the ground rising to meet the walker and answering his downward pressure with a vectorial intent of its own.

Now this 'dialogue' between foot and ground, this sense of convergence, of coincidence, involves an enclosure act quite antithetical to the kind discussed earlier. Here the act of enclosure does not take the form of drawing a line about, of scoring a surface especially prepared or preconceived for the purpose of owning it exclusively. Rather, it is expressed in terms of a region of pressure, an imprint in the earth which does not establish a sharp distinction between that which is imprinted and that which is unmarked, but on the contrary accents the earth as such. And rather than represent a marker or boundary, it celebrates the earth as a commonplace, as a space manifold whose history is composed of vibrating tracks, crossing through and over one another. Here, enclosure is the condition of becoming; footsteps lead on. A single step is a monstrosity, because it can only be interpreted as a sign of what is missing. But footsteps setting out across the ground work differently. They are not to be compared with dotted lines on a map, linking places; nor even with those imaginary lines indicating contours, pressure gradients or coastlines. They correspond more to fields and tones, the individual peculiarities of the foot's impression providing in this sense a distinct timbre.

Furthermore, these impressions do not occur 'on' the ground, or even 'in' it. They are vibrations of the ground itself – of the human ground but for which our becoming would be fixed as a timeless 'being'. In this sense, footsteps are constitutive of the ground. The ground is named as our connection with the earth; in our pressed patterning of it – and in its own differentiation – we both found ourselves and reproduce the earth's own founding; our footsteps are also footprints, our wanderings are also designs. This momentary kinetic coincidence, a form of expression that is not writerly – an enclosure act that is not semiotic, not predicated on an opposition between fleeting presence and enduring absence – enables us to understand the lie of the land as a process of enclosure, in the 'open sense' of giving to the elements a form which is their identity but which does not rupture their dependence on their surroundings. But even this understanding has to recognize the extent to which the lie of the land, like the term enclosure, has been subject to cultural (and physical) engineering.

The river is not 'enclosed' by the banks between which it flows; the sloping edges constitute it as a river. It is the lie of the land that gives the element of water a form which is its identity. The river, the directed flow of water in a narrow band, is inconceivable apart from the lie of the land that brings it into being. And yet the form of the river has been historically, as well as geomorphologically, produced. The *beau ideal* of the river – navigable, with steady currents, firm banks, deep and free of obstacles – has had to be constructed: the eighteenth-century canal, smooth, submissive, its flow turned off or minimized, and the turbine-powering waterfall are its corollaries, and recapitulate the Greek desire to interpret movement as either rectilinear or circular. Other modes of water-flow illustrate the 'open' act of enclosure in other ways. The anastomosing waters of the Australian interior – occasional, reversing the linear perspective of progress – articulate the lie of the land each time they begin to flow. And after the flowing out has lost its strength and the water lowered sufficiently to form necklaces of waterholes or billabongs, the resulting constellation of ponds reveals an inverted landscape, one where the depths are marked out with watery footsteps. It is the rocks that provide these shallow chalices, and the clouds print memories of their passage when they leave them temporarily brimming with water.

From the point of view of Lockean enclosure, the mutable aspect of the land is offensive, as it suggests an unenclosed temporality which has to be channelled or rendered circular. Enclosure translates space into place; it asks the world to quieten down, to become a surface where meanings may be planted. An environment where parts continue to discover connections with one another is not only one in which the removal of a single element is noticed, it is also one where temporarily-absent elements can be expected to return; rain will come and the country spread out, firm land evaporate. Such a forthcoming will not be at all theatrical – a chaotic departure from the 'normal'. It will be methektically countenanced by the cloud-like forms that pockmark the ground, and which human technology may also mimic. The form of the land, its design, is in this view the spirit of its creation. The declivities, rock-falls, outcrops and depressions are the shape of their own being; they do not represent the outcome of geological history, but the pattern of their own movement, their animate constitution.

This idea, expressed by Aboriginal artists, is equally congenial to physicists, who jettison the old distinction between mass and energy, content and form, realizing that the opposition is meaningless, but it remains strange to a culture whose ancient enclosure act, its translation of the world's phenomena into forms of linear writing, makes difficult the apprehension of those enclosures that disclose. While we may descry a convergent, or at least parallel, evolution between the landscape paintings of Fred Williams and the the dot-and-circle productions of the Papunya Tula school, we also have to recognize the antithetical philosophical premisses informing them. Williams looks for a grammar in a visually chaotic or grammarless nature, aiming to refine a visual impression; his paintings intend to be a representation of the essential character of the view before him. His dotted canvases mimic the distribution of trees on the stone plains of Victoria; they wonderfully explore their structureless scatter, finding there a corollary of a different way of seeing – one able to investigate reversed perspective, free of the desire to compose unilaterally.

In contrast, the Papunya dot technique originates in a *techne*, in a mode of body-painting. The dots do not stand for something, but mark the bounds and forms of patterns; the repertoire of patterns do not stand in for landscape forms, but reproduce their histories, the movement over the landscape which brought, and continues to bring, them into being. Similarly, the designs of Rover Thomas do not map the country, but offer a template of its coming into being; the patterns of dark and light, deep and pale, fringed with white dots, which themselves border pathways around and between these closed regions of colour, evoke certain tonal relationships in the history of the locality. The form the outlines take are zoomorphic or ancestor-like only in the sense that the animating forces producing the landscape assume, in becoming places, just these prodigious forms. Because of this complete coincidence, there is no reason to 'fill in' the blanks, to decorate the interiors of these sombre zones. The event, the history they contain, is coeval with the shape of the mark, with its spaciousness on the canvas, its air of gravity. Only where the land has been violated are these open grounds invaded by images – the coffin and the skull, recalling the Ruby Plains Killing, also recall the intrusion of 'history', the false and jarring ideology of signs.[173]

Williams's lightness of touch, his scatter of marks, corresponds to a moment in the evolution of a distinctively Australian landscape aesthetic. Against the European taste for the monumental, the theatrical, the picturesque, Williams explores the pleasures of a landscape whose forms are underdetermined. Like the novelist Gerald Murnane, he takes pleasure in evacuating the landscape of prior associations, histories, stories in order to project on to it an image of the modern homeless wanderer. He poses as an aesthete of mirages, flat grasslands, basalt plains; he seeks to recuperate the planar, to find in the minute variations of its surface instances of hidden or missed itineraries. This is one, characteristically modern form of lightness; but the paintings of Rover Thomas point to another kind of lightness, free of this constitutional self-enquiry – free, too, of its *alter ego*, a tendency to self-enclosure. In Thomas's work there is no sunlight, no glittering images; the surfaces are characteristically sombre, and the forms, although topologically mobile and in-wound, are themselves stable, posed and quiet. His canvases evince an enormous sense of uncentred calm, of a nuanced conviction of the earth's spread and compassion. Here, the opposition between light and dark makes no sense, any more than it makes sense to oppose left and right foot; his canvases evoke the movement-in-stillness of a world where parts are balanced, where forces flow across boundaries and down sinuous pathways, without looking to left or right – without having to see at all. To see, or at least to see panoptically, is to have lost touch with the drift-lanes – not to know where to put one's feet.

When the colonizing nations of the West sit down at the negotiating table with the world's indigenous peoples, they will need to have something to offer. It will not be enough to admit the original wrong of invasion. Legal measures acknowledging the prior occupancy of indigenous cultures, and giving back to them a degree of self-determination, cannot restore what has been taken away. And even if they could, they would merely represent a belated recognition of what colonized peoples have always known: that they were here first and, unlike the invaders, enjoyed a legitimate relationship with the land. Indigenous people say that Westerners have lost their dreaming. They deduce this from colonialism itself; had the Spaniards, the British, the Dutch been at home in the lands of their birth, they would have had no motive for seeking out and invading other countries. Even Westerners often buy into this view: we are replete with histories which show European greed and brutalization in unholy symbiosis with the historical forces of capitalism and industrialization. Around the time the cannon was invented – or it may have been the printing press, or linear perspective – Europeans shuffled off the last vestiges of spiritualism; they became rootless rationalists.

Colonialism was the consequence: a people without a dreaming, without an attachment to the land, were machines for free movement. They were robots or ghosts, these landless wanderers. Armoured in wonder-working technology, and vulnerable to the agoraphobia all must feel who have no place they can call their own, they proved a fearsome, and as it turned out irresistible, force. But this did not change the fact that the whites, the Europeans, with their gun-running, their money-changing, their sexism and their photography, were essentially unreal. Perhaps this self-flagellating logic is meant to placate the descendants of the native dead. But this latter-day self-abasement has the opposite effect: it confirms non-Western peoples in their view that we have lost our way. It is well known that traders who talk up their wares are not to be trusted, but what are we to make of men and women who say they no longer have anything to exchange except their own historical tragedy? This is hardly playing the game; and besides, there are practical issues to be sorted out, about the environment and its management, about the alleviation of suffering, the cessation of war.

As we come to the negotiating table, it will not be enough to right the wrong, to redraft the history books, to rewrite the statute books. Indigenous and non-indigenous peoples will need to find something in common; they will need to find a reason to stay together. Beyond the dictates of economic and political pragmatism, they will need to discover common interests. Hitherto, the process has been one-sided: anthropologists, educators, therapists and prophets have beaten a path to the shamans and witch-doctors and brought back remedies for a civilization sick at heart, but there has rarely been any spiritual exchange in the other direction. From the West has come solely magic technology, and while the Utopian rationalism this embodied may once upon a time have justified the displacement of peoples from their lands, it now seems an admission of failure. Guns, drugs and diseases were exchanged in the absence of anything genuinely useful to say.

It will not be enough to express an interest in their traditional wisdom. To legitimate our curiosity, we will need to bring useful knowledge of our own to swap. And this will have to be something other than the latest scientific and technological know-how; it will have to represent a return to certain dreamings which our post-Renaissance history has generally suppressed in the interests of Progress. In particular, we will need to have to hand a different conception of the land and our relationship to it. Until we can overcome our obsession with exclusive ownership, it is not only the others but we who have nowhere defensible to stand. We cannot expect those across the table to furnish us with these concepts; we need to locate them within the neglected counter-traditions of our own culture.

We could do worse than begin by reflecting on the mechanism of the negotiating table and the model of communication it implies. What does this polished, horizontal surface hoisted off the ground signify? What history of violence does its pretence of smoothness, its equalization of places, conceal? We could do worse than ask: when did we in the West leave the ground? What was it about the uneven land that inspired our need to control it, to clear it of trees, to load it with buildings, to possess it with maps as if it were flat. The very idea of invasion and colonization presupposed a theatrical conception of space foreign to non-Western peoples. While the improved technologies for travelling may have made more of the earth's surface accessible to Europe, they also tended to characterize travelling as a narrowly linear, extra-territorial activity. The idea that one might travel in order to stay at home ceased to make sense. Equally, the idea that movement might be a primary condition of human existence, and sedentary nations an eccentricity – this became inconceivable.

Yet, I have tried to intimate, within the West a persistent counter-tradition opposed the ultimately Aristotelian view that the natural condition of things, whether objects or states, was one of stasis. It is no accident that within this counter-tradition, politics and poetics go hand in hand; for here it was intuitively understood that song and dance were means of measuring the ground, of demarcating the earth socially and historically. The polity that might result from such an equation was, admittedly, different from the one predicated on the table-smooth space of the agora. For example, it could seem anti-architectural, opposed in general to the accumulation of capital and the construction of treasure-houses. More fundamentally, it depended on the free circulation of objects and their continual renewal in use. It had little time for personality cults or myths of first contact. In compensation, it was able occasionally to achieve what all the armies and outworks of Greece and Rome could never manage: a sense of being lightly grounded.

In this context, the localism of *The Lie of the Land* is practically motivated. Its preference for deepening certain historical grooves in such a way that they begin to resonate and, although physically remote from one another on the planar floor of linear history, fold into each other on the uneven ground of historical experience – this preference is perhaps constitutional. For in effect, it is an attempt to incorporate formally the rhetoric of the lie of the land. If the metaphysical 'ground' of Western science represents an ideological enclosure act, if epistemological as well as ontological value must be given to the unevenly folded nature of the environment we inhabit, a writing that embraces this shifted perspective must, presumably, also accept its implications. It will not be panoptic, not attempt to see through the 'cloudy' passages where linear lines of descent are obscured. It will be 'poetic' in the derided sense given this term by serious historians and social scientists – but only because it refuses their off-the-ground generalization, and insists on deepening the differences.

Our intellectual flat-earthism is deeply embedded in our habitual modes of thinking. The environment inhabited by even so subtle an observer as J. J. Gibson 'tends to be on average flat'.[174] Kurt Lewin's topological psychology, developed in the 1930s, is in some respects an attempt to map the interpersonal drift-lanes that old-fashioned clinical psychology ignored. Lewin was something of a 'Venetian', writing that, so far as understanding the content of mental life was concerned, 'the transition from Aristotelian to Galilean concepts demands that we no longer seek the "cause" of events in the nature of a single isolated object, but in the relationship between an object and its surrounding.'[175] Even so, Lewin's 'life space' is conceived entirely horizontally; his diagrams of psychological regions, with their zones of power, their obstructed goals, their maze-like corridors, may or may not map behavioural forces, but they certainly bear a remarkable resemblance to the design and layout of modern 1930s office spaces.

Similarly, attempts to understand space conceptions in non-Western cultures have been vitiated by a failure to recognize that space itself is a distinctively Western concept. Pinxten, van Dooren and Harvey's study of the natural philosophy of the Navajo, *The Anthropology of Space*, or Weiner's *The Empty Place*, a lyrical account of 'poetry, space and being among the Foi of Papua New Guinea',[176] may intend to illuminate the cultures under study, but their result is instead to offer Western readers a meditation on the meaning of spatiality within their own culture. In Weiner's study, the song, dance and building of the Foi provides him with an elaborate vindication of Heideggerian concepts of time and space, but the prior process of territorialization, the act of 'paramnesia' on which this strategy depends,[177] is never acknowledged. Both studies proceed as if the locally uneven ground were irrelevant to their purpose; as if the space philosophies supposedly espoused by these peoples could be wholly disembodied from their history.

Studies of these kinds need to be grounded differently. Instead of perpetuating intellectual enclosure acts (however illuminating they may be to Western readers), they should be recast as exercises in diplomacy. The approach should not be dialectical, a diplomatic balancing-act based on the stereotyping of both cultures in the interests of manufacturing a series of pseudo-equivalences. This kind of metaphorical exchange may be 'poetic' in a bad sense. A better politics involves an examination of the grounds these exchanges presuppose; only out of this self-examination can the Western powers find those wares they need to bring to the negotiating table – among which will be the insight that the table was never bare or level: it bore within its surface the textures and patterns of its history of manufacture. Always sloping, rounded and grooved, it was always delicately balanced.

Transferred from Turi in Apulia, where he had been incarcerated since 1929, to a private hospital outside Rome, the political philosopher Antonio Gramsci wrote to his wife: 'What a terrifying experience it was to look out from the train after six years of seeing nothing but those roofs and walls, those surly faces, and to realise that the vast world had gone on existing with its meadows and woods and ordinary people, its flocks of boys and girls, its particular trees and vegetable gardens!' And Gramsci added, 'most of all, what a shock it was to look into a mirror after such a long time – it made me run back to the *carabinieri* . . .'[178] Against his best intentions, Gramsci had internalized the viewpoint of the prison, where the simultaneity of multiple existences is unthinkable. He had fixed the world in an image of the past, forgetting its endless, baroque capacity for proliferating instances of ordinary forms. His own face had gone on living, ageing, growing a stranger to his former self; so that the man who hated 'tossing stones into the dark' – 'I need an interlocutor, a concrete adversary . . . I have to create a dialogue'[179] – found that in prison he had not even been talking to himself.

Seeing the 'particular trees and vegetable gardens', Gramsci grasped the tragic meaning of an imprisonment as much historical as physical. It was to substitute the false ideology of exclusive possession for that of co-existence and co-occupancy; it was to confuse stasis with order – and to make motion identical with rebellion and chaos, as if the cultivated ground did not provide a mode of existence at once mobile and stable. It was, above all, to deny the fact of multiple historical and social worlds, whose ability to face away from each other and go lightly about their own tasks alone makes the process of exchange something more than a one-sided expropriation and domination. Whether the opposite intuitions which our history's enclosure acts throw up can provide a strategy in the creation of post-colonial societies may be open to question, but that in any case is another subject. The ambition of *The Lie of the Land* is different: not to prescribe the legal and political constitution of such societies, but to explore the necessity of a concomitant form of self-redefinition, which is poetic, being based on the discovery of common interests, common grounds, and not simply a formal truce.

This is not to advocate a further rationalization of relationships, to neutralize the uneven ground further, to bulldoze its ridges and ditches, to level off its gradients, and so complete the effacement of its mobile history. It is to seek to live in the storm of becoming, whose trace is the light-dark of torrents. But the storm would be changed by this; its gale would no longer spell disaster. The charge of thunder and lightning would no longer signify chaotic flight and dispossession. Its periodic turbulences would belong to the same economy of circulation evidenced in the perturbations of the sail swelling and contracting. Where in-breath and out-breath are two slopes of a single wave, there can be no slipping away into the loneliness of the colonial condition. To be on the move, to understand the measure of motion, its poetic basis, this would be a beginning. To be 'wild' where one is, this would make sense. But as Prynne writes:

> it is a very wild and
> distant resort that keeps a man, wandering
> at night, more or less in his place.

References and Notes

Introduction: Friday's Other Foot

1 Herbert, George, *The Works in Prose and Verse,* New York, 1869, p. 337.
2 Rilke, R. M., *Letters on Cezanne*, translated by J. Agee, London, 1988, p. 23.
3 Sturt, A. G., *Journals 1890–1927*, ed. E. D. Mackerness, Cambridge, 1967, vol 1, p. 66.
4 Strehlow, T. G. H., *Journals*, South Australian Museum Archives, I, p. 153.
5 Bradley, W., *A Voyage to New South Wales: The Journal of Lieutenant William Bradley of HMS Sirius 1786–1792*, Sydney, 1969, p. 59.
6 King, P. G., in Hunter, John, *An Historical Journal of the Transactions at Port Jackson and Norfolk Island*, Adelaide, 1968, p. 401.
7 Carter, P., *The Road to Botany Bay*, London, 1987, p. xvff.
8 Arago, Jacques, *Narrative of a Voyage around the World*, London, 1823, pp. 163–5. 'In the town, I beheld Europe, for European hands had raised it . . . You would imagine that our best architects had deserted Europe, and repaired to New Holland, to re-produce their most elegant designs.'
9 Quoted by Barnard, John, *John Keats*, Cambridge, 1987, p. 11. Shelley put it another way: 'The cultivation of those sciences which have enlarged the limits of the empire of man over the external world has for want of the poetical faculty proportionally circumscribed those of the internal world; and man, having enslaved the elements, remains himself a slave.' (*Shelley's Prose: or, The Trumpet of a Prophesy*, edited by D. Lee Clark, El Paso, 1966, p. 293.)
10 Tench, W., *Sydney's First Four Years,* Sydney, 1979, p. 51.
11 Southey, R., 'Elinor', Botany Bay Eclogues, *Poems*, Bristol, 1797, p. 81.
12 Collins, David, *An Account of the English Colony in New South Wales*, Sydney, 1975 [orig. pub. 1798]), vol 1, p. 5.
13 Bitterli, U., *Cultures in Conflict*, trans. R. Robertson, London, 1989, p. 137.
14 Easty, John, *Memorandum of the Transactions of a Voyage from England to Botany Bay 1787–1793*, Sydney, 1965, p. 78.
15 See Carter, P., *Living In A New Country*, London, 1992, pp. 83–4.
16 Defoe, Daniel, *Robinson Crusoe*, ed. J. D. Crowley, London, 1972, pp. 38 and 41.
17 Ibid., pp. 58–9.

18 Ibid., p. 60.
19 Ibid., pp. 153–4.
20 Ibid., p.156.
21 Ibid., p.157.
22 See note 36 of 'About Canoes' below.
23 Defoe, Daniel, *Robinson Crusoe*, pp. 203–4.
24 But where in Montaigne? The notebook where I copied this some years ago gives no clue. In this embarrassing situation my only consolation is that Montaigne was equally careless: 'I am so outstanding a forgetter that . . . I forget even my own words and writings . . . If anyone wanted to know the sources of the verse and *exempla* that I have accumulated here, I would be at a loss to tell him.' (De Montaigne, Michel, 'On Presumption', *The Essays of Michel de Montaigne*, trans. M. A. Screech, London, 1991, p. 740.)
25 Eckermann, J. P., *Conversations with Goethe*, trans. J. Oxenford, London, 1971, entry for 11 April 1827, pp. 186–7.
26 Toffler, A., Foreword to I. Prigogine and I. Stengers, *Order out of Chaos*, London, 1984, p. xiii.
27 Mandelstam, O., 'Conversation about Dante', *Selected Essays*, trans. S. Monas, Austin, 1977, p. 37.
28 Quoted by S. Craig, *Dreams and Deconstructions: Alternative Theatre in Britain*, Ambergate (Derbyshire), 1980, p. 14. Or Mandelstam again: 'Europeans are cast out of their biographies, like balls from the pocket of a billiard table' ('The End of the Novel', *Selected Essays*, p. 87).
29 Ibid., 'Notes about Chénier', p. 108.
30 See, for example, N. C. Canclini's analysis of this trend in the border town of Tijuana in 'Scenes without Territories: The Aesthetics of Migrations and Identities in Transition' in *Art from Latin America: La Cita Transcultural*, Sydney, 1993, p. 20.
31 Clark, J. 'The lost lives of our children ploughed under our asphalt,' *The Age*, 26 November 1994, p. 19.
32 Jeans, J., *Science and Music*, New York, 1968 [orig. pub. 1937], pp. 125–6.
33 Ibid., p. 127.
34 Canetti, E., *The Human Province,* London, 1978, p. 256. Elsewhere, Canetti describes 'A fear of Aristotlizing my thoughts: of divisions, definitions, and similar empty games.' (Ibid., p. 156). He characterizes Aristotle as an extreme case of the 'ordering' mind and contrasts him with 'The illuminating mind [which] is like lightning, it flashes rapidly over the greatest distances. It leaves everything aside and shoots for one thing, which it does not know before illuminating it.' (Ibid., pp. 200–1).
35 Jeans, J., *Science and Music*, p. 126.
36 Butler, S., *The Notebooks*, ed. H. F. Jones, London, 1913, p. 9.

Part One: A Reverent Miming

1 Strehlow, T. G. H., *Songs of Central Australia*, Sydney, 1971, p. 729.

2 For these details, see Strehlow, T. G. H., *Journals*, South Australian Museum Archives, I, p. 153ff. Also W. McNally, *Aborigines, Artefacts and Anguish*, Adelaide, 1981, p. 78. An incisive account of this period, based on the Strehlow *Journals*, is Philip Jones, 'Traveller Between Two Worlds' in *The Heritage of Namatjira*, ed. J. Hardy, J. V. S. Megaw and M. R. Megaw, Melbourne, 1992, p. 122ff.

3 Strehlow, T. G. H., *Comments on the Journals of John McDouall Stuart*, Adelaide, 1967, p. 13.

4 Strehlow, T. G. H., *Journey to Horseshoe Bend*, Adelaide, 1969, p. 28.

5 David Hugo, pers.comm., July 1994.

6 McNally, W., *Aborigines, Artefacts and Anguish*, p. 145.

7 Described, for instance, by C. Ellis in *Aboriginal Music*, St Lucia, 1985, p. 82ff.

8 The rift between the Hermannsburg Mission Society in Germany and the Immanuel Synod of South Australia, referred to in B. Henson, *A Straight-out Man*, Melbourne, 1994, p. 11, and in C. Stevens, *White Man's Dreaming*, Melbourne, 1994, pp. 142–3, recapitulated structurally the dispute over the sources of authority that plagued Light in South Australia nearly a century earlier (See 'Light Reading', p. 236).

9 Strehlow, T. G. H., *Journey to Horseshoe Bend*, pp. 17–19 and p. 170.

10 According to Vladimir Propp. Lévi-Strauss criticized Propp's structuralist account of the fairy-tale for a failure to take account of historical factors influencing its transformations. Still, Lévi-Strauss, like Propp, imagined change occurring internally, diachronically, within a sedentary, territorially-delimited population. A suggestive gloss on this unquestioned assumption comes from Calvino, who noted that the fairy-tale's capacity to substitute one structural element for another perfectly fitted it out for migration, from country to country, from one class to another. (See Vladimir J. A. Propp, *Morfologia della Fiaba*, Torino, 1988, and Lévi-Strauss's essay in the same volume. Also Italo Calvino, *Sulla Fiaba*, ed. M. Lavagetto, Torino, 1988, Introduction, p. 13.)

11 Strehlow, T. G. H., *Songs of Central Australia*, p. xvi. But Philip Jones describes Carl Strehlow's policy as a 'campaign against Aranda religion' ('Traveller Between Two Worlds', p. 120).

12 Strehlow, T.G.H., 'Nomads in No-Man's-Land', An Address delivered at the 9th Summer School, Adult Education Department, University of Adelaide, 20 January 1960, p. 13.

13 Jones, P., 'Traveller Between Two Worlds', pp. 123–6.

14 Ibid., pp. 136–7, note 62.

15 Charles Chewing's translation of C. Strehlow, *Die Aranda-und-Loritja-Stämme in Zentral Australien*, n.d., p. 1280. Microfilm held at South Australian Museum.

16 Morton, J., 'Country, People, Art: The Western Aranda 1870–1990', in *The Heritage of Namatjira*, p. 61.

17 Jones, P., op. cit., pp. 122–3.
18 Strehlow, T. G. H., *Journals* I, p. 155
19 Ibid., pp. 118–9.
20 Ibid., p. 119.
21 Strehlow, T. G. H., *Songs of Central Australia*, p. 593.
22 Strehlow, T. G. H., *Journals* I, p. 58. Thus, when referring to Strehlow's encouragement of performances whose future was immediately threatened, Jones describes him as 'the most anomalous figure in these developments' ('Traveller Between Two Worlds', p. 133.). The anomaly extends to Strehlow himself. At issue was the ambiguous nature of his own coming into being. Could the father be murdered without being murdered, resurrected without dying?
23 Strehlow, T. G. H., *Journals* I, p. 119.
24 Strehlow, T. G. H., *Journals* VII, p. 56, entry for 20 May.
25 'Almost invariably the threat [of rain] is an empty one, and after a period of silence and expectancy, the whole spectacle goes into reverse. The curtain splits up into detached masses, the sun breaks through, and within two hours the last trace of cloud has melted away, leaving the sky clear and hard as in the morning.' (H. H. Finlayson, *The Red Centre*, Sydney, 1936, p. 35.)
26 Strehlow, T. G. H., *Journals* I, p. 83.
27 Ibid., p. 10.
28 Strehlow, T. G. H., *Songs of Central Australia*, p. 230, note 286, and *Book of Daniel*, 9:15.
29 Strehlow, T. G. H., *Songs of Central Australia*, p. 460.
30 Strehlow, T. G. H., *Journals* I, p. 118.
31 Ibid., p. 150.
32 Ibid., p. 150.
33 Strehlow, T. G. H., *Aranda Phonetics and Grammar*, Sydney, c. 1944, p. 62. As an example of 'the new forms of intonation . . . being evolved by christianised aboriginals' at the Hermannsburg Mission, Strehlow cites the chanting of the Creed, where 'the "chords" at the beginning of each Article are pitched higher than towards the end; and all voices descend to a lower register at the conclusion,' and comments: 'Here we have a transference of an age-old native practice to the new sacred forms introduced by Christianity.' (*Songs of Central Australia*, pp. 32–3.)
34 Strehlow, T. G. H., 'Nomads in No-Man's-Land', p. 15.
35 Robinson, Roland, *The Shift of Sands*, Melbourne, 1976, p. 135.
36 Ibid., pp. 138–9.
37 Strehlow, T. G. H., *Journey to Horseshoe Bend*, p. 213.
38 Strehlow, T. G. H., *Journals* I, p. 153.
39 Strehlow, T. G. H., *Songs of Central Australia*, p. 555 and p. 599.
40 Ibid., pp. 235–6.
41 Ibid., p. 247.

42 Strehlow, T. G. H., *Journey to Horseshoe Bend*, pp. 212–3.
43 Strehlow, T. G. H., 'Foreword' to Battarbee, Rex, *Modern Australian Aboriginal Art*, Sydney, 1951, p. 6.
44 Strehlow, T. G. H., 'Nomads in No-Man's-Land', p. 35.
45 Ibid., p. 15.
46 Carter, P., *Living in a New Country*, London, 1992, p. 71.
47 Battarbee, Rex, *Modern Australian Aboriginal Art*, p. 47.
48 Strehlow, T. G. H., *Rex Battarbee: artist and founder of the Aboriginal art movement in Central Australia*, Sydney, 1956, pp. 5 and 10.
49 Battarbee, Rex, *Modern Australian Aboriginal Art*, pp. 11–12.
50 Strehlow, T. G. H., *Aranda Phonetics and Grammar*, p. 188.
51 Strehlow, C., *Galtjindinjamea-pepa: Aranda-wolambarinjaka; nana intalelamala*, Tanunda, 1924.
52 Rouse, T., 'Painting from Memory: Art, Economics and Citizenship 1940–1960' in *The Heritage of Namatjira*, p. 179.
53 Blumenberg, Hans, *The Genesis of the Copernican World*, trans. R. M. Wallace, Cambridge (Mass), 1987, p. 202.
54 See particularly Jenny Green, 'Country in Mind: The Continuing Tradition of Landscape Painting' in *The Heritage of Namatjira*, p. 284ff.
55 Strehlow, T. G. H., *Journals* VII, p. 134.
56 Battarbee, Rex, *Modern Australian Aboriginal Art*, p. 10.
57 'The five-mile trench for the pipeline was dug across limestone country by Hermannsburg men.' (Henson, B., *A Straight-out Man*, photo caption facing p. 142.)
58 Strehlow, T. G. H., *Journey to Horseshoe Bend*, pp. 218–9.
59 Ibid., p. 219.
60 Ibid., p. 219.
61 Strehlow, T. G. H., *Journals* X, p. 22. This journal is remarkable for its fragmentary rain-song translations. Cumulatively, they form a vast midden of kennings, ruins of an epic poem yet to be written.
62 See note 198 to 'Light Reading' below.
63 Strehlow, T. G. H., *Songs of Central Australia*, p. 459.
64 Strehlow, T. G. H., Foreword to Battarbee, Rex, *Modern Australian Aboriginal Art*, p. 4.
65 Ibid., p. 5. And see also *Aranda Traditions*, p. 6, and *Songs of Central Australia*, p. 704, where Strehlow further discusses his thesis.
66 T.G.H. Strehlow, 'Foreword' to Battarbee, Rex, *Modern Australian Aboriginal Art*, p. 5.
67 Rees, Leslie, 'Modern Australian Aboriginal Art', *The Australian Quarterly*, December 1951, p. 91. I am indebted to Ian McLean for this reference.
68 As it might appear from the other direction, looking towards the water-tank at Hermannsburg where the pipe emerges above ground.
69 Battarbee, Rex, *Modern Australian Aboriginal Art*, p. 12.
70 Ibid., p. 12.

71 Ibid., p. 19.
72 Strehlow, T. G. H., 'Foreword' to Battarbee, Rex, *Modern Australian Aboriginal Art*, p. 7.
73 Battarbee, Rex, *Modern Australian Aboriginal Art*, p. 27.
74 '[Strehlow says] that of all the Australian aboriginal tribes that he knows the Arunta has the most ornamentation in its literature, art and music and that the music is full of rhythm. Some of the chants have up to thirteen beats to the bar.' (Rex Battarbee, *Modern Australian Aboriginal Art*, p. 27.)
75 Ibid., p. 23. Otto is compared to Van Gogh (p. 27).
76 Ibid., p. 44.
77 Ibid., p. 44.
78 Strehlow, T. G. H., 'Central Australian Religion', Bedford Park (SA), 1978, Special Studies in Religions Series, 2, p. 34. This essay was originally published in 1964 as 'Personal Monototemism in a Polytotemic Community'.
79 For this thesis, see T. G. H. Strehlow, 'Central Australian Religion', p. 32 and, for example, J. Harrison, *Themis,* London, 1989 [orig. pub. 1911]), p. 450ff.
80 Battarbee, Rex, *Modern Australian Aboriginal Art*, pp. 52–3.
81 Ibid., p. 52.
82 Strehlow, T. G. H., *Songs of Central Australia*, p. 658.
83 Ibid., p. 585, note 563.
84 Harrison, J., *Themis*, p. 122.
85 Roheim, G., *Australian Totemism*, London, 1971 [orig. pub. 1925], p. 337ff, also pp. 367 and 402ff. Strehlow's vigorous insistence that the Aranda exclusively worship the earth is motivated in part presumably by his determination to discredit Roheim's thesis. (See *Songs of Central Australia*, p. 435.)
86 Strehlow, T. G. H., *Songs of Central Australia*, p. 704.
87 Strehlow, T. G. H., *Rex Battarbee: artist and founder of the Aboriginal art movement in Central Australia*, p. 35.
88 Ibid., p. 36.
89 Ibid., p. 20.
90 Ibid., p. 41.
91 Strehlow, T. G. H., *Songs of Central Australia*, p. 728.
92 Ingamells, R., 'Unknown Land', *Selected Poems*, Melbourne, 1944, p. 39.
93 Ibid., p. 39.
94 See, for example, McNally, W., *Aborigines, Artefacts and Anguish*, pp. 93–4.
95 Strehlow, T. G. H., *Songs of Central Australia*, p. xv.
96 McNally, W., *Aborigines, Artefacts and Anguish*, p. 20, and Catherine Ellis, pers. comm., May 1994.
97 Strehlow, T. G. H., *Aranda Phonetics and Grammar*, p. 106. 'In the European languages the stress is laid upon a pleasing variety of moods and compound tenses; in Aranda it is laid upon a rich display of derivative

verbs, all used in one or two simple moods and tenses.'

98 Strehlow, T. G. H., *Songs of Central Australia*, p. 20.
99 Ellis, C., *Aboriginal Music*, p. 85.
100 Strehlow, T. G. H., 'Nomads in No-Man's-Land', p. 15.
101 Strehlow, T. G. H., *Aranda Phonetics and Grammar*, p. 72.
102 Ibid., p. 108.
103 Ibid., p. 105.
104 Strehlow, T. G. H., 'Anthropology and the Study of Languages,' Presidential Address, ANZAAS Perth Meeting, 1947 (Adelaide, n.d.), p. 24.
105 Strehlow, T. G. H., *Aranda Phonetics and Grammar*, pp. 108–9.
106 Strehlow, T. G. H., *Songs of Central Australia*, pp. 87–8, citing G. Saintsbury, *A History of English Prosody*.
107 McNally, W., *Aborigines, Artefacts and Anguish*, p. 106.
108 John Pfitzner, pers. comm., June 1994.
109 Dally, J., 'The Jindyworobak Movement', p. 33ff. This excellent study, still (inexplicably) unpublished, suggestively documents the spasmodic influence of Strehlow's work (notably his *Aranda Traditions*, published in 1947) on Ingamells's understanding of Aboriginal culture.
110 Cited in my *The Road to Botany Bay*, London, 1987, p. 352, here as there with the shadow-image of the hunter-historian in mind.
111 Quoted by Wise, T., *The Self-Made Anthropologist*, Sydney, 1985, p. 238. This judgement was not disinterested; when in 1951 the Commonwealth Literary Fund contacted Elkin about one of Robinson's projects to render into appropriate English a selection of Aboriginal legends, he had dismissed it, saying 'he is not a trained anthropologist.' (Ibid., p. 203). Elkin and Harney's versions may have been 'inadequate' for other reasons: on many occasions, the English versions of the singer's words were products of a complex, and necessarily makeshift, process of phonetic mimicry, verbal reconstruction, translation (often under the shadow of various taboos) and speculative interpretation. (See A. P. Elkin and Trevor A. Jones, *Arnhem Land Music (North Australian)*, The Oceania Monographs, No. 9, Sydney, 1957, p. 57ff.)
112 Dean, B., and Carell, V., *Dust for the Dancers*, Sydney, 1955, p. 209.
113 Ibid., p. 209.
114 Ellis, C., *Aboriginal Music*, p. 93.
115 Ibid., p. 93.
116 Ibid., p. 93.
117 Robinson, Roland, *The Shift of Sands*, p. 124.
118 Ibid., p. 37.
119 Ibid., p. 149.
120 Ibid., p. 125.
121 Ibid., p. 340.
122 Cornford, F. M., *From Religion to Philosophy*, New York, 1957, p. 254.

123 Ibid., p. 253ff. See also the same author's *Plato and Parmenides*, London, 1939, p. 84ff.
124 Harrison, J., *Themis*, p. 124.
125 Ibid., p. 125.
126 Lord, A. B., *General Introduction to Serbocroatian Heroic Songs collected by Milman Parry*, Cambridge (Mass), 1954, vol. 1, p. 5.
127 Ibid., p. 16.
128 Heidegger, M., writing in November 1933, cited by V. Farías, *Heidegger and Nazism*, trans. P. Burrell, Philadelphia, 1989, p. 159.
129 Ellis, C., *Aboriginal Music*, pp. 124–5.
130 Harrison, J., *Themis*, p. 335.
131 Ibid., p.xvi.
132 Ibid., p. xviii.
133 Ibid., p. xix.
134 Ibid., p. 35.
135 Ibid., p. 469.
136 Strehlow, T. G. H., *Songs of Central Australia*, p. 696.
137 See note 65 above.
138 Strehlow, T. G. H., *Songs of Central Australia*, p. 706.
139 Ibid., p. xxvi.
140 Ibid., p. xxviii.
141 Ibid., p. xxxi.
142 Ibid., p. xxxii.
143 Ibid., p. 349.
144 Strehlow, T. G. H., 'The Art of Circle, Line and Square' in *Australian Aboriginal Art*, ed. R. M. Berndt, Sydney, 1964, pp. 45–6.
145 Strehlow, T. G. H., *Songs of Central Australia*, p. 9.
146 Strehlow, T. G. H., 'Australian Aboriginal Songs', *Journal of the International Folk Music Council*, vol. 7, 1955, p. 40.
147 Strehlow, T. G. H., 'Central Australian Religion', p. 45 for example. See also 'The Sustaining Ideals of Australian Aboriginal Society' (Adelaide, 1966), where Strehlow defines the corollary of the localization of authority as 'the principles of cooperation, not subordination; of differentiation without inequality; of tolerance for the customs of other peoples in their own country' (p. 11). Further elaboration of these themes occurs in 'Geography and the Totemic Landscape' in *Australian Aboriginal Anthropology* ed. R. M. Berndt (Nedlands, WA, 1970), where Strehlow maintains that the lack of centralized authority meant that 'men and women in a sense lived in those ideal communities envisaged by Karl Marx (and by William Morris in *News from Nowhere*) . . . ' (p. 130).
148 Strehlow, T. G. H., *Songs of Central Australia*, p. 329, note 156.
149 Ibid., p. 337.
150 Ibid., p. 586.
151 Strehlow, T. G. H., 'Central Australian Religion', p. 64, note 24.

152 Ibid., p. 34.
153 Ibid., p. 64, note 24.
154 Ibid., p. 32.
155 Ibid., p. 32.
156 Cornford, F. M., *From Religion to Philosophy*, p. 254.
157 Ibid., p. 198.
158 Ibid., p. 199.
159 See Jones, F. J., *Giuseppe Ungaretti*, Edinburgh, 1977, pp. 10 and 71, where Ungaretti describes the 'orphic hallowing of reality' thus: 'There are not two parallel lines between things and words: things, when we look at them, already are no longer external, they are already within us, they are us: and they become externalised again with our words, emerging when transformed from material into moral objects.' Jones glosses this as 'the self-surprise of [Ungaretti's] modern baroque outlook'.
160 Robinson, Roland, *The Shift of Sands*, p. 133.
161 Cornford, F. M., *From Religion to Philosophy*, p. 209.
162 Strehlow, T. G. H., 'The Art of Circle, Line and Square', p. 47.
163 Cornford, F. M., *From Religion to Philosophy*, pp. 200–1.
164 See my *The Sound In-Between*, Sydney, 1992, p.8, where the 'performance logic' of certain scripts is described as 'spatial, historical and phonic. Their successful interpretation does not depend on the performers getting inside a character; it demands an ability to put on and put off "acoustic masks"' – this last phrase being derived from Strehlow.
165 Strehlow, T. G. H., *Journey to Horseshoe Bend*, p. 220.
166 Ibid., p. 170.
167 Strehlow, T. G. H., *Songs of Central Australia*, pp. 536–7.
168 Ibid., p. 537.
169 Certainly, according to David Hugo (pers.comm. July 1994), a sequel was planned.
170 That Klein's 'depressive' position might have implications for an understanding both of 'primitive' religion and of the debate between Parmenides and Plato regarding the nature of 'oneness' was clearly grasped by Adrian Stokes in *Greek Culture and the Ego*, especially chapter 6, 'Early Greek Science' (*The Critical Writings of Adrian Stokes*, ed. L. Gowing, London, 1978, vol. 3, p. 125ff). Cryptographers will naturally see a further connection - with Stokes's meditation on Giorgione's power to assure the integration of parts in their independence of one another, what he calls 'the utmost drama of the soul as laid-out things.' (*The Critical Writings of Adrian Stokes*, vol. 2, p. 129.)
171 See note 135 to 'Light Reading' below.
172 Strehlow, T. G. H., *Songs of Central Australia*, pp. 14–16.
173 Harney, W. E., and Elkin, A. P., *Songs of the Songman*, Melbourne, 1949, p. 14.
174 Pitjantjatjara music, and presumably other Aboriginal music traditions, exhibits a capacity 'for expansion and contraction of formal units within

established boundaries'. In contrast with Western music, which is built up lineally, using patterns (bars) of equal length, the Aboriginal system allows for 'varying degrees of fold' (C. Ellis, *Aboriginal Music*, pp. 84–5).

175 Strehlow, T. G. H., *Songs of Central Australia*, p. 690.
176 Ibid., p. 690.
177 Strehlow, T. G. H., 'Australian Aboriginal Songs', p. 37.
178 Ibid., p. 37.
179 Strehlow, T. G. H., *Songs of Central Australia*, p. 693.
180 Strehlow, T. G. H., 'Australian Aboriginal Songs', p. 38.
181 Ellis, C., *Aboriginal Music*, p. 99.
182 Likewise in my *Living In A New Country*: 'It was the spontaneous identification of his memory with his footsteps that moved Carlyle, the intuition that spaces were scores and historians the instruments tuned to play them.' (p. 185)
183 Cited by B. Elliott, *The Jindyworobaks*, St Lucia, 1979, p. 249.
184 Mudie, I., 'Morialta Memory', in *The Jindyworobaks*, p. 68.
185 Hart-Smith, W., 'April 28th 1770', in *The Jindyworobaks*, p. 100.
186 Robinson, Roland, 'Would That I Might Find My Country' and 'I Had No Human Speech', in *The Jindyworobaks*, p. 126 and p. 128 respectively. The former also appears as prose in *The Drift of Things*, Melbourne, 1973, p. 289.
187 Strehlow, T. G. H., *Songs of Central Australia*, p. 89.
188 Ibid., p. 714.
189 Ingamells, R., *Selected Poems*, p. 122. 'They travel through miraging morning, till,/ Beside Ulamba's soak as noon-day nears,/ . . . In single file move the Aranda men,/ . . . They must be reverent when/ Ulamba's sacred cave is visited./ . . . Ulamba's shadows lengthen on the plain;/ The sun sets fierce behind the western peaks;/ The party, down beside the soak again,/ . . .' and so on ('Ulamba', *Selected Poems*, pp. 53–5). Strehlow's own account of the visit to Ulamba (of which Ingamells' poem is little more than a stilted paraphrase) occurs in *Aranda Traditions*, pp. 1–5.
190 Strehlow, T. G. H., *Songs of Central Australia*, pp. 446–9.
191 Ibid., p. 582.
192 Ibid., p. 582.
193 Ibid., pp. 581–2 and 583.
194 Ellis, C., *Aboriginal Music*, p. 86.
195 Strehlow, T. G. H., *Songs of Central Australia*, p. 170.
196 Ibid., p. 209.
197 Ibid., p. 718.
198 Doughty, C. M., *The Dawn of Britain*, London, 1906, vol. 6, postscript.
199 Ibid., vol. 6, postscript.
200 Ibid., vol. 6, postscript.
201 MacDiarmid, Hugh, *The Company I've Kept*, London, 1966, p. 171.
202 Jones, David, *The Roman Quarry*, ed. H. Grisewood and R. Hague, London, 1981: 'The stressed accents tell bucolic song and the companion throats leave

quantity to cissy Greeks' (p. 3). Jones associates the accentual invasion with the evasion of the land's lie: 'Their Ordovician hills are yet outside the world (but shortly to be levelled to the world-plain) . . .' (Ibid., p. 56.)

203 Strehlow, T. G. H., *Songs of Central Australia*, p. 19.

204 Ibid., pp. 10–11.

205 *Ezra Pound and Music*, ed. R. Murray Schafer, London, 1978, p. 472.

206 Ibid., p. 470. Gregorian plainchant appealed to Pound, not least on account of its lack of notational precision. (see Ibid., p. 474.)

207 Cornford, F. M., *Plato and Parmenides*, London, 1939, p. 28.

208 Heidegger, M., 'The Anaximander Fragment' in *Early Greek Thinkers*, trans. D. F. Krell and F. A. Capuzzi, San Francisco, c.1975, p. 27, and Heidegger, M., *Parmenides*, trans. A. Schuwer and R. Rojcewicz, Bloomington, c.1992, p. 144.

209 Cornford, F. M., *Plato and Parmenides*, p. 29.

210 Ibid., p. 31

211 Heidegger, M., *Parmenides*, p. 95.

212 Ibid., p. 95.

213 Ibid., p. 101.

214 Ibid., p. 150.

215 Ibid., p. 151.

216 Strehlow, T. G. H., *Songs of Central Australia*, p. 703.

217 Ibid., p. 704.

218 Farías, V., *Heidegger and Nazism*, p. 271.

219 Papastergiadis, N., 'Greece at the Crossroads', catalogue essay for *Beyond Missolonghi*, exhibition curated by E. Gertsakis, Ian Potter Gallery, University of Melbourne, August 1994, pp. 10–20.

220 Heidegger, M., *Parmenides*, p. 164.

221 Strehlow, T. G. H., *Songs of Central Australia*, pp. 248–53. The resemblance between Othin and the 'Central Australian ceremonial chief' is glossed in note 15 (p. 248). Strehlow's use of footnotes is an essential ingredient of his rhapsodic mode of composition. To the extent that the footnotes expose the 'stratigraphy' of Strehlow's evolving thought, they invert, even subvert, the process of gradual unmasking that characterizes the main text. They preserve the impression, integral to Aranda poetics, that the more nearly we approach the light, the more conscious we grow of an enfolding darkness. This cultivation of textual chiaroscuro serves as a way of putting off the end, of preventing the identificatory performance from slipping into the past and the representational space of history - a point usefully explored in M. Bowie, *Freud, Proust and Lacan: Theory as Fiction*, Cambridge, 1987, p. 37.

222 Jones, P., 'Traveller between Two Worlds', p. 127, where Jones points out the ambiguously hybrid character of a mulga plaque inscribed 'Jesus': 'this Church icon resembles a stone or wooden *tjurunga*.'

223 McNally, W., *Aborigines, Artefacts and Anguish*, p. 122.

224 See Inglis, K., *The Stuart Case*, Melbourne, 1961, pp. 55–6, 229 and 296–8.
225 *The Stuart Case*, pp. 215 and 229.
226 Ibid., p. 298.
227 But to produce a performance reliable enough for the sound-recordist was already to stop performing. Colin Simpson, sound-recordist with Charles Mountford's 1948 expedition to Arnhem Land, reports his attempts to record a rain-making ceremony at Oenpelli. The men would not sing near the rain pole: 'Finally I got them a hundred feet away against a clump of lantana . . . They sang to the mike, the iron thing I held in my hand. But they were not singing to the pole of wood' (C. Simpson, *Adam in Ochre*, Sydney, 1962, p. 76). Wider social and cultural implications of this technological moment are explored in P. Carter, 'Remember Me/Mimicry' in *Art & Text*, vol. 31, 1989, pp. 43–9.
228 See note 65 above and K. Hale, 'Remarks on Creativity in Aboriginal Verse' in *Problems and Solutions*, ed. J. C. Kassler and J. Stubington, St Lucia, 1984, p. 259.
229 Ellis, C., 'Connection and Disconnection of Elements of the Rhythmic Hierarchy in an Aranda Song', in *Musicology Australia*, 1992, vol xv, p. 51.
230 Ibid., p. 63.
231 Strehlow, T. G. H., 'The Art of Circle, Line and Square', p. 50.
232 Strehlow, T. G. H., *Songs of Central Australia*, p. 674.
233 Strehlow, T. G. H., *Rex Battarbee: artist and founder of the Aboriginal art movement in Central Australia*, p. 36.
234 Rousseau, J.J., 'Essay on the Origin of Languages' in *On the Origin of Language*, New York, 1966, p. 58.
235 Carter, P., 'Baroque Identities: Migration and Mimicry' in *Identifying Australia in Postmodern Times*, ed. L. Dobrez, Canberra, 1994, pp. 2–3.
236 Charles Chewing's translation of C. Strehlow, *Die Aranda-und-Loritja-Stamme in Zentral Australien*, n.d., p. 1162ff.
237 Carter, P., *Living In A New Country*, p. 193.
238 Ibid., p. 196.
239 Strehlow, T. G. H., *Songs of Central Australia*, p. 444.
240 Ibid., pp. 445–9.
241 Ibid., p. 456.
242 Strehlow, T. G. H., *Journey to Horseshoe Bend*, pp. 131, 137 and 146.
243 Ibid., p. 132.
244 Ibid., p. 139.
245 Ibid., p. 219.
246 Ibid., pp. 218–9.
247 Ibid., p. 219.
248 Ibid., p. 220.
249 Title of photograph in C. Chewings, *Back In The Stone Age*, Sydney, 1936, facing page 50.
250 L. Morphett, pers.comm., July 1994.

251 Strehlow, T. G. H., *Journey to Horseshoe Bend*, p. 148.
252 Ibid., p. 149.
253 Ibid., pp. 146–7.
254 As Geoff Bardon has remarked of that 'new, geometrical form of abstract art' that Strehlow had prophecied (*Rex Battarbee: Artist and Founder of the Aboriginal Art Movement in Central Australia*, p. 20): 'The Papunya painters have no need for internal or external horizons; their horizons lie within the landscape' – a remark Bardon understands directly as a question of poetics. 'In the Western Desert paintings, the images do not provide a mere graphic equivalent of spoken words, thereby attaching themselves to the temporality implicit in the ordinary syntax of a sentence. Quite to the contrary, and importantly: time has become space.' (G. Bardon, *Papunya Tula: Art of the Western Desert*, Melbourne, 1991, p. 134.)
255 Strehlow, T. G. H., *Journey to Horseshoe Bend*, p. 142.
256 Ibid., p. 143.

Part Two: About Canoes

1 Spence, Joseph, *Letters from the Grand Tour*, ed. S. Klima, Montreal, 1975, p. 96.
2 'Visual facts' in a double sense as will emerge; as what is referred to here is not simply a fact of Giorgione's painting, but a fact of visual perception. The concavity of his picture-space – its refusal to accept the physical surface of the painting as a rectangular frontal grid defining the character of the represented space – preserves the sensation we have in ordinary vision: 'We see not with one fixed eye, but with two constantly moving eyes; the image which we receive on the retina is a spheroid world projected on a concave plane.' (A. G. M. Little, 'Perspective and Scene Painting', *Art Bulletin*, XIX (1936), p. 492, cited by Robert Hansen in his translator's 'Afterword' to A. Flocon and A. Barré, *Curvilinear Perspective*, Berkeley, 1987, p. 226.) Flocon and Barré's 'arc-based system' of drawing, while 'reproducing the curving appearance of the world', still fails to integrate the 'frontal plane' of the picture surface. Hansen proposes a 'hyperbolic system': 'I am convinced that every straight line appears to us like a hyperbola, a curving ligament connecting two almost straight orthogonal asymptotes.' (*Curvilinear Perspective*, p. 227).

The most thorough recent treatment of hyperbolic space is Patrick Heelan, *Space Perception and the Philosophy of Science*, Berkeley, 1983. The sense Giorgione's paintings give us of objects turning to face us suggests an analogy with Gibson's concept of visual 'affordances' (J. J. Gibson, *The Ecological Approach to Visual Perception*, Boston, 1979, chapter 8). Interesting links between hyperbolic space conceptions and late-Modernist conceptualizations of auditory space are made in D. Cabrera, 'Sound Space and Edgard Varèse's *Poème Electronique*', MA thesis, 1994, University of Technology, Sydney.

3 Williams, R., *Notes on the Underground*, Cambridge (Mass), 1990, p. 46. In the same passage, Williams points out that structuralists and post-structuralists alike share a preoccupation with hidden strata of meaning. But what if the meaning did not lie in bottomless depths but on the infinite surface? One thing is clear: in this event, it would not be reducible to networks of signs. Topological relationships would have to be taken into account.

4 Settis, Salvatore, *La 'Tempesta' Interpretata*, Milano, 1978, p. 60. On the basis of the *Tempesta*'s 'expressive landscape', the German art-historian Josef Strzygowski recruited Giorgione to the Indo-Iranian tradition, whose finest flower was, of course, Nazi Germany. (*La 'Tempesta' Interpretata*, p. 49) By the oddest of routes, though, this brings us later to the 'black forest' of Heidegger, and to that philosopher's desire to create a 'clearing', to 'ground' thought afresh.

Also in the 1930s, art-historian Federico Hermanin suggested that the *Tempesta* represented an episode in the life of Paris, and that 'the lightning and the ruins were an allusion to the fire and the destruction of Troy.' In which case, with scarcely less plausibility, we might take the gypsy for Andromache, Hector's wife, and find in the painting an allusion to Book VI of the *Iliad* and that episode of consummate pathos where Hector's baby son, frightened by his father's shining helm, 'back into the bosom of his fair-girdled nurse shrank' *(The Iliad*, trans. A. T. Murray, London, 1971, vol 1, VI, l. 467).

Then the helmless soldier is Hector: 'in his hand he held a spear of eleven cubits' (*The Iliad*, vol 1, VI, l. 161). And if Hector foresees a son growing up, then Pallas Athene foresees Hector's fate – for surely the twin *paterae* under their Byzantine eyebrows immediately above and behind the soldier represent owl-faced Athena, Troy's tutelary deity, whose image may have been enigmatic in Giorgione's day but which Schliemann found reproduced everywhere when he sank his trenches into Troy. Witness, for example, the terracotta vase Schliemann reproduces on p. 219 of *Troy and its Remains* (New York, 1976).

But there is no end of these mere coincidences, and even mere coincidences have their reasons, and must be necessary, not spuriously sufficient.

5 Lefebvre, Henri, *The Production of Space*, trans. D. Nicholson-Smith, Oxford, 1991), p. 5.

6 White, J., *The Birth and Rebirth of Pictorial Space*, London, 1972, p. 103.

7 In Bean, J., and Stampfle, P., *The Italian Renaissance*, Drawings from New York Collections 1, New York, 1965, Plate 81.

8 In Levenson, J. A., Oberhuber, K., and Sheehan, J. L., *Early Italian Engravings from the National Gallery of Art*, Washington, 1973, Fig. 19–4, p. 394.

9 Ibid., plates 127 and 161, pp. 320 and 448 respectively.

10 Ibid., Figs 19–1 and 19–2, p. 393.

11 Stokes, Adrian, 'Art and Science' (originally published in 1949) in *The Critical Writings of Adrian Stokes*, London, 1978, vol. 2, p. 204.

12 Ibid., p. 210.

13 Lefebvre, Henri, *The Production of Space*, p. 74.

14 In this sense: that capitalism, 'the atomisation of economic relationships', has as its corollary 'the atomisation of social relationships', the production of the 'bourgeois individual' (A. Wilden, 'Montaigne on the Paradoxes of Individualism' in *System and Structure*, London, 1980, p. 91). It is an apprehension of an accelerating process of 'atomisation' that, according to Wilden, provokes Montaigne's troubled reflections on the nature of selfhood; which, Wilden notes, Montaigne defines in two quite contradictory ways, first as a process of becoming, fluid, circulatory, like 'the living stream of life' (and, we would say, the Venetian economy), and secondly as an entity, stable and accumulative (and which we would associate with the coagulation of open pathways into linearly-transfixed and monumental prospects), evoked in terms of 'battling "upstream" against [the stream] towards a source of stability, towards a fixable point of origin, towards a spatial transcendence of becoming, a ME "like a neighbour, like a tree".'(*System and Structure*, p. 90.)

15 Stokes, Adrian, 'Art and Science', p. 203.

16 Lefebvre, Henri, *The Production of Space*, p. 77.

17 Boschini, Marco, *La Carta del Navegar Pitoresco* (originally published 1660), ed. Anna Pallucchini, Venezia-Roma, c.1976, stanza 72, p. 93. '*Come xe in man de sti Popieri el remo,/ Cusi el penel xe in man dei Veneziani.*'

18 Gentile's diplomatic mission to Mehmet II (1479–81) is well known. Carpaccio's sense of the circulation of images, and of the necessity to reconcile converging viewpoints, histories and ideologies may have been equally well developed. The fauna of Carpaccio's cameo of fawning women, the *Two Courtesans* in the Correr Museum, Venice, include two white doves, a peacock, a mastiff, a white lap-dog and a possibly American parrot (?a macaw).

Meditating on these and the other appurtenances of the scene, a vase, a little colonnade, Michel Serres arrives at: '*Colombe, enfant. Oiseau-colombe, paon, perroquet. Colombe, chien . . . L'icône à deux dimensions, qui en simule trois, porte infiniment plus d'information que les messages linéaires: elle les inscrit tous en sautoir. Et dessine la carte des pays parcourus, comme la toile de Pénélope faisait et défaisait les voyages d'Ulysse errant. Ce n'est pas l'explosion, c'est la gerbe totale. Non la misère et la dissolution, mais la somme des solutions, parmi l'opulence*' (*Esthetiques sur Carpaccio*, Paris, 1975, pp. 129–30).

Perhaps, in addition to Christopher Columbus, Serres alludes, with '*oiseau-colombe*', to the Bird Man reported by Torquemada which, according to the *Codice of 1576*, appeared in 1508, foretelling the speed with which the Spaniards would come and dispossess the Aztecs of the lands (*Codice de 1576 (Codice Aubin)*, trans. Charles E. Dibble, Madrid, 1963, p. 51); but evidently, certain historically significant non-linear alliterations were in the air. Serres sees Carpaccio's art as glyphic, its meaning only to be found using a non-linear reading technique comparable to the way in which the painting was put together. This is in direct opposition to the voyages (iconographic and mythical) which seek the Golden Fleece at the end of the rainbow.

19 Panofsky, E., *Studies in Iconology*, Mary Flexner Lectures, New York, 1939, p. 51.

20 See Francastel, Pierre, *Studi di Sociologia dell'Arte*, Milano, 1976, p. 201. Francastel makes the further point that, in the early fifteenth century, Flemish and Burgundian painters also achieved spatially-coherent compositions; it was simply that they did not conceive of space as unified. Similarly, throughout the fifteenth century, northern Italian, and not a few Florentine, painters continued in practice to use a bifocal perspective construction which, in tending to focus attention on a (usually divided) foreground, provided the vernacular context in which reversed perspective made immediate intuitive sense (*Studi di Sociologia dell'Arte*, p. 138ff).

21 *Encyclopaedia Britannica*, Chicago, 1989, vol. 1, p. 217.

22 Alberti memorably captured this desire to marry ancient reason and contemporary experience in his description of the artist's task as the expression of *la più grassa Minerva* (see Alberti, Leon Battista, *De Pictura*, trans. J. Spencer, Yale, 1977, pp. 18–9).

23 According to Las Casas, who transcribed Columbus's now lost diary. See *The 'Diario' of Christopher Columbus's First Voyage to America, 1492–1493*, transcribed and translated by Oliver Dunn and James E. Kelley Jr., Norman (Oklahoma), 1989, p. 29 and note, which offers an alternative explanation for the numerical discrepancies.

24 Hakluyt, Richard, *Voyages, The Principall Navigations of the English Nation*, London, 1962, vol. 5, p. 181–2. Best's denigration is an imperial pretext, his discourse aiming 'to prove all partes of the Worlde habitable'. In a remarkably circular argument, Best recommends 'new Discoveries' for, among the revelation of diverse nations and their products, 'the infinite treasure of Pearle, Golde and Silver, the newes of newe found landes, the sundry positions of the Sphere, and many others' (p. 171).

25 Sarpi, Paolo, *Pensieri*, ed. Gaetano and Luisa Cozzi, Torino, 1976, p. 33. 'The earth through its rivers, which carry sand and rocks, and through animals, which transport themselves as well as other things, changes shape, and therefore its centre of gravity.'

26 Vasari, Giorgio, *The Lives of the Artists*, trans. George Bull, London, 1965, pp. 275–6.

27 Stokes, Adrian, 'Art and Science', *The Critical Writings of Adrian Stokes*, vol. 2, p. 202.

28 Perhaps because of his early interest in the ballet, Stokes associates movement with music, the conjunction rendering both theatrical. Against a theatricalism which he frequently associates disparagingly with the baroque, Stokes advocates a multiplanar movement in stillness as a release from merely choreographic correspondences. 'It is a common experience when gazing at some successful piece of architecture or sculpture for a tune to enter the mind: that inner rhythm, the tune, denotes response to the visual experience: we incorporate it in this form of rhythm or melody,' Stokes writes, then defining his own taste quite differently: 'I myself value most highly in painting, architecture and sculpture, those very rare achievements entirely removed from any musical suggestion or correspondence. We cannot incorporate such works because their entire insistence is upon outwardness, upon the inner world in terms of spatiality that is the medium of visual art.' (*Russian Ballets*, London, 1935, p. 177.)

Why must the inner world lack a sense of rhythm? Even the process of projecting the inwards outwards implies a pulse. The statuesque retains the marks of the energetic movement that hurled it into place, compacted it and isolated it. Its very stillness poses the question of its turbulent origins.

29 White, John, *The Birth and Rebirth of Pictorial Space*, p. 208. White defines four features of such a perspective. These include 'All straight lines not passing through the point on the plane surface nearest to the eye are given a curvilinear distortion' and 'The size of objects is dependent on the visual angle and does not diminish in direct proportion to the distance, the discrepancy being greatest for wide angles.' These distortions and discrepancies of a curvilinear perspective construction are 'corrected' in reversed perspective: straight lines replace curvilinear ones, while the intuition of a curvilinear space is retained.

30 Flocon, A., and Barré, A., *Curvilinear Perspective*, p. 15.

31 Ibid., p. 23.

32 Arnheim, Rudolf, *Visual Thinking*, Berkeley, 1969, p. 24.

33 Ibid., p. 18.

34 Smith, F. Joseph, *The Experiencing of Musical Sound*, New York, 1978, p. 31.

35 Arnheim, Rudolf, op. cit., p. 14.

36 Todorov, T., *La Conquista dell'America*, Torino, 1992, p. 33ff, and Greenblatt both draw attention to Columbus the semiotician. These signs were not merely textual, 'marking a tension between the visual and the verbal.' (Greenblatt, Stephen, *Marvelous Possessions*, Chicago, 1991, p. 87.) They were directional, signifying the rectilinear rupture of curvilinear space. Columbus's always-significant birds, like those of Australian explorers, always flew towards the object of his desire (see my *The Road to Botany Bay*, London, 1987, p. 78).

37 'Columbus's Letter on His First Voyage' in *The Four Voyages of Christopher Columbus*, trans. J. M. Cohen, London, 1988, p. 216. Prior to sighting land, Columbus had expressed the view that 'nothing was

lacking except to hear nightingales' (*The 'Diario'*, p. 33) and these prognostics of Paradise were again on his mind on 7 December (*The 'Diario'*, p. 213).

38 In his rhyming chronicle, Giovanni Santi, father of Raphael, describes a statue of Minerva: '*Cum habito ligiadro altero e adorno/ Pallade io viddi, qual cinta de oliva/ Parea possente a far di nocte giorno,/ Col scudo de cristal, la donde viva/ Vedease entro la testa de Medusa,/ Che per spavento la sua bocca apriva . . .*' (Santi, G., *Federigo di Montefeltro duca di Urbino, Cronaca rimata*, Stuttgart, 1893, p. 11.)

39 *The 'Diário' of Christopher Columbus's First Voyage to America, 1492–1493*, pp. 67–8.

40 Ibid., pp. 67–8.

41 Ibid., p. 177.

42 Ibid., p. 177.

43 Cited by Edgar Wind (*Art and Anarchy*, London, 1963, p. 137) in the course of his polemic against aesthetic purists: 'Whether you take Wölfflin or Riegl and the Vienna School, or Roger Fry and Clive Bell, or Bernard Berenson, they methodically developed an exquisite skill in skimming off the top of a work without necessarily making contact with its imaginative forces, often even shunning that contact because it might disturb the lucid application of a fastidious technique.' (Ibid., p. 24).

44 Stein, Leo, *Journey into the Self*, New York, 1950, p. 196.

45 Berenson, B., *Italian Pictures of the Renaissance, Florentine School*, London, 1963, vol. 2, Plate 793.

46 Stein, Leo, op. cit., p. 197.

47 Calvino, Italo, *Mr Palomar*, trans. William Weaver, London, 1983, pp. 8–10.

48 Jaynes, J., *The Origin of Consciousness in the Breakdown of the Bicameral Mind*, London, 1990, p. 160.

49 Ibid., p.160.

50 MacCormack, S., 'In Very Ancient Times: How the Past was Remembered in Early Colonial Peru,' unpublished paper delivered at *Discovery: Meanings, Legitimations, Critiques*, conference held at University of Wisconson-Madison, 25–27 September 1992, p. 24.

51 Garcés, Maria Antonia, 'Writing the Body of Mama Waku: Primal Scenes in Waman Puma', unpublished typescript, pp. 4–7.

52 Prescott, W. H., *History of the Conquest of Peru*, London, 1847, vol. 1, pp. 362–5. For Atahuallpa's smile, Prescott follows the manuscript *Relación del Primer Descubrimiento de la Costa y Mar del Sur*, written by a companion of Hernando Pizarro and an eyewitness to the event: '*el cual a esto volvío la cabeza a mirarle sonriendose . . .*'

53 Ibid., vol. 1, p. 369.

54 Durán, Diego, *Storia delle Indie della Nuova Spagna e delle Isole di 'Tierra Firme'*, trans. from the Spanish by Pier Luigi Crovetto, in Todorov, T., and

Baudot, Georges (eds), *Racconti Aztechi della Conquista*, Torino, 1988, pp. 225–7.

55 Ibid., p. 227.

56 Todorov, T., and Baudot, Georges (eds), *Racconti Aztechi della Conquista*, p. xxvii. But this may preserve a structuralist bias towards seeing historical events in terms of binary oppositions. It is not clear what 'portents' can mean in a culture where historical time is conceived of cyclically. All the signs of ending are described in Nahuatl and Spanish writings that postdate the fall of Tenochtitlán; they retrospectively linearize the past to make it conform to, converge upon, and legitimate a Spanish future. MacCormack makes a parallel observation regarding post-conquest Incan histories: 'The European preoccupation with a single chronological schema that resulted in a unitary narrative reaching from the origin of humanity to the present thus conditioned the manner in which Pachacuti Yamqui and Guaman Poma ordered their knowledge about the Andean past' ('In Very Ancient Times: How the Past was Remembered in Early Colonial Peru,' p. 24).

The historical determinism that the hispanicized Nahuatl historians engage in may reflect cultural dispossession, not self-possession. Their willingness to cast their own past in terms of signs (portents, prophecies and other events of covert significance) may be related to their adoption of linear writing; glyphic script might bear historical witness quite differently. If memories seemed, retrospectively, to be composed of prophetic deceptions, if certain experiences now appeared to be merely signs indicating an ending, it was because a cultural space had contracted and grown thin. Historical phenomena that had formerly been 'fat', multi-dimensional and radiant (like the glyphic script in which they were recorded and performed) now seemed to be composed of orthogonals converging on a vanishing point.

57 Díaz, Bernal, *The Conquest of New Spain*, trans. J. M. Cohen, London, 1963, p. 91.

58 Ibid., p. 92.

59 Ibid., p. 93.

60 Ibid., p. 90.

61 Mullaney, Steven, *The Place of the Stage*, Chicago, 1988, p. 69.

62 Duran, Diego, *Storia delle Indie della Nuova Spagna e delle Isole di 'Tierra Firme'*, p. 226.

63 Pignatti, T., *Giorgione*, Venezia, 1969, p. 96.

64 Translated by W. M. Conway, *Literary Remains of Albrecht Dürer*, Cambridge, 1899, p. 58. Panofsky translates the same phrase rather differently: 'for the sake of "art" in secret perspective', with the stress on 'secret' (*The Life and Art of Albrecht Dürer*, 1943, p. 248). Nowadays, more stress is laid on the positive cross-influences between Northern and Venetian painting funnelled through Dürer during his 1505–6 stay in Venice. See F. Valcanover, 'An Introduction to Titian', and T. Pignatti,

'Giorgione and Titian', both in *Titian: Prince of Painters*, exhibition catalogue, Venice, 1990.

65 Joost-Gaugier, C. L., 'Jacopo Bellini's Interest in Perspective and its Iconographic Significance', in *Zeitschrift für Kunstgeschichte*, 1975, vol. 38, p. 2. Although preferring to use a single vanishing-point, Joost-Gaugier thinks that the bifocal or chequerboard method of perspective construction 'may well have been known to Jacopo, surely as a consequence of its popularity in Padua' (p. 6).

66 Klein, R., 'Pomponius Gauricus on Perspective', *Art Bulletin*, XLIII, 1961, pp. 211–30, argues that Gauricus's 'compositional perspective' was based on the bifocal system of perspective, not on Alberti's '*costruzione legittima*': 'Gauricus had never heard of a central vanishing point.' Klein also notes (p. 221) that Masolino (from whom, to judge from the fiercely-contracting orthogonals they both favour, Jacopo Bellini may have learned his perspective) paid no attention to the unification of space. The difference of Alberti's or Brunelleschi's method was that it did create a 'complete and unified space'.

67 Pignatti, T., *Giorgione*, pp. 8–9 and p. 95.

68 Gombrich, E., *The Story of Art*, London, 1972, p. 220.

69 Gombrich, E., *The Heritage of Apelles*, Ithaca (New York), 1976, pp. 33–4.

70 Berkeley, George, *An Essay towards a New Theory of Vision*, *The Works of George Berkeley*, ed. A. Luce and T. E. Jessup, London, 1948, vol. 1, p. 229. In the later 'Theory of Vision, or Visual Language, Vindicated and Explained', Berkeley rejects this view, maintaining that 'there is no more likeness to exhibit, or necessity to infer, things tangible from the modifications of light, than there is in language to collect the meaning from the sound.' (*The Works of George Berkeley*, ed. A. C. Fraser, Oxford, 1901, vol. IV, p. 398.)

71 De Holanda, Francisco, *Dialoghi Romani con Michelangelo*, Milano, 1964, p. 53. Earlier, Michelangelo says: 'Everyone, without knowing it, is painting in this world, whether creating or producing new forms and figures, as when putting on different clothes, whether in building and occupying a space with buildings and painted houses, whether in cultivating the fields, making prospects and designs [*pitture e segni*], by working the earth, in navigating the seas with sails, in fighting and dividing armies, and finally in deaths and funerals, as indeed in all other operations, gestures and actions.' (*Dialoghi Romani*, p. 48)

72 Berkeley, George, *An Essay towards a New Theory of Vision*, *The Works of George Berkeley*, vol. 1, p. 173.

73 Berkeley, George, 'Theory of Vision, or Visual Language, Vindicated and Explained', *The Works of George Berkeley*, vol. IV, p. 404. As the title indicates, Berkeley finds an analogy between seeing and thinking.

74 *Codice de 1576 (Codice Aubin)*, trans. Charles E. Dibble, pp. 9–10.

75 Herder, Johann Gottfried, 'Essay on the Origin of Language' in *On the*

Origin of Language, trans. J. H. Moran and A. Gode, New York, 1966, p. 163.

76 Sacks, O., *Seeing Voices*, New York, 1990, p. 88.

77 Ibid., p. 87.

78 LeCron Foster, Mary, 'The Symbolic Structure of Primordial Language', in *Human Evolution, Biosocial Perspectives*, ed. S. L. Washburn and E. R. McCown, Memlo Park (California), 1978, p. 117.

79 Laban, Rudolf, *Choreutics*, London, 1966, p. 48.

80 Rousseau, Jean-Jacques, 'Essay on the Origin of Languages' in *On the Origin of Language*, p. 17.

81 Ibid., p.17.

82 Settis, Salvatore, *La 'Tempesta' Interpretata*, p. 133ff.

83 Vasari, Giorgio, *The Lives of the Artists*, p. 272.

84 See C. Pedretti, *Leonardo da Vinci on Painting, a Lost Book*, Berkeley, 1966, p. 66ff. Alternatively in Venice in 1500, when, it now appears, Leonardo visited the city. See F. Valcanover, 'An Introduction to Titian' in *Titian, Prince of Painters*, p. 6.

85 Pedretti, C., *Leonardo da Vinci on Painting, a Lost Book*, p. 43.

86 Ibid., p. 37.

87 *The Literary Works of Leonardo da Vinci*, ed. J. P. Richter, London, 1970, vol.1, p. 216.

88 In *Venezia e l'Europa, Atti del XVIII Congresso Internazionale di Storia dell'Arte*, Venezia, 1955, p. 122.

89 *The Literary Works of Leonardo da Vinci*, ed. J. P. Richter, vol. 1, p. 137.

90 Vasari, Giorgio, *The Lives of the Artists*, p. 273.

91 Ibid., p. 443.

92 Settis, Salvatore, *La 'Tempesta' Interpretata*, p. 70ff.

93 De Acosta, Father Joseph, *The Natural and Moral History of the Indies*, trans. Edward Grimston (1604), ed. C. R. Markham, London, 1880, p. 280. 'The manner is with small delicate pinsors they pull the feathers from the dead fowles, and with a fine paste they cunningly joyne them together.' He further reports that 'The Indians (besides these images) did use feathers in many other most excellent workes, especially for the ornament of Kings and Noblemen, their Temples and Idolls.' Other species provide 'plumes of sundry colours, especially when they go to warre, inriching them with gold and silver very artificially, which was a matter of great price.' (*The Natural and Moral History of the Indies*, p. 281.)

94 *The Literary Works of Leonardo da Vinci*, ed. J. P. Richter, vol. 1, p. 173.

95 Muraro, M., *The Treasures of Venice*, trans. J. Emmons, London, 1963, p. 52.

96 Ibid., p. 52.

97 Ibid., p. 52.

98 Mathew, G., *Byzantine Aesthetics*, London, 1963, pp. 18–19. Further circumstantial support for the view that Venetian mosaicists drew on a

narrower range of colours than the Byzantine masters comes from a fragment of mosaic from a pillar in the chancel of St Mark's, which dates from before 1071. (See P. Toesca, *The Mosaics in the Church of St Mark in Venice*, trans. J. Templeton and G. Scaglia, London, 1959, p. 18.) Part of a Crucifixion, it represents four women, clearly distinguished from one another by the colours of their shawls: blue, flame orange, emerald green and mauve. Now, as early as the sixth century in Hagia Sophia, 'attempts were made to break the monotony of gold'. There, adornment 'consisted of the use of a precious material which conveys multiple colours in a mathematical proportion' (*Byzantine Aesthetics*, p. 89). In these four women we may like to recognize a provincial echo of this sophisticated aesthetic. If so, by the thirteenth century, when most of the mosaics of St Mark's were done, any taste for such subtleties had been lost. The images which jewel the basilica's golden vaults recall those enamels where the subject is enisled in a golden sea. Even in the later, fourteenth-century cycle at the Chora in Constantinople, where 'the pervasive influence of enamels' may be detected (*Byzantine Aesthetics*, p. 144), the figures are not so entirely detached from their surroundings as they are in St Mark's, where amid the shimmering billows they even lack a bar to stand on.

99 Ruskin, John, *Works*, ed. E. J. Cook and A. Wedderburn, London, 1903–1912, vol. x, *The Stones of Venice*, pp. 169–71.

100 See W. Wolters, *La Scultura Veneziana Gotica 1360–1460*, Venezia, 1976, vol. 1, p. 40.

101 'Il Poemetto di Pietro de Natali sulla Pace tra Alessandro III e Federico Barbarossa', *Rerum Italicorum Scriptores*, tome 22, parte 4, ed. G. Monticolo, Città di Castello, 1900, pp. 558–9. According to Monticolo, the poem was composed between 1381 and 1382 (p. 520).

102 *Mémoires de Philippe de Commynes*, ed. R. Chanteleuze, Paris, 1881, liv. VII, chapter xviii.

103 Bettini, S., 'Il Cammino dell'Arte', *Arte Veneta*, 1954, p. 31.

104 Ruskin, John, *Works*, vol. x, *The Stones of Venice*, p. 31. See also note 125 below.

105 See W. Wolters, *La Scultura Veneziana Gotica 1360–1460*, pp. 82–3.

106 *Canon Pietro Casola's Pilgrimage to Jerusalem in the year 1494*, ed. and trans. Newett, Manchester, 1907, p. 201.

107 *Mémoires de Philippe de Commynes*, liv. VII, chapter xviii.

108 Gilbert, F., 'Venice in the Crisis of the League of Cambrai' in *Renaissance Venice*, ed. J. R. Hale, London, 1973, p. 297.

109 W. Wolters, *La Scultura Veneziana Gotica 1360–1460*, p. 116.

110 Alberti, L. B., *De Pictura*, ed. C. Grayson, London, 1972, Lib. II, 49. 'On the other hand it is no error to use gold for sculptured columns, bases, capitals and frontispieces . . .': that is, for the precious frames of paintings. It is only in the business of creating a scientific illusion of depth that gold is useless. In the same spirit of avoiding the vulgar mimicry of light,

Alberti urges great restraint in the use of black and white. Because there is nothing whiter than white in the artist's palette, he should use it only to add the last highlight, to show 'the final lustre [*lustro*] on a highly polished sword.' He should use it in conjunction with black when he wants vessels to look like silver, gold or glass, so that painted they appear to shine [*risplendere*]. (*De Pictura*, Lib. II, 46.) This is advice quite congenial to the masters of the macchia.

111 Ibid., Lib. II, 48. The distinction Alberti draws between colours which dazzle and colours which set each other off is a distinction between lustre (highlights) and illumination and, as has often been pointed out (see, for instance, Adrian Stokes, 'Art and Science', p. 190 and E. Gombrich, 'Light, Form and Texture in XVth Century Painting North and South of the Alps' in *The Heritage of Apelles*, p. 21ff), it is an interest in colours that illuminate which characterizes the art of Domenico Veneziano, the master of Piero della Francesca. Piero shares with Alberti an interest in inner light, in light as mass, welling up to the surface as constant colour. For this reason, when he painted the *Legend of the True Cross* at Arezzo, he ignored Voragine's statement that the cross carried by Constantine was gold, and painted it white 'thus satisfying aesthetic rather than iconographical requirements.' (K. Clark, *Piero della Francesca*, London, 1951, p. 79, note 33.)

112 *The Fugger News Letters, 1568–1605*, ed. V. von Klarwill, trans. P. de Chary, London, 1928, p. 140. The same passage asserts: 'He has no other wish than to be of good use to his country, the Republic.'

113 Ibid., p. 146.

114 Ibid., p. 268.

115 Goethe, J. W., *Italian Journey*, trans. W. H. Auden and E. Mayer, London, 1962, p. 65. Whether it was best to colour light or to leave it to marble remained an issue for architects in Venice. Did Longhena, for instance, intend to give the Salute a polychrome interior, as he did I Scalzi? D. Lewis (*The Late Baroque Churches of Venice*, New York, 1979, p. 400, note 1) argues, against Wittkower, that he did. Possibly there is no real conflict. As Otto Benesch says ('Titian and Tintoretto', *Arte Veneta*, 1958, p. 79), 'coloured surface had in Venice the importance which plastic form had in Florence and architectural structure in Rome.'

116 Cited by Robert Southey, *Madoc*, London, 1825, vol. 1, p. 239.

117 *The Letters of Amerigo Vespucci*, London, 1894, pp. 12, 18 and 32.

118 Cited by Lauts, J., *Venezia e l'Europa*, p. 72. 'By a slight and imperceptible change, the beautiful impression of fire and gold is transformed into one not undeserving the epithet foul; and the colour of honour and joy reversed to that of ignominy,' writes Goethe (*Theory of Colours*, trans. C. S. Eastlake, London, 1967 [orig. pub. 1840], p. 308). So in Venice, the Doge's cap was golden, but the detested Jew was made to wear yellow. By a degree, use became usury; by the rise or fall of a foot, Venice's shining canals turned into foaming floods or malodorous flats.

119 Tucci, U., 'The Psychology of the Venetian Merchant in the XVIth Century', *Renaissance Venice*, p. 347. Eloquent testimony to Venice's vulnerability is found in Marin Sanuto's diaries: '*In questo anno* [1496] *fue grandissima carestia di formenti . . . Et se non fusse state le valide provision fate per la Signoria nostra mediante li proveditori a le biave, la terra haria patito grandemente*' (*Diarii*, Venezia, 1879–1903, [reprint Bologna, 1969] vol. 1, p. 507).

120 Coccius Sabellicus, quoted by P. Zagata in his *Cronaca della Città di Verona*, reprinted Bologna, 1967, vol. 2, pp. 46–7.

121 Spence, Joseph, *Letters from the Grand Tour*, p. 94.

122 Aretino, Pietro, 'Letter to Domenico Bolani, October 27, 1537', *Lettere sull'Arte*, ed. E. Camescaca, Milano, c.1960, vol. 1, p. 71.

123 Berni, F., *Le Rime*, Milano, n.d., p. 35. Written 1530 or 1531.

124 Molmenti, P. G., *Venice: Its Individual Growth from the Earliest Beginnings to the Fall*, trans. H. F. Brown, London, 1906–8, vol. 2, p. 47ff.

125 Vasari, Giorgio, *Vasari on Technique*, translated by L. S. Maclehose, New York, 1960, p. 57. Vasari adds: 'Very few works made of [breccias and other kinds of stone] are to be seen, because of the general use of Istrian stone, into which porphyry, serpentine and other sorts of breccia are often inlaid, resulting in compositions which are very ornamental.' Vasari's observations probably derive from his first visit to Venice in 1542. Writing about 1580, F. Sansovino, who ought to have known, appears to contradict Vasari: 'The stones of Verona are greatly esteemed because being red and variously marked [*con macchie diverse*] they lend beauty to buildings, and from them they make the floors of churches like chequerboards, and they make other things from them which are most appealing, like aquaria, chimneys, cornices and such like things' (*Venetia citta nobilissima et singolare descritta in XIII libri*, Venezia, 1581, p. 140ff). But Vasari makes his comment in the context of criticizing the Venetian attachment, excessive in his view, to Istrian marble as a building material. While Veronese stone was used to create jewel-like effects, Sansovino does not suggest it was used for building.

126 Rosand, D., 'Titian and Pictorial Space' in *Titian, Prince of Painters*, p. 94.

127 Lindsay, Jack, *Blast-Power and Ballistics*, London, 1974, p. 387.

128 Mathew, G., *Byzantine Aesthetics*, p. 30. And he comments: 'The custom of gazing at a decorated surface is perhaps essentially Western.' That is, not Byzantine; nor Venetian, either.

129 Lindsay, Jack, *Blast-Power and Ballistics,* p. 182.

130 Mathew, G., *Byzantine Aesthetics*, p. 31.

131 Rosand, D., 'Titian and Pictorial Space', p. 95.

132 Boschini, Marco, *La Carta del Navegar Pitoresco*, Introduction, p. xxxix.

133 Ibid., stanza 297, p. 328.

134 Ibid., stanza 299, pp. 330–1.

135 Ibid., stanza 343, p. 377.

136 Ibid., stanza 339, p. 373 and *Breve Istruzione*, p. 748 in the same volume, where Boschini spells out the point that in painting, without lights and shadows a circle is indistinguishable from a sphere or ball.

137 Ibid., stanza 340, p. 373. The 'left' and 'right' of chiaroscuro could also be understood musically, as the mastery of contrapuntal forms. (See note 167 below.)

138 In fact, '*el colorito/ Contien in si la machia.*' (Ibid., stanza 300, p. 331.)

139 Boschini, Marco, *Breve Istruzione* in *La Carta del Navegar Pitoresco*, p. 753.

140 Boschini, Marco, *La Carta del Navegar Pitoresco*, stanza 294, p. 325.

141 Ibid., stanza 338, p. 372.

142 Ibid., p. 709. '*Ben tempestato col pennello.*'

143 Ibid., stanza 162, p. 186. '*Qua si Tician, ch'ha teso dreto l'arco . . .*' Of Bassano's brushwork, he writes '*Che 'l ghiera cusi pronto col penelo, / Che se qualcun con lu fava duelo, / Quel tal dava de piato, e lu de ponta.*' (stanza 275, p. 304.)

144 See Doerner, M., *The Materials of the Artists*, trans. E. Neuhaus, London, 1969, pp. 336–7.

145 Rosand, D., and Muraro, M., *Titian and the Venetian Woodcut*, Washington, 1976, p. 9.

146 Boschini, Marco, *La Carta del Navegar Pitoresco*, stanza 339, p. 372.

147 De Montaigne, Michel, 'On Repenting', *The Essays of Michel de Montaigne*, trans. M. A. Screech, London, 1991, p. 909.

148 Rosand, D., 'Titian and Pictorial Space', p. 100.

149 Thompson, D'Arcy Wentworth, *On Growth and Form*, Cambridge, 1942, vol. 1, p. 345. Thompson himself observes, 'The water-colour painter makes good use of the surface-tension effect of the minutest trace of ox-gall' (p. 361).

150 'Oil Painting', *The Oxford Companion to Art*, ed. Harold Osborne, Oxford, 1970, p. 787.

151 Thompson, D'Arcy Wentworth, *On Growth and Form*, vol. 1, p. 359.

152 See Doerner, M., *The Materials of the Artists*, p. 166. L. Lazzarini summarizes the results of physical and chemical analyses of Titian's 'extremely complex' painting technique, in 'Titian's Technique', *Titian, Prince of Painters*, pp. 378–80.

153 Quoted by G. Nepi Sciré, 'Giorgione: Nuda' in *Giorgione a Venezia*, Milano, 1978, p. 120, who cites this passage as proof of a taste already receptive to fresco. But Dolce's remark dates from almost forty years after Giorgione's death, and suggests he stimulated the new taste rather than merely responding to it.

154 Eastlake, Sir C. L., *Methods and Materials of Painting of the Great Schools and Masters*, New York, 1970 [orig. pub. 1847], vol. 1, p. 130. Bearing in mind that Giorgione painted where a year before all had been flames (the fresco commission had been occasioned by the need to rebuild the Fondaco

after its destruction by fire in 1504), his fiery colour suggests a typically Venetian taste for ambiguity, for expressing opposite possibilities in a single form, and interpreting the mastery of their mere coincidence as a cause for self-confidence. As the frescoes have disappeared, it is difficult to assess the relationship between the figures and their architectural milieu. (But see F. Valcanover, note 158 below.)

155 Ibid., vol. 1, p. 370.

156 Ibid., vol. 1, p. 370. The property of 'fieriness' is associated with transformation, whether alchemical or aesthetic. In the poetic sphere, it signifies the ability to 'forge' striking metaphors. The warm glow of Giorgione's figures signified 'liveliness', their power to re-enact the painter's will, to project it and by this process to enhance curvilinear perceptions of the connectedness of parts.

157 Boschini, Marco, *La Carta del Navegar Pitoresco*, stanza 299, p. 330. '*Come la note ilumina dal zorno/ Vien col razo solar terso e pulito,/ Cuso podemo dir, che 'l colorito/ Da chiarezza al dessegno e 'l rende adorno.*' This passage may allude to the same play on words evident in the description of Bassani: '*Ben e vero che i nostri gran Bassani/ Con le so note, ha mostra el zorno a tuti* (stanza 137, p. 161), where Pallucchini observes that '*note*' signifies '*notturni*' or dark passages, and '*giorno*' signifies '*la luce della conquista tecnica raggiunta.*'

158 Valcanover, F., 'Gli affreschi del Fondaco dei Tedeschi' in *Giorgione a Venezia*, pp. 130–1.

159 Eastlake, Sir C. L., *Methods and Materials of Painting of the Great Schools and Masters*, vol. 1, pp. 369–70

160 Herder, J. H., 'Essay on the Origin of Language' in *On the Origin of Language*, p. 150.

161 Ramusio, Giovanni Battista, *Navigazioni e Viaggi*, Torino, 1978–88, vol. 2, p. 937.

162 Lord Byron, 'Childe Harold's Pilgrimage', *The Poetical Works of Lord Byron,* Oxford, 1952, canto IV, xxvii, p. 230.

163 See Hazlitt, W.C., *The Venetian Republic: Its Rise, its Growth, and its Fall*, London, 1915, vol. 2, p. 308.

164 Rosand, David, 'Titian and Pictorial Space', p. 100.

165 Lewin, Kurt, *Principles of Topological Psychology*, New York, 1936, p. 89.

166 Wilden, Antony, *System and Structure*, London, 1980, p. xlvi.

167 Boschini, Marco, *La Carta del Navegar Pitoresco*, stanza 294, p. 324. Stokes insisted polemically that he would write 'upon the aspect of visual art to which music offers no parallel.' ('Art and Science', *The Critical Writings of Adrian Stokes*, vol. 2, p. 207). But Giorgione was a musician, according to Vasari a skilled lutenist (Vasari, Giorgio, *The Lives of the Artists*, trans. G. Bull, p. 273). The critical issue was not the musical analogy itself, but the kind of music with which Giorgione's art should be compared. Like a musician whose accidental dissonances serve to display and heighten the

beauty and grace of the piece he is playing or improvising (Boschini, Marco, *La Carta del Navegar Pitoresco*, stanza 294, p. 324), so the artist avoids mechanical imitation.

The obvious parallel is with the art of the *frottola* practised by Willaert, the greatest of the madrigalists working in Venice in the mid-part of the sixteenth century. Einstein writes of Willaert's style: 'The diction is most painstaking and flexible without descending to mere declamation. The structure of the part writing is at once visible and hidden; it is most visible in the play of the imitation between tenor and soprano. Willaert achieves expression, the *expressivo*, with ease; he does not paint, but he attains a delicate rhetoric which appears and appeals in every phrase.' (Einstein, A., *The Italian Madrigal*, Princeton, 1947, p. 339.)

168 Hillman, J., *La Vana Fuga dagli Dei*, Milano, 1991, pp. 66–7.

169 Ibid., p. 72

170 Smith, F. Joseph, *The Experiencing of Musical Sound*, p. 168.

171 De Montaigne, Michel, 'On the Inconstancy of Our Actions', *The Essays of Michel de Montaigne*, p. 380.

172 Ibid., 'On Affectionate Relationships', p. 205–6.

173 Ibid., 'On Repenting', pp. 907–8.

174 Ibid., 'On Presumption', p. 738. 'I want people to see my natural ordinary stride, however much it wanders off the path.' ('On Books', p. 459.)

175 Ibid., 'On the Inconstancy of our Actions', p. 379.

176 Ibid., 'On Practice', p. 424.

177 Ibid., 'How We Weep and Laugh at the Same Thing', p. 265.

178 Ibid., 'On the Cannibals', p. 231.

179 Greenblatt, S., *Marvelous Possessions*, p. 147.

180 Ibid., p. 150.

181 See Hillman, J., *La Vana Fuga dagli Dei*, pp. 78–9.

182 Boschini, Marco, *La Carta del Navegar Pitoresco*, stanza 220, p. 247. '*La fazza conto che 'l gran Tentoreto/ Ande dove non serve Tramontana,/ A trovar niovi Mondi ala lontana,/ Come fece el Colombo . . .*' But maybe the point is subtler. Tintoretto went beyond the 'sunset' of colour; he went over the mountains by plumbing their depths, the folds of their shadow garments, not by putting them behind him.

183 Sartre, J-P., *Situations*, trans. B. Eisler, London, 1965, p. 57ff.

184 See Paz, Octavio, *The Labyrinth of Solitude*, trans. Lysander Kemp, London, 1985, p. 77.

185 Papini, Mario, *Arbor Humanae Linguae*, Bologna, 1984, p. 86. He continues: 'The rectilinearity of the first [Cartesian] interpretation is cancelled out by the intrinsically curviform nature of the second, and deeper, vision of reality.'

186 De Montaigne, Michel, 'On the Inconstancy of our Actions', *The Essays of Michel de Montaigne*, p. 377

187 Ibid., p. 377.

188 Ibid., p. 377.
189 Maclean, I., '"Le pais au delà": Montaigne and Philosophical Speculation', in *Montaigne*, ed. McFarlane, I.D., and Maclean, I., Oxford, 1982, pp. 124–5.
190 See note 85 above.
191 Feyerabend, Paul, *Against Method*, London, 1978, p. 21.
192 Cited by Feyerabend, ibid., p. 69.
193 Ibid., p. 24.
194 Ibid., p. 21.
195 White, E. C., *Kaironomia*, Ithaca (New York), 1987, p. 21. Like Feyerabend, White associates this art of occasions with that practised by the Dadaists (ibid., p. 20, note 12): it would also, he writes, 'approximate to "Pataphysics", Alfred Jarry's term for the mock-serious science that would examine the laws governing exceptions.'
196 Ibid., p. 21.
197 Ibid., p. 153.
198 See White's discussion, ibid., p. 153ff.
199 Maclean, I., '"Le pais au dela": Montaigne and Philosophical Speculation', p. 124.
200 De Montaigne, Michel, 'On the Cannibals', *The Essays of Michel de Montaigne*, p. 231.
201 Paolo Sarpi, *Pensieri*, Torino, 1976, p.14.
202 Ibid., p. 44.
203 Thompson, D'Arcy Wentworth, *On Growth and Form*, vol. 2, p. 675.
204 Feyerabend, Paul, *Against Method*, p. 82.
205 Ibid., p. 81.
206 Quoted by Vicente L. Rafael in 'Gods and Grammar: The Politics of Translation in the Spanish Colonisation of the Tagalogs of the Phillipines', in *Notebooks in Cultural Analysis*, Duke University, 1986, Vol. 3: A Special Issue on 'Voice', p. 98.
207 Stokes, Adrian, 'Venice', *The Critical Writings of Adrian Stokes*, vol. 2, p. 127.
208 Taviani and Varela list the 'indigenous' *ca* words in *Cristoforo Colombo, Giornale di Bordo della prima Navigazione e scoperta delle Indie*, vol. 2, pp. 54–5. F. Maldonado de Guevara, *El Primer Contacto de Blancos y Gentes de Color en America*, Valladolid, 1924, p. 30ff, has a good discussion of these phonic ambiguities.
209 *The 'Diario' of Christopher Columbus's First Voyage to America*, pp. 262–3. Taviani and Varela have 'caona'. (*Cristoforo Colombo, Giornale di Bordo della prima Navigazione e scoperta delle Indie*, vol. 2, pp. 54.)
210 Maldonado de Guevara, F., *El Primer Contacto de Blancos y Gentes de Color en America*, pp. 26–7.
211 *The 'Diario' of Christopher Columbus's First Voyage to America*, pp. 124–5.
212 Polo, Marco, *Il Milione*, Roma, 1985, p. 143, note 3.

213 *The 'Diario' of Christopher Columbus's First Voyage to America*, pp. 128–9.
214 Ibid., p. 147.
215 Wescott, Roger, 'Types of Apophony in Proto-Speech', in *Language Origins*, Silver Spring (Maryland), c.1974, p. 154. 'The Spaniards . . . employed dogs in their recent conquest of the American Indies; they paid them like soldiers and gave them a share in the booty' (Michel de Montaigne, 'An Apology for Raymond Sebond', *The Essays of Michel de Montaigne*, p. 521).
216 'Columbus's Narrative of the Third Voyage', *The Four Voyages of Christopher Columbus*, p. 218.
217 Carter, P., *The Sound In-Between*, Sydney, 1992, p. 81.
218 *The 'Diario' of Christopher Columbus's First Voyage to America*, p. 91.
219 Ibid., p. 91.
220 Ibid., p. 67.
221 Colombo, Cristoforo, *Giornale di Bordo della prima Navigàzione e scoperta delle Indie*, pp. 367–8.
222 Maldonado de Guevara, F., *El Primer Contacto de Blancos y Gentes de Color en America*, p. 47.
223 *The 'Diario' of Christopher Columbus's First Voyage to America*, pp. 67–8.
224 Ibid., pp. 67–8.
225 Ibid., pp. 222–3.
226 Greenblatt, Stephen, *Marvelous Possessions*, p. 99. Greenblatt's conclusion follows from his initial assumption of a kind of equivalence in otherness. Thus he posits: 'In the absence of a common language both Europeans and natives attempted . . . to communicate with signs' (*Marvelous Possessions*, p. 93). This is no doubt true so long as 'signs' are taken in a loose sense to cover a range of gestures, dances, vocalisations, gift-exchanges etc; but it may not be true if we suppose both parties were not seeking to signify in comparable ways.
227 *The 'Diario' of Christopher Columbus's First Voyage to America*, pp. 67–8.
228 Rousseau, Jean-Jacques, 'Essay on the Origin of Languages' in *On the Origin of Language*, pp. 11–13 and 178 and *The 'Diario' of Christopher Columbus's First Voyage to America*, pp. 67–8.
229 Ibid., pp. 67–8.
230 Arioli, A., *Le Isole Mirabili*, p. 30. Herder, of course, would have had no sympathy for an imitative theory of the origin of language. Columbus might have thought he recognized the nightingale, but no man could 'invent for himself a language by trilling the trills of the nightingale. And what a monstrosity: a human nightingale in a cave or out in the forest with the hunt!' (J. G. Herder, 'Essay on the Origin of Language' in *On the Origin of Language*, p. 136).

But hunters have been known to mimic ducks; the 'nightingale' Columbus heard was in all probability a species of mocking-bird. The point is not to derive language from the birds, but to recognize the fact that, where there is no shared language, meanings evolve dialogically, are improvised on the basis of mere coincidence. To get beyond parroting presupposes a specifically human talent for language; but a human talent for language presupposes in turn a mimetic adeptness, a willingness to yield to the sounds around.

231 *The 'Diario' of Christopher Columbus's First Voyage to America*, p. 315ff. Columbus's understanding of the story would have been influenced by his familiarity with Marco Polo's account of 'The two islands in one of which men live without women, and in the other of which women live without men' (Marco Polo, *Il Milione*, p. 271).

232 Maldonado de Guevara, F., *El Primer Contacto de Blancos y Gentes de Color en America*, pp. 36–7.

233 Dati, Giuliano, *La Lettera dell'Isole*, Bologna, 1968, stanza LXI, p. 23. See also Arioli, A., *Le Isole Mirabili*, p. 104, for other precedents.

234 *The Life of the Admiral Christopher Columbus by His Son Ferdinand*, ed. and trans. B. Keen, New Brunswick (N.J.), 1959, p. 154.

235 Ibid., p. 156.

236 Pignatti, T., *Giorgione*, p. 16.

237 *Aretino's Dialogues*, trans. R. Rosenthal, London, 1971, p. 242.

238 Cezanne, Paul, *Letters*, ed. and trans. J. Rewald, Oxford, 1941, pp. 262–3.

239 *The Literary Works of Leonardo da Vinci*, ed. J. P. Richter, vol. 1, p. 152.

240 Quoted by Adrian Stokes, 'Cezanne', *The Critical Writings of Adrian Stokes*, vol. 2, p. 263. 'He was always a very amorous man' (Vasari, *The Lives of the Artists*, p. 272).

241 Mullaney, Steven, *The Place of the Stage*, p. 47ff.

242 Spence, Joseph, *Letters from the Grand Tour*, pp. 94–5.

243 Ibid., p 95.

244 Ibid., p. 95.

245 Ibid., p. 95.

246 Ibid., p. 96

247 Ibid., p. 95.

248 Von Kleist, Heinrich. 'On the Marionette Theater', in *Fragments for a History of the Human Body*, ed. M. Feher, New York, 1990, p. 418.

249 *Dr Charles Burney 's Continental Travels, 1770–1772*, ed. G. H. Glover, London, 1927, p. 38.

250 Salmond, Anne, *Hui*, Auckland, 1990, p. 132.

251 Ibid., p.15.

252 Spence, Joseph, *Letters from the Grand Tour*, p. 96.

253 See Carter, Paul, 'Towards a Sound Photography' in *Living In A New Country*, pp. 84–5.

Part Three: Light Reading

1 *Light Papers*, State Library of South Australia, PRG Special List, Series 4, Item 171.

2 Ibid., Series 4, Item 134.
3 The biographical details are drawn from Elder, D., Introduction to *William Light's Brief Journal and Australian Diaries*, Adelaide, 1984; Dutton, G., *Founder of a City*, Melbourne, 1960; Steuart, A. F., *A Short Sketch of the Lives of Francis and William Light*, London, 1901; and Mayo, M. P., *The Life and Letters of William Light*, Adelaide, 1937. An alternative account of William Light's father is offered by Clodd, H. P., *Malaya's First British Pioneer* (London, 1948).
4 Dutton, G., *Founder of a City*, p. 171.
5 Elder, D., *William Light's Brief Journal and Australian Diaries*, p. 59.
6 Steuart, A. F., *A Short Sketch of the Lives of Francis and William Light*, p. 64.
7 Elder, D., *William Light's Brief Journal and Australian Diaries*, p. 16.
8 Mayo, M. P., *The Life and Letters of William Light*, pp. 249–50.
9 These details are derived from Light's *Last Diary* in Elder, D., *William Light's Brief Journal and Australian Diaries*. No complete catalogue of Light's drawings and paintings exists, although the South Australian Historical Pictures Index in the Mortlock Library of South Australiana is very useful. D. Elder's catalogue *William Light 1786–1839, Surveyor-General of South Australia*, Adelaide, 1966, is supplemented by his finely-illustrated *Art of William Light*, Adelaide, 1987. The latter reproduces most of the watercolours referred to here.
10 Light, W., *Last Diary*, p. 155.
11 Elder, D., *William Light's Brief Journal and Australian Diaries*, p. 49, and Dutton, G., *Founder of a City*, p. 282.
12 Some idea of how Light's agent Collard had regarded the South Australian appointment is evident from a letter dated 10 July 1836 in which Light is urged to communicate any 'opening . . . where a speculation might be entered into with a firm prospect of advantage for I consider you now almost as having started in a remarkable career - at all events I certainly look forward to your making a great deal of money as an Exporter of Wool to England in the course of a few years . . .' (Light Papers, PRG Special List, Series 1, Item 10.)
13 Dutton, G., *Founder of a City*, p. 283.
14 Whitelock, D. *Adelaide 1836–1976: A History of Difference*, St Lucia (Queensland), 1977, p. 36.
15 Dutton, G., *Founder of a City*, p. 281.
16 *Light Papers*, Series 1, Item 92.
17 Bate, W. J., *John Keats*, Cambridge (Mass), 1963, p. 680.
18 Ibid., p. 680.
19 Gell, J. P., 'South Australian Aborigines: The Vocabulary of the Adelaide Tribe', *Proc. Royal Geographical Society of Australia*, South Australian Branch, Adelaide, vol. 7, p. 97. As originally published in 1842, this article contained, immediately after the passage cited, a Latin poem commemorating the foundation of Carthage.

20 Elder, D., 'Introduction' to *William Light's Brief Journal and Australian Diaries*.
21 Whittemore, R., *Pure Lives*, Baltimore, 1988, p. 6.
22 Obeyesekere, G., *The Apotheosis of Captain Cook*, Princeton, 1993, p. 11.
23 Dutton, G., *Founder of a City*, p. 13.
24 Steuart, A. F., *A Short Sketch of the Lives of Francis and William Light*, p. 27.
25 Dutton, G., *Founder of a City*, pp. 128–32 for these details.
26 The Florentine interlude is narrated in Pope-Hennessy, J., *The Official Life of Queen Mary* (London, 1959), chapter 5. For this reference and the information concerning the 1901 visit I am indebted to Dr John Tregenza.
27 See Lord Mayor Reginald Walker's Speech of Acceptance, Civic Collection, Accession Number 685. Again, I owe this reference to Dr John Tregenza.
28 Obeyesekere, G., *The Apotheosis of Captain Cook* pp. 134–7.
29 Johnson, D.L., and Langmead, D., *The Adelaide City Plan: Fact and Fiction*, Adelaide, 1986. See also R. Cheesman's comments on the views of another pioneer descendant (*Patterns in Perpetuity*, Adelaide, 1986, p. 99). Light's own statement is not easily refuted, however, except by declaring it an outright lie: 'It has been hinted to me that Mr Kingston took to himself the credits of the site and plan of this town - if he did it is false he had nothing to do with it but marking off town acres and in doing this he blundered . . .' (*Light Papers*, Series 1, Item 114.)
30 See my 'Making Contact: History and Performance' in *Living In A New Country*, London, 1992, p. 171.
31 Elder, D., *William Light's Brief Journal and Australian Diaries*, p. 9.
32 Steuart, A. F., *A Short Sketch of the Lives of Francis and William Light*, p. 44.
33 Dutton, G., *Founder of a City*, p. 271.
34 Mayo, M. P., *The Life and Letters of William Light*, p. 20.
35 Ibid., p. 20.
36 Elder, D., *William Light's Brief Journal and Australian Diaries*, p. 10ff.
37 Dutton, G., *Founder of a City*, p. 72.
38 Stephens, J., *The Land of Promise*, London, 1839, p. 78.
39 Asked his opinion of the Kaurna's suitability as soldiers, Light responded, 'I do not think they can be made much of until the Colony becomes so populous that their very living be taken away except they work for it.' (*Light Papers*, Series 1, Item 117.)
40 Elder, D., *William Light's Brief Journal and Australian Diaries*, p. 47.
41 Light W., *Last Diary*, page entries identifiable by dates.
42 Tregenza, J., 'Colonel Light's Theberton Cottage and His Legacy to Maria Gandy: A Reconsideration of the Evidence', *Journal of the Historical Society of South Australia*, vol. 17, 1989, pp. 5–24.
43 Locke, John, *Two Treatises of Civil Government*, London, 1955, p. 132.

44 Frost, A., 'New South Wales as *terra nullius*: The British Denial of Aboriginal Land Rights', *Historical Studies (Melbourne)*, vol. 19, no.77, p. 520.
45 Bennett, Richard, *Early Days of Port Fairy*, Warrnambool, 1984, p. 61.
46 Worgan, G., *Journal of a First Fleet Surgeon*, Sydney, 1978, p. 33.
47 Locke, John, *Two Treatises of Civil Government*, p. 132.
48 'Erectness is moral, existential, no less than physical' (Sacks, O., *A Leg to Stand On*, London, 1984, p. 98.) Sacks discovers that 'severe disturbances of body-image and body-ego occur as a result of peripheral injury, disease or disorder' (p. 159). Zeno has the opposite experience: a disturbance of body-ego induces a disorder of body-image. Like his famous namesake, the author of the paradox, Zeno has difficulty in imagining himself getting from one place to another. He cannot attain spontaneity: hence, instead of walking, he can only limp. Like Sacks, Zeno associates recovery with music. 'The music that is produced by a well-balanced physique is identical with the rhythm it creates and exploits: it is rhythm itself. When I can play like that I shall be cured' (Svevo, I., *Confessions of Zeno*, trans. B. de Zoete, London, 1962, p. 136).
49 See 'About Canoes', note 181, above.
50 Pye, Henry James, *Faringdon Hill*, London, 1774, Book 1, p. 4.
51 See my *The Road to Botany Bay*, London, 1987, pp. 43–4.
52 Pye, Henry James, *Faringdon Hill*, p. 5
53 Holmes, R., *Footsteps*, London, 1985, p. 210.
54 Brownlow, T., *John Clare and Picturesque Landscape*, Oxford, 1983, p. 12.
55 Ibid., p. 12.
56 Forbes, D., Hume's Philosophical Politics, Cambridge, 1975, p. 10.
57 Dutton, G., *Founder of a City*, p. 215.
58 Haggard, H. R., *The Days of My Life*, London, 1926, vol. 2, pp. 168–71.
59 Ibid., p. 171.
60 Ibid., p. 168
61 Von Rezzori, G., *The Death of my Brother Abel*, trans. J. Neugroschel, New York, 1985, p. 208.
62 Lawrence, C., 'The Power and the Glory: Humphry Davy and Romanticism', in *Romanticism and the Sciences*, ed. A. Cunningham and N. Jardine, Cambridge, 1990, p. 225.
63 Ibid., p. 224.
64 Napier, Charles J., *Colonization particularly in South Australia*, New York, 1969 [orig. pub. 1835], pp. 77–8.
65 Ibid. p. 78.
66 Rogers, S., 'The Pleasures of Memory', *Poems*, London, 1849, p. 16.
67 Wallace, A. R., *My Life*, London, 1905, vol. 2, p. 389.
68 Brownlow, T., *John Clare and Picturesque Landscape*, p. 21.
69 Ibid., p. 34.
70 Ibid., p. 68.
71 Letter to J. Fisher, 20 April 1837, cited by Elder, D., 'Introduction' to

William Light's Brief Journal and Australian Diaries, p. 41.
72 Carter, P., 'Plotting' in *Living In A New Country*, p. 23.
73 Brownlow, T., *John Clare and Picturesque Landscape*, p. 17.
74 See *Light Papers*, Series 2, Item 111. Light's argument is amplified in subsequent letters (Items 113, 114 and 115).
75 Brownlow, T., *John Clare and Picturesque Landscape*, p. 13.
76 Kant, I., *Anthropology from a Pragmatic Point of View*, trans. M. J. Gregor, The Hague, 1974, p. 88.
77 Light, W., *Brief Journal*, p. 62.
78 Ibid., p. 79.
79 Ibid., p. 63.
80 Ibid., p. 72.
81 Ibid., p. 75.
82 Ibid., p. 76.
83 Ibid., p. 76.
84 Eliot, George, *Silas Marner*, ed. Q. D. Leavis, London, 1967, p. 51.
85 Kant, I., *Anthropology from a Pragmatic Point of View*, p. 86.
86 Vaihinger, H., *The Philosophy of 'As If'*, trans. C. K. Ogden, London, 1924, p. 101.
87 Ibid., p. 103.
88 Ibid., p. 103.
89 Ibid., p. 104.
90 Ibid., p. 15.
91 Ibid., p. 2.
92 See 'Friday's Other Foot', note 9, above.
93 So Cato committed suicide rather than submit to the dictator Caesar.
94 Elder observes '[Francis] Light was ill-served by dual control, the East India Company and British government speaking with different voices.' (Elder, D., *William Light's Brief Journal and Australian Diaries*, p. 8.) Light is said to have been disgusted with the East India Company for having 'robbed his father of the island (of Penang) by forcing him to cede it for money . . .' (H.P. Clodd, *Malaya's First British Pioneer*, p. 132.)
95 Mills, R. C., *The Colonization of Australia (1829–1842)*, London, 1968, p. 126.
96 Cited by R.C. Mills, op. cit., p. 206.
97 Wakefield, E. G., Letter from Sydney, cited by Mills, R. C., *The Colonization of Australia (1829–1842)*, p.198.
98 Ibid., p. 117.
99 Ibid., p. 107.
100 Ibid., p. 100.
101 Ibid., p. 104.
102 Bhabha, H., 'Of Mimicry and Man: The Ambivalence of Colonial Discourse', *October, the First Decade, 1976–1986*, Cambridge (Mass), 1987, p. 324.

103 Stephens, J., *The Land of Promise*, p. 73 and p. 80.
104 Ibid., p. 73.
105 Ibid., p. 69.
106 Gouger, R., *South Australia in 1837*, London, 1837, p. 52.
107 Leigh, W.H., *Travels and Adventures in South Australia 1836–1838*, London, 1839, p. 152.
108 Ibid., p. 165.
109 See Hassell, K., *The Relations Between the Settlers and Aborigines in South Australia, 1836–1860*, Adelaide, 1966, p. 30.
110 Stephens, J., *The Land of Promise*, p. 77.
111 Von Humboldt, Wilhelm, *On Language*, trans. P. Heaton, Cambridge, 1988, pp. 68–9.
112 See Boon, J., *Affinities and Extremes*, Chicago, 1990, pp. 20–3, for these passages and a discussion of them.
113 Hassell, K., *The Relations Between the Settlers and Aborigines in South Australia, 1836–1860*, p. 18.
114 Gouger, R., *South Australia in 1837*, p. 53.
115 The date of the vessel's arrival is given by Stephens, J., *The Land of Promise*, p. 116.
116 Leigh, W.H., *Travels and Adventures in South Australia 1836–1838*, p. 85.
117 See note 106, above.
118 Tregenza, J., 'The Visual Dimension of Colonial History', *Art and Australia*, vol. 19, Spring 1981, p. 92.
119 Aemilia Curran's portrait of the poet done in 1819 is reproduced in Holmes, R., *Shelley: The Pursuit*, London, 1974, Plate 38. Perhaps we should say 'apparently tubercular'; Hele-King bluntly dismisses the 1815 diagnosis as irresponsibly wrong, noting though that '"Romantic death-wishes" are only too probable if doctors pronounce death sentences whenever diagnosis baffles them.' (Hele-King, D., *Shelley: His Thought and Work*, London, 1971, p. 62.)
120 R. Holmes also reproduces Curran's 1819 portrait of Claire Clairmont (*Shelley: The Pursuit*, Plate 16).
121 Both poets quoted by A. Cunningham and N. Jardine in their Introduction to *Romanticism and the Sciences*, p. 2.
122 Dutton, G., *Founder of a City*, p. 214. Dutton explicitly rejects any possibility of a Sicilian influence on Light's plan.
123 Ibid., p. 215.
124 Cheesman, R., *Pattern and Perpetuity*, p. 103. T. Denholm takes it for granted that Light's plan is 'a basic grid pattern' (Denholm, T., 'Adelaide: A Victorian Bastide' in *The Origins of Australia's Capital Cities*, ed. P. Statham, Cambridge, 1989, p. 181. Denholm's article is perverse and perceptive: Light's plan was intended to give urban definition to a predominantly-rural population but, as Denholm admits, 'Unlike most medieval "bastides" Adelaide has no military function or town wall.' (!)

125 Elder, D., letter to author, April 1995.
126 This summary is based mainly on Canale, C.G., *Noto - La Struttura Continua della Città Tardo-Barocca*, Palermo, 1976, pp. 69–96.
127 Bentham, J., 'Colonization Society', unpublished proposals, 1831, p. 43. I am indebted to Prof John Poynter for a copy of his unpublished edition of this work. Other names that Bentham toyed with included 'New Colonia' and 'Liberia'.
128 Napier, Charles J., *Colonization particularly in South Australia*, p. 47.
129 Carter, P., *The Road to Botany Bay*, pp. 212–5.
130 Leigh, W.H., *Travels and Adventures in South Australia 1836–1838*, p. 139.
131 Richardson, L., Jr, *Pompeii: An Architectural History*, Baltimore, 1988, p. xxi.
132 Ibid., p. xxii.
133 Stephens, J., *The Land of Promise*, p. 41.
134 See 'Friday's Other Foot', note 26, above.
135 Lord Lytton, *The Last Days of Pompeii*, London, 1877, p. 393.
136 See Thacker, C., *The Wildness Pleases*, London, 1983, pp. 145–52.
137 Lord Lytton, *The Last Days of Pompeii*, p. 424.
138 Ibid., p. 424.
139 Ibid., p. 424.
140 Stephens, J., *The Land of Promise*, pp. 107–8.
141 Ibid., p. 108.
142 Light, W., Letter to George Palmer, 12 March 1839 (*Light Papers*, Series 1, Item 117).
143 Worsnop, T., *History of the City of Adelaide*, Adelaide, 1878, p. 10, quoting an early Report of the Commissioners.
144 Kant, I., *Anthropology from a Pragmatic Point of View*, pp. 85–6.
145 Ibid., p. 86.
146 Lyotard, J-F., *The Inhuman*, trans. G. Bennington and R. Bowlby, Stanford, 1991, p. 182.
147 Light, W., *Brief Journal*, p. 72. 'A vertical pillar of light or, rather, feather of light can be observed fairly often above the rising or setting sun . . . This pillar of light is in itself uncoloured, but when the sun is low and has become yellow, orange or red, the pillar naturally assumes the same tint.' (Minnaert, M., *The Nature of Light and Colour*, trans. H.M. Kremer-Priest, New York, 1954, p. 201.) But Light states that the pillar was seen in the north-east, not in the west as one would expect towards sunset.
148 Pater, W., *Gaston de Latour*, London, 1910, p. 60. 'The rain, the first streak of dawn, the very sullenness of the sky, had a power, only to be described by saying that they seemed to be moral facts.'
149 Ibid., p. 84.
150 Ibid., pp. 94–5.
151 Teichelmann, C., *Aborigines of South Australia*, Adelaide, 1841, p. 12. Teichelmann's missionary efforts and attitudes are discussed by Foster, R.,

'The Aborigines Location (*sic*) in Adelaide: South Australia's First "Mission" to the Aborigines' in *Aboriginal Adelaide*, Journal of the Anthropological Society of South Australia, vol. 28, nos 1 and 2, pp. 11–37.

152 Tench, W., *Sydney's First Four Years*, Sydney, 1979, pp. 31–2. Bearing in mind that Sarpi and Montaigne regarded Cato's unbending moral rectitude as akin to boorish pigheadedness, the character of the imperialism implicit in Tench's choice of text becomes clearer. Another cryptic connection: although Addison's *Cato* was not performed until 1713, one of his biographers suggests that the idea for the tragedy first came to him in Venice 'where he was struck by a grotesque play upon the death of Cato.' (I. Bruce Nagel, *Biography: Fiction, Fact and Form*, London: Macmillan, 1985, p. 50).

153 Goldsmith, O., 'Prologue to Zobeide', *The Poems of Gray, Collins and Goldsmith*, ed. R. Lonsdale, London, 1969, pp. 705–6.

154 Clark, R., *The Journal and Letters of Lt. Ralph Clark 1787–1792*, Sydney, 1981, p. 263.

155 Bowes Smyth, A., *The Journal of Arthur Bowes Smyth: Surgeon, Lady Penrhyn 1787–1789*, Sydney, 1979, p. 67.

156 Clark, R., *The Journal and Letters of Lt. Ralph Clark 1787–1792*, p. 101.

157 Ibid., p. 101.

158 Macarthur, Elizabeth, Letter of 7 March 1791, in *Penguin Anthology of Australian Women's Writing*, ed. D. Spender, Melbourne, 1989, p. 24.

159 Tench, W., *Sydney's First Four Years*, p. 278.

160 Collins, David, *An Account of the English Colony in New South Wales*, Sydney, 1975, vol. 1, p. 547.

161 King, P. G., in Hunter, John, *An Historical Journal of the Transactions at Port Jackson and Norfolk Island*, Adelaide, 1968, p. 412.

162 Teichelmann, C. G., and Schurmann, C.W., *Outlines of a grammar, vocabulary and phraseology of the Aboriginal language of South Australia*, Adelaide, 1841, p. 70.

163 Ibid., p. 71.

164 Light, W., *Brief Journal*, pp. 70–1.

165 Boswell's phrase. See *The Road to Botany Bay*, p. 75.

166 See the splendid and arcane summary in *Encyclopaedia Britannica* (Chicago, 1989), vol 3, pp. 398–9.

167 Forster, T., *Researches about Atmospheric Phaenomena*, London, 1812, p. 6. A few pages earlier, Forster notes, 'Our English word cloud is derived from the Anglo-Saxon word *hlithan* . . . tegere, to cover; from the same verb come glade, blot, lot and lid.' (p. 2.)

168 Ibid., p. 10.

169 Ibid., pp. 19–20.

170 Ibid., pp. 21–3.

171 Ibid., pp. 25–6.

172 Sepper, D. L., 'Goethe, Colour and the Science of Seeing' in *Romanticism and the Sciences*, pp. 196–7.

173 Ibid., p. 192.
174 Reproduced in Elder, D., *Art of William Light*, Plate 7, p. 33. Elder notes that 'much time was spent in Rome. Between December 1824 and February 1825 Light was laid up there with a serious illness.'
175 See note 18, above.
176 The same uncertainty could lend colonization a clinical fatefulness: 'If you have any friends afflicted with pulmonary diseases, pray entreat them to try this climate, when, with God's blessing, they would soon be cured,' averred one Mr Giles, writing from Adelaide in June 1838 (Stephens, J., *The Land of Promise*, p. 46).
177 The contagious theory was apparently especially popular in Italy (see Dubos, R. and J., *The White Plague: Tuberculosis, Man and Society*, Boston, 1952, pp. 29–32).
178 *Light Papers*, Series 3, Item 171.
179 Dutton, G., *Founder of a City*, p.112.
180 *Light Papers*, Series 3, Item 134.
181 Just some of the legion pseudo-cures for phthisis entertained in Light's day.
182 Duncan, A., *Observations on the Distinguishing Symptoms of the three different Species of Pulmonary Consumption*, Edinburgh, 1813, p. 146.
183 Ibid., p. 319.
184 Light, W., 'Diary of a Journey to Lynedoch Valley, December 1837', in Elder, D., *William Light's Brief Journal and Australian Diaries*, p. 133.
185 Ibid., p. 137.
186 Light, W., *Last Diary*, p. 161.
187 Sontag, S., *Illness as Metaphor*, London, 1978, p. 38.
188 Feldman, T.S., 'Late Enlightenment Meteorology' in *The Quantifying Spirit in the 18th Century*, ed. T. Frangsmyr, J. L. Heilbron and R. E. Rider, Berkeley, 1990, p. 154.
189 Ibid., p. 177.
190 Harris, W. S., *On the Nature of Thunderstorms*, London, 1843, p. 3.
191 Forster, T., *Researches about Atmospheric Phaenomena*, p. 165.
192 Ibid., p. 166.
193 Harris, W. S., *On the Nature of Thunderstorms*, p. 33.
194 Lawrence, C., 'The Power and the Glory: Humphry Davy and Romanticism', p. 216.
195 Ibid., p. 226.
196 See note 66 above.
197 Schaffer, S., 'Genius in Romantic Natural Philosophy' in *Romanticism and the Sciences*, p. 93.
198 Duncan, A., *Observations on the Distinguishing Symptoms of the three different Species of Pulmonary Consumption*, p. 50ff.
199 Keats, John, *Poems*. As doctors of the soul, poets too have their fashions: Mandelstam thought Pasternak's verses 'must be a cure for tuberculosis.'

(O. Mandelstam, 'About Poetry', *Selected Essays*, trans. S. Monas, Austin, 1977, p. 83).
200 Bate, W. J., *John Keats*, p. 636.
201 Sontag, S., *Illness as Metaphor*, p. 17.
202 Forster, T., *Researches about Atmospheric Phaenomena*, p. 219.
203 Onians, R. B., *The Origins of European Thought*, Cambridge, 1991, pp. 73–7.
204 Dubos, R. and J., *The White Plague: Tuberculosis, Man and Society*, pp. 77–87.
205 Smith, F. Joseph, *The Experiencing of Musical Sound*, New York, 1978, p. 168.
206 Light, W., *Last Diary*, p. 144.
207 Ibid., p. 146.
208 Elder ('Introduction' to *William Light's Brief Journal and Australian Diaries*, p. 47) notes that 'this was a sympathetic exaggeration.'
209 Light, W., *Last Diary*, p. 149.
210 Serres, M., quoted by Prigogine, I., and Stengers, I., *Order out of Chaos*, in a section entitled 'A Whirlwind in a Turbulent Nature', p. 304.
211 Light, W., *Last Diary*, p. 151.
212 Bergson, H., *An Introduction to Metaphysics*, trans. T. E. Hulme, London, 1913, p. 31.
213 Light, W., *Last Diary*, p. 153.
214 Sciascia, L., *The Moro Affair and the Mystery of Majorana*, trans. S. Rabinovitch, Manchester, 1987, p. 137, note 1.
215 Light, W., *Last Diary*, p. 158.
216 Sciascia, L., *The Moro Affair and the Mystery of Majorana*, p. 173.
217 Light, W., *Last Diary*, p. 161.
218 *Light Papers*, Series 1, Item 85 (dated 2 July 1838).
219 Sciascia, L., *The Moro Affair and the Mystery of Majorana*, p. 173.
220 Light, W., *Last Diary*, p. 164.
221 Ibid., p. 167.
222 Ibid., p. 167.
223 Ibid., p. 168.
224 Ibid., p. 169.
225 Ibid., p. 169.
226 Ibid., p. 169.
227 Ibid., p. 170.
228 Ibid., p. 170.
229 Ibid., p. 170.

Part Four: Drift Lanes

1 Prynne, J. H., 'The Common Gain, Reverted', *Poems*, Edinburgh, 1982, p. 88.
2 Valéry, P., 'Poetry and Abstract Thought' in The Art of Poetry, vol. 7, *The*

Collected Works of Paul Valéry, ed. J. Mathews, Princeton, 1955–70, p. 78.
3 Ibid., p. 70.
4 Valéry, P., 'Conversation on History' in History and Politics, vol. 10, *The Collected Works of Paul Valéry*, p. 322ff.
5 See 'About Canoes', note 185, above.
6 Gibson, J. J., *The Ecological Approach to Visual Perception*, Boston, 1979, pp. 128–9 and pp. 239–40.
7 Müller, M., 'Kant's Critique of Pure Reason', *Last Essays*, London, 1901, p. 237.
8 Ibid., p. 238.
9 Müller, M., 'Coincidences', *Last Essays*, p. 254.
10 Ibid., p. 254.
11 Gibson, J. J., *The Ecological Approach to Visual Perception*, p. 16ff. Stroll, A., *Surfaces*, Minneapolis, 1987, chapter 5, summarizes the evolution of Gibson's ideas well, besides offering an interesting critique of his arguments.
12 Valéry, P., 'Poetry and Abstract Thought' in The Art of Poetry, p. 62. It is an interesting question what form the flight would take. If 'straight-line natural motion' is a sublunar exception to the general rule of circular motion, Valéry's double would describe a self-meeting curve. Here, then, is a double reason for escaping the ground: flat, it is the relic of 'violent' motion (Blumenberg, H., *The Genesis of the Copernican World*, trans. R. M. Wallace, Cambridge, Mass., 1987, pp.160–1), while undulating and uneven, it is actively non-rational. 'In 1541, Reinhold [an early interpreter of Copernicus] explained that the Earth's deviations, through its mountains and deeps, from the pure form of a sphere by saying that God had abandoned rationality in His work in favour of usefulness for man.' (Blumenberg, H., *The Genesis of the Copernican World*, p. 334.)
13 Valéry, P., 'Poetry and Abstract Thought' in The Art of Poetry, p. 61.
14 Heidegger, M., 'The Origin of the Work of Art', in *Poetry, Language, Thought*, trans. A. Hofstadter, New York, 1971, pp. 41–3. 'The temple-work, standing there, opens up a world and at the same time sets this world back again on earth, which itself only thus emerges as native ground.' (p. 42)
15 Lawson, J. C., *Modern Greek Folklore and Ancient Greek Religion*, New York, 1964 [orig. pub. 1910]), p. 35.
16 See 'About Canoes', note 2, above.
17 Eco, U., 'The Poetics of the Open Work', *The Open Work*, Cambridge, Mass., 1989, p. 7.
18 Dubois, C. G., *Le Baroque, Profondeurs de l'Apparence*, quoted by Guérin, J-Y., *Le Théâtre d'Audibert et le Baroque*, Paris, 1976, p. 21.
19 Wentworth Thompson, D'Arcy, *On Growth and Form*, Cambridge, 1942, vol. 2, p. 676.
20 Tabucchi, A., *Piccoli Equivoci senza Importanza*, Milano, 1985, p. 7.
21 Carter, P., *Baroque Memories*, Manchester, 1994, pp. 159–60.

22 Eco, U., 'The Poetics of the Open Work', *The Open Work*, p. 7.
23 *Ezra Pound on Music*, p. 469.
24 Stokes, Adrian, 'Venice', *The Critical Works of Adrian Stokes*, London, 1978, vol. 2, p. 88.
25 Berio, L., *Two Interviews*, London, 1985, p. 89.
26 Ibid., p. 89.
27 A point argued in fascinating depth by J. Bardon in 'A Monograph concerning Hieroglyphs in Australian Art, and their perspectives', *Revolution by Night*, Sydney, 1991, p. 224ff.
28 See Davies, M. F., *Life in an English Village* (London, 1919), p. 14, where the 'Celtic' parish of Corsley in south-west Wiltshire is described as 'intersected by an intricate network of lanes and footpaths, which wind about in a manner which is often unintelligible at the present day . . . these lanes and pathways connect up all the hamlets and scattered dwellings.' Hoskins casts doubt on this 'racial history'. (Hoskins, W. G., *English Landscapes*, London, 1979, p. 7.)
29 Prynne, J. H., 'The Common Gain, Reverted', p. 87.
30 Ibid., p. 87.
31 Gibson, J. J., *The Ecological Approach to Visual Perception*, p. 303.
32 Ibid., p. 197.
33 Ibid., p. 202. The persistence of the hidden in the unhidden oddly recalls Heidegger's intuition of the unconcealed within the concealed. At issue for both is a being in the world that is oriented, fateful, attuned to the lightning-glance of becoming.
34 Ihde, D., *Listening and Voice: A Phenomenology of Sound*, Athens (Ohio), c.1976, p. 68.
35 Smith, F. Joseph, *The Experiencing of Musical Sound*, p. 68.
36 Prynne, J. H., 'The Common Gain, Reverted', p. 87.
37 Homer, *The Iliad*, trans. A. T. Murray, London, 1971, vol. 2, XXII, l. 299. In his *Parmenides* (trans. A. Schuwer and R. Rojcewicz, Bloomington, 1992), Heidegger interpreted this passage as evidencing the importance of the concept of 'concealedness' in Greek thinking: truth, to 'unconceal', is to bring out into the open, the clearing (pp. 23–4), to disclose (p. 49). In this view, Pallas Athene is an agent of unconcealing, revealing 'Being' as the 'groundless' (p. 150).
38 Pyne, W. H., *Wine and Walnuts*, London, 1823, vol. 1, chapter XXI, 281ff. However, what ensured that De Loutherbourg could 'create a copy of Nature, to be taken for Nature's self' was his pioneering of 'the picturesque of sound'.
39 Lindsay, J., *Blast Power and Ballistics*, London, 1974, p. 326.
40 Homer, *The Iliad*, vol. 2, XXII, ll. 274–6.
41 Lindsay, J., *Blast Power and Ballistics*, p. 249.
42 Ibid., p. 82.
43 Ibid., p. 82.

44 Homer, *The Odyssey*, trans. A. T. Murray, London, 1945, vol. 1, Book VI, ll. 232ff.
45 Ibid., vol. 2, Book XIV, ll. 199ff.
46 Vico, G., *La Scienza Nuova*, Milano, 1977, p. 400.
47 Vernant, J-P., *Myth and Thought among the Greeks*, London, 1983, p. 185.
48 Ibid., p. 130.
49 Ibid., p. 130.
50 Ibid., p. 184.
51 Basinius Parmensis, *Hesperidos*, Liber VII, ll. 250ff. in *Opera*, Rimini, 1794.
52 See 'About Canoes', note 38, above.
53 For Rhiannon, see Jones, David, *The Roman Quarry*, ed. H. Grisewood and R. Hague, London, 1981, pp. 15–16. The 'romanization' of Pallas Athene is not only associated with her statuesque reduction to symmetry; it also involves her silencing or musicalization, the neutralizing of her power to move, to reshape space in her wake. Athene's voice is described by Sophocles' Odysseus as 'Like some Tyrrhenian trumpet, brazen-mouthed' (*Sophocles*, trans F. Storr, London, 1961, vol. 2, p. 7). Jones's Roman soldiers mock the (Celtic) bugler and his type: 'They fancy they're the Darlings of Athene - to bring all the world's walls down.' (*The Roman Quarry*, p. 4.) Presumably, Athene's bugle or trumpet tone had the same properties that drew Edgard Varèse to sirens. It is the temporal symmetry of music that Prynne also objects to, its transformation of uneven ground into spaceless sound. By contrast, when Varèse experimented with sirens, he heard hyperbolae and parabolae. (See Cabrera, D., 'Sound Space and Edgard Varèse's *Poème Electronique*', especially chapter 5.)
54 Lindsay, J., *Blast Power and Ballistics*, pp. 231–8.
55 Ibid., p. 85.
56 Harrison, J., *Themis*, p. 500.
57 Lindsay, J., *Blast Power and Ballistics*, p. 381 and chapter XIII passim. Lindsay critically links the power of the thunderbolt, and man's desire to control it, to the fall of the Palladium that consecrates Athene's Troy (p. 237).
58 Ibid., p. 418.
59 Cited by B. Smith in *Imagining the Pacific*, Yale, 1992, pp. 219–20.
60 Lindsay, J., *Blast Power and Ballistics*, p. 152ff.
61 MacGillivray, J., *Narrative of the Voyage of HMS Rattlesnake*, London, 1852, vol. 1, p. 315.
62 Steele, J. G., *Aboriginal Pathways*, St Lucia (Queensland), 1984, p. 235.
63 Robinson, Roland, *The Drift of Things*, Melbourne, 1973, pp. 113–4.
64 Robinson, Roland, *The Shift of Sands*, p. 247.
65 Robinson, Roland, *The Drift of Things*, p. 423.
66 And repression of 'the feminine part of me, the part which I loved, yes loved, and yet of which I was ashamed' (Robinson, Roland, *The Drift of Things*, p. 89).

67 Ibid., p. 296.
68 Sorabji, R., *Matter, Space & Motion*, London, 1988, p. 144.
69 Ibid. p. 238.
70 Lindsay, J., *Blast Power and Ballistics*, pp. 278–79.
71 Hall, A. R., *Ballistics in the Seventeenth Century*, Cambridge, 1952, p. 53.
72 Sorabji, R., *Matter, Space & Motion*, p. 238.
73 Lindsay, J., *Blast Power and Ballistics*, p. 314ff.
74 Ibid., pp. 81–2.
75 Memorably in the fifteenth-century Catalan poet Auzias March's lines, 'Death has come out into the street with open arms, her eyes weeping from excess of joy' (March, A., *Selected Poems*, trans. A. Terry, Austin (Texas), 1978, p. 41).
76 Lindsay, J., *Blast Power and Ballistics*, p. 232.
77 Ibid., p. 234.
78 White, E. K., *Kaironomia*, Ithaca, New York, 1987, p. 17.
79 Ibid., p. 17.
80 Ibid., p. 16ff.
81 *Encyclopaedia Britannica*,1989, vol. 26, p. 805.
82 Onians, R. B., *The Origins of European Thought*, Cambridge, 1988, p. 67, note 4.
83 Ibid., p. 470.
84 Marsden, E.W. , *Greek and Roman Artillery*, Oxford, 1969, pp. 90–1 and p. 12.
85 Hall, A. R., *Ballistics in the Seventeenth Century*, p. 53.
86 Ibid., p. 54.
87 Ibid., p. 55.
88 Cavalcanti, Guido, *Rime*, ed. M. Ciccuto, Milano, 1978, p. 73.
89 *Opere di Dante Alighieri*, ed. E. Moore and P. Toynbee, Oxford, 1958, Inferno, XIV, l. 30.
90 Frederick of Hohenstaufen, *The Art of Falconry (De Arte Venandi cum avibus)*, trans. C. A. Wood and F.M. Fyfe, Boston, 1955, pp. 92–3.
91 Ibid., p. 93.
92 Ibid., p. xxxv.
93 Ibid., p. 40.
94 See Hart, C., *The Dream of Flight*, London, 1972, especially chapter 8 for discussion of Leonardo's aerodynamic theories and experiments.
95 Giacomo da Lentini in *Sonetti della Scuola Siciliana*, ed. E. Sanguineti, Torino, 1965, p. 17.
96 Ibid., p. 17.
97 Ibid., p. 17.
98 Ibid., p. 21.
99 Ibid., pp. 35 and 36.
100 Ibid., p. 30.
101 Cavalcanti, Guido, *Rime*, p. 166.

102 Ibid., pp. 166–8.

103 The term Jaynes coins to register the fact that a mutually implicating relationship exists between a metaphor and the object or concept it is used to evoke. 'Concrete metaphors' do not simply describe 'abstract concepts', they generate them. Thus, for Cavalcanti the ballistic imagery of love is not merely rhetorical (replaceable), it is a tool of analysis, actively discovering love's psycho-physical dynamics (see Jaynes, J., *The Origin of Consciousness in the Breakdown of the Bicameral Mind*, London, 1990, pp. 48–50.)

104 See Corti, M., 'La fisionomia stilistica di Guido Cavalcanti' in *Rendiconti dell' Accademia Nazionale dei Lincei*, s.viii, vol. V, 1950, p. 53ff.

105 Circutto describes them as '*una specie di proiezione potenziata dell'essere, una facoltà cosciente che rappresenta "in atto" nel farsi stesso della poesia, i desideri conoscitiva del poeta*' (Cavalcanti, Guido, *Rime*, p. 79). Once, according to Heidegger, 'in the beginning of Western thinking, the essence of language flashed in the light of Being . . . But the lightning abruptly vanished. No one held on to its streak of light and the nearness of what it illuminated' (Heidegger, M., *Early Greek Thinking*, trans. D. F. Krell and F. A. Capuzzi, San Francisco, 1975, p. 78). Whether or not this glosses a historical fact, it certainly evokes a persistent Western myth, one that Cavalcanti's poems and Giorgione's painting both enact.

106 In *La Vita Nuova*, *Il Convivio* and the *Divine Comedy* respectively.

107 Cavalcanti, Guido, *Rime*, p. 120.

108 Ibid., p. 75.

109 Ibid., p. 114. And '*Allora par che ne la mente piova/ una figura di donna pensosa. . .*' (p. 100).

110 For example, P. Bigongiari, 'Guido Cavalcanti', *Paragone*, LXXXVI, 1957, p. 28, writes of '*una sacra rappresentazione interiore*'.

111 Cavalcanti, Guido, *Rime*, p. 136.

112 Lindsay, J., *Blast Power and Ballistics*, p. 146.

113 Dennett, D. C., *Consciousness Explained*, London, 1991, p. 333.

114 Ibid., p. 334.

115 Gins, M., *Helen Keller or Arakawa*, Santa Fe, 1994, p. 99.

116 Ibid., pp. 14–15.

117 Smith, F. Joseph, *The Experiencing of Musical Sound*, New York, 1978, p. 68.

118 Ibid., p. 109.

119 Ibid., p. 110.

120 White, E. K., *Kaironomia*, p. 52.

121 Ascham, R., *Toxophilus*, in *English Works*, ed. W. A. Wright, Cambridge, 1970, p. 113.

122 Ibid., p. 112.

123 See 'A Reverent Miming', note 102, above.

124 See my *Living In A New Country*, p. 182.

125 Strehlow, T. G. H., *Anthropology and the Study of Languages*, Presidential Address, ANZAAS Perth Meeting, 1947 (Adelaide, n. d.), p. 22, note 11.

126 Homer, *The Odyssey*, vol. 2, Book XXI, ll. 419ff.
127 Prynne, J.H., 'The Common Gain, Reverted,' p. 88.
128 Prynne, J.H., 'A Note on Metal', *Poems*, p. 126.
129 Ibid., p. 127.
130 Ibid., p. 127.
131 Prynne, J.H., 'First Notes on Daylight', *Poems*, p. 69.
132 Prynne, J.H., 'A Note on Metal', p. 129.
133 Prynne, J.H., 'The Common Gain, Reverted', p. 87.
134 Prynne, J.H., 'Thoughts on the Esterhazy Court Uniform', *Poems*, p. 97.
135 Ibid., p. 98.
136 Smith, F. Joseph, *The Experiencing of Musical Sound*, p. 157.
137 Ibid., p. 102.
138 Jeans, J., *Science and Music*, New York, 1968 (orig. pub. 1937), pp. 125–6.
139 Ibid., p. 126.
140 Prynne, J.H, 'Quality in That Case as Pressure', *Poems*, p. 77.
141 Prynne, J.H, 'A Note on Metal', p. 129.
142 Jeans, J., *Science and Music*, p. 128.
143 Onians, R. B., *The Origins of European Thought*, pp. 343–6.
144 Ibid., p. 346.
145 Smith, F. Joseph, *The Experiencing of Musical Sound*, p. 154.
146 Bardon, G., *Papunya Tula: Art of the Western Desert*, Melbourne, 1991, p. 133.
147 Strehlow, T. G. H., *Songs of Central Australia*, Sydney, 1971, p. 13.
148 Ibid., p. 246.
149 Strehlow, T. G. H., *Rex Battarbee: Artist and Founder of the Aboriginal Art Movement in Central Australia*, Sydney, 1956, p. 20.
150 Ibid., p. 20.
151 Bardon, G., *Papunya Tula: Art of the Western Desert*, p. 136.
152 Ibid., p. 131ff.
153 Bardon, G., 'Notes on Obed Raggett' in letter to author, 7 September 1995, p. 1.
154 Ibid., p. 2.
155 Ibid., pp. 2–3. 'There were as many as five separate mural paintings made on the Papunya School walls as well as decorative designs and patterns on the metal railings and posts which supported the school building. The murals completed were: (a) a practice Dreaming (b) a Wallaby Dreaming (c) a Widow's Dreaming (d) a Snake Dreaming (e) a Honey Ant Dreaming, plus a number of bull's-eye motifs.' (G. Bardon, Letter to author, 17 May 1995.)
156 Bardon, G., *Aboriginal Art of the Western Desert*, Sydney, 1979, p. 15.
157 Bardon, G., *Papunya Tula: Art of the Western Desert*, p. 131.
158 Spectacularly collected in Johnson, V., *The Art of Clifford Possum Tjapaltjarri*, Basel, 1994.
159 Ibid., p. 139.

160 G. Bardon, Letter to author, 7 September 1994.
161 Ibid.
162 Bardon, G., *Papunya Tula: Art of the Western Desert*, pp. 131–2.
163 Ibid., p. 132.
164 Bardon, G., *Aboriginal Art of the Western Desert*, p. 17.
165 Conversations with Geoff Bardon, 13–14 May 1994 and Letter to author, 7 September 1994.
166 Bardon, G., *Papunya Tula: Art of the Western Desert*, p. 136.
167 Ibid., p. 132.
168 Mathews, T., *Reading Apollinaire*, Manchester, 1987, p. 107.
169 Conversations with Geoff Bardon, 13–14 May 1994.
170 Conversations with Geoff Bardon, 13–14 May 1994.
171 Harney, W. E., *Life among the Aborigines*, London, 1957, p. 52. In a similar spirit, George Borrow could write about pre-enclosed, unmetalled 'ways' in Spain as 'a medley of bridle-paths and drift-ways where discrimination is very difficult.' (Borrow, G., *The Bible in Spain*, London, 1905, p. 281.)
172 In Shaw, A. G. L., 'British Policy towards the Australian Aborigines', in *Australian Historical Studies*, vol. 25, no.99, October 1992, p. 283. Among Social Darwinists, the simile was taken seriously; endowing the Aborigines (and other non-Western peoples) with a 'sixth sense', atrophied in more 'advanced' races, that enabled them to navigate unfamiliar country, some writers at least wondered if this sense were not the same utilized by migrating birds. (see Jaccard, P., *Le Sens de la Direction et l'Orientation chez l'Homme*, Paris, 1932, p. 305ff.)
173 Thomas, Rover, *Roads Cross: The Paintings of Rover Thomas*, Canberra, 1994, pp. 40–5.
174 Gibson, J. J., *The Ecological Approach to Visual Perception*, p. 10.
175 Lewin, K., *Principles of Topological Psychology*, trans. F. and G. Heider, New York, 1936, p. 9.
176 Pinxten, R., van Dooren, I., and Harvey, F., *The Anthropology of Space*, Philadelphia, 1983; Weiner, J., *The Empty Place*, Bloomington, 1991.
177 Gilles Deleuze defines paramnesia as 'a kind of displacement by which the past is embodied only in terms of a present that is different from that which it has been.' (Deleuze, G., *Bergsonism*, trans. H. Tomlinson and B. Habberjam, New York, 1988, p. 70.)
178 Gramsci, A., *Letters from Prison*, ed. L. Lawner, New York, 1973, p. 262.
179 Ibid., p. 193.

Index